THE PACIFIC WORLD

THE PACIFIC WORLD

Its vast distances, its lands and the life upon them, and its peoples

Edited by FAIRFIELD OSBORN

With maps and illustrations by
ROBERT M. CHAPIN, JR. · ANDREY AVINOFF
FRANCIS LEE JACQUES · JOY FLINSCH BUBA
CHARLES CLARK

W · W · NORTON & COMPANY · INC ·
NEW YORK

First Edition

PRINTED IN THE UNITED STATES OF AMERICA
FOR THE PUBLISHERS BY THE NORWOOD PRESS

FOREWORD

"LOOK TO THE WEST!" This is in the destiny of the people of America. The voyage of the *Mayflower*, the building of the continent, the experiences of later years in the Pacific—all of our epic movements have been westward. As this is written, we have a far-flung battle line over the vast areas of the ocean beyond our western shore. When the battles are over, destiny will still be calling for us there. Our soldiers and sailors who are there today will be succeeded by untold numbers of American people busying themselves in the ways of peace. It is not written otherwise. All of this being true, we Americans need to know more of the Pacific—its distances, its lands, the life upon them, and its peoples.

The information presented here has been gathered together by the men of nine educational and scientific institutions. We need make no excuse for presenting so vast a subject in so small a book. It is at best but a general picture, yet one, we hope, which will give to those in our Armed Services and to their families and friends at home a clearer idea of this great area of the earth's surface from which we cannot turn our faces.

FAIRFIELD OSBORN, *Editor*
President, New York Zoological Society

This book exists because:

The American Committee for International Wild Life Protection, acting upon the suggestion of Childs Frick and Harold Coolidge, initiated and sponsored it and the series of supplementary handbooks that are now in preparation, believing that literature regarding the animal life of the Pacific islands would encourage its conservation.

Twenty-eight men of nine institutions worked tirelessly and gratuitously on gathering together the information here contained.

Robert Cushman Murphy ably prepared a large part of the preliminary data which enabled the editor to carry on from there.

Harold C. Amos and Captain Carl Von Hoffman contributed, respectively, the articles on Japan and Formosa, and information on the Philippines, the Luchus, and the Bonins; J. van Beusekom contributed information on the Netherlands Indies; Herbert S. Zim helped materially in the editorial work, and Donald Marcy in the research work.

Finally, the great Pacific—being almost half this world of ours—is worth knowing.

F. O.

The information in this book has been provided by the following:

American Geographical Society

JOHN K. WRIGHT

American Museum of Natural History

H. E. ANTHONY
W. H. BARTON, JR.
T. D. CARTER
C. H. CURRAN
CHILDS FRICK
W. K. GREGORY
J. E. HILL
FRANK E. LUTZ
ERNST MAYR
ROBERT CUSHMAN MURPHY
JOHN T. NICHOLS
HENRY C. RAVEN
H. L. SHAPIRO
G. H. H. TATE
E. M. WEYER, JR.
JOHN T. ZIMMER

Arnold Arboretum

E. D. MERRILL

Blue Hill Meteorological Observatory

CHARLES F. BROOKS

Carnegie Museum

ANDREY AVINOFF

Chicago Natural History Museum

KARL P. SCHMIDT

Museum of Comparative Zoology

THOMAS BARBOUR
ARTHUR LOVERIDGE

New York Zoological Society

WILLIAM BEEBE
CLAUDE W. LEISTER
ROSS NIGRELLI
FAIRFIELD OSBORN

Smithsonian Institution

ALEXANDER WETMORE

CONTENTS

CONTENTS

ILLUSTRATIONS

Regional Maps

THE PACIFIC IS BEFORE YOU

An Introduction to the Men of the Armed Services
by William Beebe

WELL, you're in the Pacific! And now that the Jap has been cleared out, what do you think of the island you're on? Oh, you don't know much about it! Don't worry, for this goes for almost every other American.

One thing that Americans have in common is keen curiosity about strange peoples, animals, lands and oceans, and the grand thing about this is that it has nothing to do with rank, sex, or where you came from.

It's funny, when you come to think of it, what fragments and bits of knowledge we take with us when, for the first time in our life, we go to a place like the South Seas or the Netherlands Indies. I suppose that those of us who remember World War I and the years preceding got our ideas about these islands chiefly from books, such as *Robinson Crusoe* and *Swiss Family Robinson*, *Nat the Naturalist*, *In Eastern Seas*, *Typee*, and from the singing words of Robert Louis Stevenson. We read these as boys and dreamed of Far Isles of Romance and Earthly Paradises slightly diluted with Cannibals.

You men of World War II have, instead, pictures in your mind, thanks to the vividness of the movies, and as a result these islands seem fairly familiar when you first see them. You will think of Dorothy Lamour before Captain Cook, and all who have seen *Moana* and *Mutiny on the "Bounty"* have intensely vivid pictures of coral atolls, coconut groves, thatched huts and languorous or ferocious natives. Those of us who can recall both the written descriptions and the motion pictures are doubly fortunate.

In both cases, however, a very important viewpoint is lacking.

Until you go ashore and actually walk through the jungles you never realize that all impressions of animal life have been left out: the wonderful butterflies, the lizards clad in jeweled coats of mail, sunbirds as gorgeous as they are tiny, taking the place of our hummingbirds, parrots clad in spectrum hues and doves like orchids, curious four-footed beasts, and unbelievable sea shells vying in delicacy of design and color with any tropical blossoms.

Even our most treasured boyhood's books may fall apart under the cold scrutiny of scientific criticism. For example, the Swiss Family Robinson is wrecked on a small, indefinite desert island. Yet Fritz, the eldest son, was such an indefatigable collector that he caught alive or shot ruffed grouse, parrots, hedgehogs, monkeys, wild asses, kangaroos and ostriches, thus drawing on the animal life of all the continents as well as Australia. I go into this detail to show that in one respect both Hollywood and the older classics have left an almost clean slate as regards the animal life of these islands of the Pacific.

The island people are probably the first living things to attract and hold your attention, and if they fail to come up to the glamorous mental images that you bring with you, do not blame them altogether. In time you will come to realize that the flower of the various races, sometimes 90 percent, has been swept away by the ravages of diseases brought by white men, and that untold others have been cheated, exploited and embittered by unscrupulous traders. The remaining islanders now find themselves enmeshed in a devastating war, but even under these conditions the men of these islands show their splendid character and loyalty to those they consider friends—by their enmity to the invading barbarians, and their universal readiness to help the Allied forces.

If at first you are inclined to laugh at the appearance and habits of life of these Pacific island natives, stop a minute and remember that the first Romans to reach England were amazed and diverted to see that the pre-Britons stained themselves all over blue with woad. The early South Sea explorers thought tattooing an outlandish trait of savages. Today few of our sailors are tattooless themselves. And while you gaze with astonishment and derision at the painted bodies and faces of the natives, you forget that at home your mothers, sisters, girl friends—perhaps at this moment at the movies, looking at pictures of you and your comrades among these savages, members of your own family—doubtless are daintily decorated with colored pastes, powders and paints, around the eyes, and along the eyebrows, upon cheeks and lips, while fingernails run the full gamut of the spectrum. Stevenson says, "When I desired any detail of savage custom, or of superstitious belief, I cast back in the story of my fathers, and fished for what I wanted with some trait of equal barbarism."

The quickest way to friendship with any wild native tribe anywhere in the world is through the animal life all around. If you point to a lizard and the savage says "Ug-Glub" and you say "Lizard" you both have learned something, and if you write down his name for the creature as it sounds in English, you have probably earned the thanks of some man back home whose life is devoted to the study of savage languages. If you point to your mouth and he nods at the lizard, you have learned another fact, perhaps a valuable one if you should ever become lost in the jungle; and so on.

Here, in this book, is an attempt to tell you something about these Pacific islands and their peoples, animals, birds, insects, shells and plants, and the winds and currents of the ocean around them. What you observe, or the notes that you may take and bring home with you, may prove more useful than you can guess. There is so much we do not know about the Pacific, and what you may find out may well make some really important contribution to scientific knowledge. For you will have discovered some true facts (perhaps quite new ones) about the creatures that live on the earth with you, and that, in general, is all any scientist can do.

If you have bothersome questions, or want to know what to do with the facts you have discovered, write to one of the institutions listed on page 7, and you will get all the help we can give. Even now, such letters are coming to us from Alaska, the Aleutians and from a dozen islands in the South Pacific, in some cases where battles are still raging. In this mutual exchange of suggestions, advice, and fresh notes from the field, we Americans will benefit from the scientific first fruits of victory.

I have already mentioned the terrible decimation of island tribes, in some cases almost to the point of extermination. There is nothing you can do about this, but there is something very important that concerns every soldier as a responsible American. There are many birds, lizards and other creatures inhabiting the smaller Pacific islands that are not to be found anywhere else in the world. A soldier could very likely land on one of the littler atolls and, with a gun, kill every individual bird of a certain species. That bird, which has been slowly evolving for millions of years, will then have been completely wiped off the face of the earth. This is, of course, an extreme and unlikely case, but on any island, anywhere, kill for food when necessary but please don't kill at random, or for the sake of sport. Collect all the sea shells and insects you want to, but as to the rest, track them down, sneak up on them, watch them, make pets of the lizards, the birds, the small four-footed beasts and see what habits you can discover, what notes, songs or cries you can hear, what strange nests or burrows they inhabit, how they care for their young. And find out all that the natives know of them, superstitions as well as facts. Both are interesting and valuable.

To the man who finds himself in the large islands of the Southwest Pacific and who is blessed with time and inclination to look beyond the outer fringes of the jungle, the animal life will become more and more exciting. Parrots and cockatoos fly past chattering, hornbills attract attention because of their large size and the startling loud swoosh of their wings. Bantamlike fowl that scurry out of the trail are worth stalking and watching, for they are red jungle fowl, ancestors of all the domestic poultry in the world.

In New Guinea birds of paradise scream high overhead and wave their inimitable plumes in their strange courtships; in the Aru Islands live huge cassowaries with brilliant wattles and tall helmets of horn. In Java the green peacocks greet the dawn from the

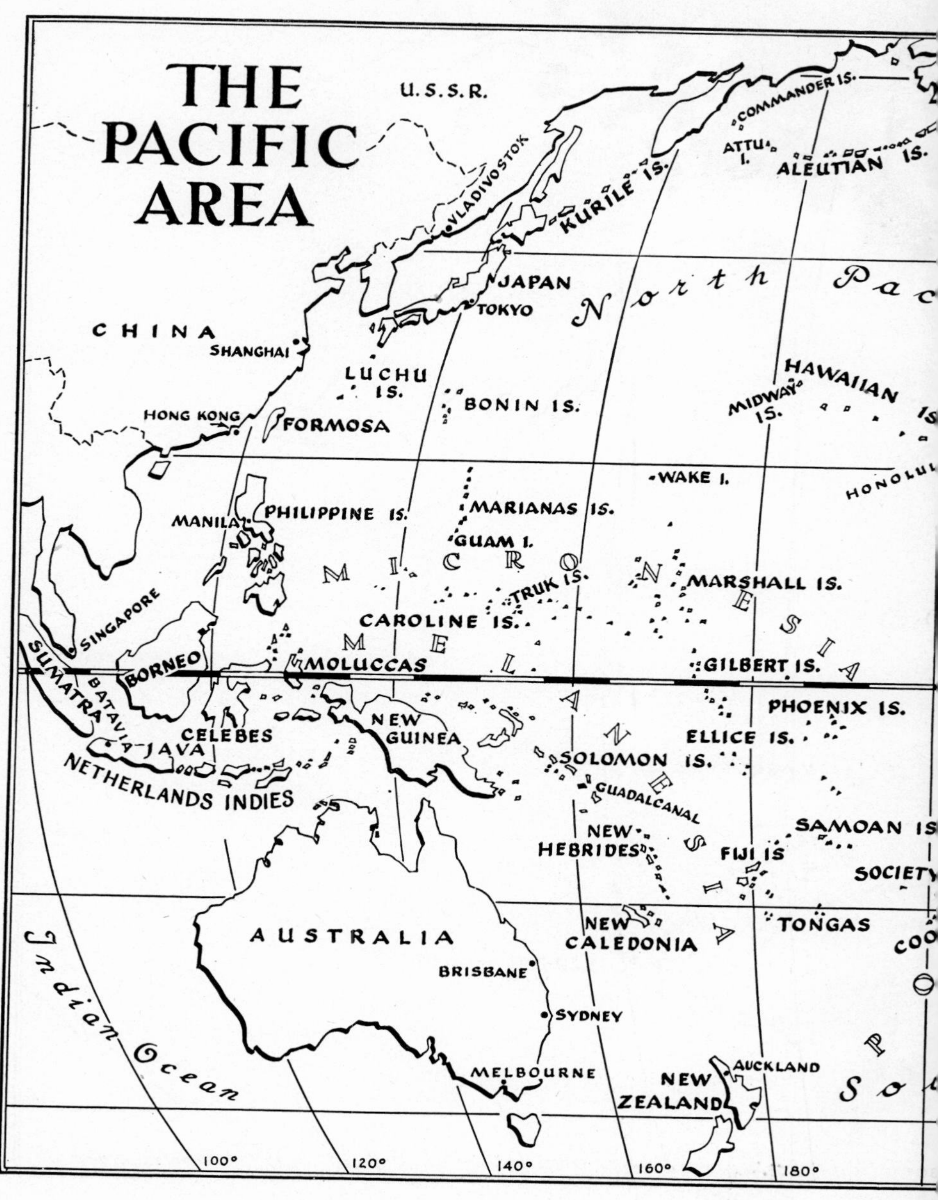

THE PACIFIC AREA
U.S.S.R.
VLADIVOSTOK
KURILE IS.
COMMANDER IS.
ATTU I.
ALEUTIAN IS.
JAPAN
TOKYO
North Pac
CHINA
SHANGHAI
LUCHU IS.
BONIN IS.
HAWAIIAN IS.
MIDWAY IS.
HONG KONG
FORMOSA
WAKE I.
HONOLULU
MANILA
PHILIPPINE IS.
MARIANAS IS.
GUAM I.
MICRONESIA
TRUK IS.
MARSHALL IS.
CAROLINE IS.
SINGAPORE
MELANESIA
SUMATRA
BORNEO
MOLUCCAS
GILBERT IS.
BATAVIA
PHOENIX IS.
CELEBES
NEW GUINEA
ELLICE IS.
JAVA
SOLOMON IS.
NETHERLANDS INDIES
GUADALCANAL
NEW HEBRIDES
FIJI IS
SAMOAN IS
SOCIETY
AUSTRALIA
NEW CALEDONIA
TONGAS
Indian Ocean
BRISBANE
SYDNEY
MELBOURNE
NEW ZEALAND
AUCKLAND
100°
120°
140°
160°
180°

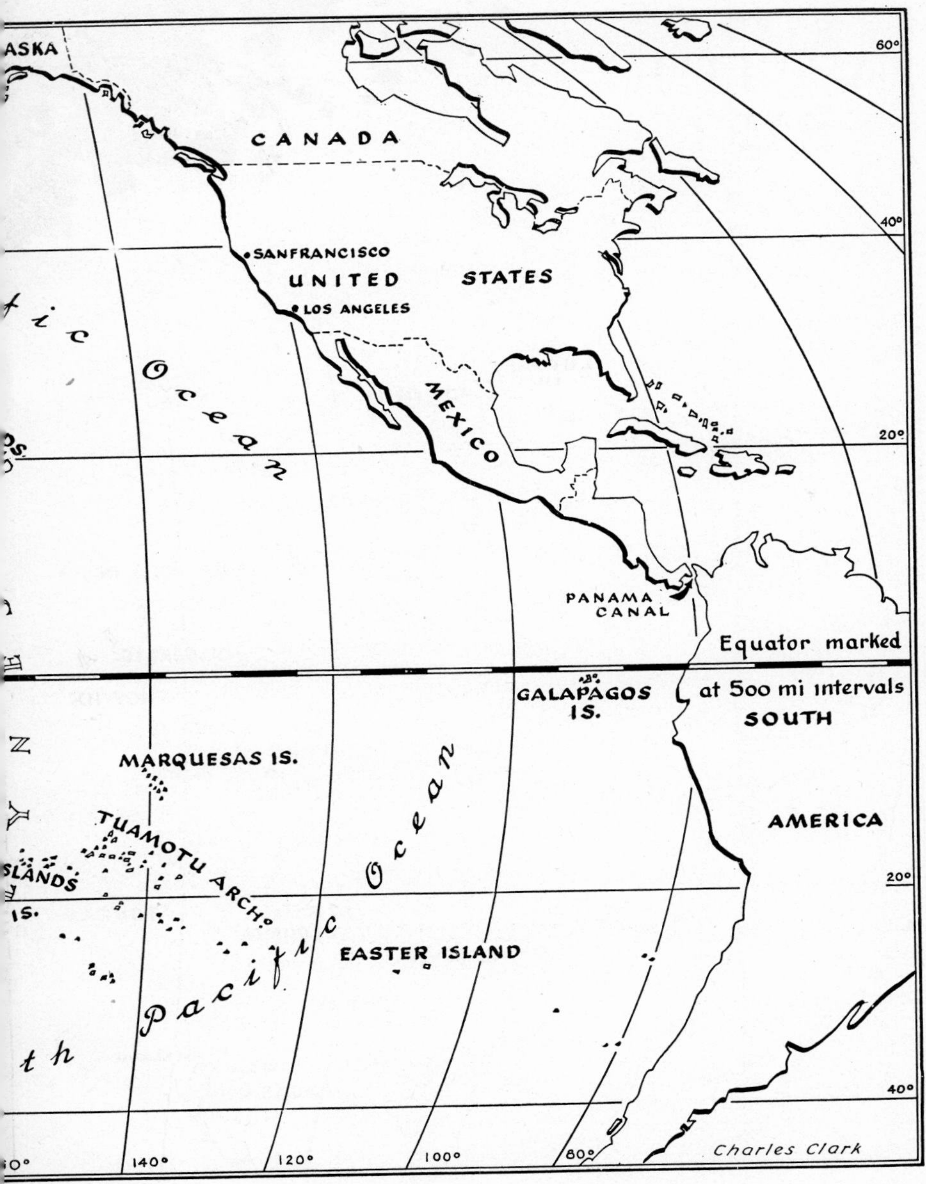

CANADA
UNITED STATES
SANFRANCISCO
LOS ANGELES
MEXICO
PANAMA CANAL
Equator marked at 500 mi intervals
GALAPAGOS IS.
SOUTH AMERICA
MARQUESAS IS.
TUAMOTU ARCH.
EASTER ISLAND
Pacific Ocean
60°
40°
20°
20°
40°
140°
120°
100°
80°
Charles Clark

highest jungle trees; Borneo, with its Dyaks, the finest savages on earth, offers to the explorers argus pheasants calling and spreading their thousand-eyed wings in their cleared arenas, and the hump-backed, red orangutans gazing mistily down from their arboreal bed of boughs. You may find the tracks of tigers, rhinos and sela-dangs in the muddy jungles of the Malay States, and you need not go far from native villages to hear the clear trumpeting of a wild elephant at midnight in the jungle. As dangerous as fully-armed Japs is the semidomesticated water buffalo, to whom the scent of a white man is more infuriating than is the flag of the matador to the bull.

When your final leave comes, when you no longer have to use your interest in birds and beasts to dim your homesickness, you embark or emplane. And now you realize vividly that the earth actually *is* round, for you are so far from Brooklyn or Omaha that you can as well start east as west.

The last and not the least exciting phase of the whole experience comes when you reach home. *What* you can tell your family and friends! And not about what they have themselves seen in the Pacific movies, but marvels never imagined or photographed by the best cinema location men.

In fact you will have trouble making anyone believe that, when cold sober, you saw lizards that took off from tree trunks, spread wide their bright membranes, rib-borne like diminutive umbrellas, and slanted smoothly as flying squirrels from tree to tree. You will hold in memory these lizards that fly and some birds that cannot, kangaroos that live in trees and mammals that lay eggs, as well as birds that bury their eggs as fast as they lay them. I have seen all these and many more, as you will too, if you use this book and your eyes.

Then, when all the first excitement has died down, a new joy develops, permanent through all remaining years, when book after book is opened, dealing with the life of these now distant lands and seas. You, the reader, will sense the great difference between the time of your visit and the times when explorers of old sailed blindly and bravely through uncharted archipelagos; you will be able to judge and condemn the exaggerations and falsities that will be found in only too many modern volumes; but you will exclaim with delight, "I've seen that very thing myself!" as you turn the magic pages of Captain Cook, Melville, Guppy, Forbes, Alcock, Darwin and Wallace.

W. B.

THE PACIFIC WORLD

Chapter I

THE OCEAN

Nearly three-quarters of our earth's surface is covered by water, and the Pacific Ocean, by far the biggest of the oceans, accounts for almost half of all the water area of the world. This vast ocean is twice as big as the Atlantic and more than twenty times as big as the United States. Further, it is a good deal larger than all the land surfaces of the world added together. The distance across the Pacific at its widest part, namely between Panama and the westernmost part of the China Sea, is about 11,000 miles, or halfway around the earth.

The Pacific is also the deepest of the oceans, with an average depth of nearly three miles. There are shallow parts, of course, some of which are occupied by many islands, large and small. On the other hand, near some of the chains of islands, and near parts of the shore of Asia, are great trenches in the ocean bottom that are tremendously deep. Northeast of Mindanao in the Philippines, for example, there is a spot 35,400 feet, or more than 6½ miles, deep. In this spot the highest mountain on earth would lie with its peak more than a mile below the surface of the water.

All places more than 18,000 feet, or slightly less than 3½ miles in depth, are known as "deeps." The Pacific Ocean has thirty-three of these, the Atlantic nineteen, and the Indian Ocean only five. Great size and depth combine to give the Pacific a volume of water that is between five and six times the volume of all the world's land that lies above sea level. This is not surprising if we consider that the average height above sea level of all the land is only half a mile, whereas the average depth of the oceans as a whole is about two and a half miles.

Do not, however, get the idea that the Pacific is *all* water. It contains innumerable islands, some of great size, some little. There are large land masses—separated from their nearby continents—such as Borneo, Sumatra and Java, once a part of Asia, or New Guinea, cut off not so long ago from Australia. Elsewhere are island groups spewed from the ocean bottom by volcanoes, or countless islands forming chains a thousand or more miles in length, islands that owe their existence to the tiny animals that build the coral reefs.

The ocean basins, despite their size, lie only on the outermost skin of our great globe. In relation to the entire earth they are not deep hollows but merely slight depressions on the earth's surface. If the world could be reduced to the size of a baseball, the depth of the Pacific would amount to less than the thickness of a sheet of paper. In other words, the earth, for all its surface difference, is practically a smooth sphere.

There is an old and familiar yarn that the bed of the Pacific Ocean is a scar caused by the tearing away of the moon from the earth. This couldn't be true. The bulk of the moon is thirty times that of even the greatest of oceans, besides which there is no good evidence that the moon was ever a part of the earth.

PACIFIC PROFILE

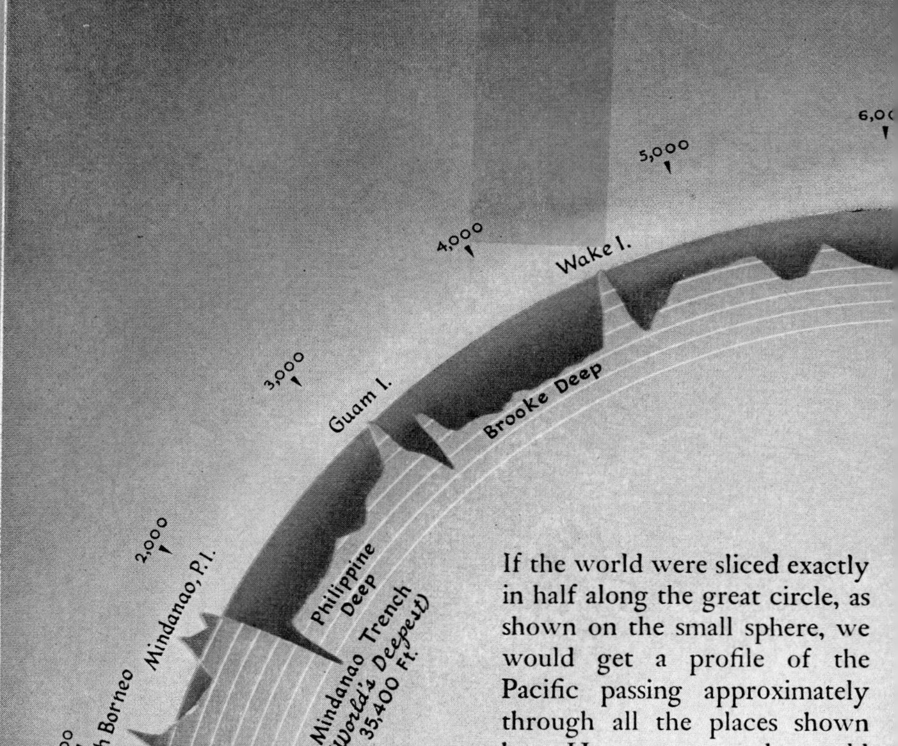

If the world were sliced exactly in half along the great circle, as shown on the small sphere, we would get a profile of the Pacific passing approximately through all the places shown here. However, were the world this size, the highest mountain and the deepest trench in the ocean would be invisible to the eye unless we greatly exaggerated the vertical scale. Here the vertical scale is exaggerated 100 times.

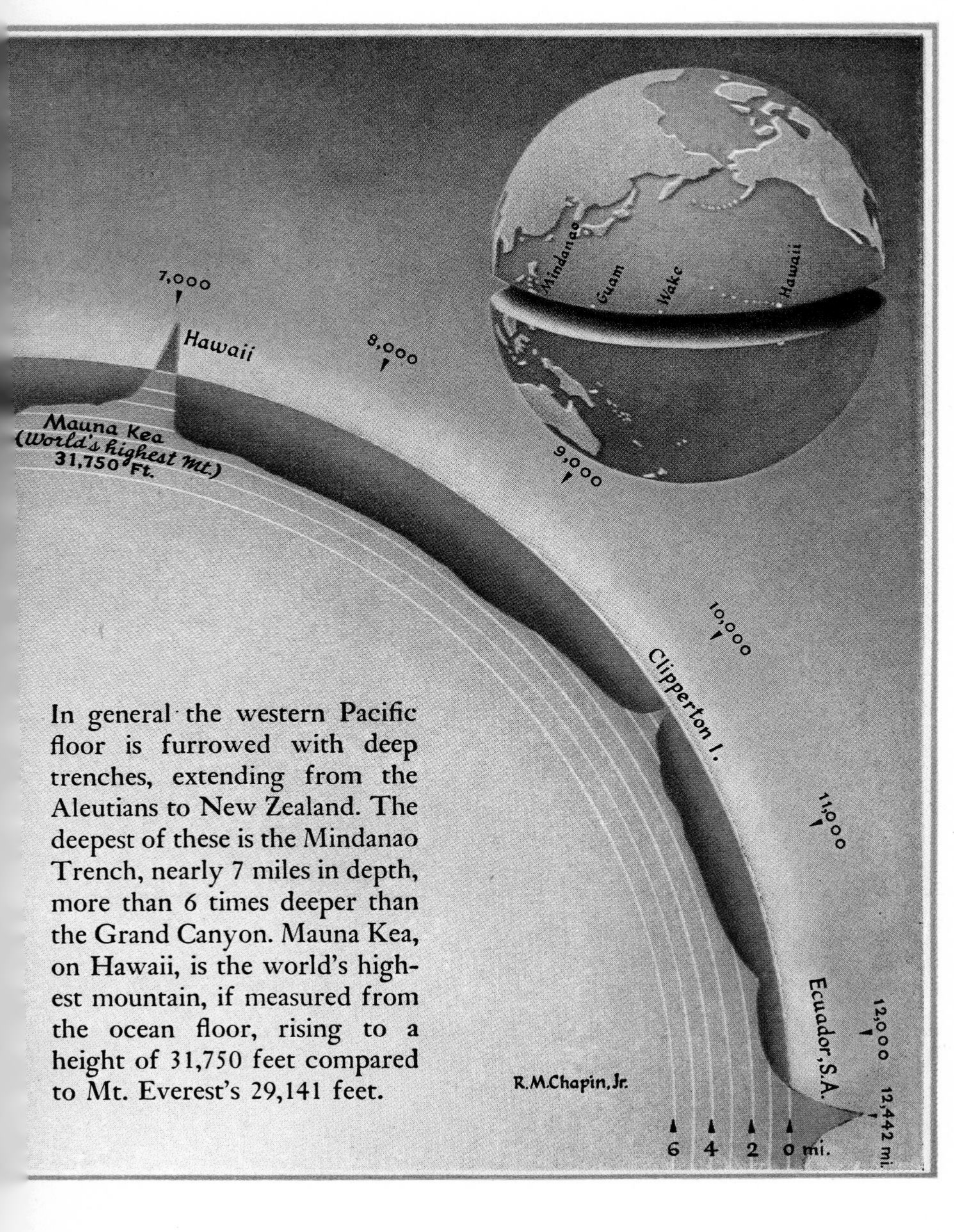

In general the western Pacific floor is furrowed with deep trenches, extending from the Aleutians to New Zealand. The deepest of these is the Mindanao Trench, nearly 7 miles in depth, more than 6 times deeper than the Grand Canyon. Mauna Kea, on Hawaii, is the world's highest mountain, if measured from the ocean floor, rising to a height of 31,750 feet compared to Mt. Everest's 29,141 feet.

Chapter II

THE ISLANDS

Large parts of the Pacific are sprinkled with countless islands, so small that they appear only as dots with a name attached. As a matter of fact there are so many islands that most of them have never been named and only a small fraction are inhabited. There are over 7,000 islands and islets in the Philippines alone. Other island groups have nearly as many. Consequently it is no exaggeration to say that the Pacific islands are "innumerable." Most of these islands are small, but many are extremely large. New Guinea, after Greenland, the largest island in the world, is a good deal larger than Texas and almost exactly ten times the size of South Carolina.

The total number of islands is difficult to estimate because an atoll of a single name may in reality be composed of a score of separate islands. However, a recent authority has listed 2,650 main islands. As an example of the smaller islands, the Tuamotu group, the native name of which means "a cloud of islands," number some eighty main bodies of land and countless smaller fragments, and yet the total land area of that archipelago adds up to only 330 square miles. No completely satisfactory classification of the Pacific island groups has been worked out. Whatever principle is chosen, such as political boundaries or climate, distribution of plant and animal life or geologic structure, the resulting classification will not work out well from the other points of view. Hence any grouping of the islands must be a compromise. The grouping as presented in Chapter Eight, based upon the geological history and the sequential distribution of animal life, is a logical and interesting approach to the subject.

The most familiar arrangement, covering many of the island groups, is based upon the distribution of the native human races within recent historic times. The islands lying east of the Philippines and north of New Guinea and its adjacent islands, inhabited principally by short, dark peoples, are called Micronesia (derived from the two Greek words, *micro*, small, and *nesos*, island). The islands inhabited by natives who are of basic Negroid stock form Melanesia (*melas*, black). These include New Guinea, eastward to the Fijis. In the Central Pacific lie the most widely scattered groups of islands, whose native inhabitants are known as Polynesians. This word is derived from the Greek meaning "many islands." The area of Polynesia extends from New Zealand, north to Hawaii, and runs far over eastward to Easter Island.

In addition there are the islands of the Northwest Pacific lying along the Asiatic continent, including Formosa, the islands of Japan, and the Kuriles. In the Northeast Pacific the most important group is that of the Aleutians reaching far oceanward from the Alaskan peninsula. Then there is the isolated Galápagos group, lying astride the equator, some 500 miles out from the coast of Ecuador. The word Oceania is used to define the ocean area and the islands of the Southwest Pacific.

GEOLOGICAL HISTORY

The Pacific Ocean is one of the oldest features of the earth. There is evidence to show that it has existed very much in its present form for perhaps 500,000,000 years.

Structurally, the Pacific can be divided into a larger eastern and a smaller western part. The eastern part, the area that lies east of a line running north from New Zealand through the Tonga Islands, is an ancient undisturbed basin. All the islands in this basin, from Samoa to Hawaii and eastward across the ocean to the Galápagos and Juan Fernández, are composed of volcanic materials that have been forced up through fissures or cracks in the earth's crust. Many of these islands are the tops of gigantic mountains, mostly submerged, rising from the ocean bed. Their purely volcanic origin is in some cases partly masked by a coating of coral rock.

The islands of the western basin have a much more complicated structure and history, representing the exposed crests of upfolds of the earth's crust lying in a series of long arcs. One of these folds sweeps southeastward from New Guinea to the Solomon, the Fiji and the Tonga Islands, New Caledonia and, perhaps, New Zealand. Another set of at least two parallel folds begins in Burma and can be traced through Sumatra and Java to the Moluccas, and possibly to the Philippines and the Palaus. The successive upfolds are separated from one another by deep downfolds or trenches. Their origin, with the exception of New Zealand, seems to be relatively recent, geologically speaking. They represent part of the mountain-building earth movements of the middle and latter part of the Age of Mammals, dating back not more than a few tens of millions of years. Many of the present islands have emerged from the ocean even more recently.

New Guinea is in fact a cut-off piece of the Australian continent, just as Borneo, Sumatra and Java are structurally a part of Asia. In both cases the islands are situated on shallow continental platforms close to their parent continent, and both were probably part of the neighboring mainlands as recently as thirty thousand to forty thousand years ago.

Though all the eastern Pacific islands are built of lava, ash and other volcanic material, active eruption is still in progress only at Hawaii and the Galápagos Islands.

VOLCANOES AND EARTHQUAKES

In the western part of the ocean a belt of volcanic activity begins in New Zealand, at the south, and continues through the New Hebrides, the Solomons, the Bismarck Archipelago and the islands north of New Guinea. A second line of active volcanoes starts at Sumatra in the west and runs through Java, the Lesser Sunda Islands, turning northward in the northern Moluccas and extending through the Philippines, finally reaching the Japanese islands, the Aleutian arc in the North Pacific, and Alaska.

The belts of volcanic activity follow the upfolds and are sharply defined. There are no traces whatsoever of present activity outside of these upfolded areas, as, for example, in Australia, most of New Guinea, and Borneo. The volcanic belt coincides also to a large extent with one of the heaviest of earthquake zones. The earthquake zone, however, is more extensive than that of volcanoes and includes also all areas of active recent mountain building such as New Guinea.

Some volcanoes erupt quietly, others explode violently. In the former kind the lava merely overflows the crater and rolls down the mountainside. Mauna Loa in Hawaii is such a volcano. Lava has run down its sides in streams up to fifty miles long. Examples of the violently explosive type of volcano are Tamboro in Java and Krakatoa in the strait between Java and Sumatra. When Tamboro erupted in 1815 it blew between twenty-eight and fifty cubic miles of lava, ash and volcanic dust into the air. Krakatoa erupted in 1883 with an explosion heard in Australia 1,500 miles away. The dust from it, rising into the upper atmosphere, extended around the world. The explosion produced huge tidal waves that swept over the low coasts of nearby islands, destroying villages and taking nearly 40,000 lives.

Pacific earthquakes have caused even more serious damage than volcanic eruptions. Probably the most devastating was the Japanese earthquake of 1703, which killed approximately 200,000 people. The Tokyo earthquake of 1923 killed half this number. There have been severe earthquakes in Formosa, the Philippines, Java and in a number of smaller islands.

CORAL ISLANDS, REEFS AND ATOLLS

A lot of land on this earth owes its present existence to animal life. Of all the land-building animals the prize must be given to the creatures that have built the innumerable coral islands, atolls and reefs of the Pacific, including the Great Barrier Reef, 1,260 miles in length, equivalent to the distance between New York and Des Moines, Iowa. This vast reef marks the edge of the submerged continental shelf along the northeastern coast of Australia. It is a little like thinking of the myriads of stars when we consider the countless trillions of small living creatures that built this vast solid structure.

The story of coral reefs, islands and atolls is briefly this. Among the chemicals found in water is calcium carbonate, or lime. Sea water contains more of this substance than does fresh water. What is ordinarily called "hard" fresh water contains more lime than "soft" fresh water does. Many animals can take calcium carbonate out of solution and use it. The oyster, clam, and snail use it to make their shells; the lobster and crab use it to reinforce their shells. It is required by man to build bones and teeth. It is needed in all the tissues of the body. Blood cannot coagulate without it. To be more emphatic, there could be no life without calcium in some form.

The sea with its myriads of visible and invisible living creatures has been the factory for the conversion of calcium into solid material. The builders range from microscopic animals, whose shells, by the billions, form chalk deposits like the White Cliffs of Dover, to the coral-building animals that are of a type related to jellyfishes and sea anemones.

The coral-building animals look like miniature sea anemones but differ from them in several respects, and particularly in the fact that they secrete lime under the base and around the sides of the body, thus forming the coral. What we call coral is the structure composed of the skeleton of these animals, and the living animal is called the polyp. Some polyps live a solitary life but most of them live in large colonies with their bodies connected to one another. Beneath the living reef where thousands of these minute organisms are clumped together in their coral-building activities are the stony remains of their ancestors extending downward hundreds of feet. In one proven case, namely at Funafuti in the Ellice Islands, these remains extend to a depth of more than 1,000 feet. In general, coral is creamy white in color but much of it is beautifully tinted in red, pink, orange, yellow, green and blue. The colors are due to the red and green algae that live within the polyps, as well as to the coloration of the polyps themselves.

While these coral-building animals are the "big builders" of reefs and islands there are many "subcontractors." Certain types of algae have the ability to produce coral-like material. These are called coralline algae and encrusting algae. All these "subcontractors" fill up the crevices of the coral and thereby convert the whole into solid limestone.

The coral-building animals require warm, shallow waters and for this reason are limited to tropical areas. They do not flourish at greater depths than twenty fathoms. When coral structures are found at greater depths it means that either a sinking of the ocean floor in that locality has occurred or that the level of the ocean surface has risen since the time of the earlier coral constructions. Because these animals do not flourish in water colder than 68° F., coral reefs are generally limited to regions within the parallels of 30° latitude on each side of the equator. In this area are found most of the Pacific islands.

A word as to atolls, which are found so frequently in the Pacific Ocean. They are coral rings without a central pile of hills. In several large Pacific groups there are islands of no other type. Atolls, however, rarely assume the form of the perfectly symmetrical palm-lined "doughnuts" that have been quaintly portrayed in certain old books. Most of them are irregular in outline and, moreover, the land that actually projects above the surface of the ocean is more often a chain of disconnected islets than a rim of continuous beach. The principal entrance to the lagoon of an atoll is usually at the leeward end because the coral-building animals thrive best and build their strongest bulwarks on windward shores, where the trade wind heaps up the waters that bring their food.

Chapter III

DISCOVERY AND EXPLORATION

In the old days of Greece, scholars had already figured out that the earth was a sphere and that an ocean must separate eastern Asia from western Europe, but there was no knowledge of the Pacific or its islands, to say nothing of the Americas that lay between. Probably the first European to set foot on any of the Pacific islands was Marco Polo, that wonderful traveler from Venice, who, in about the year 1293, spent five months in Sumatra on the way back from his famous journey to China. Although shortly after Marco Polo's trip other travelers from Europe got to the East Indies, little was known of this part of the world until more than 200 years later. Columbus had no notion of the Pacific Ocean, because in those days navigators thought that the Atlantic stretched unbroken from Spain to Japan and other islands off the Asiatic coast. When Balboa, in 1513, gazed upon the waters of the "South Seas" he is said to have "discovered" the Pacific, but little did he suspect its immensity.

When Columbus set out on the voyage in which he discovered America, he was actually trying to find a good, short sailing route westward from Spain to the East Indies over what he thought would be an "all ocean" route. Magellan had the same idea when he started his great voyage around the world in 1519. In those days the Spanish and Portuguese were far from modest! They had divided the world between them—the Spanish agreeing to confine their exploration and colonizing to the west of a line passing through the mid-Atlantic, and the Portuguese agreeing to keep to the east of it. The other boundary was to be on the exact opposite side of the world! Both countries had their eyes on the Spice

Islands (now known as the Moluccas) and the Spanish thought it a pretty good gamble that these desirable islands would fall in their half of the world. Charles V of Spain sent Magellan, a Portuguese in Spanish service, westward across the Atlantic in search of a route to these fabulous islands. Magellan hit the South American coast and sailed along it until he found the strait on the southern end of South America, which bears his name. Working his way through the strait, he came up the west coast of South America, and then turned out into the great ocean again and was carried by the trade winds to Guam and the Philippines. Magellan was killed there by the natives and his ship was taken over by his first officer, Del Cano, who made his way south to the Moluccas and home to Spain around the Cape of Good Hope at the southern tip of Africa, thus completing the first trip around the world, and the greatest voyage of discovery of all times.

Despite Spanish discovery, the Moluccas and the other islands of the East Indies were to remain under Portuguese influence until the Dutch, the pioneers of the seventeenth century and the world's great navigators, took control.

Magellan had shown that the southern Pacific could be readily crossed on a westbound course in the trade-wind zone, and a number of Spanish voyagers followed his lead from Mexico. Most of them found it impossible to get back to America against the trade winds, which, of course, always blow from the northeast or southeast. Finally, in 1565 one of these navigators, Andres de Urdaneta, tried an experiment and sailed his ship north from the Philippines to the North Pacific, where he ran into the zone of the winds that blow pretty steadily to the east. He was thus able to make the first round trip in the Pacific Ocean itself. This made possible the Spanish conquest of the Philippines during the latter years of the sixteenth century.

For more than 200 years thereafter Spanish ships, the Manila galleons, plied regularly back and forth between America and this outpost of the Spanish Empire in the Far East. The Marianas, the Caroline, and the Marshall Islands, which lay along this route, were all claimed by Spain toward the end of the seventeenth century. The Hawaiian Islands were probably sighted and may have been visited by the Spanish in those days, since they lay between the westbound and eastbound sailing routes, but for some reason the Spanish made nothing of their discovery of Hawaii.

Though a Spanish ocean highway was thus in use across the heart of the Pacific from the late sixteenth century onward, it was not until toward the end of the eighteenth century that the continental coast lines and all the principal islands of the ocean were finally discovered and charted. Vast areas both south and north of the routes of the Manila galleons were long to remain wholly unknown. We shall sketch their discovery only in the broadest outline.

Explorers seldom set sail without having some definite purpose in mind. The goal that lured the early explorers into the southern half of the Pacific Ocean was a curious fantasy—one that had its origins in the speculations of the ancient Greeks and that was expressed in many maps and books even until late in the eighteenth century. It was the belief that there was an immense continent, Terra Australis or Southern Land, in the southern portion of the world centering around the South Pole and extending thousands of miles north from there.

The great figures of the early navigators passed across the stage —Sir Francis Drake, Alvaro de Mendaña, Pedro Fernandez de Quiros, Luis de Torres and Abel Janszoon Tasman. Gradually, through voyages of incredible length and great hardship, most of the islands and land masses of the Pacific were discovered and, at the same time, the myth of the vast southern continent was exploded.

Toward the middle of the eighteenth century a new era in the exploration of the Pacific dawned, in which the advancement of knowledge became the dominant motive. It was the time when the foundations of modern science were being laid in Europe. The Englishman, James Cook, was by all odds the greatest of the trained navigators. There were also others—Russian, French, Spanish, American and British. To these the Pacific yielded the last of its larger surface mysteries, the mysteries of its depths being left to future generations. To Captain Cook, however, belongs the real credit for finally disposing of the mythical great southern continent. While Christopher Columbus found a continent where none had been suspected, Cook reversed this accomplishment by finding only vast ocean spaces where, for many long centuries, a continent had been thought to lie. The tracks of Captain Cook's voyages in the far South Pacific, his stout ships battling with the "Roaring Forties" and, as the sailors used to call them, the "Furious Fifties" and the "Shrieking Sixties," are too extensive to relate in detail here. He voyaged not only through the South Pacific but across the southern Atlantic and Indian oceans as well. He sailed around the globe in these cold, unfriendly waters, even penetrating to the Antarctic ice at three points.

In the far north of the Pacific the relationship between Asia and America long remained unknown. It was for the Russians to close the breach. Traders and Cossacks had pushed overland across Siberia, reaching the Sea of Okhotsk, on whose shores they established a station in 1639. Nine years later a Cossack named Deshnef is reported to have made his way in small boats from the Arctic coast of Siberia around through Bering Strait to northern Kamchatka. However, the truth of this report is doubted by some, and, even if true, the details of the voyage are not clear. In any case, it was not until nearly a century later that Vitus Bering, who, although a Dane, was an officer in the Russian Navy, thoroughly explored the strait named after him—the strait that separates the great continents of Asia and the Americas. He made these voyages in ships built on the remote wilderness shores of northeastern Asia. Even then it was not known whether the Alaskan coast, which Bering had visited, was actually a part of the American continent or merely a large, separate, northerly island.

To answer this question, Captain Cook again appeared on the scene, undertaking his third great voyage, which lasted four years, ending in 1780. It turned out that the most outstanding result was a rediscovery, on his outward journey, of the Hawaiian Islands, which the captain named the Sandwich Islands. After leaving Hawaii he sailed over to the little known coast of Oregon and Vancouver Island. Unfortunately, bad weather forced him to keep well out in the open sea from there up to southeastern Alaska, so he was unable to explore the shores of British Columbia. Consequently, it was left for a later navigator, Captain George Vancouver, in 1790, to demonstrate conclusively that no passage east of Bering Strait connected the Pacific with the Arctic Ocean.

Captain Cook, in the meanwhile, had made it clear that no such passage existed farther north since he had thoroughly examined the Alaskan coast as far north as Point Barrow beyond Bering Strait on the Arctic shore. Returning from Alaska, directly south across Bering Sea in the open Pacific to Hawaii, Cook eliminated the possibility of large islands existing in these waters, but mystery still hung over the unvisited northwestern Pacific between Hawaii and Siberia. He determined to explore this part of the ocean but his luck had run out. On the eve of his final departure from Hawaii he was attacked and killed by the natives. The voyage across the Northwest Pacific to Kamchatka—the voyage that solved the last great problem of the Pacific—was carried out under the leadership of Cook's second-in-command, Captain Clerke.

With the completion of these voyages "the period of discovery in the Pacific" came to a close. Subsequent voyages, made by other navigators, served merely to fill in details on the map, rather than establish its fundamental pattern. Jean François de La Pérouse, a Frenchman, should be mentioned because he was the first navigator who was equipped with and made regular use of chronometers of considerable accuracy and was, therefore, able to establish longitudes with precision. It has been said that after the time of La Pérouse, the Pacific islands "ceased to fluctuate" from one place to another!

If we mean by the word "discovery" the finding of islands and continental coast lines, the period of discovery ended in 1780. But the detailed mapping of these islands and coast lines, and the exploration of winds and ocean currents, of geological structure, of the birds, mammals, plants and fishes, of the ocean floor, of the native peoples and their histories—these investigations had hardly begun in 1780. It was the task of the nineteenth and twentieth centuries—an important task still being pursued and to which there is no end.

After the discovery of the major islands of the Pacific, it was not long before white men followed to trade or otherwise to exploit the islands' resources. These were bad days for the native peoples. Traders came, or planters, and with them adventurers of all types —beachcombers, deserters from whaling vessels, escaped convicts from the penal settlements of Australia, and the like. With no well-established government control, these men brought the worst of "civilization" with them. Diseases, firearms and "firewater" spread their devastating effects. The best native land was often grabbed or bought for a few guns or trinkets. Young men were transported from one island to another to work on plantations. Some were even kidnaped to labor in the mines of South America. A rapid decline of native population followed and continued almost to the present day.

There were, of course, better elements among the whites. The last century was the time of missionaries and the "spreading of the Gospel"—by French Catholics or British and American Protestants, who sought not only to convert the natives to Christianity but to protect them from the other whites. If in some ways and in many instances the missionaries failed to understand the native's way of life, tried to force a different kind of civilization on him before he was ready to accept it, made him wear European clothes and give up his dances and religious rites, the fact still remains that, had it not been for these earnest men, the island peoples would have suffered far more than they did; for the missionaries were in many cases responsible for helping to raise the general living standards of these people.

When the western governments finally stepped in, their primary motive was the quest for power and wealth in the form of colonies. Such ambitions have waxed and waned at different times in different countries. Toward the latter part of the last century they were particularly strong in Germany, France and Great Britain. This condition led up to the dividing of the Pacific in the years following 1870 in about the same way that Africa was being divided up at that time. The United States was the last to enter the picture. While we had taken control of a few small scattered islands—Midway was one of them—and had established a coaling station and naval base in Samoa prior to our war with Spain in 1898, it was not until after that brief conflict that we became an imperial power in both the Caribbean Sea and the Pacific Ocean.

Politically the islands fall into three main classes: (1) those that have always been completely independent, (2) those brought under the control of the western nations in the sixteenth century, and (3) those brought under western control in the nineteenth century.

The only islands of the Pacific that have maintained complete independence since the earliest times are those of the Japanese Archipelago. The story of Japan's medieval isolationism until Admiral Perry's visit in 1853, of its subsequent opening to western influences, and of the amazingly rapid adoption of the mechanisms if not the spirit of western culture has been told too often to need repetition.

The islands that were first brought under the control of western nations were the Philippines (together with Guam) and the East Indies—old colonial domains in which European influences have been powerful for some 400 years. The Philippine Islands were governed by Spain until the close of the Spanish-American War in 1898, when they were ceded to the United States. An agreement made in 1935 provides for their complete independence on July 4, 1946.

The East Indies, as we have seen, were dominated by Portugal until the Dutch gained control in the seventeenth century. On the eve of the Japanese invasion, the eastern part of Timor still belonged to Portugal, a relic of the once mighty Portuguese Empire in the Far East. This does not mean that either the Portuguese at any time or the Dutch until quite recently have actually governed all parts of the immense archipelago. Local potentates in many places long retained complete or partial independence, and much of the interiors of the larger islands—Sumatra, Borneo, Celebes, New Guinea—remained unexplored until the last few decades. Even today the interiors of some of these islands, New Guinea, for example, have not been fully explored. The Dutch, moreover, never established themselves on the northwestern coast of Borneo, where three states, Brunei, North Borneo, and Sarawak, were made British protectorates in the 1880's.

Although under the sovereignty of the Netherlands, the Netherlands Indies were largely self-governing after 1922—self-governing, that is, in the sense that the home government in the Netherlands exerted little direct control over local affairs, but not in the sense that the native peoples ruled themselves. Except for two native states in Java, the actual administration was in the hands of Europeans, assisted by native civil servants. After the middle of the eighteenth century the Dutch concentrated their attention on Java and Madura—islands of immense fertility and peopled by a civilized and docile folk. As a consequence, the population of Java and Madura, which comprise only 7 percent of the total land area of the Netherlands Indies, increased at an astonishing rate, at last reports reaching about 45,000,000 or almost 80 percent of the total population of the Netherlands Indies.

The Indies had thus become an empire in itself within the larger empire of the Dutch. Java and Madura formed the metropolitan center in which the "Outer Provinces" (as the remainder of the Indies was termed) stood in a kind of colonial relationship. From Java the exploitation of the rich mineral, forest and agricultural resources of the Outer Provinces was directed, and agricultural settlement by Javanese in the outlying islands was encouraged.

Let us now turn to the Pacific islands of the third category, those that have been brought under western control since 1800—the small islands of the "South Seas" together with eastern New Guinea and New Zealand.

Although many of the discoverers had laid claim to islands in behalf of their own countries, the home governments were often in no hurry to confirm these claims by annexation. Great Britain, France, and the United States were at first reluctant to assume the responsibility and expense of administering and defending remote and undeveloped places. Indeed, it was not until the beginning of the present century that the division of this part of the Pacific among different powers was completed, and there are still a number of tiny islands and coral reefs over which more than one nation claims sovereignty.

What, broadly, was the situation in 1900 and what have been the changes that have since occurred? In 1900 France was dominant in the east-central Pacific and also held the large island of New Caledonia, with its rich mineral deposits. The British Empire and the Germans dominated the central and western Pacific. From Spain the Germans had bought the Caroline, the Marianas (except for Guam), and the Marshall Islands after the Spanish-American War. In the eighties they had acquired northeastern New Guinea, the Bismarck Archipelago, the northern Solomons, and Nauru, where in 1897 rich deposits of phosphates were found. In 1900 they had divided the Samoan group with the United States, taking the western part. The British ruled the central and southwestern islands, except for French New Caledonia, American Samoa, and the New Hebrides, the last of which they governed jointly with the French. The United States controlled the Northeast Pacific, holding Hawaii and the Aleutians. We had also acquired the Philippines and Guam from Spain in 1898.

The principal change between 1900 and the Japanese invasion of 1941–42 was the establishment under mandates from the League of Nations of British, Australian, New Zealand, and Japanese governments. The Japanese seized the Marianas, the Caroline, and the Marshall Islands in 1914 and were given a mandate for them in 1920. The Australian mandate covered northeastern New Guinea, the Bismarck Archipelago, and the northern Solomons, and that of New Zealand covered western Samoa. Nauru became a mandated territory of the British Empire—Great Britain, Australia, and New Zealand jointly deciding from time to time as to which of the three should administer it.

Western government has brought unquestioned benefits to the islanders, but it has been a slow process. As officials have become more and more familiar with native needs, institutions, and psychology, far-reaching reforms have been carried out. Many of the evils wrought in the earlier period of lawlessness are disappearing. The decline in native population has nearly everywhere been checked and in many places reversed, partly as a result of an increasing natural immunity to disease but mainly because better regulated ways of life have been introduced. Medical care and the ending of inter-tribal conflicts have cut the death rate, and with stable government have come improved economic opportunties. In general, the western rulers now regard the welfare of the natives as a trust, and their activities are directed toward the conservation of the island peoples and the promotion of their progress along the paths of modern civilization. Policies differ and have met with varying degrees of success, but the most enlightened seem to be those that recognize that the necessary and inevitable adjustment of native life to modern conditions can be made only gradually.

Chapter IV

CLIMATES, WINDS, CURRENTS, AND TIDES

All kinds of climate, from polar cold to tropical heat, are found in the Pacific. There are the foggy, cold, wind-swept reaches of the Aleutians, the steaming jungles of Guadalcanal, and the soft and pleasing climate of Hawaii and the other mid-ocean islands. At or near the equator, the temperature remains about the same throughout the year but everywhere else there are definite seasons.

THE EQUATOR AND THE TRADE WINDS

Heat in the equatorial belt causes the air to expand and overflow poleward aloft. This results in a reduction of the total air and hence a lowered pressure at the surface on the equator and an increase in total air and higher pressure to the north and south. Consequently, there is an almost continuous equatorward flow of air, known as the trade winds. The trade winds do not, however, blow directly from the north and south because our earth is spinning to the east. The chart between pages 44 and 45 illustrates this and shows why trade winds north of the equator always blow from the northeast and why those south of the equator blow from the southeast. The region of the equator is one of prevailing east winds except near Asia, with heavy rainfalls distributed fairly evenly throughout the year.

It is an interesting fact that the heat equator lies north of the actual or geographic equator. This is due mainly to the greater amount of land in the Northern Hemisphere and to the fact that land surfaces are heated more readily by the sun than water surfaces. While this explanation accounts for the curious condition near the continents of America and Asia, another reason exists out in the mid-Pacific; namely, that the mid-ocean areas are openly exposed to the cold Antarctic Continent lying to the south, whereas north of the Pacific, Siberia and Alaska are not as cold.

Another curious fact is that the trade-wind belts shift somewhat with the seasons as they "follow the sun." In December the northeast trade-wind zone extends south to the equator or even below it. In June the southeast trade-wind zone extends in some localities as far north as 10° of north latitude. Trade winds are noted for their steadiness, and from the earliest days of ocean voyages sailors have relied upon them to carry their vessels along trade routes.

In certain parts of the ocean, trade winds are interrupted or deflected. For example, in the lee of the great Andes mountain range, these winds usually blow from west of south instead of from the southeast. Out in the western part of the Pacific the huge land mass of Asia causes the trade winds to be replaced by the alternating seasonal winds known as monsoons. The cooling of land and air during the winter produces a high-pressure area over the continent, so that the wind blows from land to sea. Along the east coast of Asia this is the northwest monsoon, which reaches its height between November and February. In summer, a low-pressure area over the continent, due to the rapid absorption of heat by land, results in the opposite, or southeast, monsoon.

There is still another, though very local, interruption of the trade-wind systems. On all mountainous islands a cool breeze usually blows down the slope and out toward the sea during the night and is replaced in the daytime by an onshore upslope wind regardless of the season.

WINDS OF THE NORTH AND SOUTH PACIFIC

On the poleward margins of the trade winds is a belt of light variable winds at about latitudes 30° N. and 30° S. These belts are sometimes called the horse latitudes, this name stemming from the tradition that in the old sailing days, ships would get becalmed there, the food supply would run low, and horses on board would die.

In the middle latitudes of the North and South Pacific are the paired zones of westerly winds. In them the tracks of storms cross the Pacific toward the American continents with considerable regularity. The wind, of course, blows from any direction but westerly winds are more common. In the Southern Hemisphere, where land areas are relatively few and small, the corresponding zone is known as the "Roaring Forties" because of the strength and persistence of the winds. The names "Furious Fifties" and "Shrieking Sixties" have been applied to belts farther south.

The South Pacific subpolar and polar regions begin near the northernmost limits of drifting ice and blend into each other. As one travels far down into the South Pacific approaching the so-called subpolar regions, the winds are chiefly from the west. Still farther south, in the polar regions, the winds are found to be generally from the south or east of south, blowing out toward the open sea from the glacier "land" of the Antarctic Continent.

These regions in the Antarctic have no counterpart in the North Pacific, which is separated from the Arctic Sea by the narrow Bering Strait, only fifty-seven miles wide between Alaska and Siberia. Because of this land barrier, the North Pacific is practically an ice-free ocean without the bergs such as drift far south from the Greenland region into the North Atlantic.

DOLDRUMS AND HURRICANES

Another belt of relatively light winds, which lies between the northeast and southeast trade-wind regions, is known as the doldrums. Its position necessarily shifts more or less during the course of the year and it is characterized by heat, high humidity, and excessive rainfall. To steamship navigation, the doldrums present no trouble, but in the days of sailing, the passage across the doldrums from one trade-wind region to the other was often slow, painful, and to be dreaded.

Tropical cyclones, which are also known as typhoons, hurricanes, and other names according to their place of origin, are limited in the Pacific Ocean to three more or less definite areas. Two of these areas lie north of the equator and one south of the equator.

In the eastern Pacific, north of the equator and off the Central American and Mexican coasts, hurricanes are by no means uncommon. Their season is between August and October.

In the western North Pacific, centering in the area of the China Sea, typhoons are likely to be very severe. Their season is from May to November, the peak period coming between July and September. Unlike some Atlantic hurricanes, they do not sweep across the whole expanse of the ocean, but may begin in the Caroline Islands district, traveling by way of the Philippines to the China coast. Here they either move inland and disappear or continue along the coast to Japan where they move out to sea again in the tracks followed by the cyclones of the zone of westerly winds.

In the western South Pacific, the tropical cyclone belt is more extensive, stretching from Australia eastward nearly half the width of the Pacific between latitudes 10° and 30° S. The South Pacific cyclones are in general less numerous and less severe than the typhoons of the North Pacific. They occur in the summer months of the Southern Hemisphere, chiefly between January and March.

Hurricanes never occur in the eastern South Pacific, the ocean off the Peruvian coast being practically storm free. Also, it is a fact that hurricanes do not originate at the equator. They usually have their point of origin in a latitude about 8° and 15° north or south of the equator, and they reach their maximum force soon after they form.

SEASONS, RAINFALL, AND CLIMATE

Rainfall at sea is determined largely by the surface temperature of the water in relation to winds and the land areas that lie in their path. The great Pacific has areas of rainlessness, other areas that have moderate to very heavy precipitation, and still others marked by alternating rainy and dry seasons. Often, however, the distinction is less one between dry and wet than between wet and "wetter."

Frequently throughout this book, reference is made to rain in terms of inches. As a basis for comparison, we may take New York, which has a yearly rainfall of 42 inches and an average rainfall of about 3.5 inches in all the months except July (4.1 inches) and August (4.3 inches).

Rainfall in the doldrums and trade-wind belts consists almost entirely of showers. Rainfall in the horse-latitude belts of light winds is infrequent. Rainfall in the zones of prevailing westerlies is produced in the traveling cyclones by the forced lifting of warm air masses over colder air masses. Over islands, rainfall is generally heavier than over the open ocean because the air is forced upward in blowing across the islands.

Change in temperature between the winter and summer of either hemisphere is almost negligible in the tropical Pacific. Wherever seasons are distinguishable, they express themselves rather through a shift in the prevailing wind or through differences in the amount of rainfall.

THE PROCESS OF RAIN

Rain is the commonest form of precipitation. A complete understanding of the phenomenon requires a knowledge of the laws of physics that govern the behavior of gases and liquids. However, the basic principles of the process are fairly simple.

When water evaporates, it passes into the air in the form of invisible vapor. At a given temperature, air is capable of holding a certain amount of water vapor. If the temperature of the air rises, more water vapor can be held, and if the temperature falls, less water vapor can be held. Sufficient cooling of the air raises the relative humidity to the point of saturation, and beyond this point the water vapor takes one of several forms of condensed moisture.

Thus, clouds are usually the result of the dynamic cooling of rising masses of air, and precipitation occurs when rapid condensation takes place after the clouds have formed. If the temperature is above 32° (the freezing point) this precipitation will be in the form of rain. Rain occurs, then, in rising, cooling, moisture-laden air currents in which exaggerated condensation is taking place.

Usually summer rain is caused by condensation in vertically ascending, or convectional, air currents. Winter rains are caused by condensation in warm air masses rising either along sloping surfaces (mountains) or on an atmospheric front of a different temperature and density. The density is indicated by the barometric pressure.

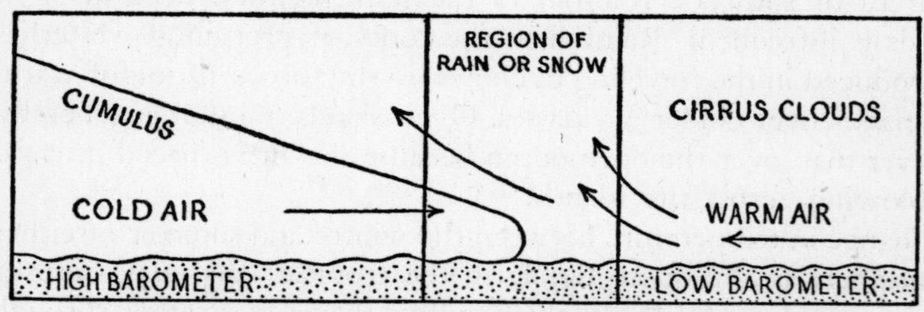

A Wedge of Cold Air Undermining and Uplifting a Mass of Warm Air *

Usually, tropical rains are convectional, but most of the exceptionally heavy rainfall records of the world are the result of forced ascent on the windward slopes of mountain ranges.

In the eastern Pacific there is a zone of fairly heavy and steady rainfall between the equator and latitude 10° N. Here the rains are remarkably uniform throughout the year, while just to the north and to the south are the trade-wind zones with relatively slight rainfall.

Although the trade winds are moisture-bearing winds and are characterized by frequent showers over the ocean, they rarely cause heavy rainfall on low islands or continental coasts, at least in the eastern part of the Pacific. A common explanation is that the land areas are apt to be of a warmer temperature than the winds that blow from a higher latitude, and the resulting heating

* This diagram is taken from *Elementary Meteorology*, by Finch, Trewartha and others (1942), p. 94, Fig. 57.

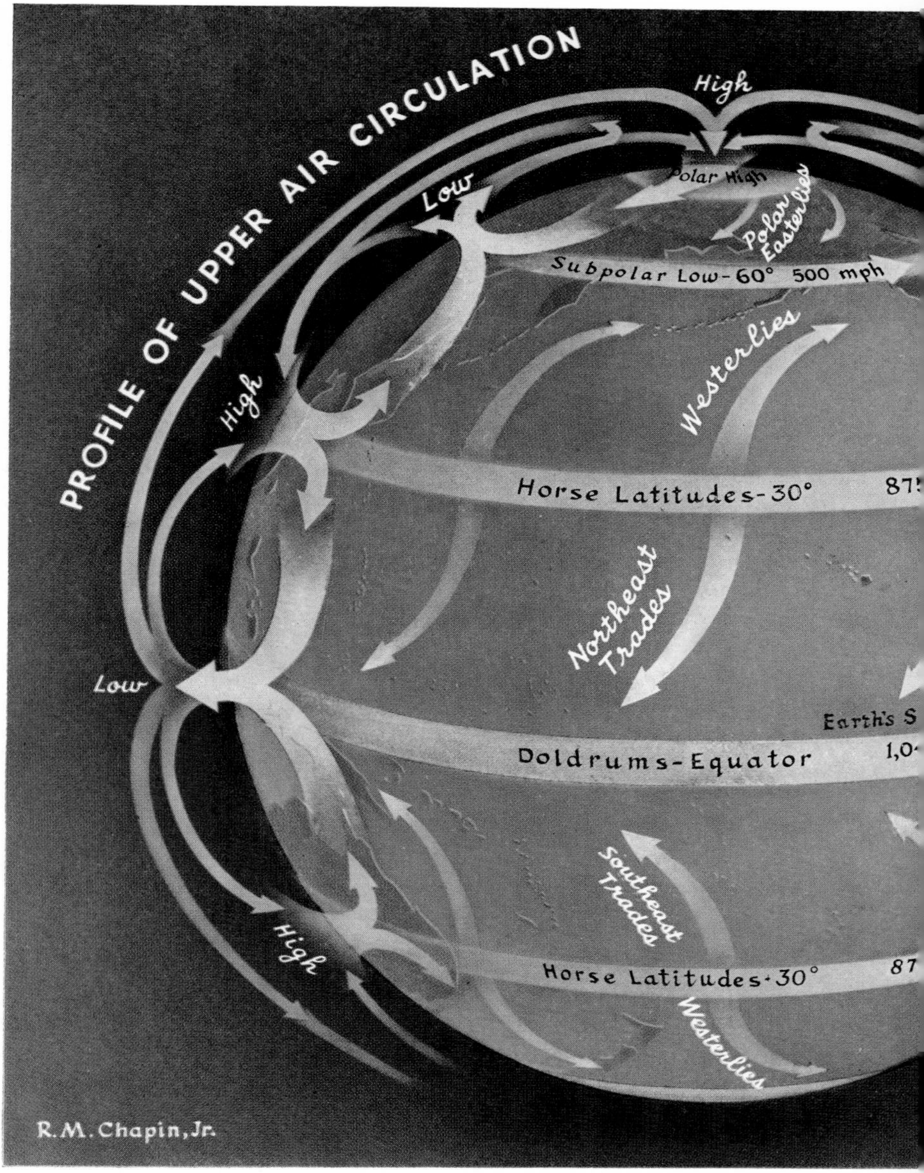

PROFILE OF UPPER AIR CIRCULATION

High

Polar High

Polar Easterlies

Low

Subpolar Low-60° 500 mph

Westerlies

High

Horse Latitudes-30° 87

Northeast Trades

Low

Earth's S

Doldrums-Equator 1,0

Southeast Trades

High

Horse Latitudes-30° 87

Westerlies

R.M. Chapin, Jr.

ORIGIN OF THE PACIFIC WINDS

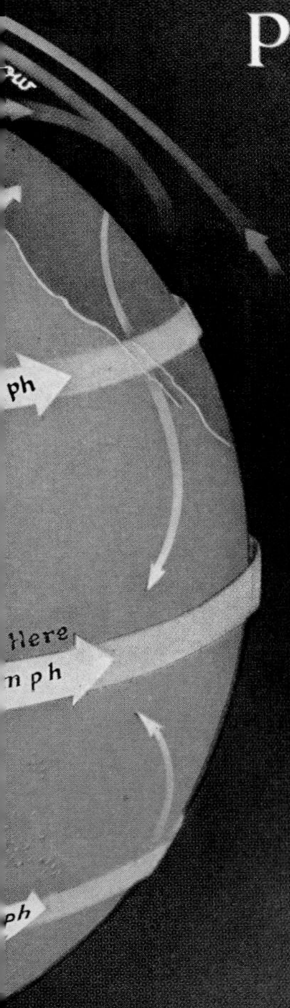

This chart presents a generalized picture of the world's air circulation. At the upper left there is shown in profile the upper air circulation. Over the face of the drawing are shown the prevailing winds at the earth's surface. Actually, the pattern is not quite so simple as this. But for the Pacific area, where water predominates, the picture is reasonably truthful.

As air is warmed, it expands. On the other hand, as air cools, it contracts. Also, warm air tends to rise, being pushed up by heavier, cooler air which moves in to take its place.

In the latitudes near the equator, the air is warmed at surface levels and the heat and humidity expand the lower atmosphere. This increases the pressure aloft so that the air there flows away from the belt over the equator northward and southward toward both poles. Thus the total air at surface levels near the equator is reduced and the pressure there is de-

(continued on the next page)

prevents much condensation of the water vapor. In many tropical localities, as at Panama, the trade-wind season is the dry season, while the rainy season is the period of calms that comes after the northeast trade-wind belt has drawn back into the higher latitudes of the North Atlantic.

In the western part of the Pacific, however, the trade winds often bring heavy rainfall even to low islands. Presumably these winds have there become more nearly saturated with moisture up to greater heights because of their long passage across warm ocean waters. Therefore only slight lifting of the air will cause enough cooling to produce condensation and rain.

Farther west in the Pacific the tropical belt broadens and becomes wetter. Here there are two seasons: north of the equator, for example, that of the southwest monsoon between May and September is the warmer and moister season, and that of the northeast monsoon between November and March is the dry period of the year.

Continued from Origin of Pacific Winds

creased, resulting in the surface low-pressure belt of the doldrums.

About a third of the way to the poles, at the horse latitudes, this air, somewhat cooled, tends to accumulate near the surface, forming the high-pressure belts of the horse latitudes. From these high-pressure belts the air again divides, some of it returning toward the equator as the northeast and southeast trade winds, some continuing toward subpolar latitudes as the westerlies.

Around the poles, the coldness shrinks the air. This reduces pressure aloft, with a consequent flow of the upper wind toward the poles from the nearby subpolar latitudes. The result is a high-pressure disk over the poles, surrounded by a belt of low pressure, with outward blowing winds at the surface.

The drawing shows that the surface winds, traveling from high-pressure to low-pressure belts, do not blow due north or south, but are deflected to the right in the Northern Hemisphere and to the left in the Southern Hemisphere. This is caused by the rotation of the earth's surface under the rather freely moving winds.

People learned this correct explanation only during the last century. Columbus discovered the trade winds. Then someone explained them as due to the greater heat of equatorial latitudes and accounted for the westward deflection as due to the atmosphere lagging behind the rotating solid earth. In 1735 Hadley pointed to the much greater eastward speed of the earth's surface at the equator (about 1,040 miles per hour, as shown by the chart) than at the horse latitudes (about 875 miles per hour), and said that the winds flowing toward the equator, the trade winds, just had to get left behind. He showed, too, that this applied to the prevailing westerlies, the winds flowing toward the poles from the horse latitudes. The prevailing westerlies travel from latitudes of comparatively high eastward velocity to latitudes of comparatively low eastward velocity (see chart) thereby putting the westerly component into these winds.

So far so good, but it did not explain a further fact that had been known since 1650 when Varenius correctly surmised that typhoons were rotating storms, and that the deflection of the winds is the same no matter in what direction they blow. But it was not until Coriolis and Poisson (in the 1830's) explained the deflective effect of the earth's rotation and Tracy and Ferrel (in the '40's and '50's) applied this fully to the winds that the "deflection" was understood as due simply to the turning of the earth's surface, as represented by a horizontal disk centered at any point, turning under the rather freely moving wind. So the deflection of the wind has to be the same no matter in what direction it blows. At the poles, this turning is about 15° per hour; at latitude 30° it is only half this, and at the equator the turning of the "disk" disappears.

Ocean currents, ships, airplanes, and shells from guns are all "deflected" by the same angular amounts in equal times, to the extent that friction with their surroundings permits.

The climate of every locality, however, varies somewhat. In the Moluccas, northeastern New Guinea and parts of the Philippines, for example, June and July are the months of heaviest rainfall.

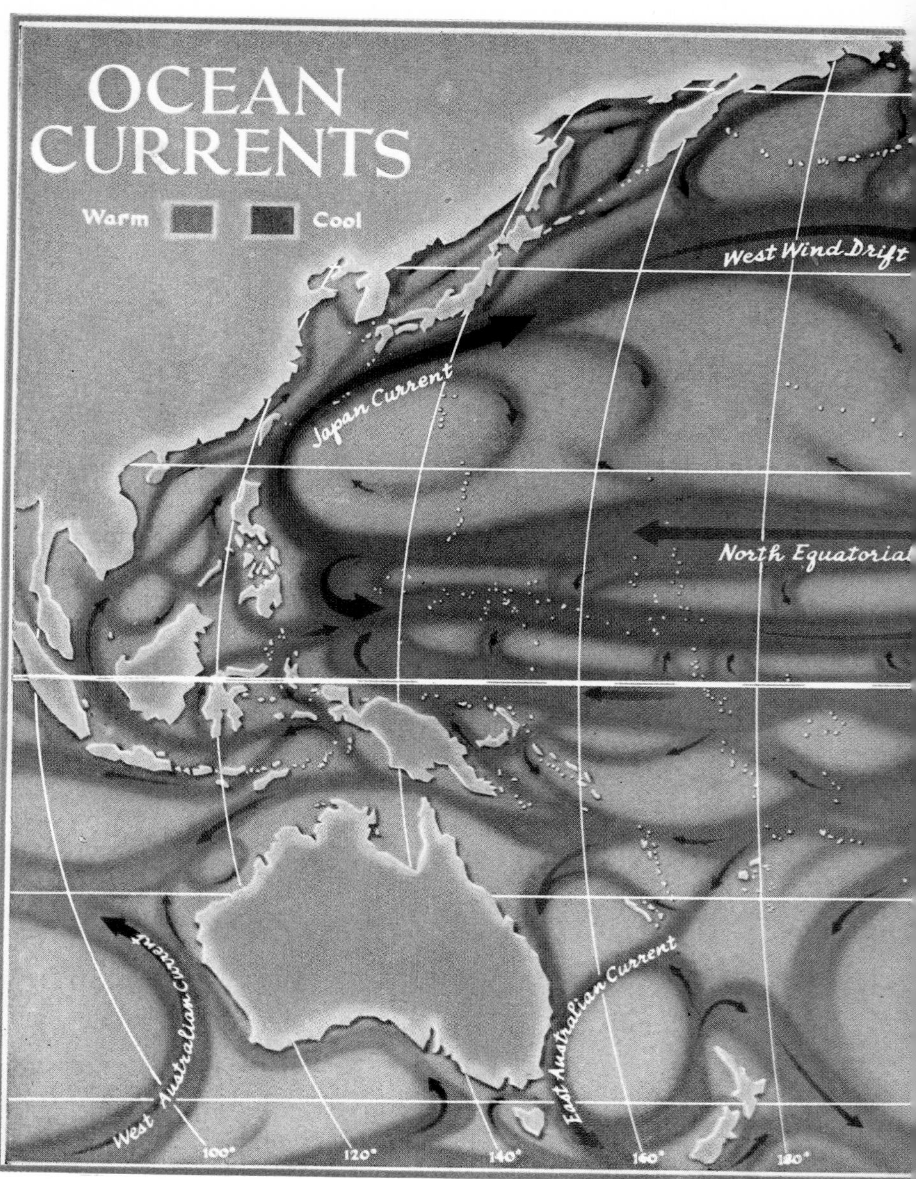
OCEAN
CURRENTS
Warm
Cool
West Wind Drift
Japan Current
North Equatorial
West Australian Current
East Australian Current
100°
120°
140°
160°
180°

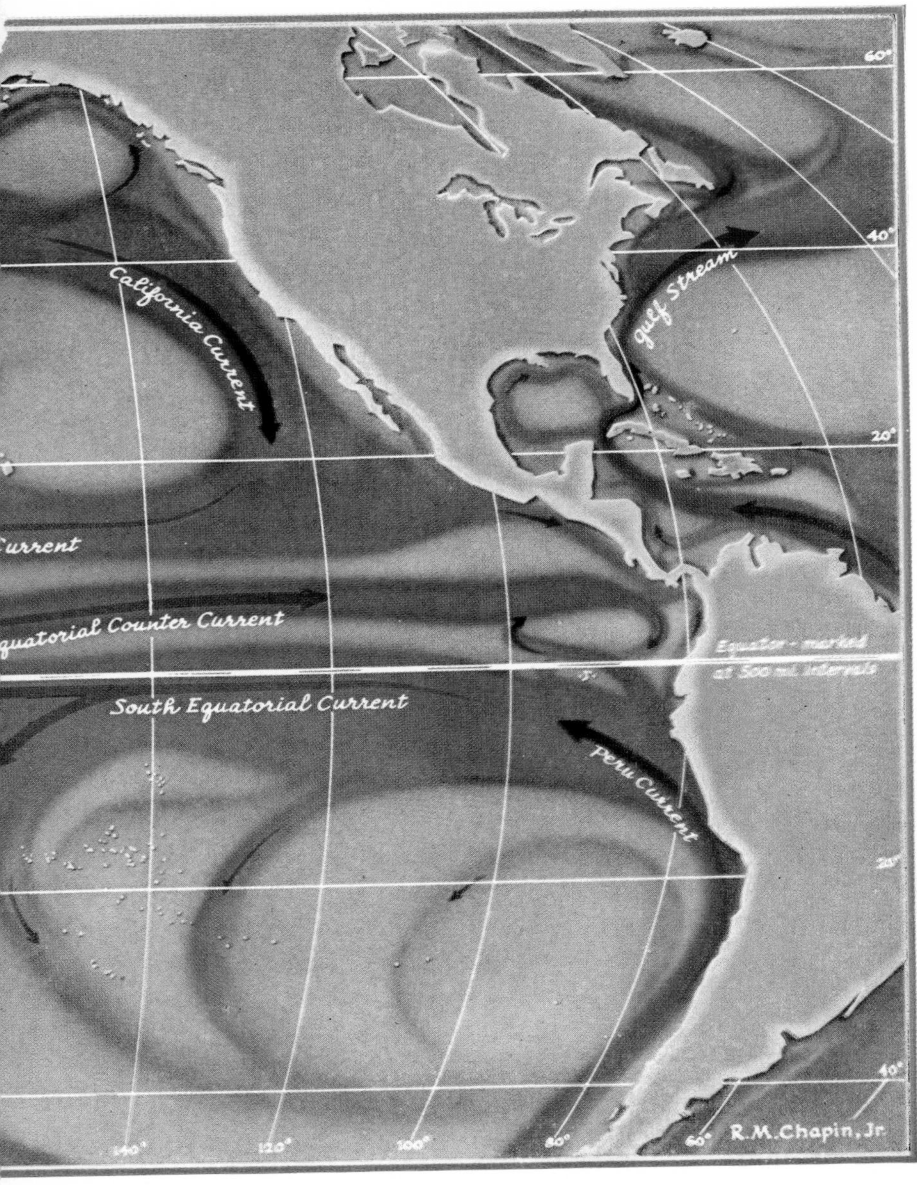

60°
40°
20°
20°
40°
California Current
Gulf Stream
Current
Equatorial Counter Current
Equator - marked
at 500 mi. intervals
South Equatorial Current
Peru Current
140°
120°
100°
80°
60°
R.M.Chapin, Jr.

At one locality on the island of Luzon, of the Philippines, 133 inches of rain were recorded in July, 1912. This is as much as New York receives in three years. The world's record is at Kauai, in the Hawaiian Islands, with an annual average rainfall of more than 450 inches.

Mountain regions generally receive much more rain than the lowlands, and quite generally in the South Pacific a cloud layer envelops the mountains above a height of 4,000 feet except during early morning. Northern New Guinea and Borneo are two of the wettest regions on earth, with an annual rainfall of at least 100 inches, ranging at certain spots to 250 inches. The northern and southern coasts of New Guinea have quite different climates and seasons, as is likely to be the case with the two sides of any large island.

South of this wet zone is a drier area extending through southern Celebes, the Lesser Sunda Islands and Java, culminating in the Timor group where there is less than three inches of rain from May to October and not more than thirty to fifty inches for the whole year. In the Solomon Islands, on the other hand, the quantity of rain received is about the same in the different periods.

OCEAN CURRENTS

All the oceans of this earth have their own systems of currents, so that if one were in a raft or boat in any spot in any ocean, one would be carried along slowly but surely even though no wind whatsoever were blowing. The only real exception exists in the center of the Sargasso Sea, which lies in the middle of the Atlantic Ocean on a line between Florida and the northwest corner of Africa. This is a true "dead spot."

One result of the current system in the Pacific, which has a movement of surface water toward the equator on the American side of the ocean and a movement largely away from the equator on the Asiatic side, is that tropical waters are squeezed into a narrow belt near the Americas but are spread out rather widely in the western Pacific. Ocean currents differ in their temperature, salt content, and other physical and chemical properties.

Temperature, which has important effects on climate and life, naturally depends upon the source of the water, the gradual effect of the air with which the surface of the water comes in contact, and the relative amount and intensity of sunlight. However, cold currents do not necessarily owe their lower temperature to the fact that they flow from cooler regions. Currents that pull away from continental coasts, such as the California Current and the Peruvian Current, are chilled by deeper and cooler water rising to replace surface water that has moved seaward. The cooling process is thus continuous for long distances, and in this case the coolness of the surface water is not due to having come from areas nearer the poles. The warm surface layers of the Japan Current, as that of the Gulf Stream, on the other hand, are composed of water that has been propelled for considerable periods by the warm winds of the tropics or subtropics.

It is well to remember, when thinking of "warm" or "cold" ocean water, that we are really referring only to the surface layers, the part that most directly concerns human beings. Afloat or ashore, man is chiefly a creature of the surface of the earth. As a matter of fact, there are no "warm" waters in the depths of the ocean, the great bulk of which is made up of water that is at a temperature just above freezing. In the tropical belt of the world, between latitude 23½° N. and 23½° S., the surface temperature of the ocean may reach as high as 85° F. Yet the average temperature of all the ocean water, from surface to bottom, within this zone is not more than 39° F. Some deep ocean waters have a temperature below 32°, the ordinary freezing point of fresh water, but still above that of sea water, the average freezing point of which, at surface levels, is 29° F.

TIDES

The tide is a periodic rise and fall of the sea caused by the gravitational pull of the moon and the more distant sun. The influence of the sun is only two-fifths that of the moon. About twice a month these two heavenly bodies pull together to produce the higher or spring tides. At the lower or neap-tide periods the sun and moon work against each other.

The range of tidal rise and fall is chiefly determined by the coastal outlines of the continents. For this reason the height of the tide is usually much less striking at remote oceanic islands than it is in certain funnel-shaped continental harbors where the long tide wave may be forced to "pile up." For example, at Midway Island the maximum change of ocean level resulting in tides is approximately eleven inches, whereas at Seattle, Washington, mean range is approximately seven feet.

Tidal influences are enormously complicated. It is known that every body of water has a natural period of "rocking" or oscillation which is proportional to its length and depth. This is as true of a bowl or a bathtub as it is of the Mediterranean Sea or the Pacific basin. Wherever the length of the oscillation corresponds to half a day, the familiar tidal effect prevails—one high tide and one low tide within twelve hours. Wherever the period approximates a full day, the situation will be reflected as a daily tidal cycle. Mixed influences produce further variety. At Honolulu in the Hawaiian Islands there is one "high" high tide and one "low" high tide each day, with low tides in between.

The effect of the tide wave in the ocean may be illustrated by tipping a dish of water, end to end or corner to corner. Under such treatment the water will, of course, alternately rise and fall at the extremities of the dish but will remain approximately at a common level in the middle. The point of stable level is called a *nodal point*. There are several such points in the vast Pacific. When an island happens to lie close to a nodal point, its surrounding waters may appear to be nearly tideless. Furthermore, at such places the normally weaker tidal pull of the sun may exert as much influence as the moon.

These complicated influences are together the cause of a variety of tidal patterns among the Pacific islands, but on all the islands the range between high and low water is usually very small when compared with the tidal ranges along continental shores.

Chapter V

STARS OVER MELANESIA

When you go out into the Pacific you will rediscover, among other things, the sky, sun, moon and stars. Whether you go to Attu in the far north or to Guadalcanal south of the equator you will see the selfsame sun, moon and planets as you do at home. But as you cross the ocean southward, over the rim of the world, many strange things come into view and none more so than the austral stars and constellations. Sailing south and leaving the equator behind, you see the glory of Canopus and Achernar at their best, or the Southern Triangle and the Magellanic Clouds, all lifting higher and higher every night as the North Star vanishes wholly from sight and the Dipper sinks closer to the northern horizon. Finally, an inconspicuous group comes into view, perhaps at first lying on its side, then slowly becoming erect, and you see for the first time the Southern Cross, which, throughout all history for the half of mankind down under, has been the guiding symbol, as the Pole Star has for us on "top" of the world.

In exchange for the Big Bear and the Little Bear you gain a whole flock of birdlike constellations—the Dove, the Crow, the Crane, the Toucan and the Phoenix, while unfamiliar glories of the Milky Way shine through the velvet, tropical night. At the equator, Scorpio, the constellation that most justifies its name, stretches far across the heavens.

Astronomical figures are not all higher mathematics. On a calm, still night, with not a breath of air stirring, the solid earth beneath you is tearing through bitter cold space at the rate of more than eighteen miles every second. Look at our only heavenly neighbor, the moon, and consider that if an airplane could fly night and day, at 350 miles an hour, it would take a month to reach the nearest lunar crater. Even so it would be a most unhappy landing, for on the sunny side of the moon the temperature is around 200° F., not far from the boiling point, while on the dark side away from the sun the mercury drops to 250° below zero.

If you look very carefully on a clear night, even with the naked eye, at the constellation of Andromeda, close to the Great Square of Pegasus, you can detect a faint smudge on the face of the heavens. This will be the spiral nebula in Andromeda, a galaxy as large as our entire Milky Way. It is 700,000 light years away (with light traveling at 186,000 miles a second), and it contains millions of suns, many of them larger than our sun. Also, while it is the only galaxy easily visible to the naked eye, it is also only one out of countless millions of other galaxies.

If these casual thoughts about stars should find you in the quiet of the night on some small island isolated in the great spaces of the Pacific Ocean, you may hear from a distant native village the sound of drums. You may think of the people of this village as good friends, contented in their daily life, but primitive in many of the ways of human beings. Look, then, to the northward, into the darkness of the open sea, and imagine the voyages that the forefathers of these same islanders made, in open canoes and without compass or sextant, steering by the stars over distances of a thousand or more miles from one speck of an island to another. And all this centuries before Columbus made his uncertain way westward, toward a New World which offered landing possibilities from north to south of 6,000 miles of continental shores!

CONSTELLATIONS

1	Cepheus	Monarch	21	Aquila	Eagle
2	Draco	Dragon	22	Ophiuchus	Serpent Bearer
3	Ursa Minor	Little Bear	23	Virgo	Maiden
4	Ursa Major	Great Bear	24	Hydra	Sea Serpent
5	Auriga	Charioteer	25	Canis Minor	Little Dog
6	Perseus	Rescuer	26	Orion	Hunter
7	Cassiopeia	Lady in the Chair	27	Cetus	Whale
			28	Capricornus	Sea Goat
8	Pegasus	Winged horse	29	Sagittarius	Archer
9	Cygnus	Swan	30	Scorpio	Scorpion
10	Lyra	Harp	31	Libra	Scales
11	Hercules	Hercules	32	Canis Major	Great Dog
12	Corona	Crown	33	Corvus	Crow
13	Boötes	Bear driver	34	Eridanus	River
14	Leo	Lion	35	Grus	Crane
15	Gemini	Twins	36	Centaurus	Centaur
16	Taurus	Bull	37	Crux	Cross
17	Triangulum	Triangle	38	Argo Navis	Ship
18	Aries	Ram	39	Triangulum Australe	Southern Triangle
19	Andromeda	Chained Lady			
20	Aquarius	Water carrier	40	Hydrus	Water Snake

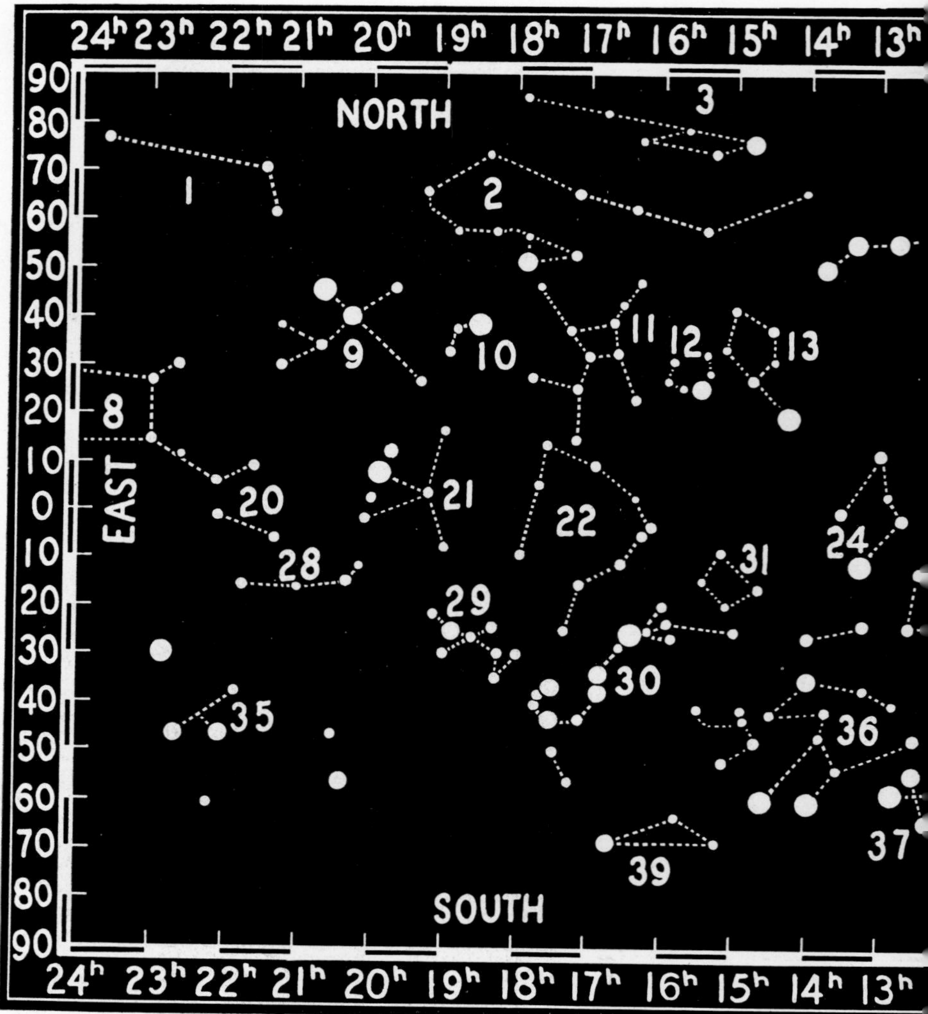

STARS OVEI

To locate the zenith point in the sky directly overhead: Add to the hours (and quarters) since noon the number of months (and quarters) since March 21. Find this sum on the hour scale top and bottom.

Draw a vertical line betw
a line across the sheet at
The intersection of the
Example: Latitude 20° S.

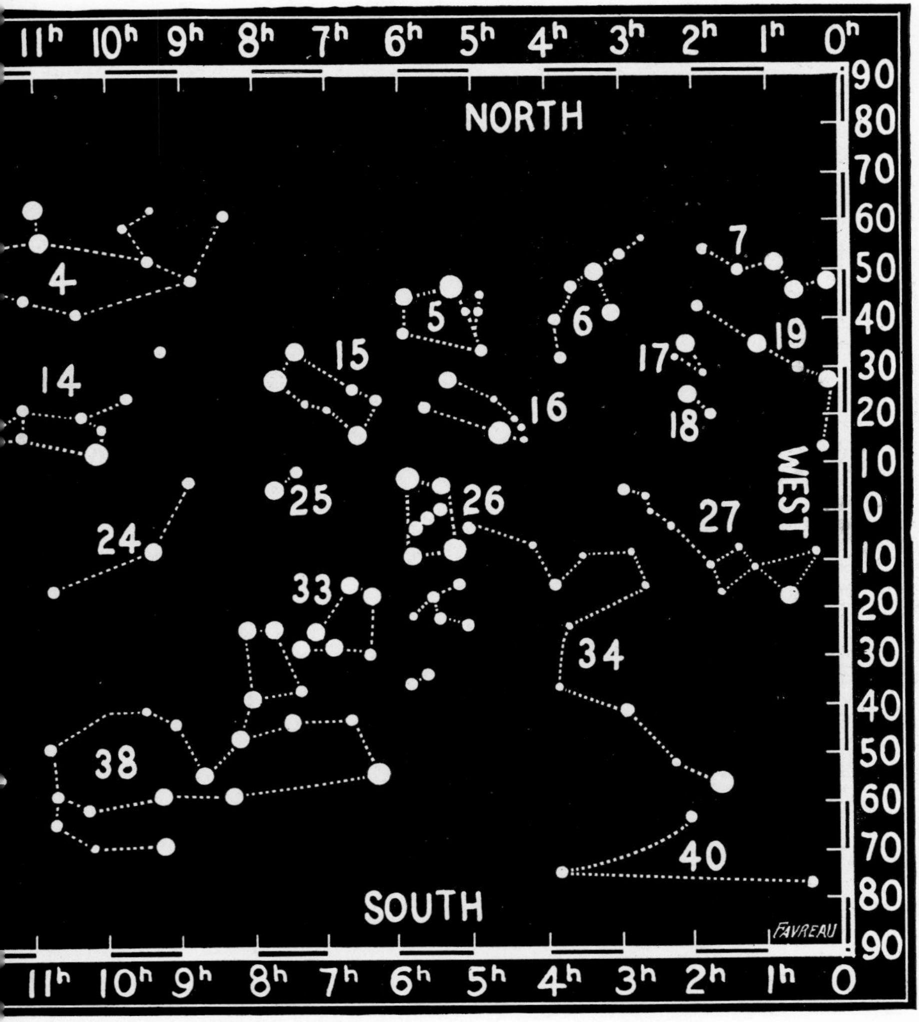

MELANESIA

hese points. Then draw
latitude north or south.
ıes locates the zenith.
o P.M., May 28. 10½ +

2 × 2¼ = 15^{h} .20° S. latitude cuts this hour line near the scales, which is approximately overhead.

See List of Constellations on the preceding page.

CHAPTER VI

THE NATIVE PEOPLES

THE ISLANDS of the Pacific, except for the Aleutians in the north, owe their populations to a series of extraordinary migrations from south and southeastern Asia. The full story of where the various native peoples of the Pacific came from will probably never be known. The voyages of some of these early people, in small primitive boats, across tremendous distances of the open ocean without navigational instruments, seem fully as wonderful as any long nonstop airplane flight today.

In the North Pacific the Aleutian Islands are inhabited by the Aleuts—an Eskimo-like people. The population of the islands is small, having diminished considerably since early times. These people live by hunting and fishing. In addition to birds and shellfish, from which they gain subsistence, they also capture seals, sea otters, walruses and occasionally whales, all of these large marine forms having once been very common in the area. They are a sturdy, isolated people who are able to obtain a meager livelihood on these cold, desolate islands with only primitive tools and weapons.

The islands of Japan have always been inhabited by people of Asiatic origin. The Ainus, who now live on the northern islands and the Kuriles, are remnants of the ancient population. They were conquered by the Japanese and now live on reservations very much like our American Indians. The Ainus have some Caucasian (white) characteristics, being lighter skinned, taller and more hairy than the Japanese. There is evidence that they once lived in northeastern Asia, and they are regarded as having an original kinship with the white race.

The Japanese themselves belong to a branch of the Mongoloid race, once widely distributed over southeastern Asia and the adjacent islands. They have mixed with the Ainu and later elements from Asia. They first developed a civilization based on farming and fishing. The arts were cultivated under Chinese influence: architecture, painting, carving in wood and bone, and literature flourished. The Japanese nation developed under a complex feudal system of government before adopting, toward the latter part of the last century, many of the methods of western civilization. Twice in their history they have consciously adopted foreign civilizations, once in the 600's A.D. from China and then in the nineteenth century from us. The people themselves are short, stocky and typically Asiatic. Their story is told in Chapter Twenty, which deals entirely with these islands.

Moving south from Japan the population becomes more mixed and new elements are introduced. At a very early time there came to the Philippines and the East Indies a number of distinct groups, each of which made its own contribution to the Pacific population. As these different peoples spread through the islands in a series of waves, they brought new blood, new customs, and new ideas. Generally they fought with the earlier inhabitants; sometimes they intermarried.

The East Indies appear to have been one of the earliest homes of man. Fossil human bones found in Java indicate the existence of a primitive man of great antiquity. There is evidence that very early savage tribes spread to Australia and to a few of the island groups. The native Australians are most primitive in their bodily development and in their use of tools. The Pygmies of the interior of New Guinea and the Negritos of the Philippines, people averaging less than four feet nine inches in height, are similarly primitive and all may be related to the earliest human races of the region.

The Dyaks of Borneo may be considered examples of another wave of people, the Indonesians, that came from southern Asia into the islands. The Indonesians are short people of fine physique

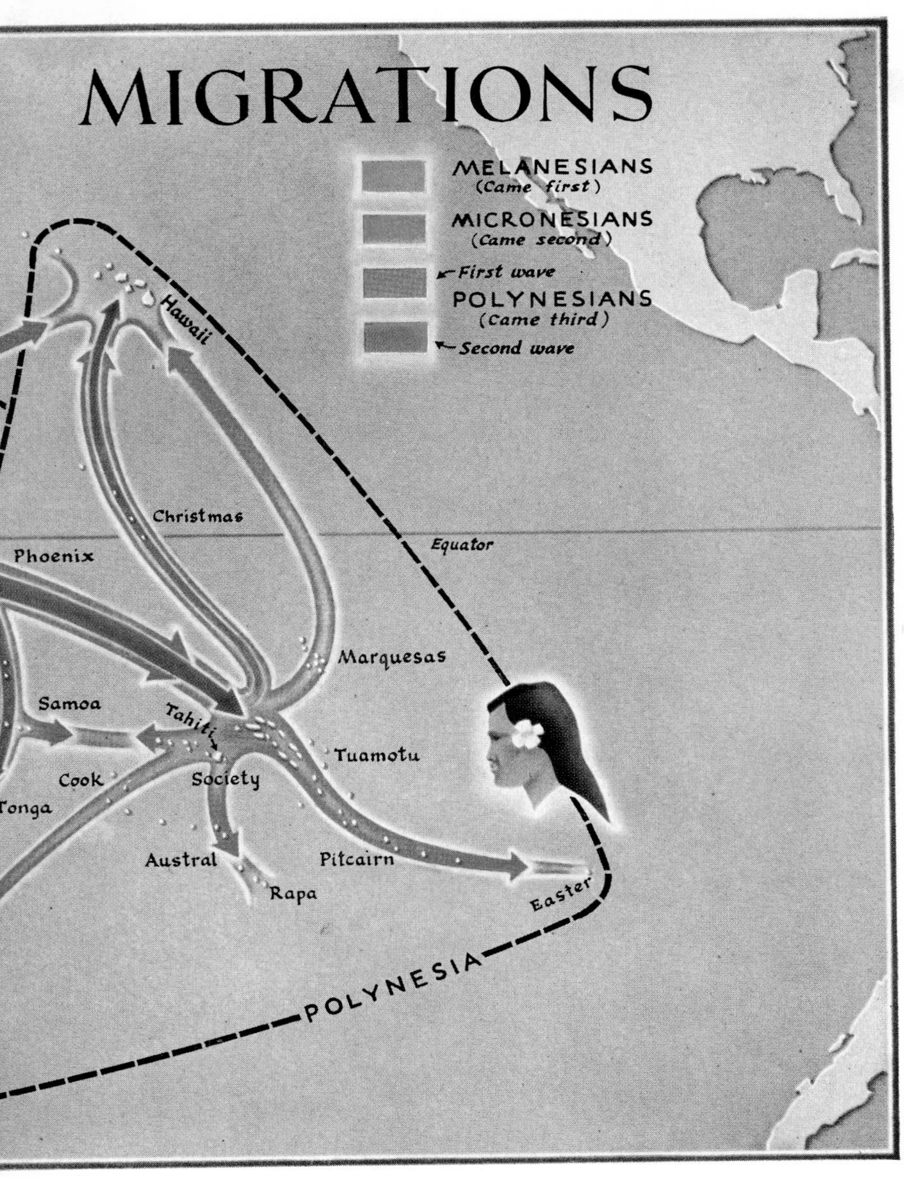
MIGRATIONS
MELANESIANS
(Came first)
MICRONESIANS
(Came second)
First wave
POLYNESIANS
(Came third)
Second wave
Hawaii
Christmas
Phoenix
Equator
Marquesas
Samoa
Tahiti
Tuamotu
Cook
Society
Tonga
Austral
Pitcairn
Rapa
Easter
POLYNESIA

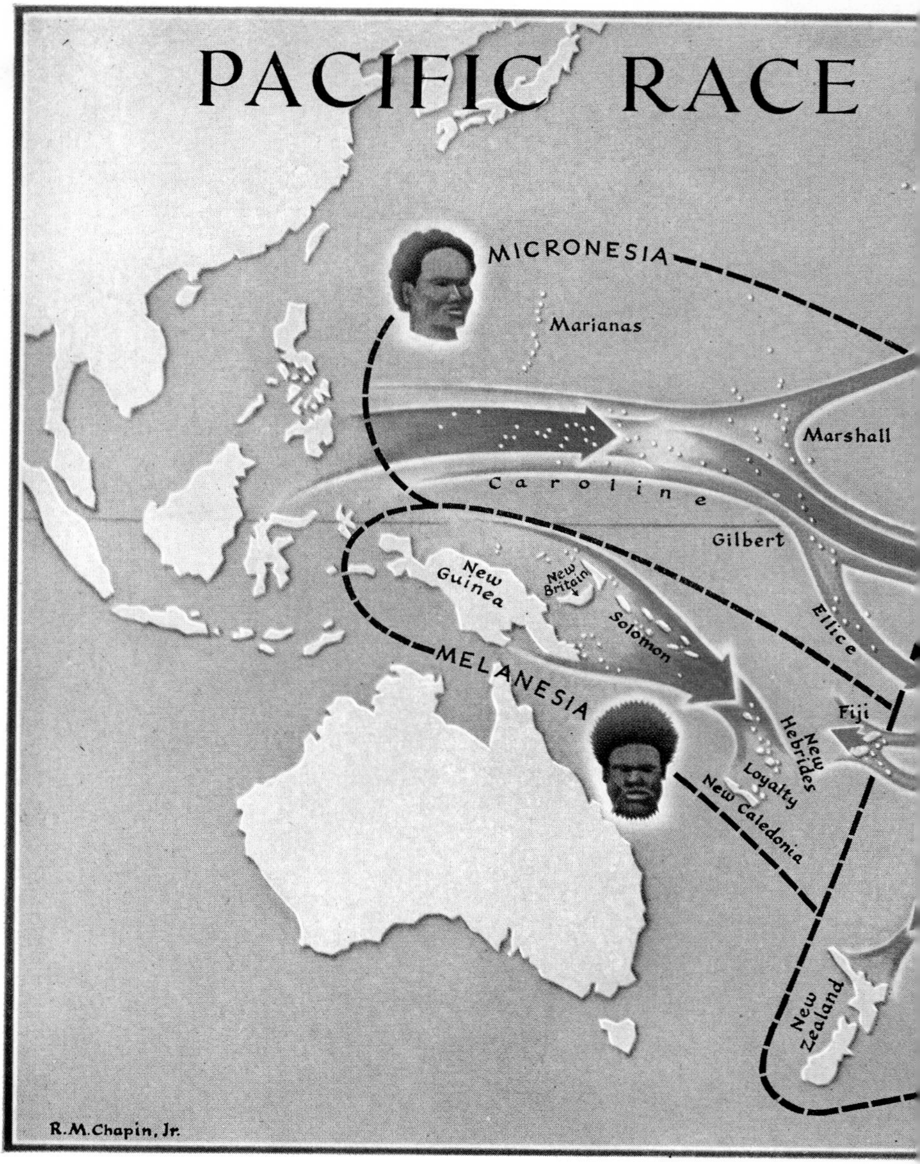

PACIFIC RACE

MICRONESIA
Marianas
Marshall
Caroline
Gilbert
New Guinea
New Britain
Solomon
Ellice
MELANESIA
Fiji
New Hebrides
Loyalty
New Caledonia
New Zealand

R.M.Chapin, Jr.

and seem related to the Polynesians. Even before historical times the Indonesians were skilled in the use of metals, in agriculture, and in hunting.

More recently arrived from Malaya were the ancestors of the people who now make up the largest part of the East Indian and Philippine population. The Malay people overran the islands, squeezing out the earlier Negritic and Indonesian populations. Their life was regulated by a social caste system controlled by the priests. These early Malays were good farmers, hunters, architects, and craftsmen.

Later, many Chinese came to the Philippines and the East Indies. Some Japanese came, too, and some Hindus from India. Much more recently whites from Europe and the Americas entered the population which is now so mixed that a more complete melting pot cannot be imagined. Most of the natives have accepted the Christian or Mohammedan religions—or parts of them. They have learned to use the trader's tools and wear store clothes, but many of the earlier beliefs and ways of life still remain, as evidenced in dances, customs, ceremonies, and local languages.

In earlier days, the waves of people who came from the mainland spread farther and farther out into the islands of the Pacific, eventually even to Hawaii and to the Marquesas and to island groups in the far southeast area of the ocean. But the history of these movements is so mixed with legend that the full story of the origin and spread of the island people is difficult to unravel. There is no doubt that the natives did cross tremendous distances of open sea in small, primitive boats, in some cases making voyages of several thousand miles.

Among the prehistoric colonists the Polynesians are most recent. They have spread farthest over the Pacific. We know more about their migration and dispersal through the islands. It is believed that by the tenth century the Polynesians had progressed as far as the Marquesas Islands. The settlement of Hawaii may have been accomplished at an even earlier date. At about A.D. 1300 the Polynesians traveled south from the Central Pacific to New Zealand and established themselves there.

As the Polynesians spread through the islands of the western Pacific with their flourishing populations, some mixing probably occurred. Moving eastward, the Polynesians found the islands less and less inhabited and on many islands east of the Fijis the Polynesians were the first to settle. It is in this area that relatively pure Polynesian stock is still to be found.

The Polynesians spread farther than any other early migrants. They established themselves throughout a vast area of the Central Pacific, extending more than 70° of longitude in the Southern Hemisphere and across 70° of latitude between the Hawaiian Islands and New Zealand, an area roughly four times that of the United States.

The Polynesians represent a race of complex origin, very different from the dark, frizzy-haired Melanesians. A great deal has been written about the relationship of the Polynesians to other groups, but it is only within recent years that the problem is beginning to be solved. Body measurements made on many islands now indicate that the Polynesians cannot be considered a uniform type. Previously certain scientists had classified them as Mongolian, others thought them to be Caucasian, while still others maintained that they are a special race. This in itself should be strong evidence that the Polynesians are a mixed people, for whenever there has been a general disagreement as to the race of any group of human beings, it has usually turned out that the group was a mixed one.

The Polynesian is a tall, handsome, well-proportioned human being, to our way of thinking. It would not, at first glance, be easy to distinguish a sun-tanned college athlete from an eastern Polynesian of the same age. They have broad faces, high narrow foreheads, noses moderately high and broad, straight or slightly wavy black hair and a golden-brown skin. The Caucasian characteristics are strongest in the easternmost islands, and the Mongoloid (yellow) characteristics in the western.

The resemblances in body and manner that the Polynesians share with people of European stock, when coupled with the charm of their romantic islands, combined to make them strongly attractive to the white men who came among them during the past two centuries.

The personal attractiveness of Polynesian women has grown into a legend. However, allowance must be made for two factors that may have colored the opinion and the accounts of the early voyagers. One of these was the fact that when the crews of the old sailing vessels landed in the Polynesian paradise, the sailors had been cut off from human society during the many months of the voyage. If, moreover, on the way they had touched at such localities as the Strait of Magellan, inhabited by American Indians of a very primitive type, or at African or Australian ports, where the natives were black, the Pacific island women would naturally have seemed, by contrast, marvels of beauty. But even if such allowances are made, there remains little doubt that the people were pleasing. Captain Cook, who visited these islands at the end of the eighteenth century, wrote that the savages of the Marquesas Islands were not only the finest race in the Pacific, but that for fair form and regular features they probably surpassed any other people in the world.

Though customs vary from island to island, the life of the Polynesians has many similarities. They are all dependent on the sea for a livelihood, supplementing this by some agriculture, hunting, and the use of a few domesticated animals, mostly pigs and chickens. Houses consist of a wood frame thatched with palm leaves and are sometimes ornamented with carvings. They make no pottery and, before contact with the whites, their primitive tools were made of wood, shell, stone and bone. The Polynesians were ingenious in design and craftwork and noted for their woodwork and their bark cloth (tapa). They were excellent navigators and brave fighters with their carved clubs. They have a remarkable oral literature, consisting of legends that are carried down from father to son. Before the western conquest the tribes were ruled by hereditary chiefs.

The Polynesians and the other island people of the South Pacific are greatly dependent upon the coconut palm. It provides them with food and drink, the leaves thatch their houses which are frequently supported by palm trunks, the husks are shredded and woven into rope and fiber articles; the shell of the nut makes cups and utensils. Copra, the dried meat of the nut, is an important article of commerce and is often the sole "money crop" of the smaller islands. The many ways that the coconut and the other palms have been used attest to the cleverness and intelligence of the race.

Melanesians are found eastward as far as the Solomons, the Fijis, the New Hebrides and New Caledonia. In the west, among the Malay islands, tribes with a Melanesian mixture are found in the Moluccas, in the Lesser Sundas and in the Timor group. These Melanesians include some of the most feared head-hunters, as well as tribes known for their craftsmanship in making ceremonial houses, masks and wood carvings. Physically, the Melanesians vary from island to island, although they are generally characterized by dark skin and frizzy hair. They are shorter and less robust than the Polynesians.

In their culture the Melanesians on the various islands have characteristics in common. They make more use of agriculture and hunting than the Polynesians, though the coastal tribes are equally dependent upon the sea. Before guns were introduced the Melanesians hunted with bows and arrows and fought with spears and clubs. In New Guinea, the Solomons, and the Fijis, the Melanesian house decoration at once catches the eye. The entire front of a dwelling may be covered with grotesque carvings and decorations. This is especially true of the men's clubhouses—and Melanesians go in for clubs and secret societies with a fervor perhaps equaled only in the United States. The Melanesians frequently chew betel nuts, the fruit of the palm, as do many of the other peoples in the Malay Peninsula. This is a custom that we with our habit of chewing gum should appreciate.

The non-Melanesian or Papuan tribes of the interior of New Guinea and of some of the neighboring islands are much more primitive and speak extremely peculiar languages. Physically they differ in certain respects from the coastal Melanesians. They have a low scale of culture and are probably very ancient inhabitants of these islands. Some of the tribes, especially in the interior of New Guinea, reveal a primitive Stone Age culture, and are skilled farmers. All the mountain people are fine woodsmen.

The people of the Micronesian islands are relatives of the Polynesians who show, however, in their racial composition more pronounced traces of Mongoloid blood. This might be expected in view of their closer proximity to the mainland of Asia. They have been studied less than the Polynesians and therefore less is known about their history and culture.

The inhabitants of the Caroline, the Marshall, and the Gilbert groups are typical Micronesians. Their culture embodies many Polynesian traits and some Melanesian. They gain their sustenance partly from the sea and partly from the cultivation of coconut palms, yams and taros. The island tribes have a well-developed caste system with nobles, commoners, and slaves.

Chapter VII

OCEAN LIFE

The surface of the ocean that rolls before one's view to the far horizons is more than just a lot of water. It is the boundary that divides two worlds—one in which man lives, the other the world of the waters, so rich, so varied in its life that, like the star systems, it is almost beyond our comprehension. That part of the life in the oceans which we human beings see or of which we have knowledge is but an infinitesimal portion of the whole. Consequently a summary of the ocean life of the Pacific, as of any ocean area, can be made only in the most general terms.

Nearly every main type of life with which we are familiar on land is found living in or on the ocean waters: in marine forests, where seaweeds reach a length of 250 feet; in pastures composed of an infinite number of small sea plants. There are large creatures of various kinds, including warm-blooded animals that suckle their young, such as seals, sea lions, and whales, together with the latter's smaller relatives—porpoises and dolphins; reptiles in the form of sea snakes and turtles; birds, just above the ocean's surface, keeping watch in the remotest parts of the sea; coral-building animals, together with other invertebrates, such as the familiar sea anemones, starfish, and shellfish. But of all the varied life of the ocean, the fishes are the most familiar, and observations regarding them will provide at least a glimpse into the life of the ocean as a whole.

In considering the fishes of the Pacific we need to recall that this ocean, inconceivably large as it is, is only a part of the one great global ocean that reaches around all the seacoasts of the continents. Many fishes are hardy navigators and it is not surprising that some types should find their way from the Atlantic around the shores of the polar seas to the North Pacific, or that others should spread northward from the Antarctic coasts across the southern ocean to the boundaries of the Atlantic, the Indian and the Pacific oceans, or that still others should swim around the southern ends of Australia and Africa. Moreover there was a time, many ages ago, before the present Isthmus of Panama was thrust up, when there was a short cut from the Atlantic to the Pacific where the Isthmus now stands.

These facts help to explain why it is that the leaping manta, or devilfish, which feeds in the bays of the West Indies, has a near relative in the Pacific; why the whale shark spreads widely over the tropical seas from the Seychelles in the Indian Ocean to the Gulf of California, and why the swordfish ranges widely over the Atlantic and Pacific; why the marlins of New Zealand are closely related to those of South America, Hawaii and the West Indies. Fishes also tend to follow the ocean currents and to establish colonies in widely separated areas. So it happens that the fishes of the various regions of all the oceans are made up of very mixed populations whose remote ancestors may have come from widely separated regions.

The great ocean currents tend to mix the populations of fishes of any given locality. However there are opposing factors that are apt to eliminate some kinds of fishes while encouraging the life of others that are better able to meet varying conditions. These factors include daily and seasonal changes in temperature of the water, its variations in saltiness or in oxygen concentration, its proximity to the mouths of great rivers, its depth, and so on.

The colder waters in both the far north and the south can absorb and hold greater amounts of oxygen than warmer waters, while as the temperature of the water rises, the oxygen content is rapidly reduced. Since oxygen is necessary for life, it follows that cold waters generally contain more of the microscopic plants and animals upon which small fishes such as herrings feed. The small fishes move in schools of countless numbers and in turn are preyed upon by and support the life of the larger fishes, the sea birds, and the whales. Such wealth of life develops especially where there is in addition to such favorable conditions some source of nitrogen and phosphorus for the plant life, which forms the base of the food pyramid. Thus it is that the cold waters of the Peruvian Current on the west coast of South America support an enormous amount of life. When, however, as a result of a weaker trade wind and a weaker cold current the warmer waters from the equatorial current take possession of the surface along the coast and flow over the Peruvian Current, the Current with its oxygen is no longer within reach of the sunshine. As a result its microscopic plants and animals die and its herrings, larger fishes and sea birds perish in millions, polluting the shores for hundreds of miles. Thus the great scythe of sudden death and destruction tends to wipe out many species over wide areas, which would be unfortunate if it did not mean that in the long run other fishes may be given a chance to increase and multiply.

A quart of water taken from the clear blue sea in the trade-wind zones, hundreds of miles from land, may show a count of only a few hundred microscopic single-celled plants and a much smaller number of tiny crustacean and other living creatures. A quart of water taken from the cool Peruvian Current close to South America, or from the far southern waters of the subpolar region, may, on the other hand, show a count of hundreds of thousands, or even a million, of similar organisms. It is therefore no accident that the world's great fisheries are carried on mainly in relatively cool waters and either close to continental coasts or on shallow banks which are only submerged parts of the continental platforms.

Such cool waters are rich in sheer quantity of life, even though the countless millions of organisms may belong to only a few kinds. The truly tropical seas, on the other hand, support an unbelievable variety of marine life, but with much less total bulk. It is said that 700 different kinds of fishes can be caught at a single locality in the Malay Archipelago, where the corals, sea shells, and other aquatic creatures are also well represented.

In the cold and foggy waters of the North Pacific the fishes tend to be either dark or pale, while in the warm surface waters of the tropics they usually take on brilliant colors. Northern fishes, living in colder waters, also tend to have longer or even eel-like bodies, with more vertebrae, or joints, in their backbones than their relatives in tropical seas. In this connection it is interesting to note that controlled experiments have shown that by lowering the temperature in which fertilized eggs of fishes are developed, the number of vertebrae is frequently increased.

The fishes of the North Pacific, such as cod, halibut, and certain herrings, are generally true to type, but local species of these fishes showing certain variations occur in the Bering Sea, the Okhotsk Sea and the North Japanese Sea. The Antarctic fishes, some of which extend north to New Zealand, are characteristic of the South Pacific and are not found elsewhere.

The fishes of the great depths are adapted to the enormous pressures in which they live. Below half a mile in depth even the actinic rays of light fade out rapidly. Consequently the energy of the sunlight that is caught by the minute plant cells near the surface is lacking at great depths except in so far as it may be stored, as it were, in the remains of plant cells that rain down from the surface. Nevertheless, in the black depths of the Pacific and other oceans swim countless schools of small, shrimplike crustaceans that presumably feed on the dead plant cells and on the remains of minute animal life. The shrimps in turn are devoured by small squids, octopuses and small fishes; but large fishes, of three feet or more in length, are either excessively rare or elude capture by the few trawling nets sent down by explorers. Notwithstanding the relative sparsity of deep-sea fishes, many hundreds of different species are already known. Even the generally uniform environment of the great depths harbors a wide assortment of body forms, whose diverse populations have evidently been derived from types of different surface and shore fishes.

Oceanic surface and offshore fishes, such as tarpons, barracudas, mackerels, bonitos, crevallés, skipjacks and flying fishes, are for the most part gracefully streamlined and fast swimmers; silver, blue and yellow sides predominate, which make them less visible from above, while white bellies help them to fade into the silvery gray ceiling when seen from below.

Sandy and muddy bottoms support flounders, skates, gurnards, toadfishes and many others that can adjust their colors to the background and so conceal themselves—an automatic or reflex response to the color of the background as seen by the fishes.

Coral reefs and the sandy bottoms near them are like seaports crowded with sailors from every clime. Here are the "voyagers" from the open seas, such as the sharks, the barracudas, and others that merely scour the shores in search of a meal; then there are the busy, quick-dodging "villagers," including demoiselles, angels, butterfly fishes and Moorish idols, which dart in and out among the coral heads. Schools of nibblers, including the triggerfishes and surgeonfishes, graze on the sea mats, while many of the snappers, basses and related families can quickly change their bands or stripes to suit the color of the nearby sea fans; snakelike morays lurk in holes or rear their writhing necks and gasp and gulp with monotonous regularity. The cardinal fish and other red and dark-striped fishes hide in the deep hollows by day and come forth at night to hunt their prey. Some of the scorpion fishes are armed with poisonous spikes and inflict dangerous wounds on incautious fishermen.

In the tide pools are the gobies, which often have suckerlike ventral fins with which they cling to the rocks. The blennies are active, keen-eyed little sprites that slither about among the rocks and corals. Such coral reefs and their life may be seen in the innumerable islands of the Central and Southwest Pacific.

It is remarkable that the great wealth of life of the East Indian region dominates the whole of the tropical Pacific, from the coast of Asia to the easternmost Polynesian islands, though diminishing to the east. The East Indian types extend northward to southern Japan and eastward to Easter Island and Hawaii. The tropical Pacific coast of the Americas, however, has many wholly different fishes and marine animals, directly allied to the West Indian forms, and evidently developed when the Panama region was a strait instead of an isthmus.

A word regarding the shark—that most notorious inhabitant of the sea. There are about fifty different species of sharks in the Pacific. Of these some are what on the land we could think of as "browsing" animals, who live on minute sea organisms, and the equipment of whose jaws and teeth would make it impossible for them to attack any larger animal, including man. Of this type there is the carpet shark which, despite its formidable appearance, has a mouth so small and teeth so blunt that it is dreaded for no good reason. The basking shark and the whale shark—the latter being the largest living fish, sometimes exceeding forty-five feet in length—are harmless and subsist by straining small creatures, many of them microscopic in size, through the sievelike portions of their gills. The sharp-toothed requiem shark, despite its funereal name, feeds chiefly on fish. On the other hand, there are large oceanic sharks, particularly the great white shark, which in some instances have been attracted by bathers and in certain isolated cases have attacked men. These animals sometimes reach a length of thirty feet or more. Many sharks will follow a trail of blood in the water, and there is no question but that an occasional shark *is* a man-eater, with all that that implies.

The sea shells of the Pacific include thousands of species, many of brilliant colors and great beauty of form. In New Zealand alone there are more than 1,600 recorded kinds of shell-bearing mollusks, and many of the other islands of the Central and South Pacific are even richer.

The most colorful are the univalves or snails, which outnumber the bivalves or clams about four to one. The snails are especially common and well developed in the coral reefs, where they prey upon one another and on the many other types of invertebrate life that find shelter there. This is the home of the cone shells of which no less than 168 kinds have been reported from the Philippines; from the Marquesas, where coral reefs are almost absent, only 14 kinds are known. The bite of many of the cone shells carries a strong poison. The brilliant cowries, the notched strombus, and a great many kinds of the spiny murex are also found in the reefs.

Of special interest are the pearl "oysters"—which are not oysters at all—which produce the precious pearls. Then there is the tridacna, sometimes known as the mantrap clam, the largest of the living clams; it grows to three feet in width and weighs up to four hundred pounds. The swimmer or diver in the reefs must be careful not to place his foot or hand within its two valves, for native pearl divers are said to have been trapped and drowned by these giant clams.

Knowledge of the mollusks of the Pacific is as yet far too incomplete. The shell-bearing animals have their own place in the general scheme of nature for they form a happy hunting ground for the fishes, and their dead shells, when ground up by the waves, will contribute largely to the limestone of future ages.

Chapter VIII

MAMMALS

Anyone who has ever seen the long-nosed proboscis monkey of Borneo is not likely to forget him—he is like no other animal on earth. This uniqueness is probably the most fascinating feature about so many of the animals of islands. The curious crested kagu, a relative of the crane, found in New Caledonia, the flightless kiwi bird, and the tuatara lizard of New Zealand, the small and peculiar buffalo of the Philippines, the babirusa boar of Celebes—to cite a few random examples—are quite different from all other birds, reptiles, and animals, and are found nowhere else in the world but on those particular islands.

Why are many of the animals and plants on islands so extremely different from those on the mainland? Where did those unique forms of life come from? If their forebears originated on the continents, when and how did they reach the islands?

SOURCE

Answering the last question first, it is believed that the ancestors of *all* things living upon islands arrived accidentally from one or more of the continents or from some other island, itself first populated from the continents. The life of the continents is the source of all island life.

DISTRIBUTION AND DEVELOPMENT

Since far back in geological time, occasional continental animals and plants have been carried through the air by storms or out to sea by flooded rivers. Of those strays, perhaps one in a thousand has been carried to some island alive and in a condition to reproduce

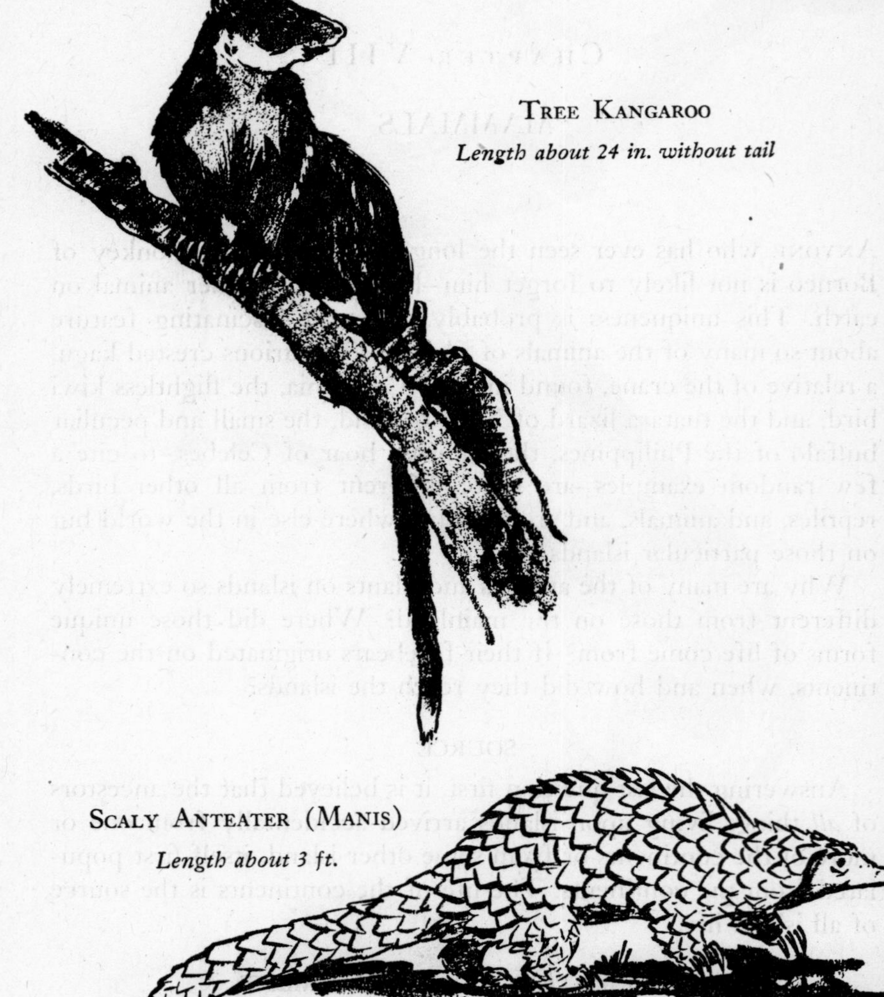

Tree Kangaroo

Length about 24 in. without tail

Scaly Anteater (Manis)

Length about 3 ft.

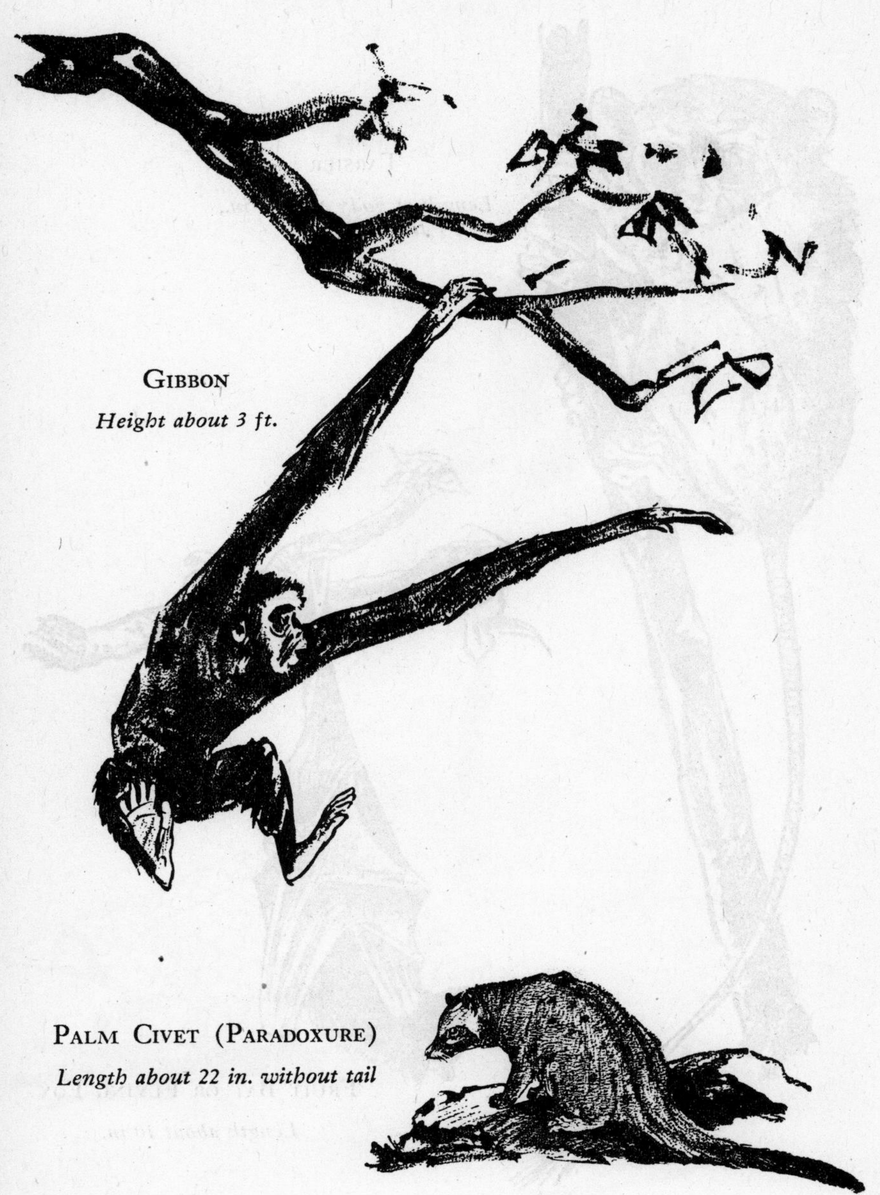

GIBBON

Height about 3 ft.

PALM CIVET (PARADOXURE)

Length about 22 in. without tail

TARSIER

Length of body about 5 in., tail about 8 in.

FRUIT BAT OR FLYING FOX

Length about 10 in.

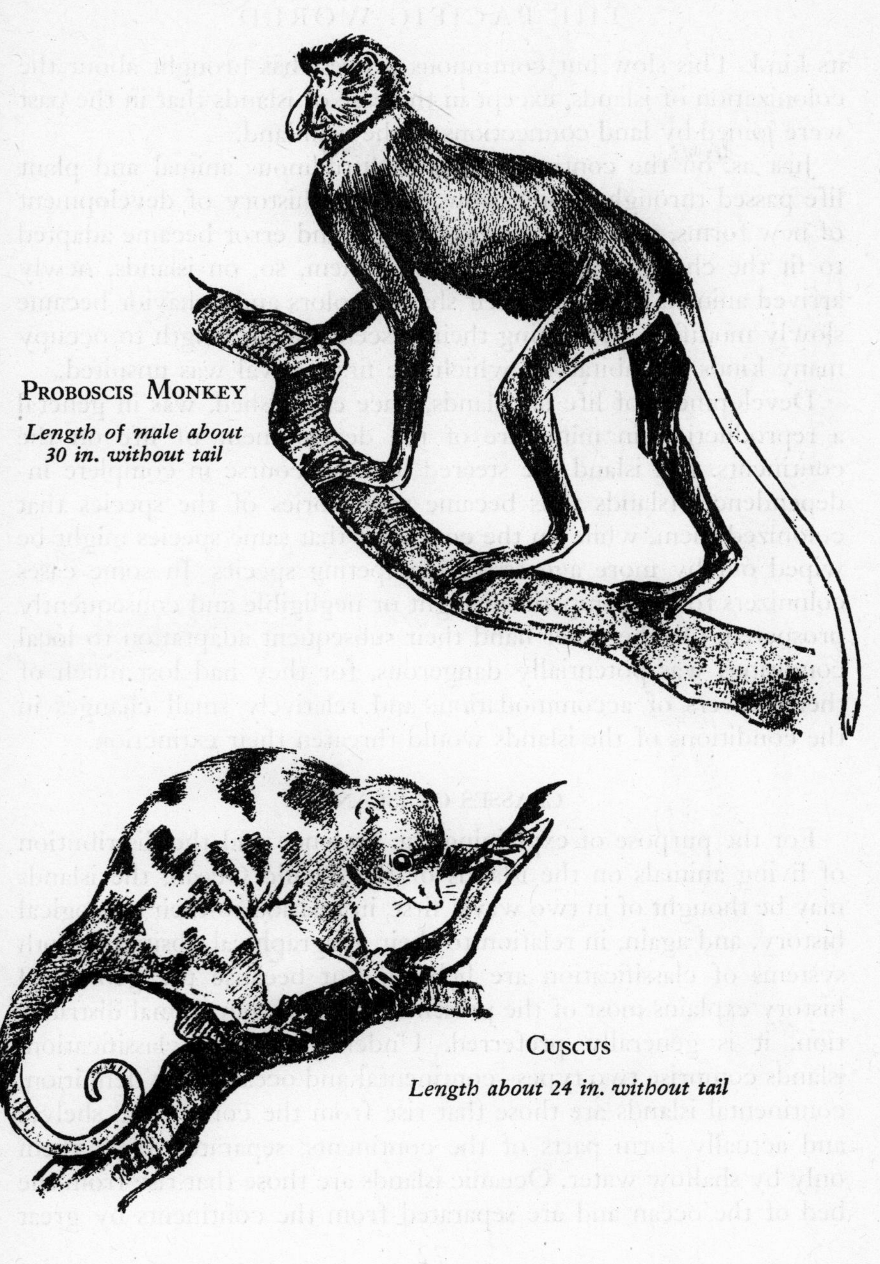

Proboscis Monkey

Length of male about 30 in. without tail

Cuscus

Length about 24 in. without tail

its kind. This slow but continuous process has brought about the colonization of islands, except in the case of islands that in the past were joined by land connections to the mainland.

Just as, on the continents, the multitudinous animal and plant life passed through a long, slow, intricate history of development of new forms, which by process of trial and error became adapted to fit the changing conditions about them, so, on islands, newly arrived animals evolved. Their shapes, colors and behavior became slowly modified, permitting their descendants at length to occupy many kinds of habitats to which the first arrival was unsuited.

Development of life on islands, once established, was in general a reproduction in miniature of the development of life on the continents. But island life steered its own course in complete independence. Islands thus became repositories of the species that colonized them, while on the continent that same species might be wiped out by more aggressive, competing species. In some cases colonizers found competition slight or negligible and consequently prospered. On the other hand their subsequent adaptation to local conditions was potentially dangerous, for they had lost much of their powers of accommodation, and relatively small changes in the conditions of the islands would threaten their extinction.

CLASSES OF ISLANDS

For the purpose of explaining the presence and the distribution of living animals on the islands of the Pacific Ocean, the islands may be thought of in two ways: first, in relation to their geological history, and again, in relation to their geographical positions. Both systems of classification are helpful. But because the geological history explains most of the present-day puzzles in animal distribution, it is generally preferred. Under geological classification, islands comprise two types—continental and oceanic. By definition, continental islands are those that rise from the continental shelves and actually form parts of the continents, separated from them only by shallow water. Oceanic islands are those that rise from the bed of the ocean and are separated from the continents by great depths of water; they may be only a few score miles from continental lands or several thousands of miles away.

CONTINENTAL ISLANDS

The continental islands were connected with their respective continents during the last ice age, which ended about 30,000 years ago. In those times such an immense volume of water from the oceans was frozen in the polar icecaps that the ocean level is estimated to have been some 300 feet lower than it is today. The direct effects of this reduction of sea level were to reunite many of the continental islands to their parent continents and to make certain of the oceanic islands larger, at the same time reducing the widths of the deep straits or seas now dividing them from the continents. The former union of the continental islands with the mainland explains how the big mammals, like the rhinoceros or orangutan, reached such large islands of the western Pacific as Sumatra and Borneo.

The animal and plant assemblages that have contributed to the population of the continental islands of the Pacific are derived respectively from three principal sources—the temperate North American and north Asiatic regions, the warm southeast Asiatic or Malay region, and the Australian region. The mammals of the Australian region, vastly different from those of the rest of the world, are the specialized descendants of the survivors of that far-distant day when pouch-bearing animals were the common inhabitants of both America and Europe.

OCEANIC ISLANDS

In the case of the oceanic islands, smaller mammals may have arrived by natural rafts—masses of trees and vegetation that were undermined by rivers and carried out into the ocean by winds and currents. Tree-living types of animals would be most easily transported in this way, although only one of such natural rafts out of perhaps thousands would reach another island. When the distances between islands were not too great, a number of the larger mammals undoubtedly swam across the water barriers. Deer and various types of wild pigs are capable of doing this. Flying mammals, the bats, would be assisted by storms or strong winds to make a longer than usual flight. The more isolated islands, however, might be successfully reached only once, or by a very limited number of mammals. Small populations are easily exterminated, and the animal life of an island may have formerly included species that were unable to persist. Large mammals are especially liable to this risk; on a small island their numbers are so limited that disease or an unfavorable year might destroy them, or in later times the human inhabitants might have killed them off. Naturally, large islands close to a continent were far more likely to receive such waifs than were tiny islands in the midst of the ocean. Furthermore, the larger islands offered a much wider choice of environment, and thus provided more frequently for the special requirements of different kinds of animals.

THE PROCESSES OF DISTRIBUTION

An interesting example of the workings of distribution is provided by the great mass of large and small islands collectively called the Indo-Australian Archipelago. This mass includes both continental and oceanic islands. Among the continental islands are Sumatra, Java and Borneo, with, as we should expect, an animal life derived from tropical Asia and the Malay Peninsula; also New Guinea, with an animal life derived from Australia.

Among oceanic islands near the continents are the Philippines, Celebes, the Moluccas, and the Lesser Sunda Islands. While the area occupied by these islands underwent great geological changes in prehistoric times, including upheavals and depressions, there is no evidence that any land connection between these oceanic islands and the continent of Asia ever existed.

This particular area has been named "Wallacea," after the naturalist, Alfred Russel Wallace; and the line of the continental shelf —which runs west of these islands from between the islands of Bali and Lombok, north through the Strait of Macassar and

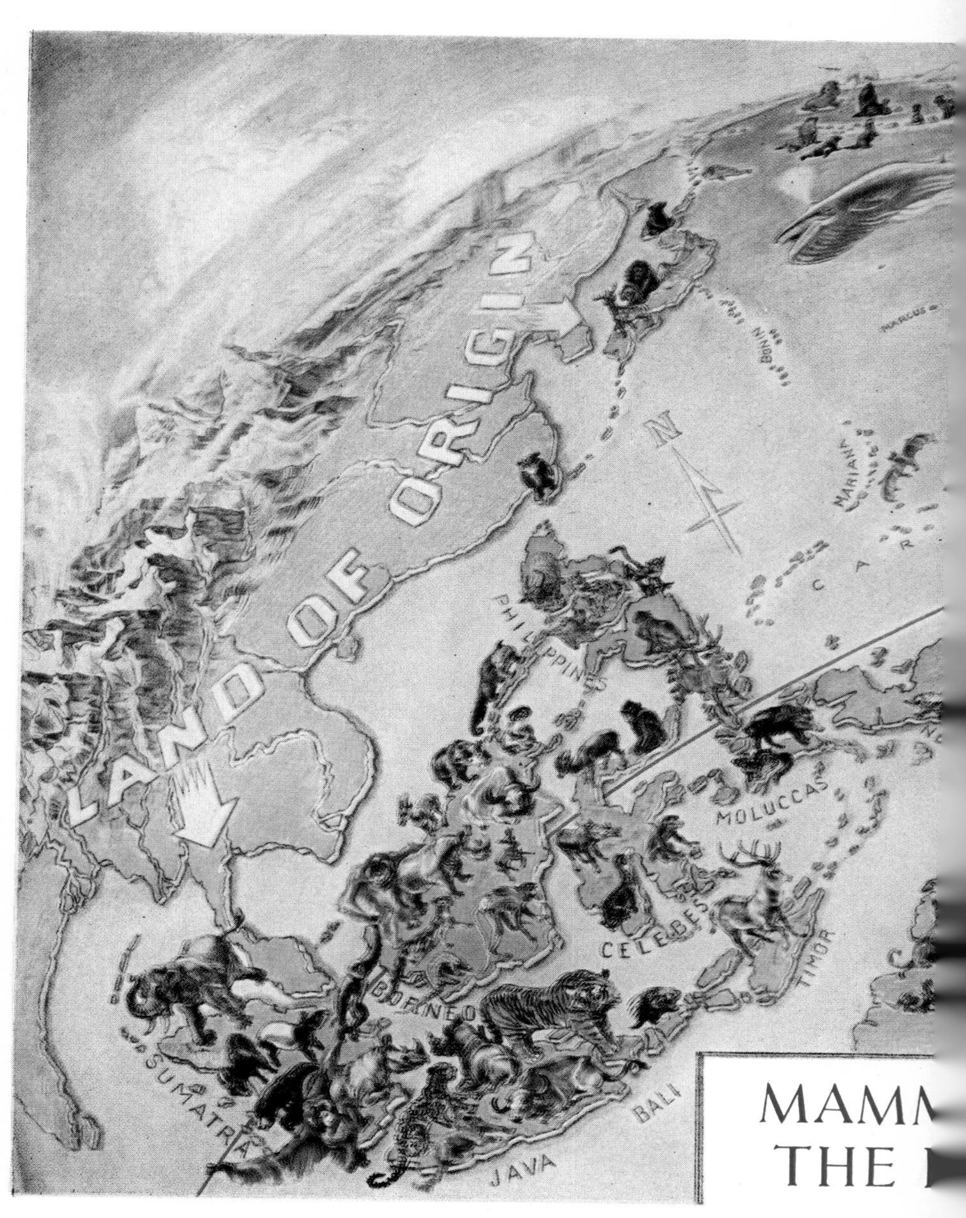

LAND OF ORIGIN
BONIN
MARCUS
MARIANA
PHILIPPINES
MOLUCCAS
CELEBES
TIMOR
BORNEO
SUMATRA
JAVA
BALI
MAMM
THE

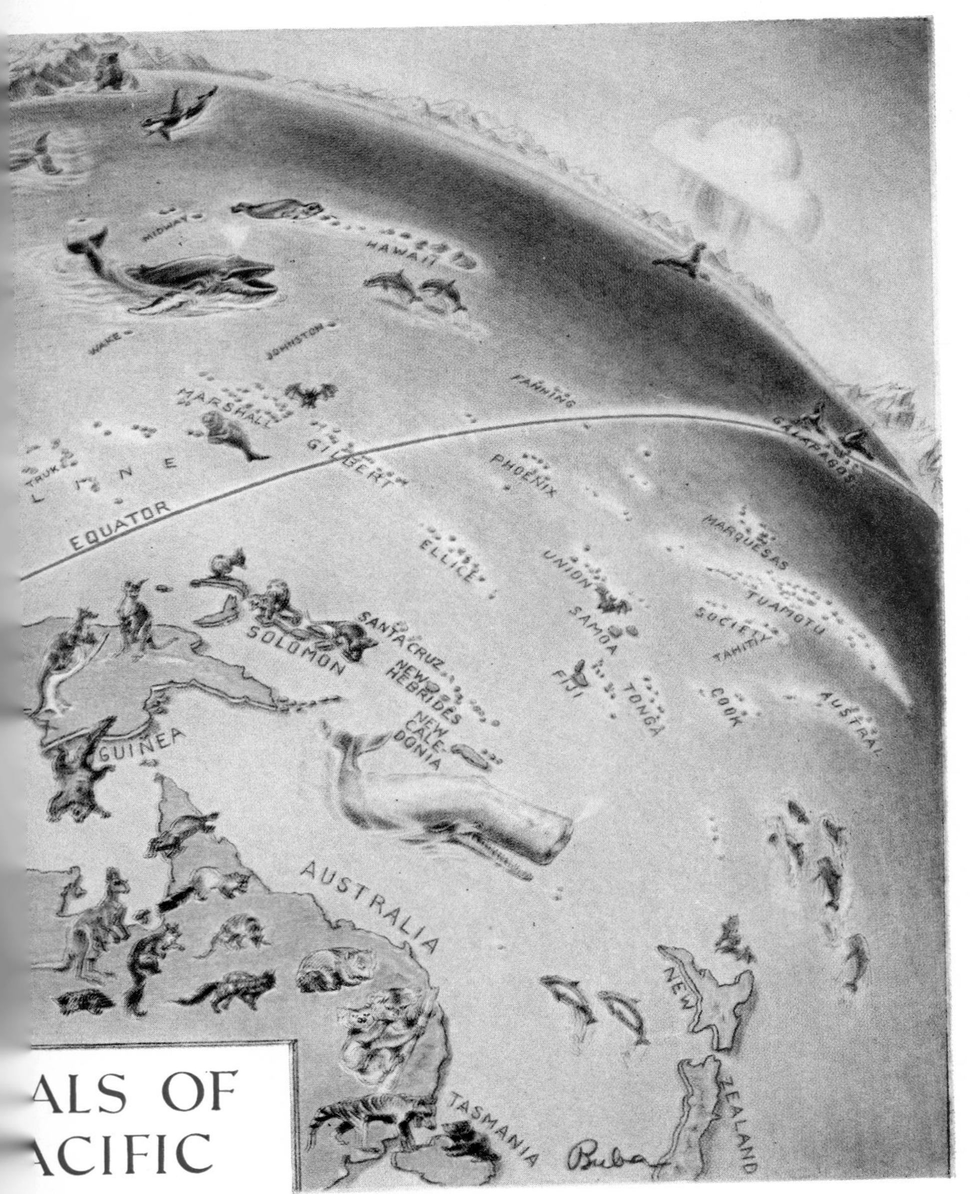

ALS OF
ACIFIC
MIDWAY
HAWAII
WAKE
JOHNSTON
MARSHALL
FANNING
GALAPAGOS
TRUK
L I N E
GILBERT
EQUATOR
PHOENIX
MARQUESAS
ELLICE
UNION
TUAMOTU
SOCIETY
TAHITI
SAMOA
SANTA CRUZ
SOLOMON
NEW HEBRIDES
FIJI
TONGA
COOK
AUSTRAL
GUINEA
NEW CALEDONIA
AUSTRALIA
NEW ZEALAND
TASMANIA
Buba

through the Sulu Sea—is commonly known as "Wallace's Line." (See maps: the Netherlands Indies, page 130, and the Philippines, page 144.) Wallace believed that this line indicated a boundary separating to a great extent the animals of Asia from those of Australia. Actually the mammals of the region are derived principally from Asia and to a very small extent from Australia.

The animal and plant life of Celebes is a case in point. This island lies only some eighty miles to the east of the continental island of Borneo (in the glacial period this distance was even shorter, reduced to approximately twenty-five miles) and more than seven hundred miles from Australia. Its mammals are predominantly of Asiatic origin. However, in parts of Celebes there are certain plants and animals so reminiscent and characteristic of Australia—the eucalyptus and nettle trees, the white cockatoo, and the cuscus, a pouch-bearing animal—that an untrained observer might think that he was in the Queensland forests of Australia.

SUCCESSFUL COLONIZATION RELATED TO DISTANCE

The nearness of the oceanic islands of Wallacea to the mainland and continental islands of Asia and Australia accounts for the profusion and variety of life dwelling on them, in comparison with the paucity of life on scattered groups of tiny oceanic islands in the mid-Pacific.

The animals and plants of any remote island are likely to be a random assortment derived from almost any part of the mainlands bordering the Pacific. In actual fact, Asia and Australia have in general contributed a much higher percentage of the animal and plant life of the oceanic islands than have the Americas. The only oceanic islands that have some mammals of American origin are the Hawaiian Islands and the Galápagos.

EVOLUTION

The process of differentiation on islands has been continuous. The species of one island became distinct from those of another, or on individual islands, mountain-living forms became separated

THE DISTRIBUTION OF REPRESENTATIVE MAMMALS FROM THREE CONTINENTAL SOURCES

Island Group	Representative Animals	Chief Sources of Animals	Remarks
NORTH TEMPERATE (NORTH ASIATIC AND NORTH AMERICAN)			
Kurile (continental) and Aleutian chain (continental and partly oceanic)	bears, weasels, wolverines, seals, rabbits, squirrels, field mice	North Asia and North America	The Aleutian Isls. contain fewer species the farther they are from the continental mainland.
Japan (continental)	raccoon dogs, foxes, deer, Japanese macaques, squirrels, shrews, moles	Temperate and subtropical Asia	Animals derived mainly from the temperate zone and to a limited degree from the cooler tropics.
TROPICAL ASIATIC AND MALAY			
Formosa (continental)	hedgehogs, bears, martens, clouded leopards, muntjacs, sambars, macaques	Tropical Asia and North Asia	Mammals scarcely to be distinguished from those of Fukien Province, China.
Luchu chain (continental)	hares, pigs, flying foxes, shrews, mice	Tropical Asia and North Asia	Animals far more limited in variety and number than those of Formosa.
Greater Sunda Isls. (continental): Sumatra, Java, Borneo, Bali	orangutan, sun bear, sambar deer, rhinoceroses, flying, tree, and ground squirrels, brush-tailed and true porcupines, pangolin	Tropical Asia and Malay Peninsula	The present-day wonderfully rich animal life is thought to have been preceded by an even richer population, known from its fossil bones, which included mastodons, primitive hyenas, and saber-toothed tigers.
Wallacea (oceanic): Philippines, Celebes, Moluccas, Lesser Sunda Isls.	tamarau and anoa buffaloes, babirusa, sambars, phalangers (part)	Tropical Asia and Malay Peninsula, both ancient and recent colonists; and Australia-New Guinea	Some of the islands contain a few Australian animals in addition to representatives of many of the continental groups. All types become fewer the farther the island is from the continent of origin.

AUSTRALIAN			
Australia, Tasmania, New Guinea (continental)	*Egg-laying forms:* duck-billed platypuses, spiny anteaters *Pouch-bearing forms:* marsupial moles, phalangers, kangaroos, wallabies, koalas, wombats, Tasmanian devils, thylacine wolves, fruit bats and insectivorous bats, peculiar genera of rats and mice, dingos	Extremely ancient to modern tropical Asia	The Australian continental group is noted for its two unique orders of primitive yet highly specialized animals: the monotremes which lay eggs and suckle their young, and the highly diversified marsupials which carry and nurse their young in pouches. During the ice age the Australian marsupials included many larger forms. Among these were kangaroos larger than the largest known today, giant phalangers with great shearing teeth, and wombats as large as tapirs.
Bismarck Arch.: New Britain, New Ireland; Solomon Isls. (oceanic)	a small wallaby, cuscus phalangers, a bandicoot, flying foxes, insectivorous bats, peculiar rats	Australia-New Guinea	These islands support a restricted animal life.
New Zealand	Two kinds of insectivorous bats	Australia, ancient and recent	Excessively ancient and isolated islands.
MID-OCEAN ISLANDS			
Micronesia, Melanesia, Polynesia	Fruit bats, a few insectivorous bats	Life fragments from various of the foregoing, through a long space of geological time	The grouping of these islands according to their native peoples has little application in zoology. The only mammals that reached the remote oceanic islands without human aid were bats.

from lowland races, and types preferring humid forests diverged from those inhabiting dry areas.

Animals that show greatest differences are believed to have descended from the earliest arrivals. Those which, on the contrary, are more like their mainland relatives are thought to have come later. The few animals and plants that are identical with those on the continents have in many cases been carried to the islands by man.

It has been shown that the fauna of continental islands is derived from the neighboring continents, that animals reached the oceanic islands by random drift from the continents, that larger oceanic islands nearer the continental sources received many more kinds of animals than smaller islands in mid-ocean, and that those continental sources are primarily three in number: north temperate (northern Asiatic and North American), tropical Asiatic and Malay, and Australian. Central and South America contributed only to the faunas of the few islands relatively close to their coasts. The Galápagos Islands received their populations mainly from Central America.

The major island groups, with some of their representative mammals, and the three continental sources from which these animals came are shown in the table on pages 76 and 77. More complete details of animal distribution are given in the table on page 204.

As stated in the opening paragraphs of this chapter the most compelling characteristic of island life resides in the remarkable difference of so many of the animals and birds and plants from those dwelling on the continents. It has been shown that islands have acted as places of refuge for many a species threatened with extinction and later wiped out by nature on the mainland. "Extinct as the dodo," is a common expression with an appalling sense of finality. It is to be hoped that, so far as is humanly possible, those fascinating and irreplaceable island species may be preserved for posterity.

Chapter IX

BIRDS

On a day in early September a strong wind from the Bering Sea, carrying the first chill of approaching winter, is sweeping across one of the ocean-girt islands of the Aleutians. A flock of fifty or sixty birds, many of them hatched only the previous May, four months before, in the remote tundra land of Alaska, are skittering along the ground in short flights, feeding as they go. The time for their great voyage is at hand. Suddenly the instinctive moment comes, the entire flock wheels into the upper air and disappears to the south over the flecked ocean to make its landfall about forty hours later on the islands of Hawaii, completing a direct and, as far as we know, nonstop flight of more than two thousand miles. This is the miraculous annual voyage of the Pacific golden plover, one of the most remarkable flights of any land or shore bird, and expressive of the distances that birds are capable of traveling.

The bird life found on the great and small islands of the Pacific is of all sorts and varieties, while the ocean itself is swept by the wings of the birds that make its broad waters their home.

The land birds, like the mammals, came originally to the islands —even to those islands that lie far out in the ocean—from one or another of the adjoining continents. The time of the first arrival of birds to the various islands no doubt varied considerably. In certain islands birds arrived quite recently, in terms of geological time. In other islands, such as New Zealand and the islands of Hawaii and the Galápagos, some birds arrived many millions of years ago. The distinctive character, for example, of the Hawaiian honey creepers or of the so-called Galápagos finches indicates a long evolutionary history. These two groups of birds are peculiar to these islands and each of the groups, since their original time of arrival, has split up into many different species.

The number of different species of land birds decreases as one travels from the islands near the continents out toward the remote islands of the mid-Pacific. As an illustration, the latest information shows that there are some 511 different kinds of resident land birds on New Guinea, 127 on the Solomon Islands, 17 on the Society Islands, and none on Easter Island.

Birds may, of course, reach distant islands from more than one original source. This is evidenced in Hawaii, where it seems probable that the family of native honey creepers is of American origin, whereas the Hawaiian honey eaters came from Polynesia. No Hawaiian land birds appear to have come directly from Asia.

As is to be expected, the birds on the islands that lie relatively near the American continents, such as the Galápagos and the Juan Fernández, are definitely of American origin. An interesting difference, however, is observed on the Aleutian Islands. Here, the native bird life is limited to half a dozen families, and these are of types found in the northern continental areas of Europe, Asia and North America, indicating the use by some birds of the bridge of land that once joined Alaska with Siberia.

On the islands of the western part of the Pacific, all the land birds show a relationship either with Australian bird life or with that of Malaya or Asia. It is interesting to note that the bird life of Japan resembles that of Asia as much as the bird life of the British Isles does that of western Europe.

Since the large amount and variety of bird life in the great Pacific region comprise more than 100 distinct families, it is obviously not possible to discuss here any one of them in detail, although much information concerning the types of birds and where they are found is given in the table on page 206. If we consider the land birds listed in the table, it will be noted that several families such as hawks, rails, pigeons, cuckoos, owls, swifts, kingfishers, swallows, and thrushes are of practically world-wide distribution. Others such as larks, titmice, nuthatches, creepers and waxwings are typically birds of the northern areas of the continents. Still others such as bustards, frogmouths, bee eaters, rollers, hoopoes, hornbills, pittas, bulbuls, sunbirds and weaver finches belong only to Asia and Europe or to one or the other of these continents. The families of hummingbirds, tyrant flycatchers, mockingbirds, wood warblers, and troupials are exclusively American. Finally, there are small families that are confined to very limited regions, such as cassowaries, emus, kiwis, kagus and birds of paradise. The kagu, for example, is a species of uncertain relationships, being found in New Caledonia and nowhere else in the world.

When it comes to sea birds, we find a simpler and more zonal type of distribution, by which is meant that they can be discussed fairly satisfactorily in terms of latitudes. The frigate birds, for instance, are tropical and subtropical and of nearly world-wide distribution in the warmer oceanic areas. The auks and loons belong exclusively to the northern part of the Northern Hemisphere, whereas the cormorants inhabit both hemispheres and occur right through the tropical belt. The penguins are exclusively southern, but they by no means deserve their wholly "antarctic" reputation. In fact most of the seventeen species belong to the temperate belt of southern Africa, South America and the Australian region, and one kind nests at the Galápagos Islands at the very line of the equator itself.

Certain sea birds are supreme in their abilities to travel over great stretches of the ocean and are likely to be found in the most remote parts of the Pacific and far away from even small islands. Among them are many albatrosses and petrels, during their nonbreeding season, tropic birds, and certain terns. Also shore birds such as snipes and sandpipers are wonderful travelers, making their long migrations from northern continental breeding grounds to their winter homes among the South Pacific islands.

Numerous other families of sea birds, on the other hand, stick closely to the coast lines and never venture far out over the ocean. One does not find, for example, loons, pelicans, cormorants, auks or murres at great distances from continental shores or from the coasts of the few remote islands upon which some of them have become established. Terns, however, may be encountered almost anywhere at sea, but their close relatives, the gulls, are entirely absent from the central parts of the Pacific Ocean. The widely advertised bird that alighted on the head of Captain Eddie Rickenbacker during his castaway experience is not likely to have been a gull, because none has ever been recorded from that part of the world. It was probably a noddy or some other species of tern, or possibly a booby.

BIRDS OF THE PACIFIC

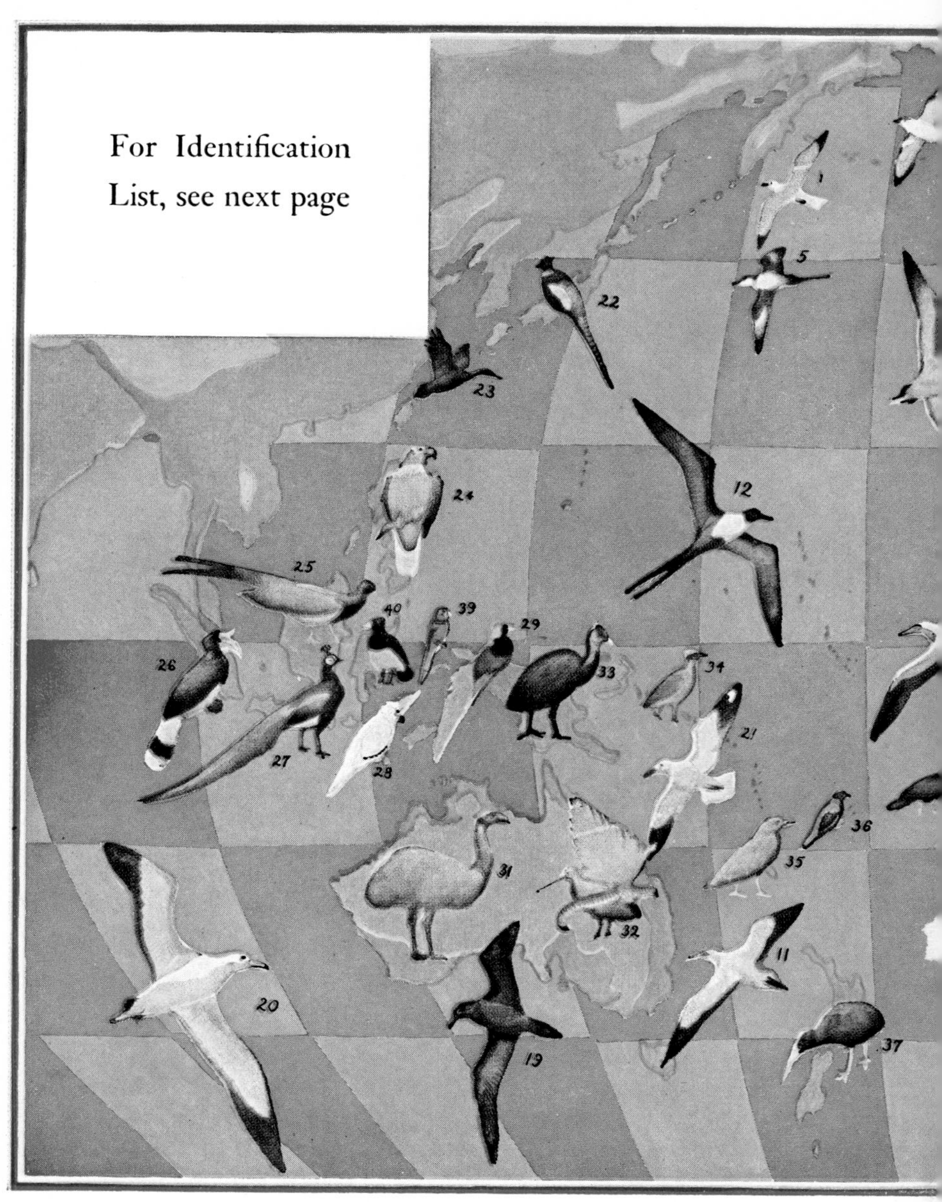

For Identification List, see next page

BIRDS OF THE PACIFIC

1. Kittiwake
2. Fulmar
3. Black-footed albatross
4. Laysan albatross
5. Parasitic jaeger
6. Hawaiian goose
7. Hawaiian storm petrel
8. Brown booby
9. Red-footed booby (gray phase)
10. Masked booby
11. Australian gannet
12. Man-of-war bird (female)
13. Man-of-war bird (male)
14. Peruvian pelican
15. Red-tailed tropic bird
16. Skua
17. Sooty shearwater
18. Cape pigeon (a petrel)
19. Sooty albatross
20. Wandering albatross
21. Silver gull
22. Japanese pheasant
23. Cormorant
24. Monkey-eating eagle
25. Argus pheasant
26. Hornbill
27. Peacock
28. Cockatoo
29. Bird of paradise
30. Tooth-billed pigeon
31. Emu
32. Lyrebird
33. Cassowary
34. Megapode
35. Kagu
36. Golden dove
37. Kiwi
38. Polynesian lorikeet
39. Lory
40. Pink-breasted mound builder
41. Tufted puffin

Chapter X

REPTILES, AMPHIBIANS, AND INSECTS

REPTILES

Unlike the birds, so much in evidence on Pacific islands, the majority of reptiles are by nature secretive. So successful are they in this matter of concealment that many persons, long resident in the tropics, remain in ignorance of their very existence.

Even such monsters as the estuarine crocodile, living in tidal waters, may be completely hidden in the muddy waters of lagoon or river. The first intimation of its presence received by some unwary stroller at the water's edge is when, his legs swept suddenly from under him by a deftly wielded tail, he is seized in the viselike grip of great jaws—to disappear in swirling waters whose surface quickly resumes its normal, placid appearance. An idea of the size attained by this man-eating reptile is furnished by records of occasional specimens over twenty-five feet long. The species ranges from India to the Philippines and through New Guinea to the Fijis.

Native tales as to the existence of a land crocodile on certain islands of the Lesser Sunda group were clarified as recently as 1912 by the discovery of the now famous Komodo monitor. Though but ten feet long, this reptile is the bulkiest of all lizards. The characteristically granular skin, in common with that of other kinds of monitors occurring throughout this region, was formerly much prized for native drums and latterly sought after for export.

LIZARDS

Almost as spectacular is the prehistoric-looking marine iguana, a large lizard, of the Galápagos. Prior to the advent of man upon the islands, immense droves of these dun-colored lizards basked upon the rough lava, swam in the surf, or followed the receding tide to feed upon the glutinous seaweed. The marine iguanas, a land iguana, some smaller lizards and harmless snakes, together with the giant tortoises, comprise the reptile life of the Galápagos. All reveal affinities with the fauna of South America. Even more remote from its American relatives is a good-sized iguanid inhabiting the Fijis.

In the western Pacific, however, one looks in vain for iguanids characteristic of the Western Hemisphere (anoles, fence lizards, and the like), for there they are represented by parallel forms known as agamids. Most intriguing of these are the so-called flying lizards. Other types in great variety are found in the arboreal, terrestrial, or river life of the islands.

Geckos are widely distributed. These small lizards have flattened toes, furnished with devices that support them while running over smooth, vertical surfaces. Though rocks and tree trunks constitute their true habitat, many geckos have adapted themselves to life in human dwellings. Hiding by day in roof or thatch, at sundown they emerge to glide easily over whitewashed walls, where they steal upon their insect prey.

Just above high-water mark on the coral of many islands, an active little lizard may be seen darting here and there as it wrests a living from the ocean. Sheltering itself from the spray of oncoming waves in a crevice of the coral, it dashes out to seize the sandhoppers or other kinds of marine life that form its daily fare. It is one of the skinks, most of which may be recognized by their glossy scales, though rough or ridged scales appear in a few kinds. Skinks are the commonest lizards throughout the Indo-Australian region and, together with geckos, are often the only reptiles on the more remote islands. In many instances their introduction may be due to man, for both geckos and skinks are particularly liable to transport by palm-thatched canoes carrying supplies of native produce. Perhaps their successful survival may be attributed to their small size and secretive ways. No non-American lizard is poisonous, though stories to the contrary are firmly believed by many native peoples. A few of the burrowing lizards have lost their limbs and consequently may be mistaken for snakes.

SNAKES

A large proportion of snakes are harmless. Nevertheless, one must not ignore the venomous kinds. Fatalities from snakebite are extremely rare—the tiny mosquito causes far more deaths—and booted, a man is usually more of a menace to the snake than the snake is to him. Also, the hero of many a "narrow escape" was dealing only with a nonpoisonous species.

All dangerous snakes are provided with one or more pairs of enlarged, grooved or tubular teeth in the front of the upper jaw. All sea snakes are poisonous, and their venom ranks among the most toxic of any snakes. Fatalities are not uncommon. Filipino fishermen, long familiar with their ways, treat the smaller sea snakes with such scant respect that onlookers are inclined, perhaps, to underestimate the risks they take. One variety of sea snake occurs in a fresh-water lake on Luzon, in the Philippines. Marine snakes may be known by the compressed, rudderlike tails with which they propel themselves through the water. Most of the species are slender and graceful. In general they average about three feet in length, but one or two kinds are known to attain nearly three times that size.

Such dimensions are far surpassed by the dreaded king cobra which, though usually about nine feet, occasionally grows to eighteen. Found in the Philippines, Borneo, Sumatra and Java, this cobra is apt to attack without warning those who trespass near its nest or mate. Until disturbed, both it and the several forms of Indian cobra present on the same islands look much like a harmless North American gopher snake. Then, raising their heads clear of the ground, they flatten the neck in the manner that has made these reptiles famous. One Sumatra-Javan form is credited with ejecting its venom at the eyes of an enemy. If the eyes be promptly and thoroughly bathed, even with plain water, no permanent injury to them will result, though for a time the pain may be agonizing.

These larger Asiatic poisonous snakes are absent from New Guinea, which has venomous snakes enough of its own. Among them is the spine-tailed death adder, whose squat form and broad head make it look more like a viper than a member of the cobra-coral-snake family to which it belongs. Of the numerous kinds of poisonous snakes in the East Indies, many are small, semiburrowing, and temperamentally rather inoffensive reptiles.

Pit vipers, whose long fangs are movable, have a range in the Pacific approximating that outlined above for the king cobra. The group is characterized by a sensory pit between nostril and eye. One species bears a distinct resemblance to its relative the cottonmouth moccasin. Others, colored green and brown, have markedly triangular heads and prehensile tails, for they are bush or tree dwellers.

Boas and pythons, both arboreal and terrestrial, are well represented, the largest being the reticulate python of Asia whose range includes the Philippines and the East Indies from Sumatra to Ceram. The maximum length for this giant among snakes is thirty-two feet, though it may be assumed that few individuals exceed twenty. Fortunately all pythons and boas are nonpoisonous, as are also the small, burrowing "blind snakes" that play a useful role in keeping down the teeming termites, so destructive of timber in the tropics.

TURTLES

The more remote islands provide a breeding place for the big marine turtles which, coming ashore, bury their numerous eggs in the sandy beaches. Among such visitors are the herbivorous green turtle, esteemed for soup, and the somewhat inedible, carnivorous hawksbill which furnishes the tortoise shell of commerce. Fresh-water forms occur in many of the larger rivers, particularly those of New Guinea. Some are akin to the flapjacks of the southern states, while one is a relative of our common snapper. Others with strangely long necks have allies in South America, while in the

East Indies certain handsome species are the local representatives of the North American terrapins. Except for two species in the East Indies and the giant forms on the Galápagos, true tortoises are absent throughout the Pacific region.

AMPHIBIANS

Toads, tree and swamp frogs will be encountered in abundance, some so similar to those at home that the relationship will be obvious. Some Pacific frogs have developed unusual breeding habits. The eggs of one Solomon Islands species are deposited in moist locations but quite away from water, which means that the embryo undergoes its entire development within the egg, from which it emerges as a perfect frog.

Two other instances where metamorphosis takes place within the egg are furnished by New Guinea frogs. The first deposits a few large eggs in a sausage-shaped membrane which the mother frog abandons in a mountain stream. In the second case nearly a score of eggs, arranged in a group, hang by a mucilaginous cord from the roof of a cavity in the tuber of a climbing plant.

Except where intentionally introduced by man, frogs and toads do not occur on islands east of the Fijis. Throughout the area newts and salamanders are unknown, but in the larger western islands certain curious, limbless, burrowing amphibians are found: snakelike, but having a tender, wrinkled skin instead of scales; wormlike, but for the tiny mouth with its fine teeth which enable the caecilian, as it is called, to hold the slugs, small worms and "white ants" on which it subsists.

INSECTS

Of all the animal life on the islands, the insects are the most numerous and the most pestiferous. Many are extremely curious in form, and some are perhaps the most beautiful of all living things.

All the large islands, particularly in the Southwest Pacific, constitute a paradise for the student of insect and related life because of the varied and strange forms that may be found upon them.

There are flies with their eyes at the end of long stalks, flies with horns on their cheeks, resembling a stag's antlers, of brilliant green and opaque black; beetles of gorgeous colors and queer shapes; butterflies of great size and dazzling color; walking sticks, inches long; mantids with queer body forms; varicolored cockroaches; brilliant dragonflies; hairy and smooth spiders; fireflies three inches long, with microscopic males and offspring that resemble the long extinct trilobites. In fact the man or woman who is fortunate enough to become interested in the insects of the islands will find a never-ending procession of surprises and an ever-increasing respect for the wonders of creation.

No one knows how many different kinds of insects there are on the islands of the Pacific, but it is safe to say that not one-tenth of them is known to man. The total number will run into many thousands, and it may be safely estimated that it will prove to be well over 100,000. Each island and group of islands has insects that are indigenous only to it, and a very great many of these are known from less than a dozen specimens—many from only a single one.

With the exception of the Netherlands Indies, the Philippines, and the Malay Peninsula, our knowledge of the insect fauna of the Pacific is due to rather spasmodic collecting by missionaries, soldiers, some settlers, and a relatively small number of expeditions to limited areas and for only short periods of time. Then, too, most collectors have gathered the large, conspicuous insects, chiefly butterflies and moths, beetles and dragonflies, roaches, bees, and so on. The butterflies and large moths are the most thoroughly known, the beetles the next best known, then the so-called orthopteroid insects, such as grasshoppers, roaches, crickets, mantids, walking sticks and, lastly, bees and wasps, true bugs and flies.

Because of the great number of insects, a review of the many conspicuous groups that occur on the islands cannot be attempted here. Instead of mentioning a large number of varied groups, there follows a very brief review of some of the moths and butterflies, with the assurance that the collector will find other types fully as strange and fully as fascinating.

BUTTERFLIES AND MOTHS

Butterflies and moths are the familiar insects with often brightly colored wings which are densely shingled with minute scales. This character is indicated in their scientific name "Lepidoptera," meaning in Greek, "scaled wings." The butterflies and moths of the Pacific area are colorful and numerous, running into many thousands of different forms.

The East Indies, the Philippines, New Guinea and the adjacent islands are among the regions richest in variety of butterflies and moths. On the other hand some of the isolated archipelagoes and isles have a very sparse population of this group of insects, but the species found there are of correspondingly greater scientific interest because of their isolation. By studying the distribution of butterflies and moths of various islands the naturalist can obtain additional information throwing light on the geological past of those parts of the globe, on former land bridges, on the breaking up of larger land areas into separate isles and the partial submergence of the land. Undoubtedly, great numbers of new forms will be discovered in the future on less explored lands and islands; for instance, the mountain ridges of New Guinea which have not yet been sufficiently investigated are certain to yield striking novelties.

New Guinea, with the Solomons to the east and the Moluccas to the west, is inhabited by some of the most spectacular representatives of the realm of butterflies and moths. Here are found the largest butterfly and the largest moth in the world, both well over ten inches in spread. This giant butterfly is the female of a species called "Queen Alexandra's bird-winged butterfly," a translation of its Latin name *Ornithoptera alexandrae*. It is of a dark-brown color with lighter markings; the male is somewhat smaller in size and is brilliantly marked in blue-green and velvet-black, displaying a conspicuous lemon-yellow color of the body. A related butterfly of comparable wing span bears the appropriate name of "goliath."

This whole group of butterflies characteristic of New Guinea and the Solomons is typified in the males by a gamut of shining

For Identification List, see next page

BUTTERFLIES
1
2
3
4
5
6
7
8
9
10

BUTTERFLIES AND MOTHS OF THE PACIFIC

BUTTERFLY PLATE

SCIENTIFIC NAME, POPULAR NAME, AND WHERE FOUND

1. *Kallima paralecta* Horsf. ♂ leaf butterfly East Indies
2. *Papilio weiskei* Ribb. ♂ (swallowtail family) New Guinea
3. *Thysonotis horsa* Gr.-Sm. ♂ (this and the next are the family of "little blues") New Guinea
4. *Amblypodia agesias* Hew. ♂ East Indies
5. *Delias timorensis* Bsdv. ♀ (this and the next are of the cabbage butterfly family) Timor
6. *Delias aruna* Bsdv. ♀ New Guinea
7. *Rhopalocampta subcaudata* Fld. subsp. *crawfordi* Dist. ♂ (skipper family) Borneo
8. *Ornithoptera alexandrae* Roths. ♂ Queen Alexandra's bird-winged butterfly New Guinea
9. *Ornithoptera alexandrae* Roths. ♀ Queen Alexandra's bird-winged butterfly (largest known butterfly) New Guinea
10. *Ornithoptera victoriae* Gray ♂ Queen Victoria's bird-winged butterfly Solomon Isls.

MOTH PLATE

1. *Cocytia durvillei* Bsdv. ♂ day-flying moth New Guinea
2. *Charagia ramsayi* Scott ♀ North Australia
3. *Apsarasa atramenta* Hamps. ♀ New Guinea
4. *Eucorma intercisa* Moore ♂ Java
5. *Coscinocera hercules* Misk. ♀ (largest known moth, related to the North American *Cecropia*) North Australia, New Guinea, and adjacent islands
6. *Actias leto* Dbl. ♂ (related to the North American luna moth) East Indies
7. *Agarista agricola* Don. ♂ North Australia
8. *Acherontia styx* Westw. ♀ hawk moth (related to European death's-head moth) India and the East Indies
9. *Alcidis aurora* S. & G. ♂ day-flying aurora moth New Guinea and adjacent islands
10. *Chionaema fulvia* L. ♀ Amboina, New Guinea, and other adjacent islands

♂ Male ♀ Female

hues of emerald green, sapphire blue, and golden yellow contrasted with jet black, while the females remain attired in modest garb. They may be compared, in the striking beauty and popularity they enjoy among naturalists and collectors, with the birds of paradise from the same region. They belong for the most part to the clan of swallow-tailed butterflies, abundantly represented in the Pacific region. In certain parts of this general territory, on Celebes for instance, a definite proportion of swallowtails often show a peculiar trait of a strangely bent front edge of the forewings. In this respect, the swallowtail butterflies are imitating in a deceptive way the appearance of totally unrelated butterflies which are considered well protected on account of a pungent taste of their bodies. Because of this similarity in appearance, swallowtail butterflies are supposed to escape bird enemies. Successful camouflage among butterflies reaches its climax in such species as the leaf butterflies which are extremely difficult to detect in the surrounding foliage when they alight on a leafy branch.

The Pacific area produces an extraordinary variety of gaudy relatives of our common cabbage butterflies. On the Philippine Islands, the East Indies, and the South Sea Islands many representatives of this group, while preserving on their upper wing surfaces the modest white attire of their relatives in America, display on the lower wing surfaces bold patterns of black, red, orange, yellow, and white. New Guinea specializes in this harlequin group. One can single out certain winged jewels as first and second cousins of our common "blues" and "coppers" of the countryside. They sparkle in tints of amethyst, aquamarine, sapphire, emerald, and topaz.

Hawk moths are fairly common throughout the islands of the Southwest Pacific. They look like the insect counterparts of a hummingbird when on the wing. They hover, usually at dusk, over flowers, on whose nectar they feed. The most conspicuous moths of another group in this region are the giant relatives of the silk moths and of the common American *Cecropia*, *Polyphemus*, and luna moths. Truly colossal proportions are reached by several members of this general group, befittingly named after Hercules and Atlas, which are the titans of the tribe. Another kind of huge moth, emerging from wood-boring larvae, is noted for bizarre patterns of the wings, adorned sometimes with markings of metallic brilliance. Still another group, whose name of Uranids suggests celestial inhabitants, consists of insects of peculiar beauty, such as the opalescent aurora moth which has the color of the sky at sunrise.

LAND LEECHES

Land leeches are among the unpleasant things that will be encountered. They occur on all the islands where there is rain forest, from New Caledonia and the New Hebrides to the Philippines, and through the Netherlands Indies into the Malay Peninsula. The land leeches are like the leeches found in American lakes and streams, but they differ from them in that they are found on the land and on the leaves of bushes. If you see them on leaves and wave your hand before them, they will stretch out and wave back and forth. They occur from sea level up to the limits of the rain forest, often in enormous numbers. They attach themselves particularly under belts or wherever clothing binds. They may not be noticed for hours. Tobacco juice, iodine, salt, a burning cigarette, or alcohol will cause them to release their hold immediately. The wounds may develop into sores which might take weeks to heal. Iodine should be applied at once.

TICKS

Ticks are another unsavory pest. They, too, will strain forward from the edge of leaves, their legs waving continually in a frantic effort to grasp your clothing as you pass. These are also removed by tobacco juice, iodine or by touching with a burning cigarette. They should not be pulled out.

CHAPTER XI

PLANTS

WHAT the pine is to New England, what the redwood is to California, the coconut palm is to the Pacific, for on the Pacific islands the coconut palm is dominant. In fact, the coconut is far more widely used in the Pacific than either of the other trees are in their own homeland. The large bud or "cabbage" of the coconut is excellent food either raw or cooked. The nut is edible and the coconut "milk," made by grating the half-ripe pulp into a watery juice, is refreshing and nutritious. The dried flesh of the nut, known as copra, is a most important source of oil, used for food in the form of lard and butter substitutes, for soap making, ammunition, and many other industrial purposes. The husks of the nuts are used for matting, the leaves for thatching, and the light wood in the construction of houses and boats. Thus the coconut palm provides natives of the Pacific islands with food, clothing, and shelter—the basic needs of life; and in its commercial product, copra, the coconut palm forms the most important cash crop in many of the Pacific islands.

Praise of the coconut should be accompanied by the emphatic statement that it is only one of thousands of interesting, beautiful, and valuable plants that grow on the Pacific islands. In the palm family alone there are scores of other species utilized by the natives for food and other purposes. Among the variety of plants to be found are the very numerous orchids, the tree ferns, the superabundant ordinary ferns, and the enormous variety of ornamental and useful herbs, shrubs and trees.

The East Indies, the Philippines and Polynesia have, it is estimated, about 50,000 different kinds of "higher plants": ferns, trees, shrubs and herbs. In New Guinea alone more than 2,500 different kinds of orchids are now known and much of the island has not yet been searched by plant explorers. In the Philippines about 900 different species of orchids occur, practically all of them being different from the New Guinea ones. This area of the western Pacific is without doubt the richest plant region in the world. In contrast, the New England and North Atlantic states have no more than 6,000 different kinds of higher plants.

These plants are not evenly distributed through the vast Pacific area. Some regions are nearly devoid of plant life. The cold Aleutians support only grasses, sedges and relatively few kinds of alpine herbaceous plants that grow and blossom during the short summer months. Another extreme is reached on the hot, low coral islets, where plant life is also limited, chiefly to a relatively few plants whose seeds may be carried by ocean currents and by migratory birds.

No matter what the island, one must bear in mind a number of factors to understand its plant life. Latitude, rainfall, soil, altitude and winds are important parts of the picture. The higher islands, for example, tend to make more rainfall and hence have richer vegetation, and on them the more interesting plants are found, mainly at altitudes of 1,000 feet or more above the sea. Features of many hillsides at medium altitudes are the thickets of wild bananas, an important source of food today as in early times. Altitude and rainfall largely determine the kind and extent of plant life within the tropics.

On low islands, or along the shores of larger ones, there may be wide beaches or, where streams empty into the sea, deep coastal swamps filled with tangles of mangrove. Beach plants include the coconut palm and the pandanus or screw pine. In fresh-water swamps are found the sago palm and in brackish swamps the nipa palm, all of which are sources of food. Morning-glories and other small plants occur too, but in general none of the handsome plants that make up the forest vegetation.

In the main islands of the Southwest Pacific the forests themselves are magnificent. Nothing quite like them occurs at home. There are often three layers of trees; first the forest giants that rise 100 feet and more before they even branch; these form the *cover* of the forest. Beneath are second-level trees whose total height is about that of the first branches of the giants. Lastly are the smaller shrubs and trees that catch only the last bits of sunlight that filters down. This old primary lowland forest is too dense for the rich growth of orchids, ferns or herbaceous plants, which are more abundant at altitudes above 2,500 to 3,000 feet where the trees are smaller. Then, especially at higher altitudes, the orchids and ferns not only cover the ground but the branches and trunks of trees as well. There is such a topsy-turvy, closely intergrown mixture of flowers, ferns, mosses and vines that the forest may be nearly impassable.

In these forests at greater heights, where the air is cooler, the climate favors plants that are more or less familiar to one who comes from the north-temperate zone. Here different kinds of rhododendrons, raspberries, oaks, huckleberries, violets, and even asters and buttercups occur, while on exposed peaks and ridges all woody plants become so dwarfed and densely interwoven that it is often difficult to penetrate these elfin-wood thickets. On the various higher mountains of the large islands in the Southwest Pacific a definite timber line occurs, and above the timber line one finds only grasses, sedges and herbs, in open heathlike formations.

In many parts of the Southwest Pacific—owing to local climatic conditions and, at times, to the destruction of the original forest by man or by natural causes, including fires—vast areas of open grassland occur. The dominant grasses are frequently very coarse, sometimes five or six to even ten or twelve feet high. Throughout the settled areas where agriculture is practiced one notes not only the cultivated plants themselves but many different kinds of weeds, the latter for the most part introduced from other parts of the tropics and within the historical period. Again, scattered in the forests, one will note various kinds of bamboos, the giants of the grass family, the stems sometimes seventy-five or more feet high;

and where the forests have been destroyed bamboo thickets may be found covering great areas. Throughout the settled areas various kinds of bamboos are actually planted, for they are among the most valuable plants in the economy of the natives, being utilized for an almost infinite variety of purposes.

The flora of that vast region extending from the Malay Peninsula to the Philippines and southeastward to New Guinea and the Solomon Islands is extraordinarily rich, both in genera and species. New Caledonia farther to the southeast also has a very varied and characteristic flora, in many respects quite different from that of the continent, and with a very high percentage of species known only from that island. As one proceeds from the western borders of the Pacific, plant life becomes more and more limited, both in genera and species. At the same time the vegetation of Micronesia and Polynesia is essentially similar to that of the Malayan region though with far fewer varieties of plants. This constant diminution of species as one goes to the farther oceanic islands is well illustrated by the orchid family, which has, roughly, as many as 3,500 different species in New Guinea and the Philippines alone, whereas in all of Micronesia and Polynesia there are only about 300 species, and as one gets as far east as Hawaii, one finds the orchid flora reduced to only three or four species.

The origin and relationships of the flora have been studied by various botanists. There is clear evidence that in the islands of the western Pacific two distinct plant worlds meet, the basis of which goes back to the time of the last great glacial age, when some of the East Indies were connected to the mainland of Asia and when New Guinea was part of Australia. This connection was of such recent time that if the sea should recede only about sixty feet, New Guinea and Australia would be reunited. Another drop of sixty or seventy feet in the sea level would bring Sumatra, Java and Borneo into contact with Asia again.

At the time of the great glacial age, plants spread eastward and south from Asia and north from Australia into the islands. There they were later isolated when the sea flooded the connecting land.

Alfred Wallace, who proclaimed the idea of evolution at the same time as Charles Darwin, first recognized a boundary through the East Indian islands where the Asiatic and Australian plants met. There is, of course, much intermingling but, in general, strictly Australian and to a lesser degree strictly Asiatic types of plants keep pretty clearly to their own side of the Wallace line.

As in all other places in the world, the peoples of the Pacific have used the land to serve their own ends. Agriculture has disturbed the native vegetation in many places. In primitive agricultural practice the trees are felled and the debris burned, and on land thus cleared food-producing plants are grown. These areas are cultivated year after year, but very often they may be abandoned, and whenever this happens the land is quickly occupied by coarse grasses, bamboo thickets, or second-growth forests made up entirely of small, quick-growing trees. This primitive agricultural practice of abandoning areas brought under cultivation for the easier method of clearing new forest areas where the soil is naturally richer has been one of the greatest factors in the destruction of the magnificent primary forests over vast areas in the tropics.

The natives of the South Pacific cultivate many plants with which the visitor is not familiar but which he will often find quite appetizing and delicious once he has tasted them. Taro is one such plant. It grows about a foot and a half high in wet, swampy land. It is a somewhat fleshy plant, related to our own Jack-in-the-pulpit, and like it taro is full of irritating, sharp, stinging crystals. The starchy tubers must be boiled or roasted before they can be eaten; they actually take the place of the potato in the Old World tropics. The young leaves, after cooking to destroy the stinging microscopic crystals, make an excellent pot herb, and thus from this one commonly cultivated plant we may secure the equivalent of potatoes and spinach. The sweet potato, familiar to us at home, is also a most important food plant and is widely cultivated. A number of different varieties occur, the tubers of all being excellent to eat; and like the taro, the sweet potato yields, in its tender growing shoots, an excellent and very widely used pot herb—a second species yielding substitutes for both our common potato and spinach.

In some regions, particularly New Guinea and the Solomon Islands, the sago palm yields a basic food that is widely used. The fairly large trunks produce great quantities of starch, the sago of commerce. The trunk is split, the soft tissues macerated, and the starch washed out into settling tanks and then dried. Bamboo shoots are also used as food. Other important food plants are yams (some weighing up to thirty pounds), arrowroot and cassava or tapioca. There are many kinds of bananas, papayas, guavas, sweetsops and soursops, custard apples, mangoes, and dozens of other fruits, berries and nuts.

The breadfruit has long been a native stand-by in Polynesia. The large fruit must be cooked or baked before eating. In olden days the islanders planted breadfruit trees upon the birth of a child in order to insure a permanent future supply of food. When the natives went exploring or on fishing trips they would plant these trees on the small islands they visited. Unfortunately, however, owing to the fact that the Polynesians are now fewer in number and that imported foods are becoming established, the breadfruit now tends to disappear over wide areas of the Pacific. The best forms produce no seeds and, unless it is planted from cuttings, the tree will not maintain itself.

Relatively few grains are grown in the East Indies and even fewer in Polynesia. Of these, rice is the best known and by far the most important. Corn is commonly planted. Grains such as wheat and barley are rarely grown. Sorghum, Italian millet and other small grains are often found in cultivation. That the East Indies have long been the producers of cereal grains is confirmed by the name of the island of Java, which is derived from the Sanskrit word "yava," meaning barley or, more broadly, cereal. Other agricultural products of the islands include coffee, tea, sugar, palm oil, quinine, pepper, nutmeg, cloves and other spices, rubber, kapoc and Manila hemp.

The importation of plants into the Pacific islands did not always prove an unmixed blessing, for with the new plants came foreign weeds which established themselves rapidly and sometimes proved an even greater nuisance than in their homeland. An interesting example of the complicated way in which plant life may be changed is the case of the American lantana. This thorny vine is now responsible for much of the "jungle" areas on Pacific islands. For many years the plant had been grown on Hawaii as an ornament in local gardens. It was cultivated and admired. Certainly it could not be considered a "problem child" of the plant world. But some time after the lantana was introduced the East Indian myna, of the starling family, was also brought to the islands. As these birds adapted themselves to Hawaiian life, they found in the berries of the lantana a favorite food. The indigestible seeds were scattered far and wide by the birds and soon very dense thickets developed all over the islands. Thus an introduced bird and an introduced plant combined to make a "jungle." An interesting if less peculiar example is found in the American miconia recently introduced into the Fiji Islands as an ornamental plant and now become a veritable pest, being known there as "Koster's curse," or merely as "the curse."

The amateur who is curious about plants has the very practical reason for learning to recognize them—for in an emergency many of them are edible.

There are, of course, some poisonous plants on the islands—those that are poisonous to eat and even fewer that are poisonous to touch—but fortunately they are few. Two plants, the seeds of which should never be eaten, are the *physic nut*, a common shrub found in cultivated areas, and the *castor-oil plant*—sometimes grown as an ornamental plant in the United States—characterized by large lobed leaves. One naturally would not eat fruits that are very bitter, or that are otherwise objectionable in taste. Whenever possible seek the advice of natives, for the average native of any island is thoroughly familiar with plants and plant uses.

Several kinds of tree nettles when touched irritate the skin, and casual contact with them may be very painful, large water blisters forming because of the irritating juice forced into the skin. Cowhage, a vine with greenish to purple flowers, is also irritating on contact, but the stinging hairs in this case are only mechanical irritants and occur only on the fruits and on parts of the flowers. There are also a few shrubs or trees related to the poison ivy and the poison oak, which do not look much like their American relatives, but which on contact may cause difficulties, the rash resulting being the same as that caused by the poison ivy or the poison oak at home.

The abundance of plant life on the Pacific islands is so overwhelming that the smaller plants, the mosses, lichens, fungi and molds, can scarcely be considered except for some varieties of mold that are a nuisance. Clothing, shoes, and other belongings may sprout a growth of mold overnight, when the temperature and moisture are right. Some of these fungi actually grow in and under the skin, and individuals so infected may require medical treatment.

Another entirely different world of plant life exists in the ocean itself, where the world's smallest plants, as well as some very large ones, are found. Billions of microscopic plants float in the ocean waters, serving as food for fish and smaller ocean animals. Some of the ocean plants help build the coral reefs. Some are edible. The northern Pacific kelp, a kind of seaweed, has been found growing over 250 feet long. From one seaweed we get *agar-agar*, a material widely used in hospitals and scientific laboratories as a medium in which to grow bacteria.

The plant life of the ocean is in itself a long story and consequently attention is here directed to the wealth of land plants that the visitor will constantly see around him on the Pacific islands.

"All flesh is grass" the Good Book says, which is only another way of stating the obvious fact that all animal life is dependent directly or indirectly on plant life. The exuberance of plant life in the humid higher islands of the Pacific, and particularly of the Malay-Melanesian regions, is reflected in the great wealth of mammals, birds, reptiles and insects. There is in these regions, as in other parts of the world, an intimate correlation of plant and animal life, and where there is an exuberant vegetation, there will be found a corresponding richness of animal life.

REGIONAL DESCRIPTIONS

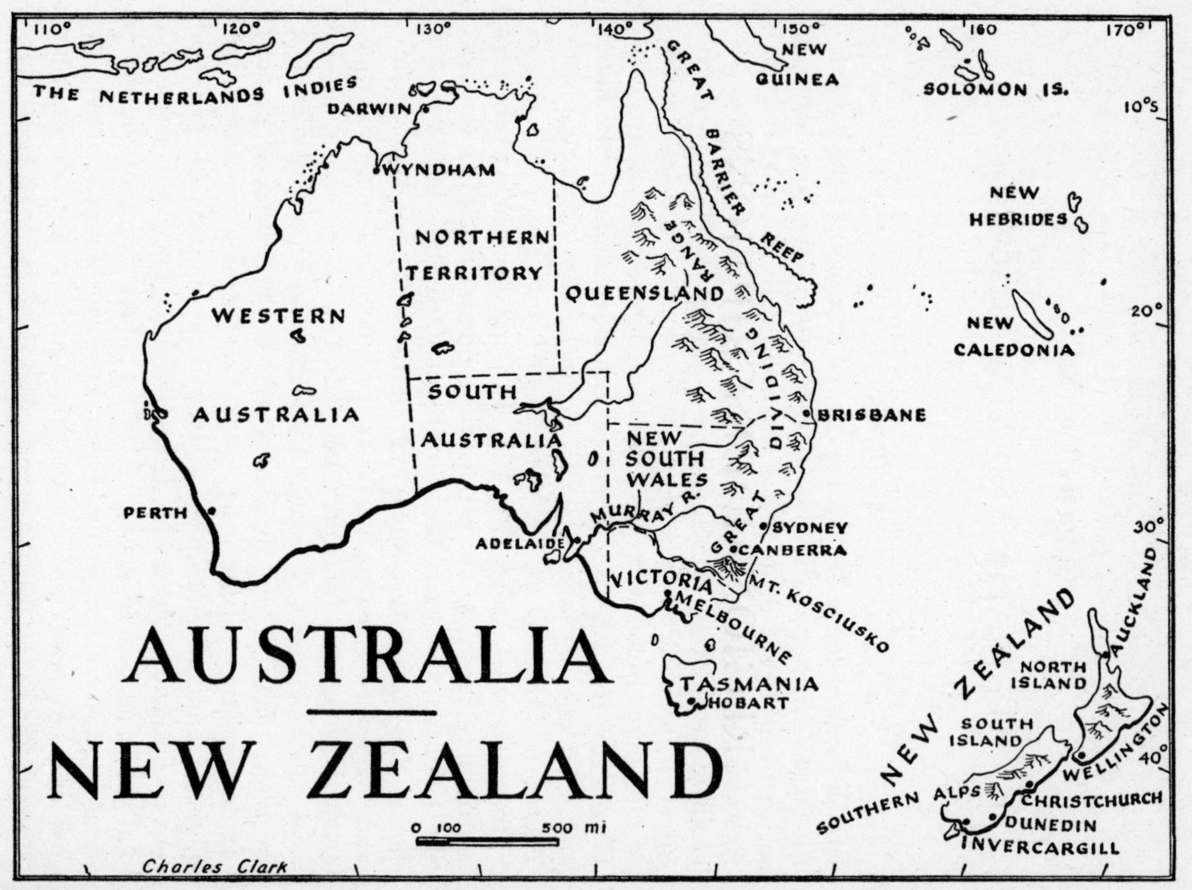
110°
120°
130°
140°
150°
160
170°
10°S
20°
30°
40°
THE NETHERLANDS INDIES
DARWIN
NEW GUINEA
SOLOMON IS.
GREAT BARRIER REEF
WYNDHAM
NORTHERN TERRITORY
QUEENSLAND
GREAT DIVIDING RANGE
NEW HEBRIDES
NEW CALEDONIA
WESTERN AUSTRALIA
SOUTH AUSTRALIA
BRISBANE
NEW SOUTH WALES
MURRAY R.
PERTH
SYDNEY
CANBERRA
ADELAIDE
VICTORIA
MT. KOSCIUSKO
MELBOURNE
AUSTRALIA
NEW ZEALAND
TASMANIA
HOBART
NEW ZEALAND
NORTH ISLAND
AUCKLAND
SOUTH ISLAND
WELLINGTON
SOUTHERN ALPS
CHRISTCHURCH
DUNEDIN
INVERCARGILL
0 100 500 mi
Charles Clark

CHAPTER XII

AUSTRALIA AND NEW ZEALAND

AUSTRALIA

IT IS difficult to convey the delight of the first sight of the Australian coast—whether the landfall is made after long, long days at sea or from a huge plane that has crossed half a world of water. Australia, meaning "southern land," lies approximately 7,000 miles southwestward from San Francisco and some 6,000 miles southeastward from Suez. It has an area approximately the same as that of the United States. On the Australian continental shelf are New Guinea, the Aru Islands and numerous smaller islands to the north and Tasmania to the south, all of which were connected with Australia as recently as 30,000 to 40,000 years ago.

In many ways Australia is like the United States; in others it is strikingly different. The people, the modern cities, the industries, the language and even the climate may remind Americans of home. Yet these same visitors will find the plant and animal life and the ways of the native Australian aboriginal quite different from anything they have ever seen before.

A geographer sees Australia as a fairly regular piece of land, a bit wider than it is long. It is comparatively flat: barely 5 percent of the land rises to more than 2,000 feet. Mount Kosciusko, the highest mountain (7,328 feet), is dwarfed by innumerable peaks of our own Rockies. The land is generally fertile, but insufficient rainfall makes all central Australia a great desert. Some of the more important rivers rise in the Great Dividing Range, a range of mountains running north and south, which in spite of its name is very close to the Australian east coast. The rivers generally flow west from here, turning north or south to the sea. Largest of these is the Murray and the Darling system, with tributaries, which flows southward and empties into the Australian Bight. But its flow is so irregular, owing to variation in rainfall, seepage and evaporation, that this generally navigable river system occasionally dries up in some places.

The climate of Australia varies from one part of the continent to another. About a third of Australia is within the tropical zone and the other two-thirds in the south-temperate zone. The southern part of Australia is the coolest region. The temperature here is controlled by the highlands and by the equalizing effects of the ocean. Northwest Australia is hottest. The desert has a great range in temperature. The thermometer may reach 110° by midafternoon and drop to near freezing at night. Wyndham, not very far from Darwin, is one of the hottest places on earth. Its *average* annual temperature is 85°.

The rainfall varies with the locality. In the north, the rainfall is about sixty inches during the hot summer season from November to April, and in the east somewhere between forty and sixty inches. Snow is rare and occurs only in the southeast mountains. However, there is sufficient snow here for winter sports. The large western and central area that makes up a third of the continent averages only about ten inches of rainfall yearly. Some parts of the western region have a rainfall of less than five inches, and a whole year may pass without a single shower. By way of contrast, there may be 165 inches yearly in northeast Queensland. Here rainfalls as great as thirty-five inches in twenty-four hours have been recorded.

Obviously the climate directly affects the vegetation, which in turn exerts control over animal life and the human uses of the land. The arid interior of Australia supports only sparse plants and brush. In the south and east are forests of giant eucalypti. The eucalyptus is characteristic of the Australian flora, and more than 300 different kinds have been identified. One species (*Eucalyptus regnans*) in Gippsland, near Melbourne, reaches a height of 300 feet and is the tallest hardwood in the world. Then there is an even greater variety of acacias. In the rich coastal area of northeast Queensland are luxuriant tropical growths that include many ferns and flowering plants similar to those of New Guinea.

The animals popularly associated with Australia are the kangaroo and the koala. These and many other strange animals inhabit the forest and brush. The kangaroo, which is distributed very generally throughout the country, is famed not only for its well-developed hindlegs and tail but for its method of caring for the young. In Australia there are many kinds of pouched animals (known to scientists as *marsupials*). At birth the young climbs by itself into the pouch, with no assistance from the mother. Here the baby feeds on the mother's milk until it is big enough to care for itself. There are many species of kangaroos and not all look like the familiar animal we see at the zoo. They range from the long-legged, man-sized red and gray kangaroos and their smaller cousins, the wallabies–some varieties of which are approximately the size of a hare–to the tiny musk kangaroos, not much larger than a house rat. Closely allied to the wallabies are the tree kangaroos of the forests of northeast Queensland.

The round-eared, woolly, and tailless koala, often spoken of as the "teddy bear," is rather closely related to the kangaroo and lives in the forests of eastern Australia, feeding only on leaves of certain kinds of eucalyptus trees.

Another curious animal is the duck-billed platypus–found in most of the rivers of eastern Australia and Tasmania–which has some of the characteristics of the duck, the beaver and the turtle. The platypus and its relative, the spiny anteater, are egg-laying mammals but are very highly specialized types, relics of prehistoric ages and rarely found today. Even their body temperature is lower and more variable than that of higher mammals. They lay eggs like reptiles and suckle their young, which hatch from the eggs. Their bony structure and various organs show them to be very primitive types.

There are dozens of other Australian animals and birds, perhaps less well known but equally interesting. This continent is the home of the emu, the cassowary, the lyrebird, and the kookaburra, a kind of kingfisher, often called the "laughing jackass." There are huge crocodiles in some of the northern rivers. One finds snakes (many venomous), lizards, turtles, giant earthworms, and strange fishes.

There is a long story behind the strange plants and animals of this continent, a story that has been many millions of years in the making. It is probable that in very early times Australia was continuous with southern Asia. Even if this were not so, the separation by water of the two continents must have been very small because so many of the plants and animals of these areas are closely related. Then when in a more recent geological period Australia became an entirely separate land mass, many of the specialized types of animals developed in the isolation of this great "island" continent.

The Australian aboriginal, or "Blackfellow," is a brown-skinned, wide-nosed person of medium height, with black wavy hair, often with prominent bony ridges above the eyes. Though dark-skinned, he is not a member of the Negro race. The tribes varied in their ways of life but most of the Blackfellows were hunters or fishermen. They had no agriculture, no domestic animals except the dingo (a dog, thought to have been brought originally to the continent by primitive man), and no towns or permanent settlements. Their simple weapons included the club, the spear, the throwing stick, and the boomerang. They had marvelous ability as hunters and trackers and were able to find food in desert lands where white men have starved. Even today the aboriginal is used by the police for tracking criminals in the way a bloodhound is used in the United States. He can see signs that escape white men and is remarkable in his knowledge of bushlore. As a rule he wears no clothing, though the weather is often cold. Although the Blackfellows are considered to be among the world's most primitive people, at the same time they have developed a complex tribal organization with many religious and social ceremonies. In 1940 the native population was recorded as approximately 50,000.

The first white settlers came in 1788, when a penal colony was founded at Port Jackson in New South Wales. In the following decades ship after ship brought other settlers from England. The discovery of gold and the excellent possibilities of agriculture and sheep raising spurred immigration by all types and classes. Gradually settlements sprang up on many parts of the coast and the colonists spread into the interior. Eventually they built fine cities, such as Melbourne and Sydney, each of whose populations today have reached more than 1,000,000. The total population of Australia today is approximately 7,190,000; 86 percent are Australian-born and 97 percent are of British stock. Nearly half the people live in the cities; the greatest concentration of the population is along the east coast of the continent.

Like Americans, the Australians have to some extent modified the English language to their own taste. Their speech is colorful and contains a peculiar brand of slang that at first seems strange to the newcomer. Even stranger than the slang are the names of places, for often they were taken from the native language, just as we took over Indian names—Mississippi, Penobscot, Mohawk, for instance. It takes time for the newcomer to get used to such Australian names as Wagga Wagga, Ninkerloo, Billeroo and Warnamboo.

Australia is primarily an agricultural country. Of the 25,000,000 acres of land under cultivation, most are devoted to wheat, sugar beet, barley, sugar cane, corn and fruit. Australian sheep ranches are justly famous, not only for the number of sheep, well over 100,000,000, but for the quality of the wool and the yield per sheep, which is the highest in the world. There are also large herds of beef and dairy cattle, yielding so well that dairy products, meats and hides are important exports.

Australia too had its gold rush, and when the excitement was over, the mining communities settled down to steady economic production. Besides gold, Australia is mined for coal, iron, copper, lead, silver, and a variety of other minerals.

Education is free and compulsory. Secondary education is well established and well organized. There are eight universities with excellent agricultural and technical schools. Australians receive better than average medical care, and the success of the sanitary and public-health measures is evident in the general excellent level of health.

Australia is a commonwealth, so proclaimed in 1901. It is one of the dominions of the British Empire and, like Canada and South Africa, is self-governing. There are six states—New South Wales, Victoria, Queensland, South Australia, West Australia, and the island of Tasmania—each with its own constitution, parliament, and laws. Also, there are a number of territories, from New Guinea to the Australian Antarctic, administered by the Australian Commonwealth.

NEW ZEALAND

New Zealand, also one of the dominions of the British Empire, lies almost exactly on the opposite side of the earth from Great Britain, and about 1,200 miles southeast of Australia. It has a total territory of 103,410 square miles (almost twice the area of Illinois) and extends 1,000 miles from north to south. In the Northern Hemisphere the position and length of New Zealand would compare with our Atlantic coast from Maine to North Carolina.

The two great islands of New Zealand are mountainous. The highest mountains on North Island are volcanoes at some distance from the main mountain range. The loftiest volcanoes rise more than 9,000 feet above the sea. Near the volcanoes are hot springs, geysers, and mud volcanoes, like those of Yellowstone Park. But New Zealand goes Yellowstone one better by featuring an occasional violent earthquake. New Zealand also boasts Sutherland Waterfalls, where the water drops 1,900 feet—nearly the world's record.

South Island is not volcanic, but is even more mountainous than North Island. Its mountains form a great snow-capped range, with peaks more than 12,000 feet high. In these New Zealand "Alps" are glaciers, mountain lakes, waterfalls, and unsurpassed mountain scenery.

Only the extreme northern tip of the long peninsula of North Island reaches the subtropics. Here mangroves grow along the coast. The rest of New Zealand has a temperate climate, somewhat cooler than might be expected in its belt of latitude. The rainfall is moderate except on parts of South Island where the prevailing sea winds from the west and the high mountains together produce heavy rains and snows. More than 150 inches of rain a year falls in this southwest corner, and from 50 to 150 inches on all the western slopes of South Island. The eastern half of South Island is much drier, but it still averages twenty-five inches of rain annually. On the whole, the climate is healthful and stimulating. The seasons are similar to those in our temperate zone, but are reversed because New Zealand is in the Southern Hemisphere.

The vegetation includes more than 1,000 kinds of plants, most of which are found nowhere else in the world. There are great forests of hardwoods, green throughout the year. In the rich undergrowth ferns, including tree ferns, grow in great variety. The gigantic kauri pine, which produces a valuable resin and is an important timber tree, occurs widely in the north.

In spite of the fact that there are no native land mammals whatever except bats, the animal life is even more peculiar than the vegetation. Snakes are absent and the two species of frogs belong to the most primitive group of frogs alive today. Among other remarkable anatomical details they have muscles for wagging the tail—though no tail is present! The tuatara, a twenty-inch lizardlike reptile, is now found on the islands in the Bay of Plenty and on Stephen Island in Cook Strait. This strange creature has a vestigial third eye which may be seen through the thin skin of the young tuatara's head, a characteristic common to many lizards. Other lizards, few and small, include the shiny-scale skinks and the big-eyed, soft-skinned geckos.

The kiwi, a remarkable flightless bird, is occasionally found. Besides its useless wings it has fluffy, hairlike feathers and a long curved bill with nostrils just behind the tip. All other birds have nostrils near the base of the bill. The moa, now extinct, was the largest of the world's land birds, reaching a height of twelve feet. It, too, was flightless and seems to have been exterminated by the Maoris, early Polynesian inhabitants of New Zealand. Other bird life includes parrots, among them the large kea, which sometimes attacks sheep with its sharp beak. There is a good variety of native songbirds, some of which are now being displaced by sparrows and other aggressive birds from Europe and Asia, or which are disappearing because they cannot adapt themselves to man and his works.

Many foreign animals, fish and birds have been brought to New Zealand. There are no less than five kinds of deer now flourishing in the islands—two from Europe, two from America, and one from India. The Alpine chamois does well in the "Southern Alps" of South Island. New Zealand's streams of salmon and trout now boast of world-famous fishing. Unfortunately, however, some of the introduced birds and mammals have become serious pests, and even domestic dogs and pigs run wild and prey upon young lambs in the sheep-raising districts.

New Zealand's main industry has been sheep raising. Pastures have been greatly improved by the introduction of European grasses. Wool was formerly the primary export, but this now tends to be displaced in importance by frozen meats (both lamb and beef), butter and cheese. Cattle raising and dairying are steadily growing industries. About two-thirds of the area of the islands is suited to agriculture.

The Maoris, who inhabited New Zealand when the islands were discovered by the Dutchman Tasman and subsequently explored by Captain Cook, are Polynesians who came by oversea canoe voyages from the Central Pacific in about the year 1300. One such voyage is reported in the remarkable oral sagas of these people, who pass stories down from generation to generation. As so often happens when white people come to distant lands, the Maoris were greatly reduced in number upon the establishment of the white settlements. Fortunately, the native population is now increasing, due in part to intermarriage with whites, and at present they number about 90,900. They are a fine people, sit in Parliament as full-fledged citizens, and have become proficient as doctors, lawyers, judges and architects.

The white population of New Zealand has grown from approximately 2,000 in 1840 to more than 1,500,000 today. The larger cities are Auckland and Wellington on North Island, and Christchurch, Dunedin and Invercargill on South Island.

New Zealand is governed by a Legislative Council and a House of Representatives. It is famed for its modern social legislation, which includes old-age benefits, family allowances, sickness, accident and unemployment benefits. There is also a national health service with a free medical plan.

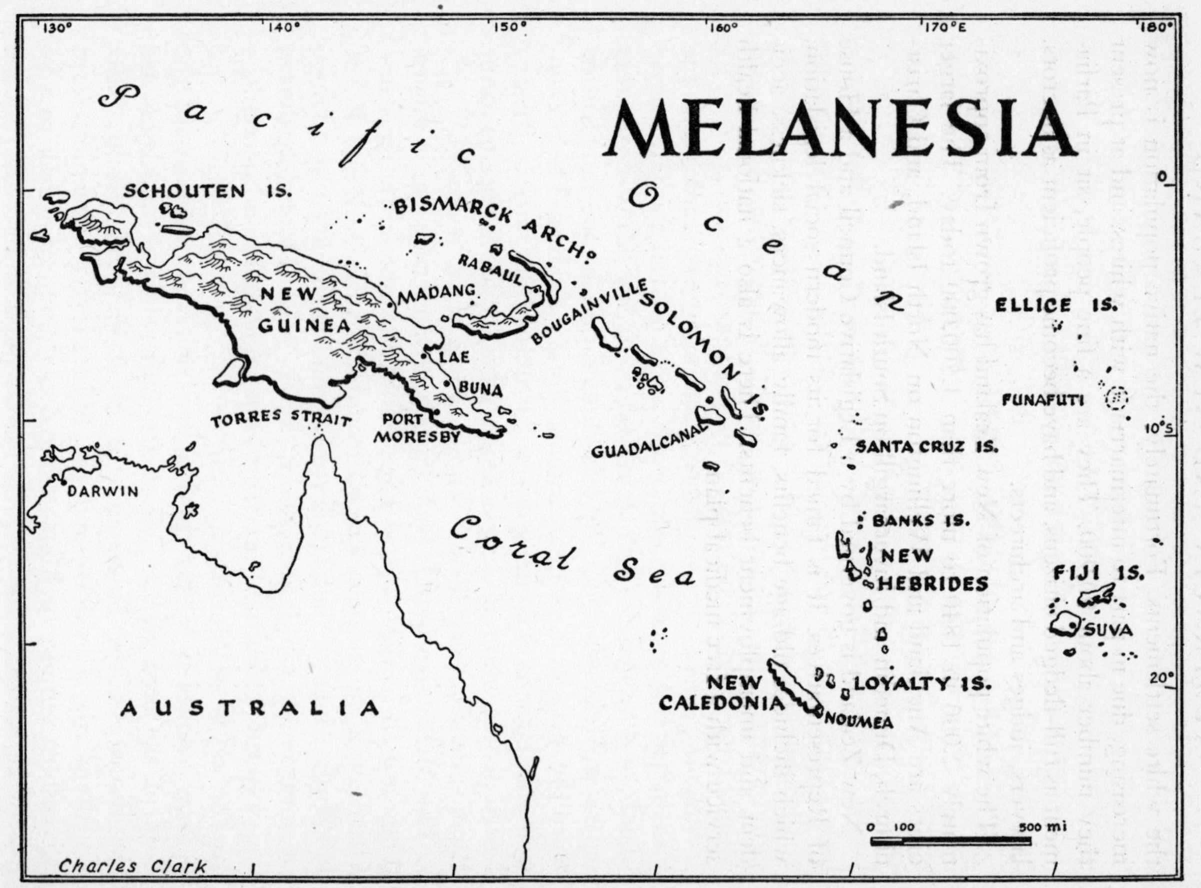
MELANESIA
Pacific Ocean
Coral Sea
SCHOUTEN IS.
BISMARCK ARCH.
NEW GUINEA
MADANG
RABAUL
LAE
BUNA
PORT MORESBY
TORRES STRAIT
DARWIN
AUSTRALIA
BOUGAINVILLE
SOLOMON IS.
GUADALCANAL
SANTA CRUZ IS.
BANKS IS.
NEW HEBRIDES
ELLICE IS.
FUNAFUTI
FIJI IS.
SUVA
LOYALTY IS.
NEW CALEDONIA
NOUMEA
0 100 500 mi
130°
140°
150°
160°
170°E
180°
0°
10°S
20°
Charles Clark

CHAPTER XIII

MELANESIA

UNTIL the war the islands of Melanesia were of comparatively little importance in world affairs. Certainly the names of many of the islands and places in Melanesia were completely unknown to most Americans. Today Guadalcanal, Bougainville, Rabaul and Munda have taken an unforgettable place in American history.

Melanesia is an arc of islands continuing eastward from the East Indies and rounding in a broad curve toward the far oceanic islands of Polynesia. There is no break in the island chain that separates Melanesia from the East Indies, and as one moves eastward the changes in plant and animal life are gradual. The population of Melanesia is composed in the main of short, stocky, frizzy-haired people who represent one distinct wave of migrations to the Pacific islands. Very little is known about their origin.

The Melanesian islands have certain characteristics in common. They are all in the tropical zone—mostly south of the equator—extending in an arc that sweeps through 20° of latitude and 40° of longitude. Many of the islands are volcanic, surrounded by a fringe of coral reefs. The larger islands are forested. Mineral resources and tropical agricultural products—rice, pineapples and coconuts—are the source of Melanesian wealth.

New Guinea is by far the largest island and accounts for the bulk of the land area of Melanesia. Other important islands are the Bismarcks, the Solomons, the New Hebrides group, New Caledonia, the Loyalties, and the Fijis, the last of which form the eastern outpost of Melanesia and the connecting link to vast Polynesia. A description of these islands and island groups follows.

NEW GUINEA

New Guinea, after Greenland, is the largest island in the world. It lies to the north of Australia, separated from it by only about 100 miles at Torres Strait, the water of which is so shallow that one could walk with dry feet from Australia to New Guinea if the ocean dropped but sixty feet.

Western New Guinea has been under Dutch control, while eastern New Guinea consists of two Australian territories, Papua and the mandated territory of New Guinea. New Guinea formed the front line of Australia's defense when the Japanese swarmed south, in 1942. A year later the island was a springboard for the counterattack.

The white population of New Guinea before the war was very small, approximately 3,200. The native peoples are estimated to number more than 600,000. Mission stations are the chief centers of white influence of the north coast. The principal city is Port Moresby, in Papua, on the south shore.

On the map New Guinea resembles a dragon, with its head pointing toward the Moluccas to the west and its tail stretching out toward the Solomons to the east. If laid over a map of the United States, with its eastern end at New York City, the western end of New Guinea would reach the middle of Nebraska. The area of the island is about 342,232 square miles.

This great island forms a small world in itself, making a brief description quite difficult. Its mountains reach to more than 16,000 feet. Its larger rivers are a mile wide in their lower reaches and hundreds of miles long, with a volume of water that makes them navigable for long distances. Several nearby islands and island groups are included within the New Guinea territory—the Louisiade Archipelago off the eastern tip, the Aru Islands to the southwest, and Japen and the Schouten Islands in Geelvink Bay to the northwest.

Most of New Guinea is mountainous. A high and broad central range of ancient, folded rocks forms the backbone of the island.

Fossil-bearing rock layers of various ages are present. Active volcanoes are found only on the islands along the northeast coast, leading to the volcanic arcs of the Bismarck Archipelago. Gold and other minerals are present in the central range.

The climate of New Guinea varies greatly from one part of the island to another, especially as one climbs the mountains. The coastal regions are hot and humid, a climate most whites find well-nigh unbearable. The amount of rainfall on the eastern and northern coast and slopes is greater than on the southern. Above 3,000 feet, the climate is, of course, cooler and it becomes bitterly cold on the high mountains above 13,000. The prevailing winds change with the seasons. They blow from the southeast from May to October and from the north or northwest during the remainder of the year. These onshore winds and the shallow coastal waters make navigation about the island more dangerous than the visitor might suspect. The coasts and the great swampy river basins are breeding grounds for mosquitoes. Malaria and other tropical fevers are present.

The forest over a large part of New Guinea is high, dense, and composed of a great variety of trees. Temperate plants, such as conifers, rhododendrons, oaks and beeches, appear in the cooler zone above 6,000 feet, while above the tree line on the higher mountains, the broad meadows–some of which have been made into landing fields for small planes–are dotted with buttercups, daisies and gentians. The lowland swamps are densely overgrown with enormously tall wild sugar cane. Where the forest fringes the rivers it is draped with great masses of vines. The sago palm, also a swamp tree, produces a readily available supply of starch, and there is a great variety of wild banana trees. On flat areas, especially in southern and southwestern New Guinea, and in the mountain districts of eastern New Guinea there are wide expanses of grass-covered plains–grasslands that develop following fires set by the natives.

The mammals of New Guinea resemble to a considerable extent those of Australia. Among them are egg-laying spiny anteaters, a few smaller kangaroos and wallabies, and many smaller pouched animals, such as bandicoots and phalangers.

Some of the New Guinea kangaroos have become true forest animals and have taken to life in the trees. They are good though clumsy climbers. There is the common native pig, apparently brought to the island by man. Lizards and snakes are far more numerous than in the islands to the east. Small, green tree pythons are found in the forests, also ground pythons and a few poisonous snakes similar to those of Australia. The largest lizards are the monitors. Many smaller kinds also occur. The bird life is extraordinary. New Guinea is famous for numerous brilliantly colored parrots, cockatoos, kingfishers, pigeons, but above all, for the gorgeous birds of paradise, of which there are about ninety different kinds. These birds are protected by law and it is illegal to own or export bird-of-paradise feathers to the United States. The flightless cassowary is the largest land bird. In all, 650 kinds of native birds, not including hundreds of subspecies, are known on New Guinea. In the insect tribe, the huge butterflies called the "Bird Wings" are among the most radiantly colored.

The native races of New Guinea are typically black and frizzy-haired and thus belong with the Melanesian tribes of the islands to the east. One group with a distinctive language, the Papuans, is often referred to as a separate race, but in coastal New Guinea, Papuans are certainly mixed with typical Melanesians. At various places in the interior mountains there are tribes of Pygmies, averaging less than five feet in height, in strong contrast with the taller Papuans.

Certain New Guinea tribes are remarkable for the elaborate carvings and decorations of their wooden tools, weapons, canoes, and houses. Animal carvings include designs based on the crocodile, the cockatoo, the hornbill, the pig, the catfish, and the human face. For their ceremonies the Papuans design fantastic costumes and masks. Stone axes and adzes, usually finely polished, were the principal tools before the arrival of white traders, and still find considerable uses.

The social life of the natives is formed about men's secret societies, which meet in enormous buildings from which women and boys are excluded. These secret societies have great influence—more so than our Masons, B.P.O.E., or Shriners. The mountain tribes are generally more primitive than the coast dwellers, although the large populations living just north of Mount Wilhelmina have developed elaborate systems of agriculture and drainage.

THE BISMARCK ISLANDS

The two long islands to the northeast of New Guinea—New Britain and New Ireland—the nearby smaller ones, and the nearby Admiralty group together are known as the Bismarck Archipelago. This island group covers about 19,650 square miles and lies between 2° and 6° south latitude.

New Britain, with an extremely irregular coast line, is 330 miles long and at most 60 wide. New Ireland is an extremely narrow island, 240 miles in length, with an average width of only about 15 miles. New Britain and New Ireland are both mountainous, with peaks that rise to nearly 7,500 feet. New Britain is spotted with active volcanoes. The Admiralty Islands, mostly very small, are clustered around Manus Island, which is about sixty miles long and twenty miles wide.

New Britain and New Ireland differ little in climate from nearby New Guinea or from the Solomon Islands. The forest vegetation of these hot and humid islands is also largely the same. There is some agriculture. Eighty percent of the cultivated land is devoted to coconuts; the remainder to cocoa, coffee, tea, rubber, and a few grain plants.

Though there are very few mammals on these islands, there is a wide variety of birds and an abundance of lizards. Snakes are few. The mammals include the introduced "wild" pig, the opossumlike cuscus, and several kinds of large bats. The birds, like those of the Solomons, are without the extreme variations in form and color that mark the birds of New Guinea. The lizards include the common and widespread black-and-yellow monitor, also found in the Solomons. The common crocodile is present along the coasts and at the mouths of the few rivers of New Britain.

The 185,000 Melanesian natives of the several islands exhibit differences in customs and physical appearance. It is evident that there has been much mixing of populations. Like their New Guinea relatives the natives make remarkable and elaborate wood carvings and extraordinary costumes and ceremonial masks. In some parts of New Ireland the natives are genuinely naked savages. The natives of the Admiralty Islands differ in language and ways of living from those of New Britain or New Ireland. They are known for their manufacture of sea-shell and tortoise-shell ornaments. On all these islands the natives are skillful fishermen, employing traps, nets, and spears.

THE SOLOMON ISLANDS

Until the Marines landed on Guadalcanal, the Solomon Islands were as far removed from the thoughts of the average American as Mars, but now many of them will find a permanent place in American history. The islands lie in two rows stretching about 700 miles southeast from New Britain, with a corridor between them approaching in beauty that of the inland waterway of Alaska. The northern, or upper, row begins at Bougainville, then Choiseul, then Santa Ysabel, and last Malaita—called by the natives Maluou. The southern row begins at Vella Lavella, then Kolombangara, then New Georgia, then Russell, then Guadalcanal—really Guadalcanar, meaning a dry river bed, and named after a city in Spain—and last San Cristobal. There are many small islands between each of these larger land groups.

The largest island is Bougainville, at the northwest, 3,900 square miles in area. This island has the highest mountain, Mount Balbi (10,000 feet), and two active volcanoes. Guadalcanal, about ninety miles long and forty miles wide, has the next highest peak, Mount Lammas, eight thousand feet high. Other islands have extinct volcanoes and nonvolcanic mountain ranges. Many of the mountains are flanked by coral limestone, which indicates a recent rise of the islands above sea level.

The islands are covered by a typical growth of jungle, hot and steamy, with a rainfall of about 120 inches a year along the coasts. It may require hours to travel several miles. Explorers speak of them as among the most impenetrable jungles of the world, containing giant trees with buttresslike roots. At midday the jungle is almost as dark as at twilight. However, there are certain areas of open fields of sharp-leaved grasses, and the shores are lined with mangrove swamps. The principal agriculture, other than the native cultivation of yams and taros in the village gardens, consists of coconut plantings.

The climate throughout the Solomons is damp and hot, the average temperature being 82°. Most of the rain falls at the time of the southeast winds, from January to March.

Much of the animal life seems related to that of New Guinea but the animals of the Solomons have so many distinctive characteristics that the islands must have been separated from New Guinea for a long time, if, in fact, they were ever connected with it. There are no large mammals. One of the smaller mammals is the cuscus, mentioned before as living in islands farther to the west. There are also other smaller phalangers which live in trees.

Among the larger birds are the black-and-white hornbill, a great variety of parrots and pigeons, and a fowl, suggestive of a small turkey, that lays its very large eggs in piles of decaying vegetation. The eggs are not incubated by the parents but by the heat of the rotting plants. There are 127 different kinds of land birds in the Solomons.

The crocodile, which occasionally is found also in the New Hebrides and the Fiji Islands, is abundant on the Solomons and lives in the larger rivers and along the coast lines. When full grown, it is definitely dangerous to men as well as to domestic animals.

There are about 95,000 native peoples living on the Solomon Islands. They are considered to be Melanesians because of their frizzy hair and dark skin. The natives, a century or more ago, received nothing but harsh treatment from the early explorers and traders. The resentment they felt toward this treatment resulted in their defending themselves so fiercely as to occasion Andrew Cheyne, in his book published in 1852, to refer to them as "without exception, the most treacherous and blood-thirsty race on the face of the Pacific." Today, with fair treatment, the opposite is the case, and many a native has risked his own life to bring American pilots, forced down behind enemy lines, to the safety of our lines.

The native art and craftsmanship, as measured by their decorated wooden tools and especially by their large seagoing canoes, are much better than those of the New Hebrides, but less elaborate than those of New Guinea. The native drums, made of hollowed logs, are handsomely carved and are used in signaling, perhaps in a "drum language," as well as in native ceremonies. There is probably very little head-hunting at the present time. On the island of Malaita, the natives of the coast are fishermen, while the inland hill people raise yams and taros. The coast people live on fortified islands and meet the hill people only on a special market day, when a truce is agreed upon to exchange their fish for yams. Some of the outer islands show evidences of contact with the Micronesians from the north.

THE NEW HEBRIDES

When the Portuguese Captain Pedro Fernández de Quiros discovered the New Hebrides group in 1606 he was sure he had at last reached the shores of the great southern continent for which all navigators had been searching. Accordingly, he named the group Austrialia del Espiritu Santo, a great name for the single tiny island to which it is now attached. When Captain Cook visited the islands again over a hundred years after their discovery, he renamed them the New Hebrides.

The New Hebrides have been governed jointly by the French and British. Lying midway between the Solomons and the Fijis and to the north of New Caledonia, they include upraised coral reefs, active volcanoes, and perhaps remnants of granite mountains in the larger islands at the north. The group includes twelve principal islands, arranged like a *Y*, between 13° and 21° S. latitude. The largest island, Espiritu Santo, with an area of only 875 square miles, has a broad, flat coastal plain, some level land at a higher latitude, and relatively good harbors. Farther north lie the small Banks Islands and the Torres group, and still farther, the Santa Cruz Islands.

The level plateaus of Espiritu Santo and Malekula are, at most, a few hundred feet above sea level. The largest of the volcanoes, Lopevi, reaches 6,195 feet. The highest land is in the mountainous western part of Espiritu Santo. This island has the only river worth mentioning, the Yoro, that flows into Big Bay on the north. The largest of the Banks Islands, Gaua, has a large fresh-water lake, two miles wide by six long, evidently in the crater of an extinct volcano, about 1,000 feet above sea level.

The climate is hot and humid throughout the year, although more moderate along the coast. The wettest season is from November to May.

All the New Hebrides islands are well watered; they are well covered with rich tropical forests, cleared away only for the few coconut plantations on the coast. In addition to coconuts, cocoa, cotton, coffee, bananas, sugar cane, and spices are grown in limited quantities. The forest vegetation usually extends to the edge of the narrow sandy beaches or coral reefs. It includes tropical hardwoods, fig trees, palms, and tree ferns. The southern islands from Tanna to Erromango are drier, with some grasslands and a few stands of kauri pine.

The animal life includes many insects and birds, a few lizards, a single kind of snake, and no frogs. The common East Indian crocodile is known to live in the Yoro River. The mammals include a considerable variety of fruit bats (flying foxes) and a few of the small insect-eating kinds. The land mammals proper are only two: the native ratlike rodent and the pig, both of which appear to have reached the islands with the native tribes. The pig is highly valued by the natives as food, but has run wild, as has the house rat, which probably came from European ships.

The only snake is a small, harmless boa like that of the Fiji Islands. The lizards are all small—several kinds of smooth-scaled skinks, some of them extremely abundant, and several types of geckos, with toe pads that enable them to climb trees and even to run across the ceilings of houses.

The bird life includes some fifty-eight different kinds of land birds. Eight kinds of pigeons, some of good size, are an important source of food. The largest bird is the brush or scrub fowl, like that of the Solomons. There are a few small, bright-colored parrots, starlings, thrushes, flycatchers, honey eaters, and finches.

The marine life of the coasts is typical of that of the tropical eastern Pacific, with richly developed coral reefs, where clams, sea snails, crabs, and other crustaceans, worms, and fishes live with the coral animals.

The only tropical diseases that appear to have occurred in the New Hebrides prior to the arrival of the white man are yaws and malaria. Unfortunately, as in so many of the other islands in the Pacific, the white man brought with him dysentery, syphilis, influenza, measles, and tuberculosis, which have caused a serious decline in the native population.

The New Hebrides natives are primarily of Melanesian stock. They are kinky-haired and black-skinned, and their language varies from island to island, as do certain minor physical characteristics. The islands have been the scene of great missionary effort, but there are wild tribes on the larger islands that have resisted white influence, whether from missionaries, traders, or coconut planters. The native life is less rich than in the Solomons or New Guinea. Families have fewer material possessions. They have less clothing and build simple, low, tentlike houses. Pigs play a more important part in their lives than automobiles do in ours. There is much ceremony connected with pig killing, and such ceremonies increase the prestige of the pig's owner.

NEW CALEDONIA

The island of New Caledonia ends the southern swing of the Melanesian arc. It lies about 700 miles east of the Queensland coast of Australia, extending from southeast to northwest. It is 220 miles in length, has an average width of 30 miles and an area, including adjacent islets, of 6,300 square miles, about that of Connecticut and Rhode Island. It lies at the southern border of the tropical zone, about 20° to 22° S. latitude.

At the ends of the island two parallel mountain chains enclose open valleys. Over the rest of the island, except for a flat coastal plain on the southeast, these ranges connect to form a confused upland tangle of low mountains, at an altitude of a little more than 5,000 feet. There are no active volcanoes. The mountains include ancient rocks like those of New Zealand, rich in minerals, especially nickel. The whole southwestern coast is paralleled by a barrier coral reef at some distance from the shore, so that along this coast there is a protected navigable channel five to eighteen miles wide. The reef on the northwestern coast is not continuous.

Numerous small rivers carry off the abundant rainfall, about seventy inches annually. This climate is subtropical, with an ill-defined rainy season from January to June and a rather hot summer from December to March.

The forest cover is not as dense as in the New Hebrides or Solomons. There are bare and arid areas, and areas partially covered with bushes and with the peculiar araucarian pines, which may reach a height of 150 feet with only a tuft of branches on top. Some of the mountain ranges to the north are covered with continuous forest, including fig trees, palms, and tree ferns. The plant life is remarkable if only because most of the species of native plants are found only on this island. The principal plantations are of coconuts and coffee.

The animal life of New Caledonia seems to have developed on an old but always isolated island. There are no native mammals except the widespread rat of the Pacific and a few kinds of bats, one of which is a large fruit eater. There are no reptiles except lizards, and some of these are peculiar forms found nowhere else. There is a good variety of birds: some allied to those of Australia, but with many more closely related to those of New Guinea. The heronlike kagu, with no near relatives anywhere in the world, is the most distinctive bird. The marine life of the coral reefs is rich and varied, like that of the Australian Great Barrier Reef. A few small ocean fish enter the fresh-water streams. These include several kinds found only in the waters of New Caledonia. The beautiful land snails are remarkable in having no relationship at all with those of Australia.

There is little or no malaria in New Caledonia. The malaria-carrying anopheles mosquito is not known to occur on this island. The common diseases seem to be primarily those introduced from Europe.

The natives of New Caledonia, referred to as Kanakas, number only about 30,000 and are confined to reservations similar to those of the American Indians. They are a black race of distinctive Melanesian type, related plainly to those of the New Hebrides and the Solomons. They are an advanced group, skilled in woodcarving, fishing, and agriculture. Their houses are well made, usually circular and with high conical roofs.

The French population totals approximately 16,500. Fortunately, the use of the island as a penal colony was discontinued in 1898 and most of the convicts have now disappeared or have been absorbed into the general population. New Caledonia, the Isle of Pines, and the Loyalty Islands are French Colonies. Nouméa, the capital of New Caledonia, is an active commercial port. From it are exported such mineral products as nickel, chrome, cobalt, iron, copper, platinum, and lead. The island also produces and exports copra, coffee, cotton, wheat, rice, tobacco, and fruit.

THE LOYALTY ISLANDS

The Loyalty Islands form a chain paralleling New Caledonia to the north at a distance of some sixty miles. There are three principal islands, Maré, Lifou, and Ouvea, all formed by the uplift of coral reefs. They are flat tables of limestone, about 200 feet high. Lifou is the largest, about thirty miles long; Maré nearly as large; and Ouvea much smaller. In spite of abundant rains, water soaks quickly into the porous limestone and is unavailable. The natives are said to be dependent for their needed liquids partly on green coconuts and partly on various devices for catching rain-water. Deep wells now supply sufficient water at plantations and settlements. The natives are evidently much more like the New Hebrideans than like the New Caledonians. Animal life also resembles that of the New Hebrides.

The Isle of Pines off the southwestern tip of New Caledonia is so named for the araucarian pine that formed its original cover of vegetation. It was long used as a colony for the "lifers" among the transported convicts.

THE FIJI ISLANDS

The Fiji Islands, forming the eastern outpost of Melanesia, lie at the southern edge of the tropical zone, between 15° and 19° S. latitude. They are centered on the 180th meridian of longitude, exactly opposite Greenwich, England, are about 600 miles southwest of Samoa, and 500 miles northwest of the Tonga Islands.

The Fijis include about 250 islands, of which most are small and only about 80 inhabited. Two of the islands, Viti Levu and Vanua Levu, are much larger than the rest. Viti Levu is 98 miles long and 67 miles wide; Vanua Levu is 117 long and 30 wide. In addition to these two main islands, only Kandavu, Taveuni, Koro, Ngau, and Ovalau are of considerable size. The larger islands are mountainous, with very little level land, while many of the smaller ones are coral atolls or the remnants of single volcanoes. The heavy rainfall (up to 160 inches a year) produces surprisingly large rivers on the main islands.

The mountains on the two large islands are composed of deposits of volcanic ash and lava that seem to overlie old granite rock. This granite base of the Fijis is the most eastern spot in the

Pacific, where the mountain structures resemble those of the continents. Gold has been mined there in recent years. Some of the smaller Fiji Islands are formed of extinct volcanic craters, but there are no active volcanoes in the group at present. There are occasional light earthquakes, and hot springs are present on several of the larger islands, evidence of past volcanic action.

The climate of the Fiji Islands, though tropical, is so much modified by the sea winds as to be pleasant and healthful. The average yearly temperature is about 78°. The hotter rainy season, from November to April, tends to have unsteady winds from the north and west. The cooler season, from June to the end of October, with regular winds from the east, is drier. The northwestern slopes of the higher islands are screened from the more regular winds and are drier than the sides facing east and south. The total rainfall on the south side of Viti Levu is about 110 inches annually.

The islands are on the whole healthful, with little malaria. European diseases have, however, come in and dysentery is fairly prevalent.

The southern and eastern mountain slopes of the Fijis are covered with a great variety of forest trees. The drier northwestern parts of the larger islands are more open, with grassy areas dotted with casuarina trees and screw or pandanus pines. The smaller islands and the coasts of the larger ones have been planted with coconut plantations. The other crops are sugar cane and fruits, the latter mainly exported to Australian markets.

As is to be expected of these remote islands, there is not a great variety of animal life, but what there is shows a clear relationship to the animals of continental Asia and Australia. The Fijis have two kinds of frogs, a small poisonous snake (probably not dangerous to man) and a sharp-clawed green lizard, related to the iguanas of tropical America. While there are a few species of bats, there are no land mammals other than introduced rats and mice. The bird life is rich in pigeons and parrots. The surrounding seas have the characteristically rich marine life of the coral reefs.

The native Fijians are black-skinned and frizzy-haired and are remarkably well built. These descendants of the most famous of the cannibals of the South Seas have now adjusted themselves to a kind of civilized Christian life of their own. They have their own version of the Bible in Fijian, their native pastors, and their own village governments. Unlike the Polynesians, farther east, the Fijians scorn mixing with the whites or any other race. They do not care to work on plantations, so large numbers of Hindus have been imported to do the work. The present status of the Fijians under British colonial rule is an example of the enlightened treatment of a native people at its best. The population of the Fiji group consists of about 4,000 white persons, 104,000 Asiatics, and 107,000 native Fijians.

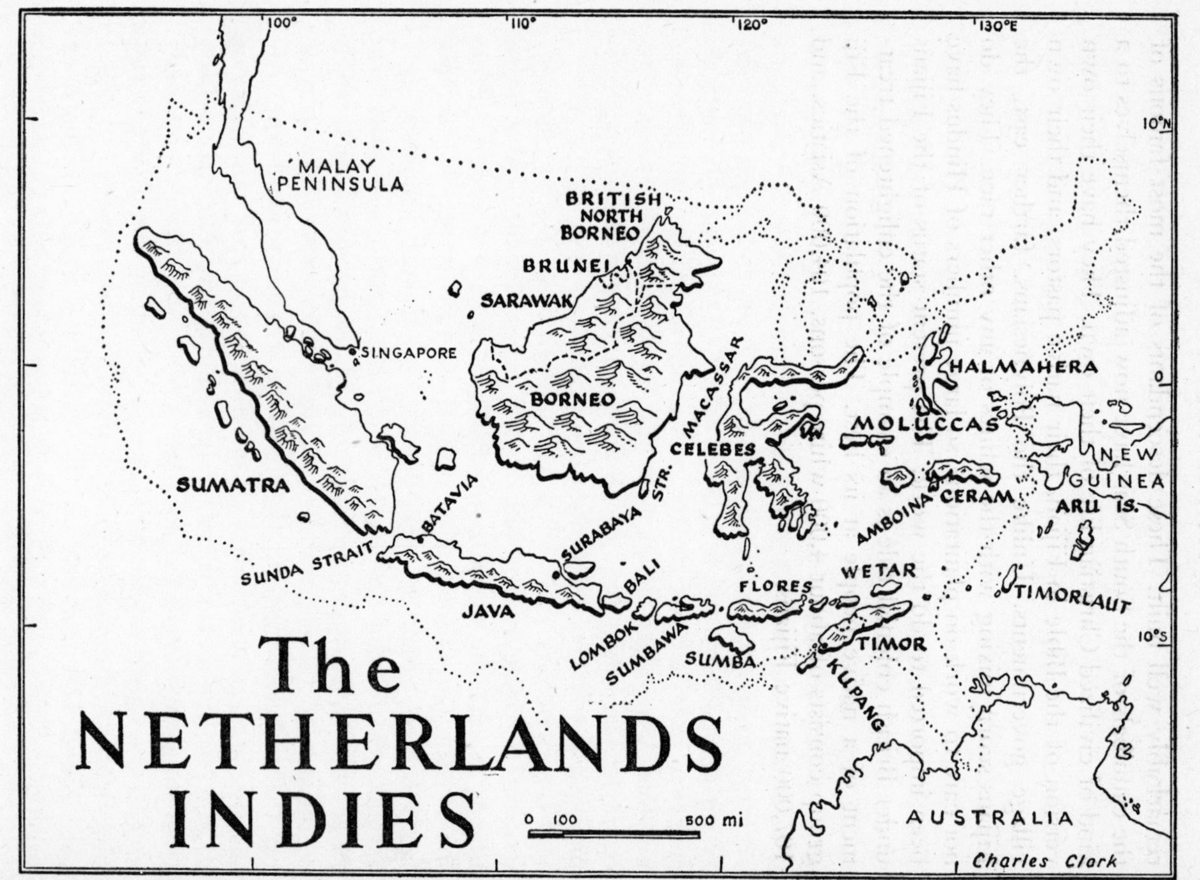

The NETHERLANDS INDIES
100°
110°
120°
130°E
10°N
0
10°S
MALAY PENINSULA
BRITISH NORTH BORNEO
BRUNEI
SARAWAK
SINGAPORE
BORNEO
SUMATRA
MACASSAR STR.
CELEBES
HALMAHERA
MOLUCCAS
NEW GUINEA
AMBOINA
CERAM
ARU IS.
BATAVIA
SUNDA STRAIT
SURABAYA
BALI
JAVA
LOMBOK
SUMBAWA
SUMBA
FLORES
WETAR
TIMORLAUT
TIMOR
KUPANG
0 100 500 mi
AUSTRALIA
Charles Clark

Chapter XIV

THE NETHERLANDS INDIES

The Netherlands Indies, for many centuries, have spelled adventure and the riches of gold, silk, spices, pearls, precious stones and tea. Today these natural riches or resources are one of the objectives, if not one of the causes, of the great war. In addition to the luxuries sought by the European nations since the sixteenth century, modern civilizations have become dependent on the rubber produced there and to a lesser extent on the valuable minerals and even upon oil, for the Indies are one of the few areas in the Far East where petroleum is found. In addition, they export to countries the world over other products such as tea, kapoc, quinine, sugar, tobacco and tapioca.

If the immensity and variety of the Pacific area needs a symbol, it is to be found in the Netherlands Indies. This group of large islands is, like the ocean itself, laid out on a grand scale. Four major islands and innumerable smaller ones constitute the Netherlands Indies. Sumatra, Java, Borneo and Celebes, totaling over 500,000 square miles, make up the great proportion of land area. As shown on the accompanying map, the distance from the western to the eastern boundaries of the Indies equals that of the span of the United States from the Pacific to the Atlantic oceans. Approximately 70,000,000 people live on these islands, of which about 47,800,000 live on the island of Java alone. This fact makes Java, with about 900 people per square mile, the most densely populated area in the entire world. The varieties of living things, from elephants and orangutans to unique orchid plants, express, to a degree found nowhere else on this earth, the infinite richness of nature.

The Netherlands Indies lie along the equator between the mainlands of Asia and Australia. Sumatra, Java and Borneo, together with some of the adjacent smaller islands, are sometimes referred to as the Greater Sunda Islands. To the east of Java stretches a chain of islands known as the Lesser Sunda Islands, including Bali, Lombok and Timor, and northerly from these lie the Moluccas or Spice Islands.

The backbone of the islands is formed by mountains. A chain of volcanoes, many of them active, runs from the northern tip of Sumatra along its west coast, thence through Java, Bali and Lombok, and from there to the east and north. These mountains are in most cases skirted by extensive lowlands and marshes such as those in the eastern part of Sumatra and along the northern parts of Java and southern and western Borneo. These plains, particularly those in Sumatra and Java, are extremely fruitful owing to the volcanic soil of which they consist. There is no winter and summer in these regions. Instead it is possible to distinguish a so-called dry monsoon season from April to October and a wet monsoon season from November to March, although in the regions close to the mainland of Asia, such seasons are almost reversed, and in some regions there is little or no distinction between dry and rainy seasons.

The islands are a melting pot of several races, of which the Malayan predominates by a large majority, although the earliest settlers, long ages before historic times, are thought to have been people similar to the aborigines of Australia.

Of interest is the fact that the celebrated fossil remains of one of the earliest and most primitive types of man, the *Pithecanthropus erectus*, was discovered between 1890 and 1892 in Java near Trinil. This fossil has come to be known as the "Java ape-man" and is considered by many scientists to be a progenitor of man.

Agriculture is the main activity of the inhabitants and rice the main staple of the native diet. So expert are the people in methods of irrigation used in the cultivation of this crop that even in the densely populated island of Java there is sometimes a surplus crop. There are fishing industries along the coasts of all the islands but particularly along the north coast of Java. Cattle breeding is important but cattle are used primarily for work on the farms rather than for meat consumption.

The Netherlands Indies have been controlled by the Dutch since the seventeenth century and the islands are divided, for administration purposes, into provinces, some that are directly governed by the Dutch, and others that are self-governed territories, namely, regions where native princes rule, although under conditions mutually agreed upon with the Dutch. A great majority of the people live in communities that have been maintained throughout the years in their original form. The villages and groups of villages have self-governing powers, which generally have one characteristic in common: they are to a high degree both democratic and communal. The chiefs are usually chosen by vote of the villagers, although much value is attached to heredity.

Ninety percent of the Indonesians adhere to the Mohammedan faith, which was brought in during the fifteenth century by traders from India. Paganism is found only in the interiors of the larger islands and especially in the more eastern part of the archipelago. Christianity has been adopted principally by these former pagans, the number of Christians today approximating 2,500,000. In general the character of Mohammedanism in the Indies is influenced by old Indonesian customs, and in Java and some of the other islands many traces of old Hindu influences persist.

SUMATRA

Sumatra is the westernmost of the great islands in the chain between Asia and Australia. It is about 1,150 miles long, with a maximum width of 250 miles. The equator cuts the island almost exactly in half. A line of good-sized islands parallels the southwest coast at a distance of some fifty miles from shore. On the northeast the Strait of Malacca, also about fifty miles wide, separates Sumatra from the Malay Peninsula and Singapore. The Sunda Strait between Sumatra and Java is a mere channel, only fifteen miles wide at places.

Mountains with volcanic peaks up to 12,000 feet extend the length of Sumatra. They lie close to the southwestern coast, with steep slopes to the southwest and more gradual slopes to the northeast. On the northeast side the mountains descend to a low, broad plain crossed by numerous rivers. The mountains are formed of ancient rocks mixed with flows of lava. Active volcanoes have broken through the older rocks and still pour out fumes and lava today. Coal, petroleum, and a great variety of metals are mined.

The climate is both hot and wet. The monsoons bring rain and there is no general dry season. As in any mountainous country, there are great differences in climate. In northeastern Sumatra drier conditions prevail because the moistest wind from a southerly direction has lost much of its moisture earlier in its passage over the land and mountains.

Sumatra has great woodlands of the tropical rain forest type, like those of Borneo, Java, and the Malay Peninsula. There are also broad open areas covered with thick grasses that have taken possession of every natural or man-made clearing. In the markets one finds a wide variety of tropical fruits, including mangoes, breadfruits and coconuts, together with other agricultural products. The principal exports are pepper, coffee, tobacco, and rubber.

The Sumatran forests are rich in animal life, much of it similar to that of the nearby Malay Peninsula. There are many kinds of large mammals: the elephant, the Malayan tapir, the two-horned rhinoceros, the tiger and the wild pig, and a great variety of monkeys and deer. Orangutans build their nests in the forest trees and search the woods for edible fruits. Long-armed gibbons swing from branch to branch with an agility born of untold generations of living in trees. The smaller mammals, rodents, insect eaters, bats and others are less conspicuous but more numerous.

The birds are as beautiful as one expects tropical birds to be. There are frogs, toads, lizards, and snakes. There is the giant python, powerful but rarely dangerous to man. Then there are a few poisonous snakes, especially the cobra, the king cobra, and the pit viper. The common East Indian crocodile is abundant on the coasts.

The native tribes of Sumatra are largely Malay and exhibit close similarities to the population of Malay. Traces of earlier populations persist in the remote areas. Culturally, also, the range is great, from the civilized Menangkabau to the tribes retaining savage customs. Most of the peoples of the nearby islands are not of the Malay type, but are either Polynesian or Indonesian. The Indonesian population is estimated at 8,900,000. The island was under Dutch control until seized by the Japanese.

JAVA

The island of Java is the most famed and the best known of all the Netherlands Indies. Great active volcanoes, tropical plants, strange animals, extraordinary Hindu temples, and a friendly, progressive people—all contribute to Java's reputation. The length of the island is 622 miles but it is less than one-fifth as wide. In area it is 51,000 square miles, not much less than the State of Illinois.

Java is mountainous from end to end, with abrupt slopes on the side toward the Indian Ocean. Some lowlands border the north coast. There are more than fifty volcanoes, about half of them active. The larger volcanoes are over 10,000 feet high. The Javanese know the terror of the thundering eruptions that have destroyed their villages and taken a frightful toll of human life. Hot springs and sulphur springs are found near the volcanoes. These and the frequent earthquakes indicate that Java is part of an extremely unstable region.

Like Sumatra, Java has a variety of climates, largely because of the mountains and elevated plateaus. The *west monsoon* winds bring rains from November to March and the *east monsoon* winds blow during the drier season from April to October. The southern parts of Java are wettest, with a rainfall of as much as 327 inches in a single year, or about seven times that of New York. At Batavia, to the northwest, the rainfall is seventy-two inches, while the eastern part of the island is much drier, its climate being similar to that of Bali.

During the changeable period between the monsoons there are violent thunderstorms but no true hurricanes. The heat is relieved by the winds at all the elevated parts of the islands. In spite of the heat and the great density of the population there is no undue amount of disease.

The native vegetation forms a dense tropical forest in western Java, with a wealth of tropical timber trees, including teaks, gigantic figs, various palms, and bamboos, but over vast areas below an altitude of 4,000 feet this primary forest has been destroyed to make land for agricultural purposes. Tree ferns are common at higher altitudes. The forest trees are hung with vines, orchids and other air plants.

Nearly half of Java is cultivated. The principal food crop is rice, grown mainly in the western part of the island. There is a great variety of tropical fruits and vegetables. Coffee, tea, cacao, sugar, tobacco, indigo, tapioca, cinchona, kapoc, and rubber are grown for export. The great rubber plantations represent a new agricultural development.

The animals of Java are very much like those of Sumatra, but there are fewer varieties. The elephant, the tapir, and the bear are absent. The rhinoceros is one-horned like that of India. In addition to the rhinoceros, there are other large animals such as a wild ox, two kinds of wild pigs, various deer, and the tiger, leopard, and wild dog. Smaller animals, including many kinds of monkeys, abound. The tropical bird life includes the beautiful green peacock, two kinds of jungle fowls, partridges, pigeons and hundreds of kinds of smaller birds.

Snakes, lizards, turtles, and frogs are common. Of the approximately ninety-three kinds of snakes the common cobra and the king cobra are the most dangerous. These two and eight other snakes are dangerously poisonous, though only the bite of the cobra and the krait is apt to be deadly.

Java has a population of about 47,000,000 Indonesians and consequently practically all parts of the island are densely populated. It is hard to conceive of one-third of all the people in the United States being crowded into an area the size of the State of Illinois, but this is exactly the situation in Java where there are more than 900 people to each square mile of land. Besides the Indonesians, there are 200,000 Europeans and 600,000 Chinese. The natives are the Sundanese in western Java, the Javanese proper in the central part of the island, and the Madurese in eastern Java. These peoples are by nature quiet and peace loving. Their docile nature has perhaps developed as a consequence of their being so intensively engaged in agriculture.

The capital of Java is Batavia, a city with a population of nearly 500,000, while Surabaya, the great port of the eastern end of the island, has more than 333,000.

The conquest of Java by the Japanese is not the first invasion that Java has suffered. Invaders from India in the sixth century established a regime of Hindu civilization and religion, marked by high cultural achievements, that was maintained to the time of the Mohammedan conquest in the year 1478. The ruined temples of central Java are among the most remarkable monuments to this past civilization.

BORNEO

Borneo ranks as the third largest island in the world, with an area of about 280,000 square miles. Set over the United States, Borneo would cover all of New England and all of the Atlantic states as far south as Georgia. This vast tropical area, which in recent times has been partly under Dutch and partly under British rule, has large sections that are still unexplored.

The mountain ranges of Borneo spread out like spokes of a wheel. Between the ranges are broad belts of lowland, each of which is drained by one or more large rivers. These valleys and rivers form the principal means of reaching the little-known interior. The mountains are, in the main, from 3,000 to 7,500 feet high, with only a few higher peaks. Mount Kinabalu (13,451 feet), near the northeastern corner of the island, is the highest. Already a great variety of mineral wealth has been found, including coal and the richest oil field in the Netherlands Indies. As the island is further explored, new discoveries may be expected.

The coastal strip of the island, which is best known, has an extremely uniform hot and damp climate. The annual rainfall on the coasts is about 100 inches. The climate is not particularly healthful and there is a considerable amount of malaria and other tropical diseases.

Nearly all of Borneo is covered by tropical forest, though the kinds of trees vary from one part of the island to another. Gigantic trees, their trunks often supported by broad buttresses, rise to great heights before breaking into branches. From the branches hang vines, the climbing rattan palm, and a great variety of air plants, including ferns, orchids, and pitcher plants. There are large areas of valuable tropical timber, including teaks, and the usual richness of tropical fruit and nut trees and smaller plants. Rubber has become the principal plantation crop in recent years.

The animal life is rich and is in many ways similar to that of southeastern Asia, but there are a few striking exceptions. The tiger is absent from Borneo; the rhinoceros is the Sumatran type, with two horns. The orangutan is abundant in the forests. The long-nosed or proboscis monkey, found near the coast, is a living caricature of man. The elephant is present only in northeast Borneo, and it is thought to have been brought to the island by man. There is a wild ox; wild pigs and the small Malayan bear are found. Birds are present in rich variety. There are many kinds of turtles, lizards and snakes and a great number of frogs. Insect life here as elsewhere in the Malay Peninsula is remarkably developed.

When in the forest, one must guard against the ever-present land leeches, a pest common to the islands of the Southwest Pacific.

They usually attach themselves where the clothing binds and may fill themselves with blood. They are not poisonous, but secondary infection frequently follows their puncturing the skin.

The Indonesian population of Borneo is estimated at 2,300,000. There are about 200,000 Chinese and 6,000 whites. The coastal peoples are mostly Mohammedan Malays. The wild tribes of the interior belong to several racial groups, apparently Indonesian. The Dyaks of the interior are typical head-hunters. The Chinese have also settled on the coast and have mixed with the other inhabitants. Chinese blood has penetrated far into the interior, since Chinese trade and immigration into Borneo began as early as the seventh century. On some of the offshore islands there are a few traces of the original frizzy-haired Negrito natives of Borneo.

CELEBES

The four spider-leg peninsulas of Celebes give this great island a most unusual form and character. With the small nearby islands, its area is about 83,810 square miles—a little more than that of Kansas. The northern peninsula of the island is nearly 500 miles long, with an average width of 40 or 50 miles; the three other "arms" are each about 300 miles in length.

Each peninsula is a mountain chain, and the highest peaks rise to more than 10,000 feet. Only the northern arm has active volcanoes. In the central mountains and in the southern and eastern peninsulas are numerous extinct volcanic peaks. Little is known of the rocks deep below the surface that have been greatly contorted and changed by volcanic activity of the past. Celebes is unique in having several large fresh-water lakes, which are rare in the Netherlands Indies.

The climate of the narrow and mountainous arms of Celebes is more healthful than that of the swampy river bottoms of Borneo, though malaria and dysentery are by no means unknown. The difference between a dry and wet season is most marked in the southwest part of Celebes, where Macassar has a dry season from April to October, during which time many trees lose their leaves. In the rainy season much rain falls in violent storms. The skies empty as much as 150 inches of rain a year. In the northern peninsula, the rainfall drops to approximately 100 inches, and this is distributed evenly throughout the year.

Forests much like those of Borneo and the Philippines cover most of Celebes. On the northern peninsula where agriculture is best developed are many nutmeg plantations and areas devoted largely to coffee growing.

The animal life is remarkable. In addition to the abundant wild pigs and deer, there are rare and unique creatures: the babirusa, a wild pig with both pairs of tusks curving upward; a tailless black ape; a dwarf forest buffalo; and a special type of small animal called the cuscus, related to the pouch-bearing animals of Australia. About two-thirds of the some 220 kinds of land birds are allied to those of the islands toward the west and one-third to those of New Guinea to the east. There are approximately sixty different snakes, forty different lizards, and twenty-two kinds of frogs. Seven of the snakes are poisonous.

On Celebes there seems to be no trace of the primitive inhabitants who preceded the Malays. The present Malays include a number of tribes in the more remote mountain areas, collectively known as the Torajas. The coastal and city populations are Mohammedan. The northern peninsula has responded to efforts of missionaries and is largely Christianized. The population of Celebes consists of about 3,089,000 Indonesians, less than 5,000 whites, and about 30,000 Chinese.

The government has been a Dutch protectorate with native rajas as the immediate rulers, who govern in eastern splendor under the supervision of the district "residents" of the Netherlands Indies.

THE LESSER SUNDA ISLANDS

Borneo, Sumatra, Java and Celebes are the Greater Sunda Islands, and the chain of smaller islands extending east from Java is commonly referred to as the Lesser Sunda Islands. Actually there are two parallel rows of islands which differ in their geology. The inner chain is a continuation of Java and consists of the islands of Bali, Lombok, Sumbawa, Flores, Alor, Wetar, and some smaller islands. The entire chain is volcanic. The active volcanoes of Bali and Lombok rise to 6,000 and 12,000 feet. The volcanoes on Sumbawa rise from 5,000 to 9,000 feet. The highest, Tambora, is said to have been 13,000 feet high before a tremendous explosion in the year 1815 blew its top off and caused widespread destruction.

The second or outer chain of islands is not volcanic. The rocks here are marine limestones, with occasionally a core of older rock. The main islands are Sumba, Savu, Timor, the Sermattas, and the Babars. But the chain continues through the Timorlaut Archipelago and the Kei Islands and finally ties up with the southern Moluccas.

The Lesser Sunda Islands thus extend nearly 1,000 miles to the east of Java, and are almost entirely between 8° and 10° south latitude. Timor lies opposite the northwest coast of Australia at a distance of 350 miles. Of all these islands, only Bali was widely known before the present war. Timor is not only the largest island of the group but is of considerable strategic importance. It is about 300 miles long and 60 wide. Part of Timor was controlled by the Dutch, the outer part being a Portuguese colony, all that remained of the early Portuguese possessions in the archipelago.

The Lesser Sundas are very different from the tropical Greater Sundas and Moluccas. The climate is relatively dry, probably because of the southeast winds from the Australian desert, resulting in less forest and more open land. Aridity increases from Bali, which is still much like eastern Java, to Timor with its scrubby growth and to the extremely barren Wetar Island.

The animal life of the Lesser Sundas differs from that of Java. Malay forms are fewer and some of the animals and birds are related to those of New Guinea. Komodo Island and the nearby Flores are remarkable for a gigantic monitor lizard, the Komodo "dragon." It attains a length up to 10 feet and a weight of 300 pounds. It was unknown to scientists until 1911.

The native peoples of Bali, Lombok, Sumbawa and Sumba are entirely Malay; and Malays have more or less invaded the coastal areas of the remaining islands. Flores and the islands east of Timor have a few primitive natives, who appear to be of the Melanesian type. There seems to have been much mixture of races on many of the islands, presumably with a strong element of the Polynesian.

Some of the Lesser Sundas are densely inhabited. Bali and Lombok at the western end of the chain, about a seventh of the total area, have a population of 1,800,000.

THE MOLUCCAS OR SPICE ISLANDS

The islands between New Guinea and Celebes may be grouped together under the name "Moluccas." The largest are Ceram and Halmahera, respectively 200 and 240 miles in length. Halmahera, like Celebes, is composed of four mountainous peninsulas joined at a common center. The high active volcanoes of Ternate and Tidore lie just to the west. Ternate is the seat of the Dutch Government in this part of the Netherlands Indies, as Amboina is of the region of the south. These islands, the goal of early explorers, are truly the "Spice Islands," for the clove was originally native to Halmahera. All of the islands produce nutmeg and mace.

It is evident from the many coral reefs found high on the mountainsides that the islands have recently been uplifted from the sea. The region as a whole—lying between the islands that are outposts of Asia and those that belong to the Australian and New Guinean continental region—is geologically one of the most unstable island areas of the world.

The climate of the Moluccas is wet and tropical, but its discomforts for the white man are greatly tempered by the fresh sea winds. For the most part the islands are forested, with only occasional areas of grassland. The Malays have introduced the growing of rice, but the abundance of the sago palm makes it the most important food-producing plant in both Halmahera and Ceram.

The islands' plant and animal life is more closely related to that of New Guinea, with the tree-living cuscus (a small opossumlike animal), the cassowary (a large, nearly wingless bird), and the bird of paradise. Some Asiatic mammals, especially wild pigs and deer, have reached certain of the Moluccas, and there are even monkeys on the island of Batjan. All these mammals may have been introduced by man.

There are remnants of the primitive Melanesians in Ceram and Halmahera. Otherwise the inhabitants are mostly Mohammedan Malays. The total population of the Spice Islands numbers about 284,000.

These islands were the goal that attracted first the early Portuguese explorers and later the Dutch, for the spice trade was immensely important to the Europe of four or five centuries ago, and control of the Spice Islands involved a control of the spice trade. It was on the basis of this trade that the Netherlands East India Company was established and prospered until the islands were taken over by the Netherlands Government at the beginning of the nineteenth century.

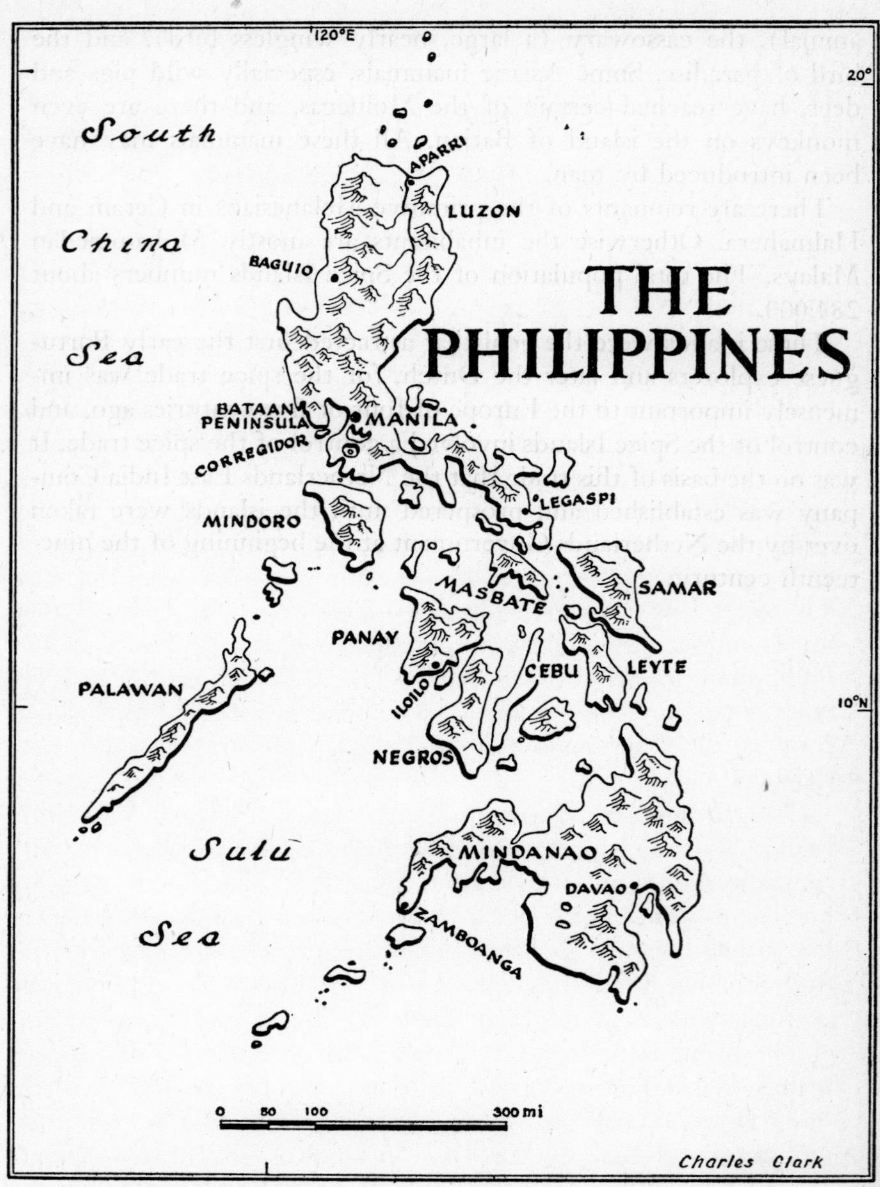
THE PHILIPPINES
120°E
20°
10°N
South China Sea
Sulu Sea
APARRI
LUZON
BAGUIO
BATAAN PENINSULA
MANILA
CORREGIDOR
LEGASPI
MINDORO
MASBATE
SAMAR
PANAY
CEBU
LEYTE
PALAWAN
ILOILO
NEGROS
MINDANAO
DAVAO
ZAMBOANGA
0 50 100 300 mi
Charles Clark

Chapter XV

THE PHILIPPINE ISLANDS

The Philippine Islands are probably better known to Americans than all other Pacific islands, except perhaps Hawaii. They lie about 7,000 miles west of San Francisco and about 700 miles east from Indo-China across the China Sea. More than 7,000 islands make up the Philippines, many of them very small. Only about 460 of the islands have an area of more than one square mile, and only 2,441 bear names. The largest islands, Luzon at the north, with 41,000 square miles, and Mindanao at the south, with 37,000 square miles, are about as large as Indiana and Tennessee, respectively. The total land area of the entire island group is about 114,400 square miles, considerably more than that of the British Isles. The Philippines are wholly within the Torrid Zone, extending 1,150 miles north and south, from 4° to 20° north latitude. Island chains connect the Philippines with Formosa, with Borneo, and with Celebes.

Other important islands are Samar, Panay, Palawan, Mindoro, Leyte, Negros, Cebu, and Masbate. Some of the island towns with romantic-sounding Malay names, like Iloilo and Zamboanga, are familiar to every sailor in Far Eastern waters, while other names, like Isabella, Puerto Princesa, and Corregidor of eternal fame, reflect the long Spanish occupation of the country. The population of the islands is about 16,000,000.

The islands' largest city is Manila, with a population of approximately 350,000. It is situated on Manila Bay, at the mouth of the Pasig River, on the west coast of the island of Luzon. The most picturesque section of Manila is Intramuros, or the old Spanish Walled City, lying along the left bank of the Pasig and filled with ancient buildings, many of which were erected three and four centuries ago. Intramuros is like a bit of Old Spain. The wide moat surrounding its ancient, turreted, moss-grown stone wall has been filled in and seeded with grass.

The islands were discovered by Magellan in 1520, and it was here, on Mactan Island, near Cebu, that the famous explorer was killed by the natives. In the city of Cebu there is a large wooden cross, known among the Filipinos as "La Cruz Creciente," erected on the spot where the first Mass is supposed to have been said after Magellan's landing. According to popular superstition it increases in height year by year. It is regarded as a shrine, and candles are burned and prayers said before it daily by the faithful.

The islands are largely mountainous with a number of active volcanoes. The low crater of Mount Taal, rising in the middle of a fresh-water lake, not far south of Manila, has an unsavory record. It has erupted more than a dozen times, and with violent explosions, during the recorded history of the Philippines. The victims of the 1911 eruption totaled 1,300. Mount Mayon (8,970 feet), near the southern end of Luzon, is one of the most perfect volcanic cones in the world. The highest peak is Mount Apo on Mindanao (10,312 feet) and there are 6 other mountains above 7,000 feet and 49 mountains above 5,000.

The climate is not unduly hot for the tropics, and from November to March, immediately following the rainy season, it may be quite pleasant, even in the lowlands. In the dry season (January to May) the temperature reaches a maximum of 100° F. in the shade. The average annual temperature is 80° F. with an average range of 53° to 100°. The northern part of the Philippines lies within the hurricane belt and is occasionally devastated by destructive storms, known locally as typhoons.

The few large rivers of the islands are navigable over a considerable distance by river steamer and smaller craft. The Cagayan River in northern Luzon is the longest. The Rio Grande de Mindanao is 200 miles long. The Pasig River that flows through Manila is a short stream emptying out of a shallow lake, the

Laguna de Bay, about fifteen miles away. There are about 500 miles of railroads and 4,200 miles of first-class highways on the main islands.

The vegetation of the Philippines is as rich as that of the Indies. It varies from the salt-beach and mangrove swamps on the shores to the cool rain forest of the mountains, and from the dense lowland forest of gigantic trees to open plains of the coarse grass known as cogon. About two-thirds of the land area is forested by over 600 kinds of trees, of which over 100 are of commercial value. Rice, tobacco, sugar cane, coconuts, and Manila hemp (abacá) are among the most important crops, grown in the 10,000,000 acres of land now under cultivation. The Manila hemp produced from a kind of banana plant is distinctively Philippine and is successfully grown in only a few other places. The picturesque rice terraces of the Mountain Province of northern Luzon are among the most remarkable agricultural sights in the world, carved out of the steep hillsides and watered by an elaborate system of irrigation. Tropical fruits, both wild and cultivated, are abundant, and include oranges, pomelos, limes, bananas, lansones, santols, jack fruits, papayas, guavas and many others.

The mineral deposits of the islands have been exploited to a very limited degree. They include gold, silver, iron, copper, bismuth, chromium, mercury, platinum and nickel.

Though wild animals are plentiful the large creatures of the Asiatic mainland are lacking. The largest native wild animal is the tamarau, a dwarf buffalo found only on Mindoro. The domestic buffalo, or carabao, and humped cattle have occasionally run wild in places. The Philippine pony is not native. Deer and wild pigs are the principal game animals. The flesh eaters include the civets and a small wildcat. Bats—both fruit bats, or flying foxes, and the smaller insect-eating kinds—are quite common. There are several species of monkeys. The remarkable tarsier, with enormous eyes, and the so-called flying lemur are of particular interest. Native rodents are numerous.

The birds total more than 750 different kinds, if subspecies are included, some of them restricted to a single island or island group, and others more widely distributed. Eleven "districts" have been recognized, each with characteristic kinds of bird life. The principal game birds are the wild jungle-fowls and a variety of pigeons, quails, ducks, rails, and snipes. There is a large and unique monkey-eating eagle. Several kinds of hornbills are among the more conspicuous forest birds both because of their size and their noisy calls. Lorikeets and parrots, including a curious racket-tailed parakeet, are found in the forests, and there is a white cockatoo, of interest because it is closely related to a similar bird from the Australian region. Palawan and several smaller islands have birds that probably came from Borneo and, similarly, Formosan birds are found in the Batanes group at the northern end of the Philippines. A considerable number of the Philippine birds are found only on the islands, but the majority show a strong relationship to Asiatic birds.

The reptiles include monitors and other good-sized lizards; a dozen kinds of flying lizards, with beautiful colored winglike membranes, that glide from tree to tree; and a variety of snakes. The only dangerous snakes are the cobras and a variety of small, green pit vipers. Poisonous snakes are generally confined to the big islands. Large pythons occur on some of these islands, too, but are rare. Small pythons are sometimes kept in the native houses as pets to catch rats and mice.

Insect life is abundant. Besides mosquitoes and other pests, the islands are plagued by the migratory locust or grasshopper that occurs at times in great numbers. From time to time the adult locusts sweep over the countryside in immense swarms, break bamboos and other plants by the weight of their densely packed numbers, and devastate the land, leaving desolation and famine behind.

The seas around the Philippines teem with coral-reef animals, colorful fishes and other kinds of marine life. Pearl oysters are found in the more southern waters.

A better understanding of the social aspects of the Philippines may perhaps be reached by the following observations regarding the peoples. The population of approximately 16,000,000 may be divided roughly into four major groups with a total of some eighty tribal divisions. According to figures supplied by the Philippine Bureau of Education, eighty-seven distinct native dialects have been recorded, the three most important of which are Tagalog, Visayan, and Ilokano, all with well-developed literatures and newspapers, periodicals and books. In the south, among the Moros, the Arabic system of writing is used.

The earliest inhabitants of the Philippines are the Negritos, a Pygmy race with black skin and wooly hair, living at a primitive stage of material culture. They build no dwellings, but construct rude shelters of boughs and leaves. They subsist largely on game, chiefly deer and wild pig, which they kill with poisoned arrows. The Negritos are very shy, seldom venturing from the deep recesses of the forests and jungles where they dwell.

In prehistoric times Malay invaders came across the China Sea to the west shore of Luzon, drove the Negritos back into the forests of the low hill region, and settled along the coast. Probably some centuries later they, in turn, were driven back by a new wave of invaders, also Malays. The defeated tribes—principally the Igorots, and including also the Kalingas and Apayaos—fled to the high mountains of what is now the Mountain Province, where they are known as the Mountain Tribes.

The newcomers settled in the lowlands of Luzon and spread to the neighboring islands to the south, particularly Leyte, Cebu, Negros and Mindanao. They were Christianized by the Spanish friars and became generally known as "Filipinos," as distinct from the Moros and Igorots. It is this group of which we naturally think when we read or speak of the Filipino people. It is they who control the government, the churches, and the educational institutions. They constitute the majority of members of the legislative houses, the courts, and the learned professions. It is in their chief dialects, Tagalog, Ilokano, and Visayan, that most of the newspapers and periodicals are printed and the greater part of the native literature is written. Because of their close association with Americans in recent decades, they are much more nearly like us in their civilization, religion, education, and manner of living than are the other groups.

The Moros were still another wave of Malay immigrants who were converted to Mohammedanism by the Arabs. They settled in the south, where they now inhabit parts of Mindanao, Palawan, Basilan, and the islands of the Sulu Sea. This Mohammedan invasion occurred only about a century before the Spaniards arrived.

Thus we have the four main groups—Filipinos, Moros, Igorots and Negritos—of which only the first three need be considered, as the Negritos are negligible in number and importance.

The Christians, or lowland Filipinos, have felt both the Christian-Spanish influence and that of industrial American life. They have taken to politics as ducks to water; and while ardently desiring their independence they are, in the main, appreciative of what America has done in the way of sanitation, hospitalization, education, and economic betterment. This appreciation was evident in the way Filipino troops stood shoulder to shoulder with American soldiers on Bataan, and with them the loyal Igorot soldiers, who shouted their old pagan battle cries as they rode the tanks through the jungles.

The Moros have never had political ambitions. They have fiercely resented intrusion on their islands and have asked only to be let alone. They are a fierce and warlike people. They are fanatic in their beliefs and, though Mohammedan, their religion is still mingled with pagan practices and superstitions. The religious leader of the Jolo Moros is the sultan of Sulu who together with other tribal sultans constitutes the only royalty—if one excepts the Hawaiian royal family—under the American flag. In days of old the Moros were dread pirates, sailing up the coast of Luzon and even raiding the shores of China and Japan. Their graceful vintas—boats with outriggers and particolored sails—are still among the swiftest sailing craft afloat.

The Filipinos and the Moros are similar physically, though the Moros continue the custom of filing their teeth to a sharp point and chewing betel nut, which stains them brown. Igorots are very different. They are shorter and more squat, with powerful legs and torsos. The face is broader and flatter, in many instances resembling that of the American Indian. One cannot help admiring the Igorots, though they do an occasional bit of head-hunting. They are mountain people, living in high altitudes, with hot sun, chilly rains, and mountain mists. Their worldly possessions are generally confined to a cheap, moldy blanket, a few cooking pots, a spear, a head-ax, and a gansa or tom-tom. Their religion emphasizes the belief in powerful spirits. Many of their waking hours are spent in pacifying the evil spirits that fill the mountains and wait for a chance to do people harm.

The Igorots are divided into tribes and subtribes. They all inhabit the high hills of the Mountain Province in northern Luzon. As one climbs the famous zigzag trail to Baguio, in the subprovince of Benguet, one meets the Benguet Igorots on the road—a shy little people, trotting in single file along the roadside, the men ahead, the women bearing huge burdens on their heads or baskets on their backs, supported by a band across the front of the head, similar to the tumpline of the Canadian woods. They are a peaceful, agricultural folk, who do not practice head-hunting or intertribal warfare unless attacked. They smoke the bodies of their dead in a sitting posture and seat the mummies on the floors of caves, where they remain for years without disintegrating.

Farther north, up the Mountain Trail, lies Bontoc, capital of the province and center of the Bontoc Igorots, fierce head-hunters of the old days, who still live in primitive fashion. The Bontocs evidence a curious mixture of Spartan training and ultramodern ideas. Bontoc children, both boys and girls, are taken from their mothers at an early age and placed together in long huts, or *ulags*—one for the boys and one for the girls—until old enough to marry. When the young man fancies a maiden he goes to her hut and stays with her, the temporary union being recognized by the tribe. If a child is born, the marriage becomes permanent. If not, both parties are free to seek other mates.

The Ifugao, also head-hunters and mighty warriors, are chiefly noted for their magnificent rice terraces, the most impressive of which are found near Banaue. These terraces rise for thousands of feet up the mountainside and with their irrigation system constitute one of the greatest engineering feats ever accomplished by a primitive people.

The Kalingas, a very fierce and warlike tribe, are still regarded as the most unstable of the mountain people. Incurable head-hunters, they have been the slowest of all the tribes to adopt the white man's ways.

Among all the tribes of head-hunters, the taking of heads was carried on against hostile tribes, mostly by sudden forays. The heads were, of course, regarded as trophies. A youth did not become a man until he had taken a head, nor would a maiden consider him as a possible husband. The heads were not cured, but the flesh was removed and the skulls alone retained. The lower jaws were severed and greatly prized as handles for tom-toms.

Head-hunting was discouraged under American rule and, while it is undoubtedly practiced occasionally, it was very rare up to the time of the Japanese occupation.

Heads of white men were never taken. The late John C. Early, for many years the beloved governor of the Mountain Province, once said that he had heard of only one white man being slain by Igorots. The story is as follows.

In the early days an American drifted up into the Igorot country, took a wife after the native custom, and reared a family. As he grew older he thought more of home, and finally informed his family of his decision to return to America. Good-bys were said and he started down the trail. His sons followed and just outside the village they killed him. According to their belief the spirit of the dead remained near the scene of death. Hence their father's spirit would always be near them and watch over them. They killed him because they loved him.

The dress of all the Mountain Tribes is essentially similar, differing only in detail. The men wear a loin cloth, or G string, while the women wear a short length of cloth, a tapis, reaching to the knees and tucked in at the waist like a sarong. The different tribes can be distinguished by the way of dressing the hair, by head, arm, and leg ornaments, and by the shape of the head-axes or other weapons.

Although primitive in their manner of living, the Igorots are intelligent and when educated are capable of becoming good doctors, teachers, ministers, and farmers. The rice terraces of Banaue are evidence of their skill. Their ingenuity is demonstrated in the primitive Igorot fire maker, which consists of a cylinder and plunger made of carabao horn. There are very few in existence now that even Igorots use safety matches.

It might seem that these different peoples, with their diversity of language, custom, and religion, would find occasion constantly to be at odds and never be welded into a nation. But the American influence has made itself widely felt. The English language, taught in all the public schools, has supplied a common medium of communication.

The system of free education provided by America to the people of the Philippines is more extensive than that found in any other colonial government, and the people have responded to it. This is substantiated by a comment made not so long ago by the district governor of Sandakan, British North Borneo, in reviewing the list of public officials in his area. At the head of each department was, of course, an Englishman; next below him came a Filipino; while lower in the list were Chinese and Malays. When asked by a visitor why the Filipinos were given such preference, the governor replied: "Because the American system of educating the Filipinos has done more for them than anything that we have done in our own colonies. The Filipinos, naturally intelligent, are better fitted to take responsibility than any other people available."

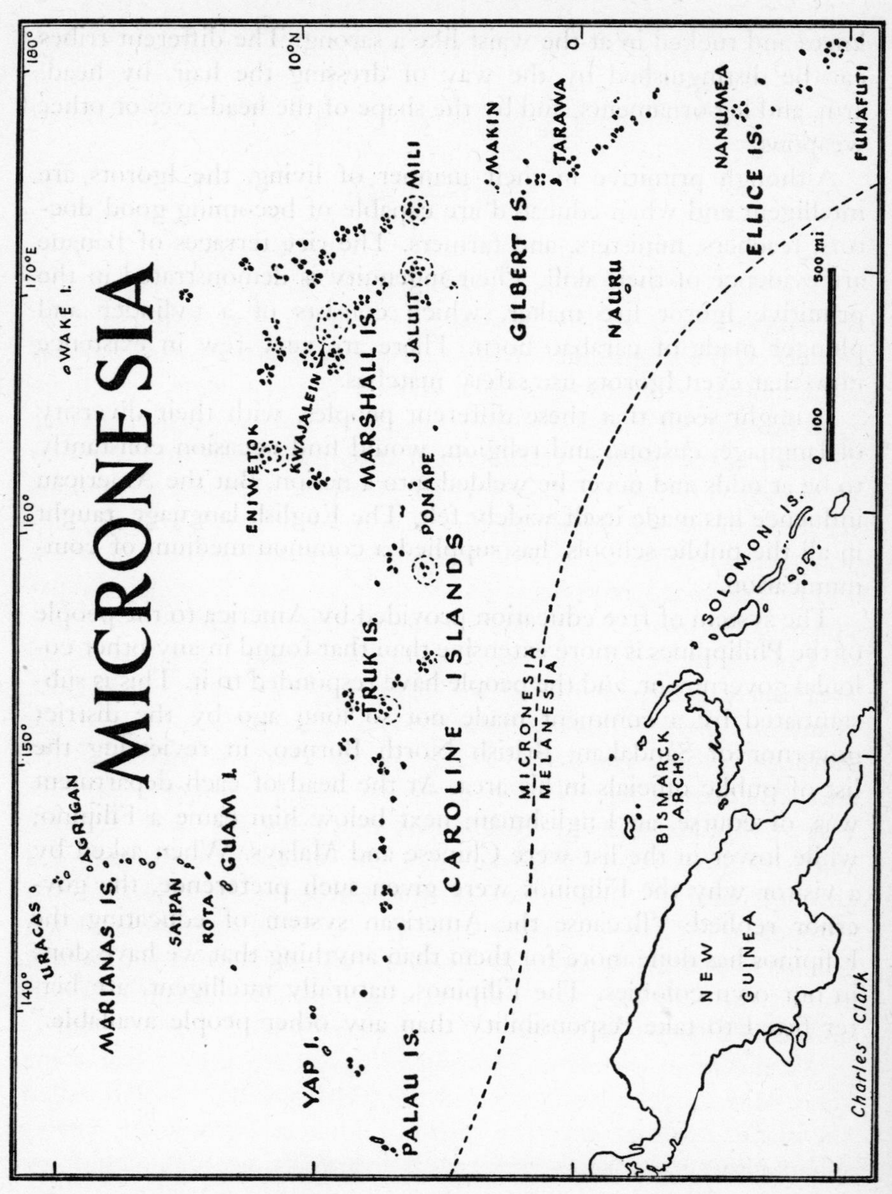

MICRONESIA
140°
150°
160°
170°E
180°
10°N
0
URACAS
AGRIGAN
MARIANAS IS.
SAIPAN
ROTA
GUAM I.
WAKE I.
YAP I.
PALAU IS.
TRUK IS.
CAROLINE ISLANDS
PONAPE
ENIWETOK
KWAJALEIN
MARSHALL IS.
JALUIT
MILI
MAKIN
TARAWA
GILBERT IS.
NAURU
NANUMEA
ELLICE IS.
FUNAFUTI
MICRONESIA
MELANESIA
SOLOMON IS.
BISMARCK ARCH°
NEW GUINEA
100
500 mi
Charles Clark

CHAPTER XVI

MICRONESIA

MICRONESIA is so called because of the small size of the islands. However, the importance of some of these islands in world affairs is far out of proportion to their size. Yap and Guam were once vital links in our Pacific cable system. Earlier, Guam was a regular stopping place for the westbound Spanish galleons from Acapulco to Manila. Truk in the Carolines has been the Japanese naval center and key to the South Pacific. These islands will probably always serve as important naval bases, airports, and weather stations.

The combined land areas of all the tiny islands of Micronesia come to less than 2,000 square miles, about the size of the State of Delaware. Yet these bits of land are scattered over an ocean area nearly as large as that of the whole United States. Most of the islands are low coral atolls; some have been uplifted to respectable elevations, and a few have volcanic peaks rising as high as 3,000 feet. Micronesia begins with the Palau Islands, about 500 miles east of Mindanao in the Philippines, and about the same distance north of New Guinea. From here the islands stretch eastward through nearly 2,000 miles of the Carolines, then northward through the Marianas toward Japan, thence through the Bonin Islands to within 500 miles of Tokyo. Farther south, at the eastern end of the Carolines, are two other groups: the Marshall Islands and the Gilbert Islands.

All the small islands of Micronesia have been known for some time. Magellan's sailors landed in the Marianas in 1521 and called the islands *Los Ladrones*, the Island of Thieves, because the natives when visiting the ships carried off every article they could lay hands on. The Carolines were first discovered in 1527 and were later named after King Charles II of Spain. The Marshall Islands and the Gilbert Islands were first seen in 1529 and were named some 250 years later after two British captains who explored them.

For hundreds of years after their discovery many of the Micronesian islands were literally forgotten. Great Britain and France claimed some and we acquired Guam from Spain at the end of the Spanish-American War, at which time Germany purchased the Carolines. The Treaty of Versailles doled out most of the German islands to the Japanese who during the 1920's and 1930's extended their control over Micronesia and proceeded to fortify the islands in direct opposition to treaty agreements.

All of the Micronesian islands have a tropical "oceanic" climate, tempered by the wind from the sea and by frequent rains. The annual average temperature is about 80° F., with a range of about 10° either way. Though climatic conditions are favorable, the variety of plants of these islands is limited. Coconuts and other palms occur, with a number of shrubs and grasses, but none of the exotic plants that make up the rain forests on islands farther south.

The animals on these small and remote islands are also few, though the coral lagoons and surrounding waters are rich in fish and sea life. Small lizards are common on the islands and on Palau the larger monitor lizard occurs. The banded sea snakes that occasionally come ashore at the tide level are venomous but are not apt to strike at man. These islands have peculiar land snails that scientists at our museums are anxious to study and ask only that the shells be collected and carefully labeled to show exactly where they were found.

Except for bats that flew to the islands, or rats that were carried by ships, the mammals are scarcely worth noting. Birds are more common but they are mostly sea birds, some of which nest on the islands in vast numbers. These birds have been a peculiar and valuable asset. Returning year after year to nest on the same small islands, their droppings, known as guano, reach into the limestone and form deposits of phosphates. These deposits are valuable as fertilizers, and the search for such phospate islands was a kind of treasure-island search for generations. In the early days natives were kidnaped from their homes in Micronesia and Polynesia to work these deposits. More recently, Annamite natives have been employed by the French and brought to the Polynesian island Makatea for the same purpose.

The origin of the inhabitants of Micronesia is not well known, nor has as much study been made of them as of their neighbors to the west and south. There is an obvious trend from the nearly pure Polynesian stock in the Gilbert Islands to Malayan or even Melanesian stock in the westernmost islands.

The original inhabitants of Micronesia suffered severely after their first contacts with the whites, smallpox, influenza and other European diseases almost destroying entire populations.

Most Micronesians, especially those from the Marshall Islands and the Gilbert Islands, are noted for their skill in woodcarving. Highly ornamented paddles, clubs, staffs, house posts and canoe prows are frequently seen. The palm and coconut is widely used. Many of the tools and implements used by the islanders are made of shell.

THE BONIN ISLANDS

This small group deserves special mention at this time because it lies along one of the two routes to Japan from the south, the other route being nearer the Asiatic coast running northward from the Philippines through Formosa and the Luchu Islands.

The Bonin Islands consist of three groups: Muko-jima, Chichi-jima, and Haha-jima (jima meaning island in Japanese). They range from north to south and lie about 500 miles south of Yokohama. There is a fourth, the Io-jima (Sulfus Islands) that the Japanese have included under the same administration as the Bonin group. Altogether, these islands total ninety-seven in number but cover an area of only forty square miles and hold a population of only fifty-seven hundred. They are of volcanic origin and are profusely forested.

The plants of the islands consist of palms, ferns, banyan trees, wild beans and taros. The animals are chiefly bats. The climate is semitropical.

The name Bonin is a corruption of the Japanese *Munin,* "empty of men," for such was the condition of the islands when sighted by a Japanese explorer in 1593. Almost two and one-half centuries later, in 1827, the islands were rediscovered by Captain Beechey of *H.M.S. Blossom.* Captain Beechey, on landing on Chichi-jima, nailed a sign on a tree denoting it as Peel Island and a possession of the Crown. Three years later an expedition to settle the islands was organized by the British consul in Honolulu, who set out in the company of two Americans, one Dane, two Englishmen, seventeen Hawaiians, and a Portuguese. Then in 1853 Commodore Perry arrived in Chichi-jima to establish a coaling station he had bought from Nathaniel Savory, one of the American settlers—a strip of land, 1,000 feet long along the waterfront—and anchored his warships in the harbor near the present village of Kiyose. Finally, in 1861 Japan advanced its claim and the United States and Britain relinquished ownership of the Bonins.

The largest island, Chichi (Father Island), is twelve and a half miles in circumference. Its harbor is an extinct volcanic crater that is now surrounded by heavily forested hills rising over 800 feet above sea level. Ships in the harbor are entirely obscured from outside view by mountainous walls. The waters are crystal clear. The eye can follow to the bottom of the crater and observe sharks and large turtles swimming around the anchors. Pineapple, banana, and sugar-cane plantations line the harbor shores. The Japanese are experimenting with cattle raising here.

The capital city of the Bonins, Omura, is located on Chichi-jima. Descendants of the first white settlers still live here, though through intermarriage with the Japanese they have become more Oriental than Occidental. Europeans were excluded from the Bonins for some time because the Japanese did not want others to find out what they were doing in the way of military and naval installations.

Thirty-five miles to the south of Chichi lies Haha-jima (Mother Island or Bailey Island). It is one and a half miles long and has no harbor. Here Okimura Hill rises to 1,470 feet above sea level. In other respects Haha resembles Chichi.

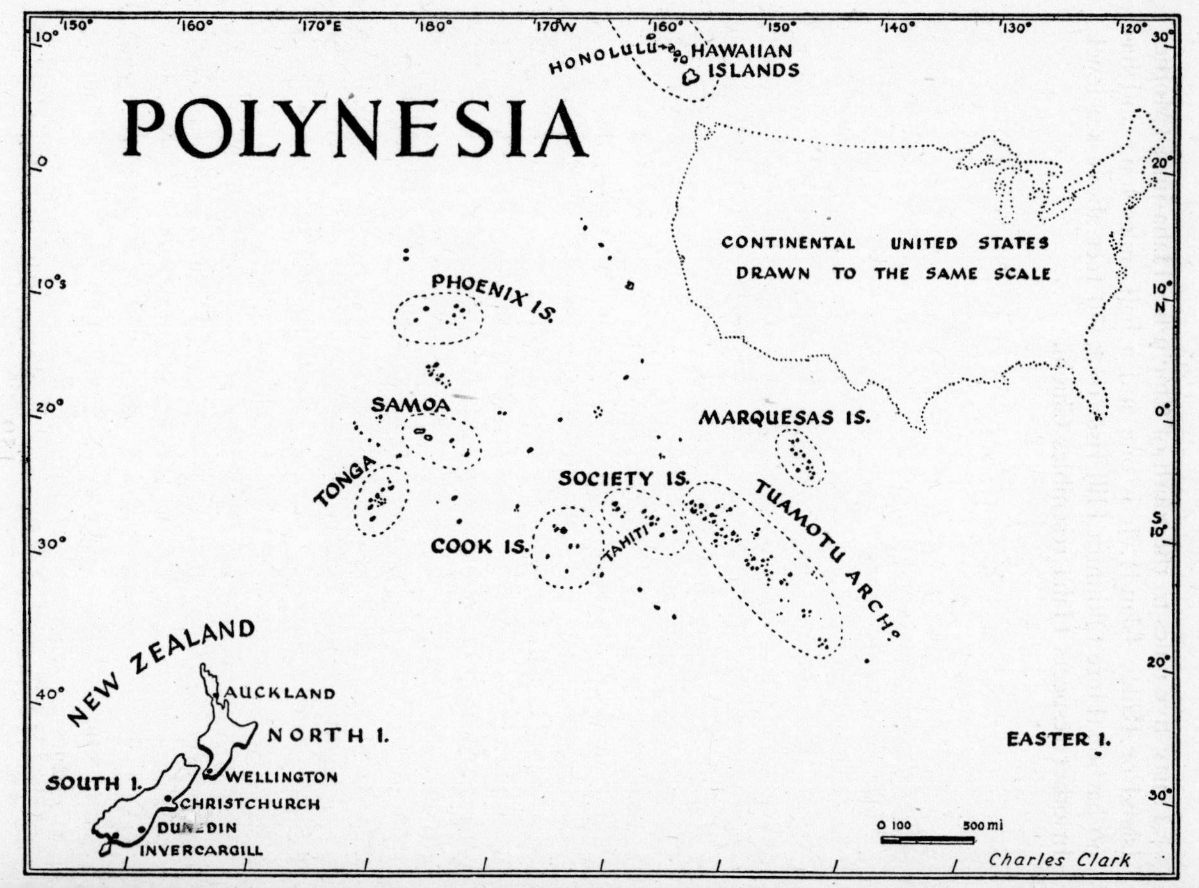
POLYNESIA
HAWAIIAN ISLANDS
HONOLULU
CONTINENTAL UNITED STATES
DRAWN TO THE SAME SCALE
PHOENIX IS.
SAMOA
TONGA
MARQUESAS IS.
SOCIETY IS.
TAHITI
COOK IS.
TUAMOTU ARCH°
NEW ZEALAND
AUCKLAND
NORTH I.
WELLINGTON
SOUTH I.
CHRISTCHURCH
DUNEDIN
INVERCARGILL
EASTER I.
0 100 500 mi
Charles Clark
150° 160° 170°E 180° 170°W 160° 150° 140° 130° 120°
10° 0 10°S 20° 30° 40°
30° 20° 10° N 0° S 10° 20° 30°

Chapter XVII

POLYNESIA

To the western world, the palm-covered coral islands of Polynesia, inhabited by picturesque and handsome natives, symbolize the beauty and languor so romantically associated with the "South Seas." The stories of the mutiny on the *Bounty* and the settlement the mutineers established on Pitcairn Island, of Melville's escape from his ship in the Marquesas, of Robert Louis Stevenson's years at Samoan Vailima, for a while so happy and later so tragic, surround these islands with an atmosphere of romance and adventure.

Polynesia provides the crowning proof of the great expanse of the Pacific, for the sides of the triangle forming its boundaries are each more than 4,500 miles in length. The islands in Polynesia, large and small, are innumerable, yet their aggregate land area, excluding New Zealand, is only about 10,000 square miles. One needs to imagine, then, an amount of land equal to that of Vermont or Maryland broken up into bits and peppered over an ocean surface equal to about four times the area of the United States.

The historic line dividing Melanesia and Polynesia in the tropical South Pacific is drawn between the Fijis and Samoa. In earlier times there was intermarriage among the native peoples, and Polynesian blood in varying degrees is evident among the dark Fijians, particularly in the ruling families. Likewise, there is a slight Melanesian strain in certain Polynesian peoples, as for example, the Tongans. At any rate, the dividing line is a practical one if not completely accurate. All Central Pacific islands from Samoa eastward are regarded as lying in Polynesia.

The Polynesians who became the first inhabitants of these remote ocean islands came to them over uncharted seas centuries before the explorations of the Vikings or Columbus. Their long and daring voyages in primitive boats guided by the stars mark them as among the first and probably the greatest of the world's oceanic explorers.

At one time the native races were estimated to number more than 1,000,000 people. By 1900, however, four-fifths of the original native population of Polynesia had disappeared. These people, who had developed an ideal culture for their own purposes, were decimated by European diseases to which they had no immunity, and injured by the treatment they received from foreigners. Since the beginning of the present century, however, there has been a moderate recovery in the numbers of the native inhabitants, and for the last several decades the western governments represented there have sought to do everything possible to compensate for earlier wrongs.

The islands of Polynesia lie in an ancient and long-undisturbed ocean basin and owe their existence to volcanic materials that have been forced up through the earth's crust. The islands are, in fact, the peaks of mountains, some of them gigantic, rising from the ocean bed. Many of the mountaintops are masked by coral rock, which forms the atolls, and in many cases the islands themselves as well as the reefs around them.

The principal Polynesian islands and island groups include Samoa, the Phoenix, the Tonga, the Society, the Tuamotu, and the Marquesas Islands, Easter Island and Hawaii. (New Zealand is often associated with Polynesia because its aborigines are Polynesians. In this book it is described in the chapter that includes its sister-dominion Australia.)

SAMOA

The Samoan group forms part of an arc, about 2,000 miles east of Australia and 4,000 miles southwest of San Francisco. The basic rock structure of the islands is volcanic. There are no active craters, although a submarine eruption did take place near

Olosega in 1866. Savaii is the largest of the three principal islands.

The animal life and vegetation of these islands are considerably less varied than those of the Fijis and the Solomons to the west, but are somewhat more abundant than in eastern Polynesia. There is one unique bird, the tooth-billed pigeon, which is noted for the toothed tip of its upper bill. The manumea, as this pigeon is known to the islanders, was almost exterminated many years ago by domestic cats which the natives obtained from whaling ships for pets, and which subsequently ran wild.

Western Samoa is under New Zealand control, while eastern Samoa, including the island of Tutuila, is American and administered by a naval commandant. The seat of our government, a small village of less than 1,000 inhabitants, is on the splendid harbor of Pago Pago. The harbor, a mile and a half long by three-quarters wide, occupies the submerged crater of an ancient volcano—beneath mountains crowned with coconut palms.

The natives, of whom there are about 49,000, formerly engaged in bitter political wars, and consequently are probably better off under the present more peaceful system of government. They own most of the land and raise coconuts for export. Their food consists largely of vegetables, coconuts, breadfruits, bananas, fish and pork.

Samoans are often praised as being the perfect Polynesian type. Indeed, everyone who has seen them has been impressed by their light-brown skin, splendid physique, and handsome features. They are a simple, intelligent, honorable and brave people. Though nominally Christian, most Samoans cling to many of their primitive beliefs. Their language has been called the "Italian of the Pacific" because of its soft, liquid quality. Full of idioms and delicate inflections, it is difficult for strangers to learn, yet delightful to hear.

THE TONGA OR FRIENDLY ISLANDS

This group, a British possession, lies south of Samoa and on the same island arc. It was discovered by Tasman, in 1643, and many years later Captain Cook gave it the name "Friendly Islands" because of the welcome he received from the native Polynesians. There are nearly 150 islands and islets in this group, which is about 200 miles long and has an area of approximately 250 square miles. The average annual temperature is 73° to 76°, and rainfall ranges from seventy-eight to eighty-eight inches a year.

There are about 32,800 native Tongans on the islands, and about 1,200 others, mostly whites and half-castes. There are no commercial fisheries, mines or factories, for the activities of the people are principally agricultural. The chief product is copra, although bananas, citrus fruits, pineapples and yams are also raised.

Between the Tonga and the Society groups lie the Cook Islands, a small group; and to the north, in the direction of the Line group, are a considerable number of scattered atolls and coral islands that are of slight importance, although several of them have had exciting histories. Tongareva, for example, was almost depopulated in 1863 by a raid of Peruvian slavers in search of laborers for the guano islands.

THE SOCIETY ISLANDS

This beautiful group of islands in the heart of Polynesia has attracted the attention of Europeans for well over 100 years and it is here the first efforts were made by Protestant missionaries to convert the natives. Of the dozen or more main islands in the Society group, Tahiti, Moorea, Huahine, Raiatea and Borabora are probably the best known. During the eighteenth century the Societies were visited by most of the European explorers who entered the Pacific. The stories they took back gave these islands top place in the earlier literature of discovery, history and romance.

Tahiti, 33 miles long and 600 miles square in area, is beyond any doubt one of the most widely known small oceanic islands in the world, and has often figured in the tales of adventurers and writers of romantic fiction. Here Paul Gauguin settled after leaving his home in France and it was here and in the Marquesas that he painted the pictures that later made him famous. Incidentally, the mutineers of the *Bounty* took six male and twelve female islanders with them from Tahiti to help them populate the colony they established on Pitcairn Island.

The population of Tahiti numbers around 19,000, of which approximately half live in Papeete, the chief town. The climate, although damp and hot, is not unhealthful. The main industries are the preparation of copra and sugar, and the exporting of mother-of-pearl and phosphates.

There are no native mammals other than bats, and no reptiles except lizards and sea turtles. There are only a few kinds of birds and insects. The lagoons, however, are alive with fishes and there are many kinds of crabs, shrimps and other shellfishes. There is a central peak—an extinct volcano—on the island, rising 7,400 feet above sea level. The island is almost entirely surrounded by a barrier reef, so that there is a broad shallow lagoon between the outer coral ridge and the island proper.

Although early influence at Tahiti was British, the group has been a French colony since 1844. In 1888 Tahiti was made the capital of the French Pacific island colonies, which include the Marquesas, the Tuamotu, and the Austral Islands. The last named group lies south of the Societies, extending south into the south-temperate zone. Rapa, the best known island, is temperate rather than tropical.

THE TUAMOTU ISLANDS

The French-owned Tuamotu group is the largest and most far-flung archipelago in the world. It lies in the central South Pacific, remote from any continent and stretching from the longitude of the Society Islands southeastward for about 1,300 miles. If all the small islets are counted, the Tuamotus number several hundred distinct islands. They are all of coral origin and most of them have an altitude of only a few feet above sea level, although several, such as Makatea, show evidence of considerable uplift, reaching a height of 1,300 feet. Rainfall in the region is not extreme, being between sixty-two and eighty-seven inches per year, but hurricanes frequently occur from November to March.

The great distance from Australia, Asia, and the Americas, the character of the soil, the dearth of standing fresh water, and the destructive violence of hurricanes to which most of the Tuamotus are exposed, all combine to limit the kinds of plant and animal life that have found a permanent home on the islands.

Far to the east of the Tuamotus lies Easter Island, or Rapa Nui, the outpost of Polynesia closest to America. It is famous for its huge and remarkable stone heads and other carved images, the relics of ancient inhabitants whose history is yet to be unfolded.

THE MARQUESAS ISLANDS

The Marquesas Islands, French possessions, lie to the northeast of the Tuamotu Islands. They, too, are of ancient volcanic origin, but, despite the fact that they lie not far south of the equator, no coral reefs line the rugged shores. The great cliffs that rise straight from the sea are frequently crowned with rich forests, made alive by white-foamed waterfalls.

Knife-edged ridges separate most of the valleys on the larger Marquesas Islands, a fact that isolated the original Polynesian inhabitants into a number of hostile communities. These people, who once may have numbered 75,000 or even considerably more, are now reduced to about 2,500. A book of fascinating interest about the Marquesas Islands at the time of their savage glory is *Typee*, by Herman Melville, which created a sensation in literary circles when it was published in 1846. Then forty years later Robert Louis Stevenson gave a charming account of the islands in his book, *In the South Seas*.

HAWAII

The Hawaiian Islands have been famous for many things—their delightful climate, lovely beaches, mighty volcanoes, luxuriant vegetation, fine native people, fruits, of which pineapples are the most prized—and today for their importance as a strategic outpost. Stretching in a 1,500-mile chain from northwest to southeast, the archipelago includes both volcanic and coral islands. Its total land area is 6,412 square miles. Most isolated of the important island groups of the Pacific, it is 2,100 miles from San Francisco, 4,700 miles from Panama, 4,400 miles from Sydney, 4,800 miles from Manila, 3,400 miles from Yokohama, and 2,100 miles from Unalaska in the Aleutians.

The volcanoes of Hawaii are known to geologists as the "quiet" type. To the layman these awe-inspiring mountains may seem far from quiet, but to the geologist the description means that the lava is very hot and very liquid and hence tends to overflow and run down the sides of the craters, instead of being hurled aloft in tremendous explosions.

Mauna Loa is regarded as the greatest of the world's volcanoes. At 13,686 feet it is nearly as high as Mauna Kea (13,835 feet) and is generally in a state of activity. Its lava flows, of a temperature between 1,000° and 2,000° C., have spread as much as fifty miles. Mauna Loa usually erupts through craters and vents on its flanks rather than through its summit, and the pits of molten lava in Kilauea, one of the craters, are truly immense. The boiling and bubbling and the eruptions of gas and melted rock are an indescribable sight.

The eight inhabited islands—Hawaii, Maui, Molokai, Lanai, Kahoolawe, Oahu, Kauai, and Niihau—are at the southeast end of the chain. The remaining islands—as a whole they are so small that they total only six square miles—extend northwestward over 1,300 miles. Nikoa and Necker retain remains of stone platforms of Polynesian origin. Laysan was formerly the home of five kinds of land birds known nowhere else in the world, and previous to 1909, when the chain of islands was proclaimed bird reservations by President Theodore Roosevelt, the gathering of bird feathers for millinery purposes had seriously threatened them with extinction. A single cargo of Japanese feather pirates, captured by an American naval patrol boat, included 260,000 pairs of albatross wings and the skins of at least 40,000 additional other birds.

Due to the isolation of the Hawaiian Islands, a small bat of American origin is the only native land mammal. Many other mammals, however, have been introduced by man, including dogs, rats and mice, cattle and horses. The so-called Hawaiian rat is a species that apparently has been spread widely through the Pacific by the early voyages of the Polynesians, just as the gray and black rats have traveled with the ships of the Europeans. Wild goats, believed to be descendants of domestic animals brought by Captain Cook, occur on Molokai, as do deer, which were introduced in 1867. One large valley on Molokai is inhabited by pugnacious and wild descendants of once-tame water buffalos.

The isolation of the Hawaiian Islands has led to striking evolutionary changes among certain native birds, an example of which is to be found in the family of Hawaiian honey creepers, believed to be of American origin. The varied species of this family supposedly are descended from a short-billed, finchlike ancestor, yet the bills of the various Hawaiian species now range from short and stout to extremely long, slender and curved. No one would suspect at first sight that such different-looking birds were actually members of the same family.

Vegetation is luxuriant on the islands, and the number of plants is unusually large. For example, there are about 900 different kinds of flowering plants, of which about one-third are trees. The forests, tropical in character, abound with ferns, mosses, lichens, fungi and climbing vines. Among the introduced plants are coconuts, breadfruits, taros (from which poi, one of the principal foods of the natives, is made), yams, bananas, citrus fruits, dates, sugar cane, and pineapples.

Sugar cane has become the basis of Hawaiian prosperity, for the soil and climate are ideal for its growth. Scientific methods have increased the yield from 2 to 3 tons to 20 tons per acre, and 1,000,000 tons are produced annually. Second only to sugar in importance is the pineapple-growing and canning industry, and third is cattle raising to which some 1,300,000 acres are devoted. Principally an agricultural country, Hawaiian manufacturing is on a small scale. There are no valuable minerals on the islands.

The original Hawaiians are believed to have migrated to their present homes via Micronesia in about the middle of the first century, and centuries later Tahitians came to add to their number. Hawaiians are a handsome, well-built, brown-skinned, black-haired race. They are often large in stature; some of them—especially the chiefs—are said to have weighed more than 300 pounds. They speak the same soft, liquid Polynesian as do the Tahitians and Samoans. The alphabet is limited to five vowels and seven consonants. The natives originally had no writing, but were fond of chants, poetry, and storytelling; and the knowledge of one generation was passed on to the next by specially trained orators and singers, whose ability to memorize lengthy stories was extraordinary. Weapons and utensils were skillfully fashioned of wood, shell, stone, tooth, and bone. Beautiful feather capes and robes of considerable artistic quality were worn by the chiefs. The natives have been noted for their skill in sailing and fishing, for their prowess as swimmers, and for their fondness for athletics, dancing, and both vocal and instrumental music. The ukulele, so commonly associated with the Hawaiians, is actually of Portuguese origin.

Religion played an important role in native Hawaiian life, for all objects and forces had their individual gods, to whom the Hawaiian appealed before any action was undertaken. When Captain Cook, the discoverer of the islands, landed in 1778 the natives took him to be a god, and so treated him until he was killed the next year in a fight between his sailors and the natives.

Since 1898 the Hawaiian Islands have been a Territory of the United States. The Territorial Legislature, consisting of fifteen senators and thirty representatives, meets every two years. A governor, secretary, and justices are appointed for four years by the President of the United States with the consent of the Senate. The excellent educational system ranges from the kindergarten through the university.

Many of the people of Hawaii are now of mixed stock, for the islands have attracted immigrants of many nationalities who have interbred more or less freely. For this reason it is increasingly difficult to classify the present inhabitants by race. Americans, northern Europeans, Spaniards, Portuguese, Puerto Ricans, Filipinos, Chinese, Japanese and Koreans have settled there and in many cases intermarried. Interestingly enough, the mixture of races has worked out well, considered from either the strictly physical or the broader social point of view, and racial antagonism is at a minimum.

At the time of discovery, the islands are believed to have had a native population of about 300,000, but unfortunately this number has decreased to the extent that estimates of 1940 place the figure at only 21,000. Other races are now estimated as follows: white 88,200; Asiatic 237,600; part Hawaiian 37,600.

CHAPTER XVIII

THE ALEUTIAN, THE PRIBILOF, AND THE GALÁPAGOS ISLANDS

IN THE previous chapter, the review of the Polynesian islands has carried us eastward toward the American continent. In this chapter a brief description is given of three of the most interesting of the island groups lying close to the Americas, before turning to the islands of the Northwest Pacific, including Japan.

Two widely divergent island groups are described: the Aleutians and the adjacent Pribilofs in the far north extending westward from Alaska, and the Galápagos, lying astride the equator and having remote associations with Central and South America. There are other sizable islands or island groups lying near the Americas, such as those off the coast of British Columbia, or Juan Fernández, lying 430 miles off the coast of Chile. But these groups are either, as in the first instance, similar to the adjacent continent, or, as in the case of Juan Fernández, not significantly different from other remote islands described elsewhere.

THE ALEUTIAN ISLANDS AND THE PRIBILOF ISLANDS

The Aleutian Islands are truly a part of North America, extending as a pointed finger 1,200 miles across the Pacific toward Asia. Though on the map the Aleutians appear as a prominent element in the Pacific island scheme, their unfavorable climate with continual fogs and their rough terrain have combined to keep them relatively unknown.

The famous Danish navigator, Commander Vitus Bering, while exploring for Russia, sighted some of the islands in 1741. Russian traders and missionaries followed him and maintained their con-

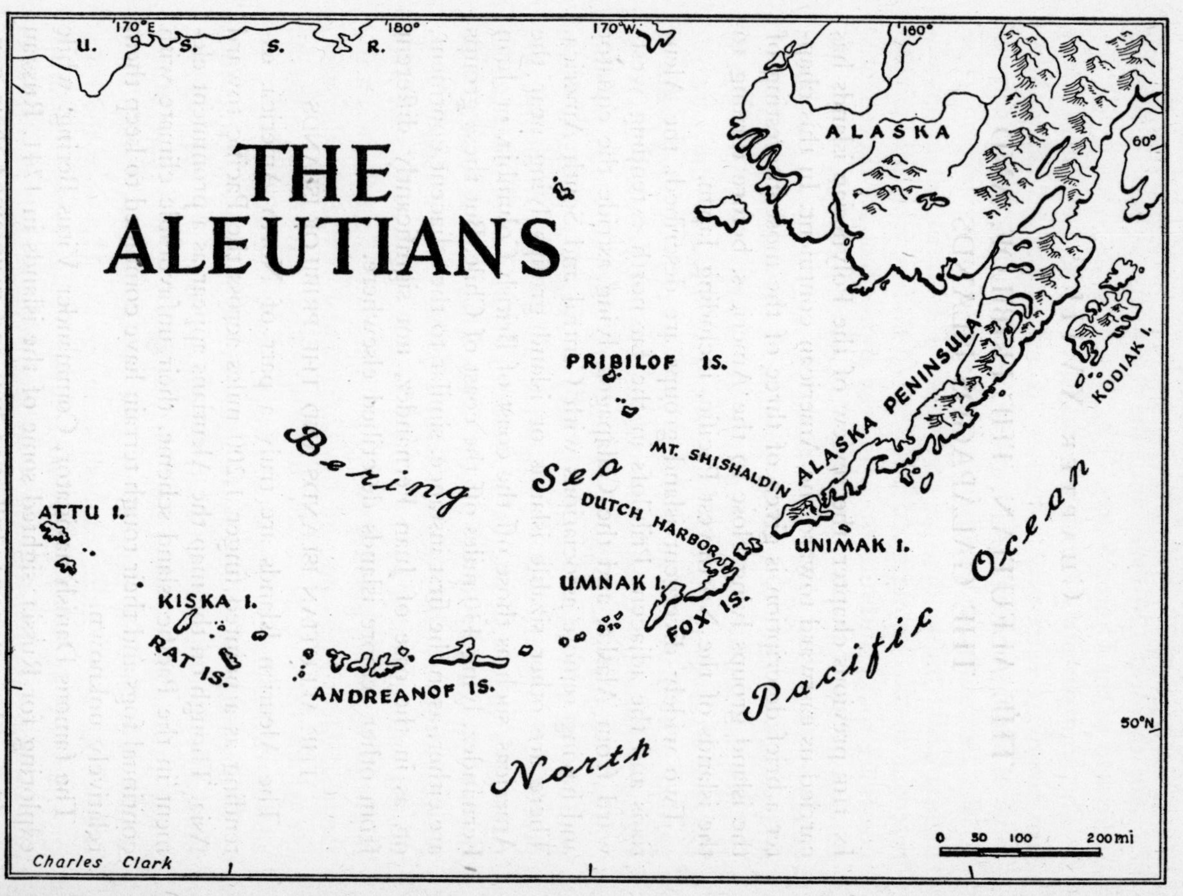
THE ALEUTIANS
U. S. S. R.
170°E
180°
170°W
160°
60°
50°N
ALASKA
ALASKA PENINSULA
KODIAK I.
UNIMAK I.
MT. SHISHALDIN
DUTCH HARBOR
FOX IS.
UMNAK I.
PRIBILOF IS.
Bering Sea
North Pacific Ocean
ANDREANOF IS.
RAT IS.
KISKA I.
ATTU I.
0 50 100 200mi
Charles Clark

tact for the next 120 years until the Aleutians, as part of Alaska, were sold to the United States.

The approximately 70 islands and islets in the 1,000-mile Aleutian chain are extremely mountainous, and many volcanic peaks, some of them smoking, are found among them and on the narrow Alaska Peninsula, of which the Aleutians are an extension. The highest peak, Shishaldin, on the island of Unimak, affectionately referred to as "Smoking Moses," is 9,387 feet in altitude. The coasts are rocky and surf worn and the approaches are exceedingly dangerous, the land in most places rising immediately from the coasts to steep, bold mountains. Strong currents between the islands and numerous reefs add to the hazards of navigation.

These islands are the home of the Aleuts, who are related to the Eskimos in language and culture, though physically they are regarded as a separate group. Today the Aleuts show the results of extensive mixing with Russians and other white people.

The Aleutian chain has received much attention as a possible pathway of primitive man from Asia to America. It is far more probable, however, that the important movements of people between the two hemispheres in prehistoric times took place across the narrow Bering Strait, about 1,000 miles farther north. The native culture of the Aleutian Islands is much more closely connected with the mainland of North America than with Asia. This might be expected because of the 250-mile water gap between the farthest Aleutian island and the Commander Islands to the west, on which there is no trace of early native settlement, and the additional 140 miles from there to the Asiatic mainland.

The remains of ancient settlements in the Aleutians, long since buried by time, unearthed and explored by scientists, have yielded much information concerning man's history in this part of the world. The ancient people lived by fishing and hunting. They used covered-over skin "canoes" similar to the kayaks of the Eskimos, as well as larger skin boats. Seals, whales, sea otters, birds and fishes were vital to their everyday needs, as well as shellfishes which are abundant. The present-day traveler, if he is forced to fall back upon what food he can get from nature, may find shell-fishes most welcome.

The mammals found on the Aleutians, particularly on the islands nearest the mainland, are very similar to those that live in the adjacent areas of Alaska, with such types as caribou, bears, wolves, hares, lemmings and ground squirrels. As one proceeds farther oceanward in the chain of islands and the water barriers between each island become greater, mammalian life naturally diminishes, so that beyond Unimak Island only a few and relatively smaller forms of mammals are found.

The Aleutians are justly famed as the home of many sea birds, such as cormorants, auklets, puffins, and others that come by the tens of thousands to nest in the islands during the summer.

The sea is rich in fishes because of the wealth of food content found in northern waters (see Chapter Seven), and in recent years Japanese fishermen have encroached on Aleutian waters to fish for crab, halibut, and salmon. Other sea animals include colonies of seals and sea lions. Occasionally a sea otter may be seen. The latter is a remarkable creature, four or five feet long and beautifully adapted to a marine life. In general form it resembles its smaller cousin, the land otter. The sea otter has been brought close to extinction because of its valuable fur and it is strictly against the law to kill these animals.

The Pribilof Islands, which lie 180 miles north of Umnak in the Aleutian chain, are notable for the great herds of fur seals that use the islands as their breeding grounds. It is now illegal to kill this handsome and interesting animal except under the strict government regulations that are helping to keep the herds safe from the depredations which, until recently, fur sealers made upon them.

The climate of both the Aleutians and the Pribilofs is stormy and foggy. In place of spring, summer, and autumn there is a long autumnlike season, with little sunny weather. The winter is raw but not extremely cold. Umnak, one of the most important of the Aleutian Islands, averages some 250 rainy days a year and is said to be the rainiest place within the territory of the United States.

The prevailing fogs, rain, and strong winds make a climate that is generally very disagreeable. Except for a few negligible groves in cultivation, the islands are practically treeless but are covered with a profuse growth of herbage including grasses, sedges, and many flowering plants.

The Aleutians, which lie close to the shortest route from the United States to Japan, have become of military significance as an outpost of American defense. The dramatic struggle that occurred at Attu and the final occupation of Kiska without a struggle will cause the names of these islands to be remembered long after the remainder of the group is forgotten, and some day, perhaps, native hunters will return to use gun emplacements and dugouts for their rude shelters.

THE GALÁPAGOS ISLANDS

The Galápagos Islands, grouped on both sides of the equator about 600 miles off the coast of South America, possess characteristics suggestive of an old-fashioned idea of hell on earth. They have fire and brimstone, and even the vegetation bristles with torturing spines. Yet they are among the most interesting places in the world and, in some aspects, among the most picturesque.

Superficially, an island in the Galápagos resembles an unfinished adolescent planet. With its primitive organic skeleton still exposed, it might be a little older than Mars or somewhat younger than the moon. Every one of the five principal islands, nineteen islets and forty-seven rocks is completely volcanic, much of the surface consisting of great loose slabs of iron-hard lava plates. These natural mantraps are so sharp that progress over them wears out leather shoes in a few days, and their incredibly delicate balance makes each step uncertain and perilous. Sprouting from earth-filled crevices are dense growths of cacti and thornbushes.

The lava fields are hot under the sun during the day but the climate in general is remarkably temperate, its untropical character being produced by the cool Peruvian, or Humboldt, Current which flows past and around the islands, making the temperature of the

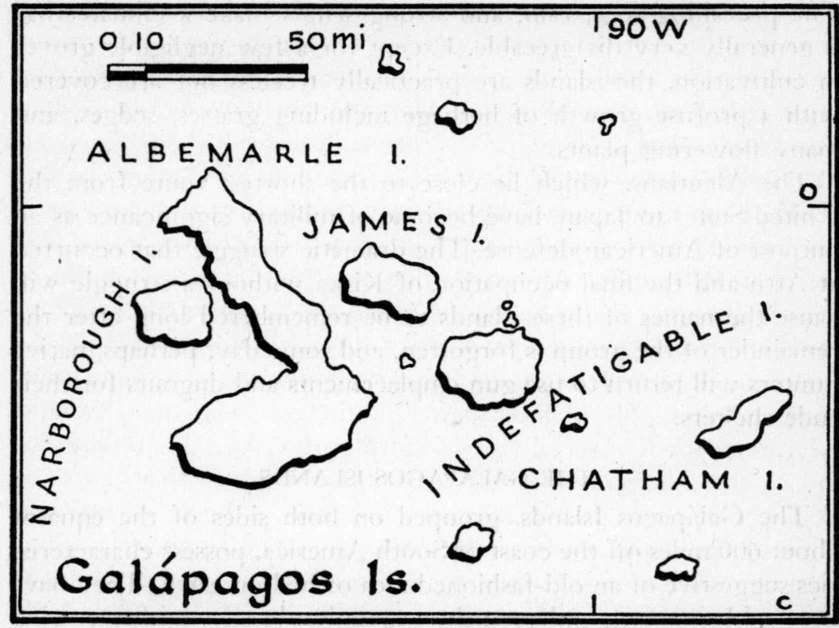

water actually below that of the air. A constant trade wind from the southeast blows the year round except for a few days of doldrums which occur intermittently at almost any season of the year.

Darwin estimated that there are more than 2,000 craters in the Galápagos and occasionally a new one erupts, filling the air with steam and fumes of sulphur and pouring floods of molten lava down to the water, where sea lions and fishes are known to have been boiled alive.

Markedly deficient rainfall makes almost a desert of the coastal lowlands, but precipitation increases inland on the higher slopes, beginning at about 500 feet above sea level, resulting in increased fertility and an almost tropical growth of trees and herbaceous vegetation.

The primitive appearance of the Galápagos extends even to some of the animal life, for the islands have been isolated for such a long time that the native reptiles and birds have evolved into forms found nowhere else in the world. Sea lizards, or iguanas, two or three feet long, lava-black in color and curiously roundheaded, haunt the water's edge by the thousands, feeding on seaweed and diving below the surface at the first hint of danger. In the shade of the cactus, crested, yard-long, red and yellow land iguanas bask. Huge tortoises, weighing up to 500 pounds, were formerly to be found in enormous numbers. The tenacity of life of these *galápagos,* as the Spaniards called them, was their undoing, for the tortoises would live in the holds of vessels without food for six to eight months, providing, in the absence of refrigeration, an abundant supply of fresh meat. Pirates, privateers, whalers and even more modern naval and pleasure craft have taken enormous toll of these helpless creatures. The final result is that the very existence of these primitive, majestic reptiles is being threatened, some of the island species being already exterminated.

In the course of the visits of all these ships, domestic animals have escaped or been put ashore, and at present we find dogs, cats, hogs, goats, donkeys and cattle running wild on the islands. Curiously enough, these animals have become exceedingly shy and wary, whereas the native birds, such as hawks, owls, finches, doves and mockingbirds, are so unaccustomed to the sight of man that they are delightfully tame, sometimes lighting on one's shoulder.

The great variety of black and brown ground finches, varying in bill and other characteristics from island to island, are famous out of all proportion to their size because of the important part they played in the mind of Charles Darwin in crystallizing his ideas concerning the evolution of species. This resulted from observations on the occasion of his visit to the Galápagos in the *Beagle* in 1834.

The peculiar Galápagos fauna was originally derived from the American continent, probably from Central rather than from South America. An exception is the penguin, descended from southern ancestors, and here thriving on the equator in the cool waters of the Peruvian Current. There are many sea birds, such as pelicans, boobies, various petrels, tropic birds, albatrosses and man-of-war birds. Flamingos, ducks and the flightless cormorants are also to be found in small numbers.

The waters around the Galápagos contain some of the finest fishing grounds in the world. Tunas, groupers, bonitos, sierra mackerels and wahoos are numerous and easy to catch. Big game fishes such as sailfishes and marlins are fairly common. Sea turtles are extremely numerous and come ashore to lay their eggs on sandy beaches.

The Galápagos Islands were discovered accidentally by the Bishop of Panama in 1535 when his ship was blown off its course during a voyage between Panama and Peru. The early history of the islands, however, is almost wholly English and it is for this reason that all the islands bear English names. British pirates in the seventeenth and eighteenth centuries used the islands as an operating base against the Spaniards. The islands were formally acquired by Ecuador in 1832. Today Spanish names are used almost exclusively in the islands, although most of the literature about them uses the older English names.

When first discovered, the Galápagos were uninhabited by man, but later Ecuador established a penal settlement, and in recent years sporadic attempts at limited colonization have been made. Human occupancy will always be on a limited scale, for although the total land area is about 2,800 square miles, the fertile, inhabitable portion is exceedingly small. The islands now form the base for a considerable commercial fishery.

Chapter XIX

FORMOSA, THE LUCHU, THE KURILE, AND THE SAKHALIN ISLANDS

FORMOSA OR TAIWAN

To the south and north of Japan proper are numerous islands, most of which for fifty years or more have been controlled by Japan. In fact, the only exception is Sakhalin. In 1905 a treaty gave Japan the southern half of Sakhalin, the northern half going to Russia. The most southerly of these island possessions of Nippon before 1941 is the large island of Formosa, or Taiwan, which lies about 660 miles south of Japan and about 200 miles north across the Bashi islands from Luzon in the Philippines. Formosa stretches from north to south for a distance of 260 miles and from east to west 90 miles, at is widest part. It covers an area of 13,887 square miles, or almost twice as much as the State of Maryland.

Formosa first became known to the western world five centuries ago when Portuguese navigators discovered this radiant island and called it Ilha Formosa, "Beautiful Island." The Chinese, who came later to the islands, called it Taiwan, "Terrace Bay," because of the natural green terraces rising like giant steps thousands of feet out of the sea. It is the magnificence of the east coast that justifies the Portuguese name of Formosa, "the Beautiful." Giant cliffs rise perpendicularly out of the Pacific to a height of 6,000 feet and for a distance of about 25 miles. They are said to be the highest in the world, arising directly from the sea. A scenic motor road cut in the wall of the cliffs has long been a tourist attraction.

There is a legendary history of Formosa that dates back many hundreds of years and appears in ancient Chinese manuscripts.

The old Chinese geographers believed in all seriousness that a dragon was responsible for the origin of Formosa. The dragon, an animal of unusual strength, lived in Foochow on the South China coast. While frolicking in the depths of the ocean one day, the dragon brought up mud and rock from the bottom and began to mold a semblance of itself. Thus the island was formed. Keelung, on the north end, resembles its head; the central mountain range with its high peaks represents its bristling back; and Cape Carambi its tail.

Formosa has two widely different areas: the eastern part, representing about two-thirds of the island, which is mountainous, and the western part, which is covered by fertile plains. The principal mountain chain runs lengthwise from the north to the south, near the east coast. Mount Morrison or Nitaka rises to 13,075 feet. The mountainous parts of the island are covered with primeval forests that cover over 6,000,000 acres. The mountain ranges have become the home of the native tribes, while the terraced foothills, valleys, and plains are inhabited by the Asiatic agriculturalists.

Formosan natives are of Malay and Indonesian origin and are believed to have inhabited the island for over 2,000 years. The real aborigines of Formosa number about 150,000 and are divided in two groups: 95,000 Chi-huan (green or wild savages), and 65,000 Pepo-huan (ripe or semicivilized barbarians). There are seven important tribes occupying some 670 villages in an area of over 7,000 square miles in the central mountain range.

The population of Formosa is 94 percent Chinese. More than 5,000,000 people live on the alluvial plain that stretches from north to south on the west coast. The Hok-Lo speak a native Chinese dialect called Amoy. In the lower ranges of the mountains and at the south cape are the Hok-Ka or "strangers," who speak the dialect of the mandarin or court Chinese. The second part of the population is made up of Japanese, totaling approximately 300,000 (not counting military forces) or 5.3 percent.

The Dutch, in 1624, were the first to attempt to bring Formosa under foreign control. They erected a fort near the town of Tainan. In the meantime, the Spaniards established themselves in the north and built two forts, but were finally driven out by the Dutch who became the absolute rulers. At the overthrow of the Ming Dynasty, in China, more than 100,000 Chinese fled to Formosa. Later, these Chinese immigrants became discontented with the Dutch rulers and rebellions followed.

When, in 1661, Cheng Ch'eng-kung, better known as Koxinga, was driven out of China by the Manchu forces, he set out with a large fleet and an army of 25,000 to capture Formosa. Supported by the rebellious Chinese, he besieged the Dutch fortress. The Dutch were overwhelmed and were forced to capitulate the following year. For more than twenty years the island was ruled by the conqueror. In 1683 China again took over Formosa and it remained part of the Manchu Empire for over 200 years. But the Chinese have a saying about Taiwan: "Every three years an uprising and every five years a rebellion." In 1874 the Japanese landed a military force, and withdrew only after the intervention of European powers. In 1895, following the Chino-Japanese War, Formosa was ceded to Japan and became the first Japanese colony.

The climate of Formosa is tropical and subtropical. Snow is rare even on the lofty mountaintops. May to August is the rainy season; September to December has rain to a lesser degree; January to April is the dry season. The agricultural regions suffer periodically from too much rainfall. Winter brings the northeastern monsoon from the Pacific and in the summer the southwestern monsoon blows in from the China Sea with its rain. This also is the typhoon season, these violent storms originating in the Pacific. Earthquakes are common, though seldom of great violence; sometimes there are as many as 300 a year. The last major earthquake occurred in 1935, when 15,000 people were injured and 54,000 houses were damaged.

The most important and modern harbor of Formosa is Keelung, situated on the northeastern point of the island on the Tansui River. Taihoku, eighteen miles south of Keelung, with a population of more than 250,000, is the largest city and the seat of the government. The city is divided into three walled sections, of which Jonai is the most modern, with its streets widened for motor traffic and with other modern improvements. Jonai is the Japanese residential section, and here, too, are the government buildings and the University of Taihoku.

Most of the forests on the mountains of Formosa are virgin stands of Chinese juniper, taiwania, cypress, red cedar, ebony, camphor, and oak. Some of these trees are estimated to be more than 2,000 years old and the taiwania is a giant in size. The forests yield rich tropical woods and have long been a principal source of camphor. The remaining forest vegetation is typical of the tropics. The cultivated western plain produces a large crop of rice, also sweet potatoes, pineapples, bananas, sugar and jute. The famous tea plantations are higher in the hills. Here the tender leaves of Formosa tea are picked by native women.

The forests are inhabited by monkeys, wild boars, deer, Asiatic bears and squirrels. Bats of various species are exceedingly common. The bird life is abundant though not so much as on the islands farther south. There are lizards and snakes and a great variety of insects.

The west-coast plain is overpopulated with Chinese immigrants who first covered the lowlands, then crowded the valleys and, finally, the foothills of the mountains, where their advance was stopped only by fear of the savage tribes in the mountain fastness. These aborigines are greatly feared by the Chinese who call them Seban, head-cutters, and even today head-hunting is not unknown. They live on inaccessible mountain slopes, reached only by narrow trails that wind through the camphor jungles and cross chasms by means of swinging suspension bridges made of bamboo and vines.

Actually, the natives are not unfriendly. They love bright beads and expect gifts from strangers. Though now disarmed by the Japanese, they were once past masters of jungle warfare, and no enemy was safe in their mountain haunts. They gave the Japanese a good deal of trouble before they were brought under control in 1910, and they have not forgotten their treatment by the conquerors.

THE LUCHU ISLANDS OR THE RYUKYU ARCHIPELAGO

The Luchu Islands form steppingstones from Japan proper south to Formosa. They are divided into two groups: the Okinawa, northern, and the Sakishima, southern.

The Luchus are mountainous and composed mainly of elevated coral reefs formed into tablelands and isolated hills. Near the northern end of the Luchus are two islands with active volcanoes, Nokono-Shima (3,500 feet) and Suwanose-Shima (2,700 feet).

The archipelago of 55 islands, with a land area of only 935 square miles, has a population of more than 577,000. The climate is semitropical, with very heavy summer rainfall. The summer is not too hot, owing to prevailing southerly winds. The maximum temperature reaches 96° F. and the minimum 38° F. In spite of the unfavorable climatic and physical conditions, the islands are heavily populated and almost every available piece of land is under cultivation. Sugar cane and sweet potatoes are the chief crops. Pineapples, bananas, indigo, and vermillion lacquer are also produced.

Okinawa, the largest island of the two groups, is 268 miles in circumference. On it are two cities: Naha, the capital and principal harbor, with a population of 60,500, and Shuri, three miles from Naha. From Naha a small railway runs to Yonabara and a branch line to the famous fishing village, Ichuma. Ichuma is of interest because here the women enjoy equal rights with the men, a thing unheard of anywhere else in the Orient until fairly recently, when China incorporated "equal rights" provisions in some of its civil codes.

Up to the seventeenth century, when the northern group was conquered by the Japanese, the Luchu Islands were under Chinese rule. In 1879 the Luchu king was deposed and sent to Japan, where he was given a noble title and no responsibility. In this way, all the Luchus became a province of Nippon.

THE KURILE ISLANDS

The Japanese-owned Kurile Islands extend in a 710-mile chain from the southern tip of Kamchatka Peninsula, a part of Siberia, to the northern end of Japan. Straits only a few miles wide at either end of the chain separate the islands from the territory of Russia and the larger Japanese islands. There are seven principal islands in the group and about twenty-five others of medium size; the total area is 3,944 square miles—a land area a little smaller than Connecticut, with a coast line, however, that would reach from Maine to Florida.

The Kuriles were discovered in 1634 by the Dutch navigator Martin de Vries. They have been a subject of dispute between Russia and Japan, as has also been the large island of Sakhalin lying between them and the mainland of Siberia. However, in 1876 Japan and Russia reached an agreement whereby Russia withdrew from the Kuriles and Japan withdrew from the northern half of Sakhalin.

Hot springs, boiling lakes and other volcanic features are found among the islands. The name Kurile itself is derived from the Russian *kurit*, "to smoke." Dense fogs surround the islands and hide the volcanic mountains that rise to a maximum of 7,783 feet.

The climate, though relatively temperate in the south, is, in general, harsh, because of the wind and fog. The temperature does not drop very low, averaging in the south from 22° in the coldest month (February) to 63° in the warmest month (August). The months from December to March average below freezing. Precipitation averages about forty inches per year.

Strong currents and masses of seaweed characterize the waters surrounding the island. Seals and sea otters were formerly found in abundance, but unrestricted hunting has almost completely destroyed them. Innumerable birds make the islands their home, and salmon abound in some of the streams. Bears are said to be numerous on the southernmost island, Kunashiri, which has extensive forests of pines. Wolves, foxes, sables, beavers, and other animals are also found in the Kuriles, but there is no rich variety of animal life. Iron, copper and sulphur are the best-known mineral resources.

The population of about 15,000 is made up mainly of Ainus, Kamchadals, or Kamchatkans, and Japanese. The Ainus differ considerably from the Japanese and other native groups of northeastern Asia. It has even been suggested that they have a remote connection with the white race, their complexion being sometimes fair and their features European. Although once warlike, they were conquered by the Japanese long ago and are now said to be gentle and rather spiritless.

SAKHALIN

The large island of Sakhalin, with a land area of 24,560 square miles, equal approximately to that of the State of West Virginia, lies north of the Japanese island Hokkaido, and is separated from the mainland of Asia by the Strait of Tatary, which varies in width from about 25 miles to 190 miles and often freezes at its narrowest part during the winter. Mountain ranges on the island rise in height from 2,000 to more than 5,000 feet. There are numerous fresh-water lakes and several short rivers, of which one, the Poronaya, is navigable for small craft for more than thirty miles. Much of the island is forested, with conifers predominating; the unforested areas form a bleak tundra.

Among the animals found on the island are bears—of which there is a very large type resembling the great Kadiak or Alaska brown bear—reindeer, musk deer, ermines, sables, otters, martens and foxes. The bird life is varied and is in the main similar to that of the Russian Asiatic mainland.

Soil and climate are both unfavorable to agriculture. Fishing is the most common occupation and fish provides the main food of the native population.

In 1905 the Treaty of Portsmouth gave Russia the northern part of the island and Japan the southern part. Recent figures on the population of the Russian half of the island are not available. The population of Karafuto, as the southern or Japanese half is called, was reported in 1938 as totaling approximately 340,000, of which about 330,000 were Japanese, the balance of the population including Koreans and Ainus. The Japanese have developed the coal deposits which are reported to be abundant and of good quality. Iron and gold are also mined.

THE COMMANDER ISLANDS

The Commander Islands, owned by Russia, lie between Kamchatka and the Aleutians. It is a matter of 250 miles eastward from the Commanders to the nearest Aleutian island and 140 miles to Kamchatka on the Siberian coast. It is said that the peaks of Kamchatka (which rise from 10,000 to 15,000 feet) can be seen from the Commanders on a clear day. The group consists of only two islands: the larger Bering Island and the smaller Copper Island.

Bering Island is fifty miles long and about ten miles wide. Its highest peak, Mount Steller, is 2,200 feet high. Copper Island is thirty miles long and averages only about two miles in width. Mount Stejneger is 2,100 feet high.

In spite of their proximity to the Asiatic mainland, there is no evidence that primitive men ever reached the Commander Islands. They were first mentioned in the journal of Commander Bering, who discovered the islands in 1741.

The fur seals that formerly frequented these islands in great numbers brought the islands to the public eye, especially in the last decade of the past century. With the year 1892 began a terrible slaughter on the open sea surrounding the islands, which depleted the herds at the rate of about 100,000 a year. Japanese poachers were active, and any attempt to follow a plan for conservation of the herds was frustrated for a number of years. As a result, by 1922 the rookeries were practically wiped out.

Another animal for which islands of this region have been known is the sea otter, which has one of the finest furs known. In recent years the Soviet Union has established an experimental station on Copper Island for the conservation of sea otters. The lonely little settlement consists of fewer than a dozen houses and a headquarters building under the direction of a Russian biologist.

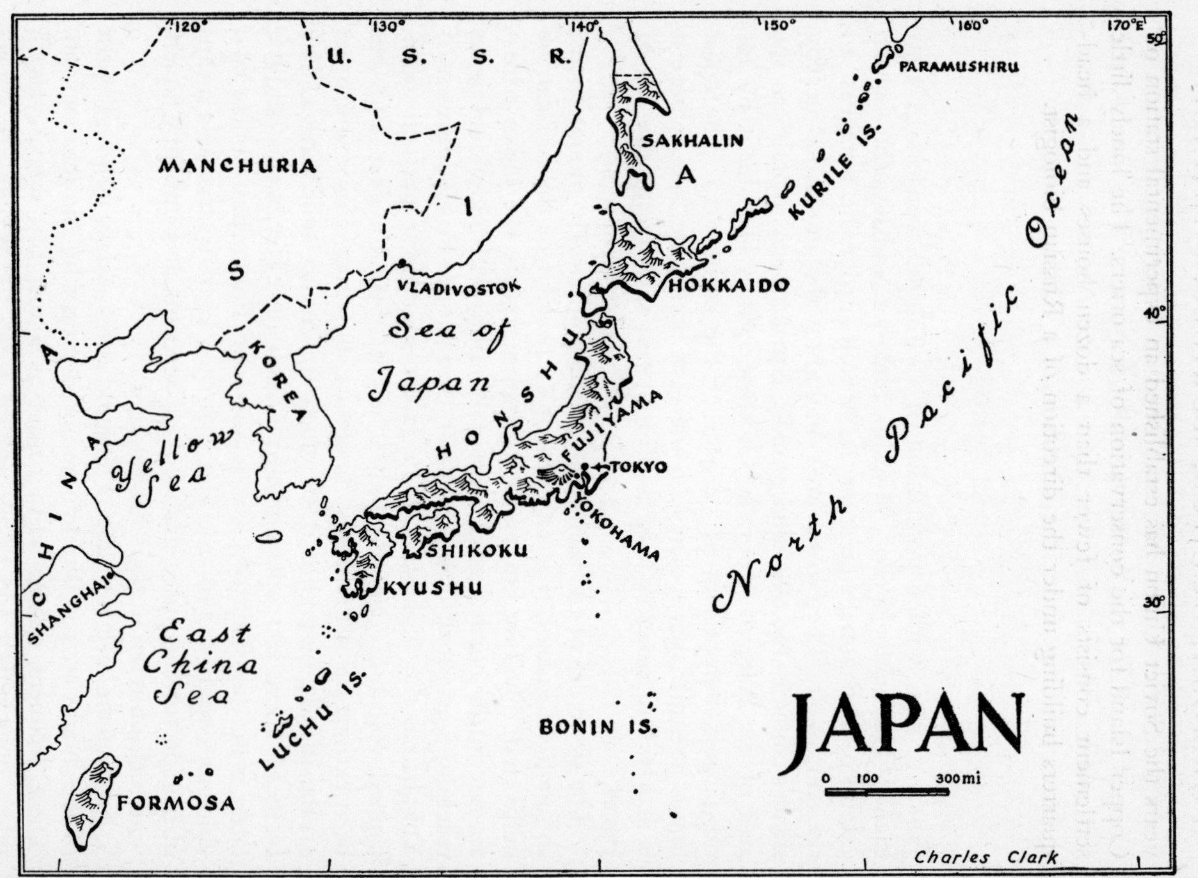
JAPAN
0 100 300mi
Charles Clark
U. S. S. R.
MANCHURIA
KOREA
VLADIVOSTOK
Sea of Japan
SAKHALIN
HOKKAIDO
KURILE IS.
PARAMUSHIRU
HONSHU
FUJIYAMA
TOKYO
YOKOHAMA
SHIKOKU
KYUSHU
BONIN IS.
LUCHU IS.
FORMOSA
SHANGHAI
CHINA
ASIA
Yellow Sea
East China Sea
North Pacific Ocean
120°
130°
140°
150°
160°
170°E
50°
40°
30°

Chapter XX

JAPAN

Japan proper, with a population of 72,223,000, consists of four islands—Hokkaido (Yezo), Honshu, Shikoku, and Kyushu—which extend in a diagonal line some 1,240 miles from the northeast to the southwest. Their total area, including the numerous nearby small islands, is 146,690 square miles, equal, approximately, to the area of the State of Montana. Of these islands Honshu is by far the largest, comprising 62 percent of the entire area. The coast line is irregular, particularly on the east, or Pacific, side, where it is nearly four times as long as on the west side, facing the Sea of Japan.

The structure of the islands is volcanic and largely mountainous; so much so, indeed, that only about 20 percent of the soil can be cultivated. The best known of the mountains are the Japan Alps—a range in the north-central part of Honshu, with individual peaks reaching a height of over 9,000 feet—and Mount Fuji, southwest of Yokohama, the highest peak in Japan, an almost perfect snow-capped volcanic cone rising to a height of 12,400 feet. Fuji has been extinct for many years. There are, however, active volcanoes on the islands, best known of which are Asama and Mihara. The former is about 100 miles north of Tokyo, near Karuizawa, and the latter is on the island of Oshima, south of Tokyo Bay. These two volcanoes are noted for the fact that their craters serve as a means of suicide for the many unsuccessful students and unhappy lovers who seek oblivion in their fiery depths.

Earthquakes are frequent, averaging three a day, although most of the shocks are too slight to be noted except by the seismograph. These frequent quakes seem to act as a sort of "safety valve"; when none is felt for any length of time, the people are apprehensive, fearing a severe quake, such as the one that wrought such havoc in Tokyo and Yokohama in 1923.

The range of climate is great. In the north, in Hokkaido, the summers are temperate and the winters cold, with deep snow. In the northern part of Honshu, snow falls heavily, but in central and southern Honshu the winters are mild and damp, with little snow, and the summers are hot and humid. Tokyo, the capital, is 3° of latitude south of Washington, D. C., and has a fairly similar climate, while that of Kyushu, farther south, approaches the tropical.

The plant life of Japan is varied. In the north are found forests and pasture lands well adapted to the grazing of cattle; many of the trees and flowers are similar to those found in the northern parts of the United States. The grass dries up in the autumn, and remains dead, brown, and brittle until the coming of spring. On Honshu and Kyushu are rice fields and the more hardy varieties of palms, as well as the plants and trees of the temperate zone. There are many flowers, both native and imported, some of which are so typical of Japan that when one sees the flower, one thinks of the land. Most of the flowers are seasonal. The seasons of their blooming are accompanied by special festivals and made the subject of poem and painting. The plum blooms in late February or early March, followed in turn by the camellia, the flowering cherry, the wistaria, the azalea, and the iris. At these times the country is literally a bower of bloom. Of the nonflowering trees, the giant cryptomeria, akin to the redwood, is the most impressive, the weeping willow the most graceful, and the maple, somewhat resembling the cut-leaf maple of the United States, the most colorful.

More than fifty species of mammals are found in the islands. In Hokkaido lives a form of Asiatic brown bear. The polar bear is a very rare visitor to the island, driven down with the northern ice packs. Black bears inhabit northern Honshu. There are other mammals of considerable variety, such as wild boars, deer, foxes, monkeys, hedgehogs and hares. There are eight species of land snakes, one of which, the mamushi, is poisonous and fairly common in the country districts. Besides a number of varieties of songbirds, there are such larger birds as ducks, pheasants, snipes, cranes, herons and ravens. Insect life abounds. In the summer months the cicada, the grasshopper, and the dragonfly are omnipresent. A favorite sport of children is to catch dragonflies on twigs smeared with a sticky gum. There are many flies and mosquitoes. The bite of the abu, or horsefly, is very painful, but soon passes; that of the buyu, or small black fly, cannot be felt at the time, but later becomes very irritating and, if scratched, may develop into a serious sore.

Although only a small percentage of the soil is arable, agriculture is one of the four great industries of the islands, the others being fishing, manufacturing, and production of silk through growing silk worms. The latter industry has, however, greatly diminished in recent years. In Hokkaido are grown the hardy cereal grains, as well as potatoes and apples, which have been introduced from North America. Most of the country's limited dairy products come from this region. Because of the lack of grain for dairy feed, the war has killed this last industry, which was beginning to make some progress.

In northern Honshu, wheat, barley, and millet are grown, as well as rice. Rice fields are everywhere. Before the war there were thousands of fields of mulberry trees, whose leaves were used to feed the silkworms; but they have now been cut down, for the most part, and rice planted in their place. Many fruits, such as apples, pears, peaches (as distinct from the native Japanese pear and peach), plums, grapes, cherries and strawberries, have been introduced from America, while such fruits as mandarin oranges, tangerines, persimmons, loquats, and many varieties of melons are grown and find a ready market. Bananas are brought in from Formosa. In the southern parts of Japan are the tea plantations. All the common vegetables are grown. Cabbages, potatoes, peas, beans, corn, soy beans, beets, carrots, lettuce, and celery find a prominent place in the diet, as well as taro and lotus root and edible seaweed.

The arable regions of Japan are cut up into thousands of tiny farms, of from a half acre to several acres, each farm supporting a family. Intensive cultivation is practiced, and the soil is constantly fertilized, much human excrement being used. As a result of unremitting labor, as many as four or five crops of some foodstuffs may be produced in a single year. Since the average farm is too small to be divided among the children, the eldest son usually inherits it, while the younger sons go to the city to find work in the mills or shops, where the most modern machinery is found side by side with some of the most primitive methods of manufacture.

Hydroelectric power is widely used, being produced by the many waterfalls found throughout the islands. Most of the manufacturing has been done with imported raw materials, including iron, cotton, wool, and rubber.

Markets for manufactured goods were sought abroad, with great success at first. Later, as foreign markets dwindled, goods were poured into the now subject countries of Asia, where at present the Japanese have no competition. The desire for raw materials, as well as the need for markets, has played a large part in Japan's policy of acquiring territory by aggression.

Fishing boats swarm over the Inland Sea, the Pacific, the Sea of Japan, and the waters of north Russia. Immense quantities of salmon, tuna, and other fishes are canned and dried for domestic and foreign consumption. The Pacific lobster, which is really a crayfish, is abundant, as are also crabs, shrimps and prawns. Whaling is an important industry, in which no attention is paid to the appeals of other nations to conserve the supply of whales, as has been the case with seal poaching in the Aleutians and elsewhere. In addition to oil, whales supply leather which, with sharkskins, has replaced cowhide and horsehide, both of which have disappeared from the civilian market. Whale meat is also sold in markets and put up in cans. The squid and the octopus are found in all market stalls. Mollusks are abundant and all kinds are used for food.

The production of cultured pearls has grown into a prosperous industry. Seed pearls or bits of pearl shell are inserted in the pearl oyster, which in the course of years covers the unwelcome substance and produces a pearl.

The Japanese people are a mixture of Mongolian and Malay with probably some trace of Ainu, the aboriginal race of Japan, now confined to reservations in Hokkaido and the Kuriles. The race is short and thickset, the trunk long in proportion to the legs, which are frequently bowed. The head is large in proportion to the body and is of a distinctive shape. Contrary to general opinion, the eyes do not slant; this is an illusion caused by the thick fleshy fold of skin at the inner end of the upper lid, making it seem to point downward. Lips and teeth are frequently prominent and protruding.

The diet of the people consists of little or no meat, some fish, and vegetables with rice, barley, millet, and seaweed. They do not eat bread or butter. Very little milk is produced, and cheese is not eaten—they consider it offensive and say that not even the Japanese rats will touch it! Such dairy products as have found a market have been consumed by foreigners and Japanese who have lived in foreign countries and acquired a taste for foreign foods. The diet seems meager, but the people perform prodigies of work on it.

The custom of eating polished rice has been responsible for a considerable amount of beriberi, a disease caused by a lack of vitamin A. There is a great deal of tuberculosis, caused at least in part, no doubt, by the fact that the people live in unheated houses during the cold, damp winters. There also seems to be a great deal of defective vision, as judged by the fact that almost every third individual among students and clerks wears glasses. This may be caused by deficient diet, or by the severe eyestrain brought about by the constant poring over intricate Japanese writing. Physical perfection, however, is an obsession with the Japanese, and to obtain it they subject themselves and their children to various "hardening processes," many of which are physically harmful. At any rate, those who survive them must be tough indeed, which is possibly the idea behind the system.

At the top of the social structure is the imperial family, the head of which is the emperor, who is known as *Tenshi* (Son of Heaven) or *Tenno* (Heavenly King). He is said to be the direct descendant of Jimmu Tenno, who, legend states, ascended the throne in 660 B.C., and who was the grandson of Amaterasu Omikami, the sun-goddess. It is true that the written history of Japan does not go back beyond 700 A.D., but all these things, even the divine descent of Jimmu, are taught in the schools as historical facts. The present emperor, Hirohito, is the 124th in line. After the imperial family comes the peerage, the army, the navy, and the people. The emperor, who is supposed to be a divine figure, is at once the embodiment of the sun-goddess and the father of his people, and theoretically owns the land and all its inhabitants. He is a mysterious figurehead; his person is considered so sacred that on one occasion the court physician could not even touch his flesh; he had to take the imperial pulse through a bit of thin silk. The emperor's name is never spoken. He is never discussed. Whoever has occasion to refer to him or to report an audience with him does so "with deepest awe."

In every Japanese school there is a vault—in many cases built like a temple or shrine, fire- and earthquakeproof—in which the emperor's picture is kept, with that of the empress. These pictures are brought out at stated times for adoration. If anything should happen to them, the principal would certainly resign, and might even commit hara-kiri. In a Tokyo primary school, attended by some 7,000 pupils, there was a serious fire several years ago. After the fire an American neighbor, the head of the American school, called on the principal; he sympathized, offered to do what he could to help, and expressed the hope that the children were all safe. The reply was typical: "You will rejoice to hear that the emperor's picture was unharmed, and that not a child was hurt."

When the emperor drives abroad in his maroon car the streets are cleared for two blocks in all directions, and the blinds of all windows above the first floor must be drawn—no one may look down upon him. The spaces in front of the gates of the Imperial Palace are filled with thousands of his subjects, their heads bowed in prayer.

And yet, in spite of the reverence and awe with which his subjects regard him, the emperor is powerless. His seal must appear on all imperial decrees, but he is told when and to what to affix it. For a number of years the nobility also has been quite without power, and the Diet or Parliament is no better than a rubber stamp. The army is in the saddle and has ruled the country since the occupation of Manchuria in 1931. Not the least of the reasons to account for this unhappy state of affairs is the series of assassinations of certain liberal statesmen who were not in sympathy with the policy of the mailed fist.

The country as a whole is orderly and law-abiding. Personal honesty seems to be the rule: articles left in public places are almost invariably returned. Crimes of violence, excepting political violence, are rare, and sex crimes are almost unknown. There are two principal reasons for this. First, the people have been trained through centuries to be patient with their lot. Second, the police are extraordinarily efficient and exercise a close supervision over all the actions of the people. The police make their own regulations, and then enforce them. They know everything that goes on in the home, the place of business, the school. Two instances will suffice. When the home of a certain American was robbed some years ago, everything stolen was returned by the police within two weeks, including some things he did not know had been taken. Sometime later, the American and a friend went on a three-day motor trip. The first night they stayed at an inn on the top of Mount Haruna, and answered the many questions of the long questionnaire that every guest has to fill out. The next morning they started out, with no definite objective, and got lost several times during the morning. About the middle of the afternoon they were passing through a small village, the name of which they never learned, when a policeman held up his hand and stopped the car. He called them both by name. He told them that they had spent the night in the inn at Haruna. He then informed them that in filling out the questionnaire they had neglected to give the names of the institutions with which they were connected. "Will you please fill these in?" he asked, giving them the proper forms. The police are omnipresent, omniscient, and omnipotent. The people respect and fear them, for they are incorruptible and harsh in their methods.

The greater part of the wealth of the country is in the hands of five great families, of which the best known are the Mitsui and the Mitsubishi. These are bankers, shipbuilders and operators, financiers and manufacturers. Between their prosperity and the poverty of the common people "there is a great gulf fixed." Salaries and wages are, in comparison with those earned in the United States, pitiful. A university professor may earn as much as $40 to $45 a month; a clerk or bookkeeper $18 to $25 a month; a laborer or farmer $8 to $12. The salary of the premier is $2,250 and that of a cabinet member $1,500. The emperor receives a fixed grant of $1,125,000 yearly, in addition to the income from his vast investments in the form of office buildings, hotels, and other property. (At the outbreak of the war, the yen was worth about twenty-three cents, which figure has been used in expressing the above incomes in dollars.)

There is no prosperous middle class such as we find in the United States. Most Japanese are forced by low incomes to live frugally. And even though the yen should mean as much to the average Japanese as a dollar does to us, salaries and wages are low by our standards. The people are content with little. The increasing scarcity of food and other commodities simply makes them tighten their belts and smile a little less spontaneously.

Of the Eta, or outcast, class, there are comparatively few remaining. This class originated among those who slaughtered animals for food and dealt in flesh and hides, which in the early days, according to Buddhist teachings, made a man unclean. There are still a few Eta villages in Japan, but their numbers are decreasing, for an Eta may, and occasionally does, migrate to some other part of Japan and start life afresh as a normal person.

At the outbreak of the war, three religions were recognized by the Japanese Government: Shinto, Buddhism, and Christianity, although it is true that the last two were subject to constant investigation and restriction. Shinto, the Way of the Gods, is the official religion, and is a cult of emperor and ancestor worship, with its own gods and demons. Shinto is very cleverly superimposed on other faiths, on the ground that bowing to the Imperial Palace and participating in other rites do not in any way conflict with either Buddhism or Christianity. In fact, in many houses both the Shinto shrine and the Buddhist altar may be found.

There is, in addition, a vast amount of superstition. Fox shrines are found everywhere, even on the roofs of the great department stores. Prayers and incantations are still said to ward off evil spirits. Certain seasons or days of the year are lucky or unlucky. For example, a girl who has had the misfortune of being born in the Year of the Horse finds it difficult to get a husband—so unlucky are the children supposed to be who were born in that year.

The educational system of Japan, to which American scholars have substantially contributed, is thorough and efficient. When one realizes that all learning has to be superimposed on the cumbersome system of character writing used by the Japanese, it is amazing that they have accomplished so much, and that the percentage of literacy is one of the highest in the world. Education is compulsory through the sixth grade, even though there are no free schools. Even in the government schools fees are paid—small, it is true, but large for a father who earns a wage of forty yen a month. The primary schools, which go through the sixth grade, are coeducational, although boys and girls never sit together. There is no coeducation in the middle, high, or normal schools, or in the universities, several of which have enrollments of well over 10,000.

This educational system is directed toward creating a state of individual repression. From the primary schools on, everything is regimented. The children are little automatons, and the principal orders his teachers about as a general does his officers. Even the sports are cut and dried, and entered into with deadly seriousness.

The people themselves are dominated by two forces—tradition and repression. The heavy hand of tradition may be illustrated by their capital city. The census of 1940 gave Tokyo a population of well over 7,000,000. It has large business districts and several large newspapers with a daily circulation running into the millions. Its modern subways are cool and clean, have indirect lighting and are decorated with vases of artificial flowers. The railroad trains coming into its three large stations arrive and start with such promptness that people set their watches by them. Yet, in this great city, the streets, with a very few exceptions, are not named, and the houses in a given area are numbered in the order of erection, without regard to their relative position. For years the newspapers have tried to bring about an adequate system of naming and numbering streets, but to no avail.

The hold of tradition is also evidenced in the written language. While there are two "alphabets" consisting of phonetic syllabic symbols, they are used only for special purposes. Books, magazines, and newspapers still use the Chinese-type characters, or ideographs, of which there are some 50,000. Even an educated man cannot write anything but comparatively simple sentences without a dictionary of characters at hand. The Japanese typewriter has been "simplified" to 3,000 characters, and a girl can learn to operate one in three years! Many societies and individuals have tried to institute a modern system of phonetic writing, but the force of tradition is too strong.

There is no such thing as individualism in Japan. From the time the child is old enough to go to school, he ceases to be an individual and becomes a unit in a group—a cog in a machine. First he belongs to the family. All his doings are decided for him by family council—his education, his subsequent occupation, his marriage, his future. If he fails he may commit suicide—not because of discouragement, but because through his failure his family has lost face. If his parents lose money and cannot see him through his education, it becomes an obligation upon the whole family or clan, not because of sympathy with the young man, but because the family would lose face if one of its members started something that he could not finish. If a Japanese businessman in a foreign city is about to become insolvent, the other Japanese merchants in the city will unite to help him out, for the same reason. These impersonal relations hold in all areas of life—family, school, university, place of business, state.

The Japanese is docile, law-abiding, uncomplaining, and long-suffering. His motto seems to be "*Shikata ganai*"—"It can't be helped." It is these very qualities that make him dangerous as an enemy. At present the civilian in Japan cannot get cotton, wool, leather, rubber, meat, or enough rice or vegetables to feed himself and his family. He does not, however, think of complaining. It would not even occur to him. He will carry through until the job is done or he is destroyed in the process. Knowing this, it is easier for us to understand the self-denying tenacity and perseverance of the Japanese civilian and the Japanese soldier. If the soldier cannot win, he will die rather than be taken prisoner. Not that he wants to die—life is as sweet to him as it is to us—but to be taken prisoner is disgraceful, and to give up his life for his emperor is glorious.

In Tokyo there is a great shrine, the Yasunkuni, where the names of all Japanese soldiers who have given their lives in battle are inscribed. They are thus deified, and, according to general belief, their spirits help the living in their struggle against the enemy. On the eve of battle, comrades fill their canteen cups with cold water and drink the toast, "Till we meet at Yasunkuni!" Then they charge the enemy. It is all part of a pattern that was cut for them centuries ago, and from which the Japanese people have not deviated. Nor will they, until the military power of Japan is destroyed and the people develop or are exposed to a new philosophy of life.

Children and adults alike are always in earnest. One will never see a group of Japanese laughing, joking, or "wise-cracking" as do Americans. Their conversation is always serious and earnest. "Earnest" is one of the most overworked words in their language. Nor have the Japanese a sense of humor such as the Chinese have. Slapstick comedy will appeal to them, as it does to a child; but a subtle joke or innuendo leaves their faces blank; and when the point is explained, the inevitable response is "*Ah, so desu ka!*" ("Is that so!"). We see a people sheeplike in their enthusiasm to follow, amenable to propaganda, who believe with fierce fanaticism that they are the seed of the sun, the beloved of the gods, the predestined saviors of civilization.

It is curious to recall that before and even after the Manchurian incident—as late as 1936, in fact—Japan was following the western path. It appeared to worship everything American. The streets of its cities were filled with American motorcars, the shops found a ready sale for American books and periodicals, and theaters showing American motion pictures were crowded. American styles of dress were copied by young men and women. Democratic ideas received a certain amount of sympathy. Even chewing gum began to be sold in the stores, and rhythmically moving jaws were actually seen in the streets.

Reactionary leaders, however, particularly in the army, viewed these tendencies not without alarm. Then followed the infamous incident of February 26, 1936, when young army officers murdered a number of cabinet ministers and made an attempt on the life of the premier. From then on the change began to make itself felt. The army and its satellites stirred up hatred against everything foreign. From that to Pearl Harbor was but a step.

TABLES AND FACTUAL SUMMARIES

FACTS ABOUT AUSTRALIA AND THE ISLANDS OF THE PACIFIC

	Number of Principal Islands	Ownership Prior to Dec. 7, 1941	Approximate Population	Approximate Length (statute miles)	Approximate Land Area (sq. miles)	Maximum Height (feet)	Annual Average Temperature (degrees Fahrenheit)*	Annual Average Rainfall (inches)*	Miscellaneous Information on Weather and Climate
AUSTRALIA	1	British Dominion	white 7,137,000 native 47,960	2,400	2,974,581	7,328	63° to 82°	5 to 165	Semitropical in north; cold months are June, July and August. Seasons vary with location.
NEW ZEALAND	2	British Dominion	white 1,600,000 Maori 90,900	1,000	103,410	12,349	50° to 60°	15 to 200	Climate temperate but cool; wettest months are May, June and July.
MELANESIA									
New Guinea	1	Netherlands, Great Britain, Australia	native 647,000 white 3,200 Asiatic 2,000 half-caste 200	1,500	342,232	16,404	80°	41	Climate tropical, varies with location. June to Oct. dry, Jan. to March wet.
Bismarck Arch.	2	Australian mandate	total 185,000 (mostly Papuans)	520	19,650	7,456	80°	75 to 105	Practically no change in seasons.
Solomons	10	Great Britain, Australian mandate	native 95,000 white 500 Chinese 200	720	14,600	10,171	82°	94 to 180	Climate damp and hot. Jan. to March rainy, June to August driest.
New Hebrides	12	Great Britain, France	native 60,000 Asiatic 1,000 white 1,000	535	5,700	6,195	76°	73 to 132	Climate damp and hot. Rainy season Nov. to May, driest season June to Oct.
New Caledonia	1	France	native 30,000 Asiatic 8,000 white 17,500	220	6,296	5,413	69° to 75°	32 to 109	Warmest months are Dec. to March. Rainfall varies with location.
Fijis	2	Great Britain	Fiji 107,100 Asiatic 104,000 white 4,000	325	7,083	4,450	78°	69 to 160	Climate tropical but pleasant. Rainy season Nov. to April.
NETHERLANDS INDIES									
Borneo	1	Netherlands, Great Britain	Indonesian 2,300,000 Chinese 200,000 white 6,000	875	280,000	13,451	80°	140	Climate tropical. Rainy season Nov. to May.
Sumatra	1	Netherlands	Indonesian 8,900,000 white 21,000	1,150	167,480	12,550	80°	95 to 139	Climate hot, damp. In the north Oct. wettest month; in south Dec. to Feb. wettest.
Java	1	Netherlands	Indonesian 47,000,000 Chinese 600,000 white 200,000	622	51,000	12,060	79°	80 to 327	Climate tropical, varies with location. Dec. to Feb. rainiest, May to August drier.
Celebes	1	Netherlands	Indonesian 3,089,000 white 4,550 Chinese 30,000	800	83,810	11,467	70° to 90°	21 to 116	Climate tropical. East monsoon May to Nov., west monsoon Dec. to April.
Lesser Sundas	6	Netherlands, Portugal	total 6,215,000	1,000	59,732	12,221	78°	60	Climate relatively dry. Dry season July to Oct.
Moluccas Proper	2	Netherlands	total 284,000	475	12,796	4,000	78°	118	Climate tropical, wet. Monsoons irregular.
PHILIPPINES	2	United States	total 16,000,000	1,150	114,400	10,312	80°	90	Climate tropical. Jan. to May dry season, June to Oct. rainy. April and May hot season.

MICRONESIA Palaus	1	Japan	Kanaka 6,360 Japanese 9,500 Chamorro 200	90	175	643	81°	137	Climate tropical. May to Dec. rainiest months.
Carolines	4	Japan	native 36,000 Japanese 3,000	1,775	380	3,000	82°	119 to 254	Climate tropical. April to August rainiest months.
Marianas	2	United States, Japan	native 4,300 Japanese 39,000	503	450	2,700	80°	80 to 100	Climate semitropical. July to Oct. rainy.
Marshalls	2	Japan	native 9,900 Japanese 500	700	160	33	80°	77 to 158	Climate tropical. In north, May to Oct. warmest; in south, Oct. to Feb. warmest.
Gilberts	16	Great Britain	native 27,300 half-caste 200 white 100	500	166	20	82°	40 to 100	Climate tropical. Dec. to Feb. rainy season.
Bonins	10	Japan	total 5,700	250	40	1,471	72°	62	Climate semitropical. May rainiest month, Jan. and Feb. coolest.
POLYNESIA Tongas	2	Great Britain	Tongan 32,800 white 400 others 800	200	250	3,020	77°	78 to 88	Climate semitropical. Dec. to March wettest, May to Nov. driest.
Samoa	3	United States, New Zealand	native 49,000 white 3,000	228	1,295	4,000	79°	90 to 185	Climate semitropical. Oct. to March rainy months.
Societies	6	France	native 24,800 white 6,200	450	657	7,349	78°	55	Climate warm, pleasant. Dec. to April rainy season.
Marquesas	8	France	total 2,500	235	490	400	70° to 90°	61 to 94	Nov. to May rainy season.
Hawaiian	8	United States	Asiatic 237,600 half-caste 37,600 native 21,000 white 88,200 others 8,400	1,578	6,412	13,835	75°	25	Climate warm, pleasant. No rainy or dry season.
Tuamotu	3	France	total 4,500	1,300	330	1,315	80°	62 to 87	Climate warm. Hurricanes likely from Nov. to March.
ALEUTIANS	30	United States	Aleut 1,000 white 300	1,200	.....	9,387	39°	63	Climate foggy, damp, windy, stormy, cold.
GALÁPAGOS	5	Ecuador	total 2,000	275	2,800	5,000	74°	8	Climate hot and dry.
FORMOSA	1	Japan	Asiatic 5,609,000 white 200	260	13,887	13,075	71°	54 to 200	Climate semitropical, varies with location. Dec. and Jan. rainy.
LUCHUS	3	Japan	total 577,000	985	935	3,485	71°	84	Climate mild. Most rain May to Oct.
KURILES	7	Japan	native 500 Japanese 14,500	710	3,944	7,783	50° to 68°	39	Climate foggy, damp. Sept. to June coldest months.
JAPAN	4	Japan	total 72,223,000	1,240	146,690	12,400	36° to 50°	31 to 125	Central Japan temperate; climate varies with location.

* In some cases the annual average temperature varies greatly at different stations on the same island or island group. Thus, in Japan, "annual average temperature 36° to 50°" means that the annual average temperature at a northerly station in Japan is 36°, while that at a southerly station is 50°.

Likewise, the annual average rainfall may vary with latitude, mountain ranges, etc. Where the variation is considerable it is shown by giving the minimum monthly mean and the maximum monthly mean.

For comparison, the annual average temperature in New York, N. Y., is 52° and the annual average rainfall in the same place is 42 inches.

	North Temperate					Malay Regions							
	Aleutians	Kuriles	Japan	Luchus	Formosa	Philippines	Malay Peninsula	Sumatra	Java	Borneo	Lesser Sundas	Celebes	Moluccas
Elephants							×	×		*			
Rhinoceroses							×	×	×	×			
Tapirs							×	×					
Wild cattle						×	×	*	×	×	*	×	*
Goat antelopes (serows)			×		×		×	×					
Deer (sambars and sikas)			×		×	×	×	×	×	×	×	×	×
Barking deer (muntjacs)					×		×	×	×	×			
Mouse deer						×	×	×	×	×			
Wild pigs			×	×	×	×	×	×	×	×	×	×	×
Babirusas												×	
Sea cows (dugongs)				×	×	×	×	×	×	×	×	×	×
Bears	×	×	×		×		×	×		×			
Weasels, Martens	×	×	×		×		×	×	×	×			
Otters, Sea otters	×	×	×		×	×	×	×	×	×			
Badgers			×		×	×	×	×	×	×			
Wild dogs, Wolves, Foxes	×	×	×				×	×	×				
Civets and civetlike animals					×	×	×	×	×	×	×	×	×
Mongooses					×	×	×	×	×	×			
Tigers							×	×	×				
Leopards and other cats		×			×	×	×	×	×	×	*		
Seals, Sea lions, Fur seals	×	×	×										
Orangutans								×		×			
Gibbons							×	×	×	×			
Monkeys			×		×	×	×	×	×	×	×	×	
Proboscis monkeys										×			
Loris, Tarsiers (lemurlike)						×	×	×	×	×		×	
Flying lemurs (colugos)						×	×	×	×	×			
Fruit bats (flying foxes)				×	×	×	×	×	×	×	×	×	×
Insect-eating bats		×	×	×	×	×	×	×	×	×	×	×	×
Tree shrews						×	×	×	×	×			
Shrews	×	×	×	×	×	×	×	×	×	×	×	×	×
Hedgehogs					×	×							
Gymnures (ratlike insectivores)						×	×	×	×	×			
Scaly anteaters (pangolins)					×	×	×	×	×	×			
Rabbits	×	×	×	×	×			×	+				
Squirrels and flying squirrels	×	×	×		×	×	×	×	×	×	×	×	
Rats and mice	×	×	×	×	×	×	×	×	×	×	×	×	×
Old World porcupines					×	×	×	×	×	×	×		
Kangaroos and Wallabies													
Tree kangaroos													
Flying phalangers, Phalangers											×	×	×
Koalas (native bears)													
Wombats													
Bandicoots													×
Marsupial wolves, Tasmanian devils													
Marsupial cats													
Marsupial mice													
Marsupial anteaters (banded anteaters)													
Marsupial moles													
Spiny anteaters (echidnas)													
Duck-billed platypuses													

THE ISLANDS OF THE PACIFIC

Micronesia						Australia, New Zealand, Melanesia									Polynesia						South America	
Bonins	Marianas	Palaus	Carolines	Marshalls	Gilberts	New Guinea	Australia	Tasmania	Bismarck Arch.	Solomons	New Hebrides	New Caledonia	Fijis	New Zealand	Samoa	Tongas	Marquesas	Tuamotu	Societies	Hawaii	Juan Fernández	Galápagos
							+															
												+		+						+		
						*	*		*	*	*	*	*	+	*	*	*	*	*	+		
×	×	×	×	×		×	×		×	×												
						*	*															
								×	×					×						×	×	×
×	×	×	×			×	×		×	×	×	×	×		×	×						
×	×	×	×	×		×	×	×	×	×	×	×	×	×	×	×				×		×
							+							+								
*	*	*	*	*	*	×	×	×	×	×	*	*	*	*	*	*	*	*	*	*	+	×
						×	×	×	×													
						×	×															
						×	×	×	×	×												
							×															
							×	×														
						×	×	×	×													
								×														
						×	×	×	×													
						×	×	×														
							×															
							×															
						×	×	×														
							×	×														

× Native.
* Introduced by man long ago.
\+ Introduced by man recently.

	Aleutians	Kuriles	Japan	Luchus	Formosa	Philippines	Malay Peninsula	Sumatra	Java	Borneo	Lesser Sundas	Celebes	Moluccas	Bonins	Marianas	Palaus	Carolines	Marshalls	Gilberts	New Guinea	Australia	Tasmania	Bismarck Arch.	Solomons	New Hebrides	New Caledonia	Fijis	New Zealand	Samoa	Tongas	Marquesas	Tuamotu	Societies	Hawaii	Juan Fernández	Galápagos
Cassowaries													×							×	×		×													
Emus																					×															
Kiwis																												×								
Penguins																					×	×						×								×
Loons	×	×	×		+																															
Grebes		×	×	×	×	×	×	×	×	×	×	×	×							×	×	×	×	×	×	×		×								
Albatrosses, Petrels	×	×	×											×	×	×					×	×	×	×	×	×	×	×			×	×	×	×	×	×
Tropic birds														×			×	×	×		×		×	×			×		×	×	×	×	×	×		×
Pelicans					×	×		×	×	×										×	×	×														×
Boobies						×			×	×	×	×	×			×	×		×	×	×		×	×	×		×	×	×	×	×	×	×	×		×
Cormorants	×	×	×			×	×	×	×	×	×	×			+	×				×	×	×	×	×												×
Frigate birds						×	×	×	×	×	×	×	×		×	×	×	×	×	×	×	×	×	×	×	×	×		×	×	×	×	×	×		×
Herons, Bitterns		×	×	×	×	×	×	×	×	×	×	×	×	×	×	×	×	×	×	×	×	×	×	×	×	×	×	×	×	×	×	×	×	×		×
Storks			×		×	×	×	×	×	×	×	×								×	×															
Ibises, Spoonbills		×	×	×	×	×	×	×	×	×	×	×	×							×	×	+		×												
Flamingos																																				×
Ducks, Geese	×	×	×	×	×	×	×	×	×	×	×	×	×	×	×	×	×	×	×	×	×	×	×	×	×	×	×	×	×	×	×	×	×	×		×
Hawks, Eagles	×	×	×	×	×	×	×	×	×	×	×	×	×	×	+	×	+			×	×	×	×	×	×	×	×	×	×	×			×	×	×	×
Falcons	×	×	×	×	×	×	×	×	×	×	×	×	×			+				×	×	×	×		×	×	×	×							×	
Megapodes						×			×	×	×	×	×		×	×				×	×		×	×	×											
Grouse	×	×	×																																	
Quails, Pheasants		×	×	×	×	×	×	×	×	×	×	×	×		+					×	×	×	×					×								
Bustard quails				×	×	×	×	×	×		×	×	×							×	×	×	×	×		×										
Cranes			×		×	×	×													×	×															
Rails, Coots		×	×	×	×	×	×	×	×	×	×	×	×	×	×	×	×		+	×	×	×	×	×	×	×	×	×	×	×	×	×	×	×		×
Kagus																										×										
Bustards			×																	×	×															
Jaçanas						×	×	×	×	×	×	×	×							×	×															
Snipes, Plovers, etc.	×	×	×	×	×	×	×	×	×	×	×	×	×	×	×	×	×	×	×	×	×	×	×	×	×	×	×	×	×	×	×	×	×	×		×
Skuas, Jaegers	×	×	×	×	×																×	×					×									×
Gulls or Terns	×	×	×	×	×	×	×	×	×	×	×	×	×	×	×	×	×	×	×	×	×	×	×	×	×	×	×	×	×	×	×	×	×	×		×
Auks, Murres	×	×	×																																	
Pigeons		×	×	×	×	×	×	×	×	×	×	×	×	×	×	×	×	×		×	×	×	×	×	×	×	×	×	×	×	×	×	×			×
Parrots, Lories						×	×	×	×	×	×	×	×				×			×	×	×	×	×	×	×	×	×	×	×	×	×	×			
Cuckoos		×	×	×	×	×	×	×	×	×	×	×	×	×	×	×	×	×	×	×	×	×	×	×	×	×	×	×	×	×	×	×	×			×
Owls	×	×	×	×	×	×	×	×	×	×	×	×	×		+	×	×			×	×	×	×	×	×	×	×	×	×	×				×		×
Frogmouths							×	×	×	×										×	×	×		×												
Owlet frogmouths													×							×	×	×				×										
Nightjars			×	×	×	×	×	×	×	×	×	×	×			×				×	×	+	×	×		×										
Swifts		×	×	×	×	×	×	×	×	×	×	×	×		×	×	×			×	×	+	×	×	×	×	×	+	×	×	×		×			
Hummingbirds																																			×	
Kingfishers		×	×	×	×	×	×	×	×	×	×	×	×		×	×	×			×	×	×	×	×	×	×	×	×	×	×	×	×	×			
Bee eaters				+		×	×	×	×	×	×	×	+							×	×		×	+												
Rollers		×	×	+	+	×	×	×	×	×	×	×	×							×	×	+	×	×				+								
Hoopoes		×	×	+	+		+	+		+																										
Hornbills						×	×	×	×	×	×	×	×							×			×	×												
Trogons						×	×	×	×	×																										
Barbets					×	×	×	×	×	×																										
Woodpeckers, etc.		×	×	×	×	×	×	×	×	×	×	×																								

THE ISLANDS OF THE PACIFIC

	Aleutians	Kuriles	Japan	Luchus	Formosa	Philippines	Malay Peninsula	Sumatra	Java	Borneo	Lesser Sundas	Celebes	Moluccas	Bonins	Marianas	Palaus	Carolines	Marshalls	Gilberts	New Guinea	Australia	Tasmania	Bismarck Arch.	Solomons	New Hebrides	New Caledonia	Fijis	New Zealand	Samoa	Tongas	Marquesas	Tuamotu	Societies	Hawaii	Juan Fernández	Galápagos
Broadbills					×	×	×	×	×	×																										
South American ovenbirds																																		×		×
Tyrant flycatchers																																			×	×
Pittas			×	×	×	×	×	×	×	×	×	×	×							×	×		×	×												
Lyrebirds																					×															
Larks		×	×	×	×	×			×	×	×									×	×															
Swallows		×	×	×	×	×	×	×	×	×	×	×	×			+				×	×	×	×	×	×	×	×	+					×			×
Cuckoo shrikes			×	×	×	×	×	×	×	×	×	×	×			×	×			×	×	×	×	×	×	×	×	+	×	×						
Bulbuls			×	×	×	×	×	×	×	×	×		×	×													+									
Wagtails, Pipits	×	×	×	×	×	×	×	×	×	×	×	×	+							×	×	×						×								
Dippers, Wrens	×	×	×	×	×																															
Mockingbirds																																				×
Thrushes		×	×	×	×	×	×	×	×	×	×	×	×	×		+				×	×	×	×	×	×	×	×		×					×	×	
Accentors		×	×		×																															
Babblers					×	×	×	×	×	×	×	×								×	×	×					×									
Warblers		×	×	×	×	×	×	×	×	×	×	×	×	×	×	×	×			×	×	×	×	×	×	×	×	×			×	×	×			
Flycatchers		×	×	×	×	×	×	×	×	×	×	×	×	×	×	×	×			×	×	×	×	×	×	×	×	×	×	×	×		×	×		
Whistlers						×	×	×	×	×	×	×	×			×				×	×	×	×	×	×	×	×	×	×	×						
Shrikes		×	×	×	×	×	×	×	×	×	×									×																
Wood swallows						×		×	×	×	×	×	×			×				×	×	×	×		×	×	×									
Starlings		×	×	×	×	×	×	×	×	×	×	×	×	×	×	×	×			×	×		×	×	×	×	×	×	×	×						
Orioles					×	×	×	×	×	×	×	×	×							×	×															
Drongos					×	×	×	×	×	×	×	×	×							×	×	+	×	×												
Bell magpies																				×	×	×														
Crows		×	×	×	×	×	×	×	×	×	×	×	×		×					×	×	×	×	×		×								×		
Bowerbirds																				×	×															
Birds of paradise													×							×	×															
Parrotbills			×		×																															
Titmice		×	×	×	×	×	×	×	×	×	×																	×								
Nuthatches		×	×		×	×	×	×	×	×										×	×															
Creepers		×	×			×														×	×															
Waxwings		×	×	×	×																															
Flowerpeckers					×	×	×	×	×	×	×	×	×							×	×	×	×	×												
Sunbirds						×	×	×	×	×	×	×	×							×	×		×	×												
White-eyes			×	×	×	×	×	×	×	×	×	×	×	+	×	×	×			×	×	×	×	×	×	×	×	×	×							
Honey eaters											×	×	×		×	×	×			×	×	×	×	×	×	×	×	×	×	×				×		
Wood warblers																																				×
Troupials																																				×
Finches	×	×	×	×	×	×	×	×	×					×																						×
Hawaiian honey creepers																																		×		
Weaver finches					×	×	×	×	×	×	×	×	×			×	×			×	×	×	×	×	×	×	×		×				+			

The symbol × means that one or more species are either resident or present at certain seasons. In the case of seabirds, particularly albatrosses and petrels, it may mean that examples have been observed in neighboring waters rather than *on* the islands. The indicated presence of a seabird therefore offers no assurance that it nests at the island referred to.

Gulls are listed with their family relatives, the terns, but there are no gulls at any of the Central Pacific islands.

The symbol + means that the birds have been recorded from the islands indicated but that they are unlikely to be found there regularly.

Blank spaces represent in certain instances gaps in present knowledge rather than the assured absence of the birds.

DISTRIBUTION OF REPTILES AND AMPHIBIANS AMONG THE ISLANDS OF THE PACIFIC

FAMILY	PHILIPPINES	NETHERLANDS INDIES	MELANESIA	POLYNESIA	MICRONESIA	GALÁPAGOS
Leathery turtles *Dermochelyidae*	×	×	×			
Sea turtles *Cheloniidae*	×	×	×	×	×	×
Terrapins *Emydidae*	×	×	×			
Tortoises *Testudinidae*		×				×
Snappers *Chelydridae*			×			
Snake-necked tortoises *Chelyididae*			×			
Pitted-shell tortoises *Carettochelydidae*			×			
Soft-shelled tortoises *Amydidae*	×	×				
Crocodiles *Crocodylidae*	×	×	×		×	
Geckos *Gekkonidae*	×	×	×	×	×	×
Iguanids *Iguanidae*			×			×
Agamids *Agamidae*	×	×	×			
Skinks *Scincidae*	×	×	×	×	×	
Limbless skinks *Dibamidae*	×	×	×			
True lizards *Lacertidae*		×				
Monitor lizards *Varanidae*	×	×	×		×	
Scale-footed lizards *Pygopodidae*		×	×			
"Blind worms" *Anguidae*		×				
Bornean lizards *Lanthanotidae*		×				
Blind snakes *Typhlopidae*	×	×	×	×	×	
Boas; pythons *Boidae*	×	×	×	×		
Cylinder snakes *Anilidae*		×				
Iridescent snakes *Xenopeltidae*	×	×				
Ordinary snakes *Colubridae*	×	×	×			×
Cobras; corals &c *Elapidae*	×	×	×			
Sea snakes *Hydrophidae*	×	×	×	×	×	
Pit vipers *Crotalidae*	×	×				
Wormlike amphibia *Caeciliidae*	×	×				
Disk-tongued frogs *Discoglossidae*	×					
Toad-frogs *Pelobatidae*	×	×				
Toads *Bufonidae*	×	×				
Southern frogs *Leptodactylidae*		×	×			
Tree frogs *Hylidae*		×	×			
Ranid tree frogs *Polypedatidae*	×	×				
Ordinary frogs *Ranidae*	×	×	×	×		
Narrow-mouthed frogs *Brevicipitidae*	×	×	×			

INDEX

INDEX

INDEX

INDEX

INDEX

INDEX

INDEX

INDEX

INDEX

Books That Live

The Norton imprint on a book means that in the publisher's estimation it is a book not for a single season but for the years.

PART 1

FREE YOUR MIND

CALL TO ADVENTURE

1. Becoming Limitless
2. Why This Matters Now
3. Your Limitless Brain
4. How to Read and Remember This (and Any) Book

PART 2

LIMITLESS MINDSET

INITIATION

DISPELLING THE 7 LIES OF LEARNING

1. Intelligence is fixed
2. We only use 10% of our brains
3. Mistakes are failures
4. Knowledge is power
5. Learning new things is difficult
6. The criticism of other people matters
7. Genius is born, not made

PART 3

LIMITLESS MOTIVATION

REVELATION

PURPOSE

ENERGY

SMALL SIMPLE STEPS

FLOW

PART 4

LIMITLESS METHODS

TRANSFORMATION

FOCUS

Calm Your Mind
Breathing
Schedule Time for Distractions

STUDY

Active Recall
Manage the State You're In
Music for the Mind
Take Note of Taking Notes

MEMORY

Visualization
Association
Emotion
Location

SPEED READING

Visual Pacer
Peripheral Vision
Comprehension

THINKING

The Thinking Hats
How Are You Smart?
Your Learning Style
Mental Models
Thinking Exponentially

LIMITLESS YOU

THE REWARD & RETURN

Praise for

LIMITLESS

"Jim Kwik knows how to get the maximum out of me as a human being."

— **WILL SMITH**

"While many authors claim to teach some amazing skill, no skill is as powerful as learning how to learn. It is the superpower from which all others grow. . . . I've seen with my own eyes what can be done with this book's triad of motivation, mindset, and method. Read on and apply what you learn. You just might amaze yourself."

— **ERIC SCHURENBERG**, CEO, Fast Company & Inc.

"My research on Alzheimer's underlines the importance of not only protecting your brain from injury but also of challenging yourself through continued learning. Jim Kwik has lectured, with great feedback, at the Cleveland Clinic Lou Ruvo Center for Brain Health to our staff, caregivers, and patients; he is the expert on brain fitness and accelerated learning."

—**JEFFREY L. CUMMINGS, M.D., SC.D.**, Founding Director, Cleveland Clinic Lou Ruvo Center for Brain Health; Director, Center for Neurodegeneration and Translational Neuroscience; Professor and Vice Chair for Research, Department of Brain Health, University of Nevada–Las Vegas (UNLV)

"Where I empower women about money matters, Jim Kwik empowers people to take learning into their own hands. Our mind is our greatest wealth-building asset. When you read *Limitless*, you'll not only get smarter, you'll accomplish things you never thought possible."

— **NICOLE LAPIN**, TV news anchor, money expert, and #1 *New York Times* best-selling author of *Rich Bitch, Boss Bitch* and *Becoming Super Woman*

"Warriors throughout time prepare and focus. They are unrelenting. Jim Kwik helps you to conquer your brain and hold your ground against the forces of distraction and negative thinking. His book *Limitless* is a must-read for an unstoppable mind."

— **GERARD BUTLER**, award-winning actor and producer

"While I was at GE, Jim Kwik coached our executive team and spoke at many of our company meetings with high reviews. He is a world-class expert at delivering the training and tools that high-impact teams need to elevate their organization."

— **BETH COMSTOCK**, former Chief Marketing Officer and Vice Chair at General Electric and best-selling author of *Imagine It Forward*

"*Limitless* is an uplifting exploration of our natural human gifts and a groundbreaking toolkit for how to make the most of them."

— **SIR KEN ROBINSON**, educator and *New York Times* best-selling author

"I hang on every word out of Jim Kwik's mouth. . . . He has such a powerful ability to help people unlock abilities that they never even knew they had."

— **TOM BILYEU**, CEO of Impact Theory and co-founder of Quest Nutrition

"*Limitless* is the perfect companion to anyone who wishes to spark meaningful change. In this book, Jim will show you how to unleash your mind, your drive, and your life."

— **LISA NICHOLS**, speaker, CEO, and *New York Times* best-selling author of *No Matter What!*

"When achieving breakthroughs, we must face skepticism and the deeply held conventional thinking that's been drilled into so many of us. *Limitless* teaches you how to dispel the 7 lies of learning that are holding your true genius back. . . . Your brain won't be the same after this book!"

— **NICK ORTNER**, *New York Times* best-selling author of *The Tapping Solution* and *The Tapping Solution for Manifesting Your Greatest Self*

"In *Limitless*, Jim Kwik shares methods for unlocking your potential. He guides you, step by step, to become the person you want to be with his simple-to-start brain-enhancing and learning habits."

— **BJ FOGG, PH.D.**, founder of the Behavior Design Lab at Stanford University and *New York Times* best-selling author of *Tiny Habits*

"Jim Kwik is like a personal trainer for your brain. He had coached my team on accelerated learning strategies to help them sharpen their focus, productivity, and mental performance. I've always believed you win in your mind first, then step onto the playing field, not the other way around. Read this book, there are no limits."

— **ALEX RODRIGUEZ**, 3-time MVP, 14-time All-Star, World Series Champion, and CEO of A-Rod Corp

"Transformation begins with preparing your mind for change. By the end of *Limitless*, you will believe in your untapped potential. New levels of success are possible and achievable with Jim Kwik as your guide."

— **JACK CANFIELD**, award-winning speaker, co-creator of the Chicken Soup for the Soul® series, and *New York Times* best-selling author of *The Success Principles*

"Memory is crucial to happiness, as Jim Kwik so beautifully explained during one of my most popular podcasts episodes ever. In his book *Limitless,* he"ll challenge you to do some crazy ish, but I swear you'll train your mind to conquer your days to live your best life. Best of all? You'll realize you are enough."

— **JEANNIE MAI**, Emmy & NAACP award-winning entertainer/producer, co-host of *The Real*

"In the same way that I help students and adults overcome their fears related to numbers and arithmetic, Jim Kwik helps people overcome their limiting beliefs about learning. *Limitless* contains the practical and proven speed-reading, studying, and memory methods we can all count on!"

— **SCOTT FLANSBURG**, The Human Calculator®, Guinness World Record holder, founder of the National Counting Bee, and best-selling author of *Math Magic*

"If you think you can't read faster, remember more, or get unstuck, this book is for you. It will change your mindset, motivate you, and help you achieve what you never thought possible."

— **DAVE ASPREY**, CEO, founder of Bulletproof 360, Inc., and *New York Times* best-selling author of *Super Human*

"Sleep has a huge impact on brain health, and so does training your mind for memory, learning continuously, and defeating negative thoughts. *Limitless* gives you the toolkit for long-lasting cognitive health. The 10 recommendations Jim shares for generating limitless brain energy are worth the price of the book alone."

— **MICHAEL J. BREUS, PH.D.**, Clinical Psychologist, a Diplomate of the American Board of Sleep Medicine, a Fellow of The American Academy of Sleep Medicine, and best-selling author of *The Power of When*

"The goal of the USC Performance Science Institute is to help students, entrepreneurs, and organizations compete and excel through applied, science-based practices. Jim Kwik's workshop at USC was among our most valued and highest-rated. Jim's accelerated learning strategies are proven and powerful. *Limitless* is essential reading for anyone who wants to challenge the limits of mental performance."

— **DAVID BELASCO**, co-founder of the USC Performance Science Institute, Executive Director, Lloyd Greif Center for Entrepreneurial Studies, and Adjunct Professor, Entrepreneurship

"When it comes to learning faster and keeping your mental game strong, Jim Kwik is the guy. Get *Limitless* for a better brain. Save the brain!"

— **STEVE AOKI**, two-time Grammy-nominated artist, musician, DJ, music producer, entrepreneur, founder of the Aoki Foundation for brain science and research and author of *Blue*

"Our organization empowers people to change the world. Engaging 4.5 million change-makers requires focus, discipline, and fast thinking. Jim Kwik's three-pronged Limitless model has helped our team upgrade their minds to better solve challenging problems and create greater social impact."

— **MARC KIELBURGER**, co-founder of the We Movement, humanitarian and activist for children's rights, columnist, and *New York Times* best-selling author of *Me to We*

"Exponential change requires a mental toolkit that amplifies creativity, rapid learning, global thinking, and optimism. *Limitless* is essential reading for anyone looking to expand the potential of their mind and advance beyond what is believed possible."

— **PETER H. DIAMANDIS**, Chairman and founder of XPRIZE Foundation, co-founder and Chairman of the Singularity University, and *New York Times* best-selling author of *Abundance*

"Taking care of our brains is an integral part of health and well-being. *Limitless* gives you the power to train and optimize your mind so you can realize your full potential."

— **MAIA AND ALEX SHIBUTANI**, two-time Olympic medalist figure skaters, three-time world medalists, two-time U.S. champions, and authors of the Kudo Kids series

"Jim Kwik's methods for learning, memory, and thinking are so empowering. . . . Producing a record amount of content, globally, requires incredible attention to detail. Thanks to Jim's teachings, our hosts are thinking better, recalling more, and prioritizing brain health for our success as well as their own. This book is a must-read!"

— **MARIA MENOUNOS**, host of the *Better Together with Maria* podcast, CEO of @afterbuzztv, Emmy Award–winning journalist and *New York Times* best-selling author of *The EveryGirl's Guide to Diet and Fitness*

"As somebody who puts lots of emphasis on exercising the brain and not just the body, I found Jim Kwik's work very empowering. *Limitless* will take you to incredible places you never expected."

— **NOVAK DJOKOVIC**, professional tennis player, winner of 17 Grand Slam singles titles

"My research on Alzheimer's disease has taught me that we must continually strive to invent new ways to use our brains . . . . Jim Kwik's *Limitless* is a revelation in learning how to learn. You'll discover new possibilities to challenge your mind and live your best life."

— **RUDOLPH E. TANZI, PH.D.**, Professor of Neurology at Harvard University, director of Genetics and Aging Research Unit at Massachusetts General Hospital, and *New York Times* best-selling author of *Super Brain*

"Achieving your goals in life is as much a mental game as it is physical. Do you want to grow your skills and improve your focus? *Limitless* is your book. Jim Kwik is your coach."

— **APOLO ANTON OHNO**, eight-time Olympic medalist, speaker, and *New York Times* best-selling author of *Zero Regrets*

"As a young girl, I dreamed of traveling to space. Dreaming big is something I'm passionate about teaching others, especially today's youth. Jim shares that same vision that nothing can hold you back once you realize your limitless potential. *Limitless* will not only make you smarter, but help you dream bigger."

— **ANOUSHEH ANSARI**, CEO of XPRIZE Foundation, first female private space explorer, and first space ambassador

"Jim Kwik is the world's elite trainer when it comes to your brain. In *Limitless*, he lights a path toward a transformation that strengthens your mental game, makes you think faster, and leaves you smarter than when you started."

— **TRACY ANDERSON, CEO**, fitness pioneer, and author of *Tracy Anderson's 30-Day Method*

"When my son suffered a life-threatening traumatic brain injury, I learned that mindset is everything. In *Limitless*, Jim Kwik shares the mindset and methods that are essential to thriving in a world of change. Even when the odds seem stacked against you, this book will show you anything is possible."

— **JJ VIRGIN**, celebrity nutrition and fitness expert and *New York Times* best-selling author of *The Virgin Diet*

"When you connect to your true self, something magical happens. I help people express themselves through movement and dance. Jim Kwik's *Limitless* taps into that same reservoir of belief that anything is possible."

— **JULIANNE HOUGH**, Emmy award-winning dancer, actress, singer, and creator of KINRGY

"In competition and in life, the finest performers stay patient, consistent, and relentless. Jim Kwik's *Limitless* will help you reach a whole new mindset—one that helps you achieve your dreams."

— **DEREK HOUGH**, two-time Emmy award winner, six-time Dancing with the Stars champion, and *New York Times* best-selling author of *Taking the Lead*

"Jim Kwik is an expert in achieving mental stamina and clarity of focus. *Limitless* will give you sustainable results in whatever you pursue."

— **MIKE BRYAN**, professional tennis player, all-time doubles team record holder

"We know full well the importance of food as fuel for a healthy brain. What you do to sharpen your cognitive abilities matters too. In *Limitless*, Jim Kwik teaches you the mindset and metalearning strategies that help you reach genius levels."

— **MAX LUGAVERE**, host of the Genius Life podcast and *New York Times* best-selling author of *Genius Foods*

"I've worked with on-screen superheroes throughout my career, and Jim's ability to level up your learning and life is one of the world's great superpowers. . . . *Limitless* is for any person or organization looking to unlock exceptional mental productivity and performance."

— **JIM GIANOPULOS**, Chairman and CEO of Paramount Pictures

"There's a whole science behind brain fitness, memory enhancement, and mental acuity, and Jim Kwik is the ultimate guide. This book is a must-read for anyone who wants to maximize their cognitive potential and learning abilities."

— **LISA MOSCONI, PH.D.**, director of the Women's Brain Initiative and associate director of the Alzheimer's Prevention Clinic at Weill Cornell Medical College, associate professor of neuroscience in neurology and radiology, and author of *The XX Brain*

"There's no genius pill, but Jim gives you the process for unlocking your best brain and brightest future."

— From the foreword by **MARK HYMAN, M.D.**, Head of Strategy and Innovation for the Cleveland Clinic Center for Functional Medicine and 12-time *New York Times* best-selling author

"Jim Kwik is just amazing. In my book *Use Your Brain to Change Your Age*, I wrote a whole chapter about him because one of the strategies to reverse brain aging and prevent Alzheimer's disease is to work on your brain. And there is no one that I trust more than Jim Kwik and his programs to optimize brain functioning."

— **DR. DANIEL AMEN**, physician, double board-certified psychiatrist, and 10-time *New York Times* best-selling author

"I'm keenly aware of how important it is to keep your mind and memory sharp. Jim Kwik's tools and techniques in *Limitless* are your brain's best friends."

— **MARIA SHRIVER**, Emmy award–winning journalist, founder of the Women's Alzheimer's Movement, and *New York Times* best-selling author of *I've Been Thinking*

"As a person who has quested for knowledge his entire life, I fully embrace what Jim Kwik has to teach in *Limitless*. When you learn how to learn, anything is possible, and Jim is the best in the world at showing you how."

— **QUINCY JONES**, music producer, recipient of Grammy Living Legend Award, and *New York Times* best-selling author of *Q*

"I want to thank my friend Jim Kwik for all his support of the Stan Lee Foundation's commitment to literacy and education. I believe there is a superhero in each of us, and at Kwik Learning you will discover how to unleash your superhero powers."

— **STAN LEE**, Marvel Chairman Emeritus

"Jim Kwik is by far the world's best Memory Trainer. Our program with Jim on Mindvalley became the number one program of the year, and in a study of almost 1,000 students, the average increase in reading speed was an astonishing 170% in just 7 days of 10-minute-a-day lessons."

— **VISHEN LAKHIANI**, founder and CEO of Mindvalley and *New York Times* best-selling author of *The Code of the Extraordinary Mind*

"Jim Kwik has the ability to expand your mind and shine a light on your inner genius. Like my song 'Unwritten' says—your life is your story. *Limitless* will help you write yours with new possibilities."

— **NATASHA BEDINGFIELD**, Grammy Award–nominated singer and songwriter

LIMITLESS

UPGRADE YOUR BRAIN, LEARN ANYTHING FASTER, AND UNLOCK YOUR EXCEPTIONAL LIFE

JIM KWIK

HAY HOUSE, INC.
Carlsbad, California • New York City
London • Sydney • New Delhi

Published in the United States by: Hay House, Inc.: www.hayhouse.com®
Published in Australia by: Hay House Australia Pty. Ltd.: www.hayhouse.com.au
Published in the United Kingdom by: Hay House UK, Ltd.: www.hayhouse.co.uk
Published in India by: Hay House Publishers India: www.hayhouse.co.in

Cover design by: Rodrigo Corral
Interior design by: Claudine Mansour Design
Photograph on page 39: Used under license from Shutterstock.com
Photograph on page 43: liliegraphie © 123RF.com
Diagrams: Jose Alonso
Other illustrations courtesy of the author
Author photo credit: Nick Onken
Indexer: J S Editorial, LLC

Cataloging-in-Publication Data is on file at the Library of Congress

Hardcover ISBN: 978-1-4019-5823-7
E-book ISBN: 978-1-4019-5824-4
Audiobook ISBN: 978-1-4019-5825-1

18 17 16 15 14 13 12 11 10 9
1st edition, April 2020

Printed in the United States of America

For my readers and students
and the limitless heroes inside you.
Thank you for your time and trust.
This one's for you.

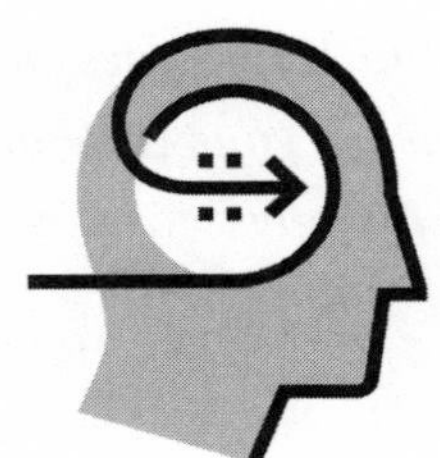

CONTENTS

FOREWORD

Our most precious gift is our brain.

It is what allows us to learn, love, think, create, and even to experience joy. It is the gateway to our emotions, to our capacity for deeply experiencing life, to our ability to have lasting intimacy. It allows us to innovate, grow, and accomplish.

Yet few of us realize that, by applying a handful of practical methods, we can enhance our brain and supercharge our ability to learn. Most of us know that we can improve our cardiovascular health through exercise and diet, but most of us do not realize that we can also greatly improve our brains, and in doing so, our life.

Unfortunately, our world doesn't foster a healthy environment for our brain. Before Jim Kwik provides a road map to become limitless, he indicts the four growing villains that are challenging our capacity to think, focus, learn, grow, and be fully human.

The first is *digital deluge*—the unending flood of information in a world of finite time and unfair expectations that leads to overwhelm, anxiety, and sleeplessness. Drowning in data and rapid change, we long for strategies and tools to regain some semblance of productivity, performance, and peace of mind.

The second villain is *digital distraction*. The fleeting ping of digital dopamine pleasure replaces our ability to sustain the attention necessary for deep relationship, deep learning, or deep work. I recently sat next to a friend at a lecture and noticed her picking up her phone multiple times within a few minutes. I asked for her phone and pulled up the screen time app. She had picked up her phone more than one thousand times and had one thousand notifications in one day. Texts, social media notifications, e-mails, and news alerts, while important in context, can derail our concentration and train us to be distracted from what matters most in the moment.

The next villain is *digital dementia.* Memory is a muscle that we have allowed to atrophy. While there are benefits to having a supercomputer in your pocket, think of it like an electric bicycle. It's fun and easy but doesn't get you in shape. Research on dementia proves that the greater our capacity to learn—the more mental "brainercise" we perform—the lower our risk of dementia. In many cases, we have outsourced our memory to our detriment.

The last brain-damaging villain is *digital deduction.* In a world where information is abundantly accessible, we've perhaps gone too far in how we use that information, even getting to the point where we are letting technology do much of our critical thinking and reasoning for us. Online, there are so many conclusions being drawn by others that we have begun to surrender our own ability to draw conclusions. We would never let another person do our thinking for us, but we've gotten far too comfortable with letting devices have that very power.

The cumulative effects of these four digital villains robs us of our focus, attention, learning, and, most importantly, our ability to truly think. It robs us of our mental clarity and results in brain fatigue, distraction, inability to easily learn, and unhappiness. While the technological advances of our time have the potential to both help and harm, the way we use them in our society can lead to an epidemic of overload, memory loss, distraction, and dependency. And it's only going to get worse.

The message of this book couldn't be more timely. You were born with the ultimate technology, and there is nothing more important than the health and fitness of our brain—it controls everything in life. Learning how to filter all the data, to develop new methods and skills for thriving in a distracted world drowning in a flood of information, is what is needed to thrive in the 21st century. Learning and the ability to learn faster and more easily makes everything else in life possible, which means that it's never been a better time to train your brain the way you do your body. Just like you want a healthy body, you want a flexible, strong, energized, and fit brain. That's what Jim does for a living—he is the personal trainer for the mind.

The four supervillains are just an example of the limits you'll learn how to overcome in this book. The key to living an exceptional life, as Jim states, is a process of unlimiting ourselves. And he has cracked the code for personal transformation with his Limitless Model. If you are struggling to reach a goal in any area, you must first ask: Where is the limit? Most likely, you're experiencing a limit in your mindset, motivation, or methods—which means that it's not a personal shortcoming or failure pointing to any perceived lack of ability. And contrary to what we tend to believe, our barriers are not set. We're in full control and can overcome them at any time.

If our mindset is not aligned with our desires or goals, we will never achieve them. It's critical to identify your limiting beliefs, stories, and deeply held beliefs, attitudes, and assumptions about yourself and what's possible. Examining, excavating, and expunging those beliefs is the first step to having a limitless mindset. I was told I could do anything by my mother, that I was smart, capable, and could be the best at anything I tried. That deeply held belief allowed me to succeed beyond my wildest dreams. But I also had the belief that relationships were hard and filled with pain and drama from witnessing my parents' divorce and marriages. It took me nearly 50 years to erase that belief and find real happiness in my marriage.

The second secret to a limitless life is your motivation. Jim outlines three key elements to motivation. First, your purpose. The reason why matters. I want to age well and am committed to lifting weights and getting stronger even though it is not my favorite thing to do. The purpose supersedes the discomfort.

The second key is the ability to do what you want. This requires energy, and energy requires something called energy management. The science of human performance is critical to achieving your purpose—eating whole unprocessed food, exercise, stress management, quality sleep, and skills at communication and building healthy relationships (and eliminating toxic ones). And lastly the tasks must be bite-size, small steps that lead to success. Floss one tooth, read one page of a book, do one push-up, meditate for one minute, all of which will lead to confidence, and ultimately bigger successes.

The last key to being limitless is using the right method. We have been taught 19th- and 20th-century tools for functioning in the 21st century. *Limitless* teaches us the five key methods to achieve whatever we want: Focus, Study, Memory Enhancement, Speed Reading, and Critical Thinking. Using these upgraded learning technologies allows us to harness our mindset and motivation to more easily and effectively reach our dreams.

Jim is no stranger to limits. After a head injury as a child impaired his focus, concentration, and ability to learn, an insensitive teacher pointed to him and said, "There's the boy with a broken brain." Jim has spent his life learning how to overcome and heal from this injury and turn his challenges into a superpower of learning. We all suffer to some degree or another from broken brains. *Limitless* is the prescription for healing our brains, reframing limiting beliefs, and upgrading our life. Learning how to learn is the ultimate superpower, the one that makes every other skill and ability possible, and teaching this to you is this book's goal.

In *Limitless,* Jim Kwik provides a road map for doing exactly this. Most of us are not raised with the tools we need, but Jim is generously sharing everything he's learned in this book. Jim has spent three decades working in the trenches with people from all walks of life—students, teachers, celebrities, construction workers, politicians, entrepreneurs, scientists. He has worked with some of the most advanced educational systems around the world, training educators, superintendents, and students in his methods. His teachings truly work and can benefit us all.

There is no pill for genius, but there is a process to get there, and you'll find it within these pages. *Limitless* is a blueprint for upgrading your brain, for not only learning how to learn faster, better, and more effectively, but also for healing your physical brain through nutrition, supplements, exercise, meditation, sleep, and more to increase the creation of new brain cells and the connections between them.

Jim delivers three books in one. If your current mindset, motivation, and methods are limiting your ability to achieve your dreams, then *Limitless* is the owner's manual to a better, brighter, brilliant brain and future. Your learning and life will never be the same.

—MARK HYMAN, M.D.
Head of Strategy and Innovation
Cleveland Clinic Center for Functional Medicine
Author of 12 *New York Times* best-selling books
December 2019

"You know when you're
a child and your
imagination is limitless
and you really
believe in magic?
I thought I had
super powers."

—MICHELLE PHAN

INTRODUCTION

What is your one wish? Seriously, if a genie offered to grant you one wish, but only one, what would you ask for?

Limitless wishes, of course!

Now, imagine that I'm your learning genie and I can grant you one learning wish—any one subject or skill. What one thing would you want to learn? What subject or skill would be the equivalent of asking for infinite wishes?

To learn how to learn, right?

If you really knew how to learn smarter, faster, and better, then you could apply that to everything. You could learn to master your mindset or your motivation, or use the methods to pick up Mandarin, marketing, music, martial arts, mathematics—there would be no limit! You'd be a mental superhero! Anything would be possible, because you would be limitless!

My mission with this book is to grant you this wish in the pages that follow. Let's start by saying how much I respect and admire you. By investing in this book and now reading it, you are far ahead of most of the population who simply accept their present conditions and constraints. You are part of a small group of individuals who not only want more for their lives but also are willing to do what it takes to get results. In other words, you are the hero of this story; you've answered the call to adventure. I believe the ultimate adventure we are all on is to reveal and realize our fullest potential and inspire others to do the same.

I have no way of knowing how your life's journey has taken you to this book. I'm guessing that at least part of that journey is accepting the confines put upon you, either by others or by yourself: You can't read fast enough to keep up with everything you need to know. Your mind is not agile enough to succeed at work.

You're not motivated to get things done or you lack the energy to reach your goals. And so on.

The nature of this book is transcending—ending the trance: the mass hypnosis and lies that we learned from our parents, programing, media, or marketing, that suggests we are limited. That, somehow, we are not enough, not capable of being, doing, having, creating, or contributing.

Belief that you are limited might be holding you back from your biggest dreams as well—at least up until now. But I promise you that none of your beliefs truly constrain who you are. We all have vast potential inside of us, untapped levels of strength, intelligence, and focus, and the key to activating these superpowers is unlimiting yourself. For more than 25 years, I've worked with people of all ages, nationalities, races, socioeconomic statuses, and education levels. What I've discovered is that no matter where you come from, no matter what challenges you face, you have incredible potential that's just waiting to be tapped. Every person—regardless of age, background, education, gender, or personal history—can advance beyond what they believe they deserve and is possible. And that includes you. Working together, you'll come to think of your own limitations as an outmoded concept.

Now in this book, I refer to superheroes and superpowers. Why is that? First, I am a bit of a geek that way. Because of my childhood brain injury and learning challenges, I escaped into comic books and movies to inspire me during my struggles. I realized that my favorite ones all shared the same pattern—the Hero's Journey. Joseph Campbell's classic plot structure appears in nearly all famed adventures, including *The Wizard of Oz; Star Wars; Harry Potter; Eat, Pray, Love; The Hunger Games; Rocky; The Lord of the Rings; Alice in Wonderland; The Matrix*, and more.

Think of your favorite story or one of the films or books I just mentioned. Does this sound familiar? The hero (for example, Harry Potter) starts out in the ordinary world, the world they've always known. The hero then hears the call to adventure. They have a choice—to ignore and stay in the ordinary world, where nothing will change, or heed the call and enter the new world of the unknown. If they heed the call (as Neo did with the red pill in

The Matrix), they meet their guide or mentor (such as Mr. Miyagi in *The Karate Kid*), who trains and prepares them to overcome obstacles and realize new levels of fulfillment. The hero is introduced to new powers and skills, and encouraged to utilize their current abilities like never before. They transcend perceived limitations, learn a new way of being, and eventually face their trials. When they return back to the ordinary world (like Dorothy going back to Kansas), they take with them the ultimate boon—the treasure, emotions, strength, clarity, and wisdom they discovered from their adventure. They then share their lessons and gifts with others.

The Hero's Journey is the perfect structure to lend power and purpose to your personal story. In *Limitless,* you are the superhero.

One of my core beliefs is that human potential is one of the only infinite resources we have in the world. Most everything else is finite, but the human mind is the ultimate superpower—there is no limit to our creativity, imagination, determination, or ability to think, reason, or learn. Yet this resource is also among the least tapped. All of us can be the heroes of our own story, dipping into the well of our potential every single day and never having that well run dry. But so few of us approach our lives this way. That's why I wrote this book—to help you realize that no matter where you are, or where you've been, you absolutely can free yourself and go from limits to liberation. That might be the only "extra" you need to transition from the ordinary world to the *extra*ordinary world.

This book is going to provide you with that extra. What you'll get within these pages is a series of tools that will help you cast off your perceived restrictions. You're going to learn how to unlimit your brain. You're going to learn how to unlimit your drive. You're going to learn how to unlimit your memory, your focus, and your habits. If I am your mentor in your hero's journey, then this book is your map to master your mind, motivation, and methods to learn how to learn. And once you've done that, you will be limitless.

Here's the door; you know what's waiting on the other side. Walk through it.

"If an egg is broken

by an outside force,

life ends.

If broken by an inside

force, life begins.

Great things

always begin

from the inside."

—JIM KWIK

PART I

FREE YOUR MIND

"We do not need magic to transform our world. We carry all of the power we need inside ourselves already."

—J. K. ROWLING

1

BECOMING LIMITLESS

"I'm so stupid."

"I don't understand."

"I'm too dumb to learn."

These were my mantras growing up. There wasn't a day that went by that I didn't tell myself that I was slow, dumb, and that I would never learn to read, much less amount to anything later in life. If a pill existed that could supercharge my brain and make me smarter in one swallow (as there was in the 2011 movie *Limitless*, starring Bradley Cooper), I would have given anything to take it.

I wasn't the only one who felt the way I did about myself. If you'd asked my teachers when I was a kid, many would have said that I was the last person they'd expect to be writing this book for you. Back then, they would have been surprised to know that I was *reading* a book, let alone writing one.

This all stems from an incident in kindergarten that completely altered the course of my life. I was in class one day, and there were sirens outside the window. Everyone in the classroom took notice, and the teacher looked out and said she saw fire trucks. The entire class responded to this information the way kindergarteners do: We immediately rushed to the windows. I was particularly excited because, by that point, I was already obsessed with superheroes (I still am). To me, firefighters were the closest thing to real-life superheroes I knew. I bolted to the window with everyone else.

The only problem was that I wasn't tall enough to be able to look down at the fire trucks. One kid went to grab his chair to stand on, and that inspired the rest of us to do the same. I ran back to my desk to get mine, pushing it right up against the huge iron radiator that ran along the bottom of the windows. I got up on my chair, saw the firefighters, and completely lit up. This was so exciting! My eyes stared and mouth gasped as I watched these courageous heroes in action with their seemingly impenetrable uniforms and their bright red vehicle.

But then one of the other kids grabbed my chair from beneath me, which caused me to lose balance and go flying head-first into the radiator. I hit the metal heater extremely hard and I started losing blood. The school rushed me to the hospital, where doctors tended to my wounds. But they were candid with my mother afterward; the injury to my brain was not mild.

My mother said I was never quite the same after that. Where I had been an energized, confident, and curious child before, now I was noticeably shut down and had a new difficulty learning; I found it extremely hard to focus, I couldn't concentrate, and my memory was awful. As you can imagine, school became an ordeal for me. Teachers would repeat themselves until I learned to pretend to understand. And while all the other kids were learning to read, I couldn't make any sense out of the letters. Do you remember getting in those reading circles, passing around the book, and having to read out loud? For me, that was the worst—nervously waiting as the book crept closer and closer, only to look at the page and not understand one word (I think that's where my crippling fear of public speaking initially came from). It would take me another three years to be able to read, and it continued to be a struggle and an uphill battle for a long time after that.

I'm not sure I ever would have learned to read if it weren't for the heroes I met and saw in comic books. Regular books couldn't hold my attention at all, but my fascination with comics drove me to keep pushing myself until I could read their stories without waiting for someone else to read them to me. I would read them by flashlight under my covers late at night. Those stories gave me hope that one person could overcome impossible odds.

My favorite superheroes growing up were the X-Men, not because they were the strongest, but because they were misunderstood and weirdly different. I felt I could relate to them. They were mutants, they didn't fit into society, and people who didn't understand them shunned them. That was me, minus the superpowers. The X-Men were outcasts, and so was I. I belonged in their world.

I grew up in Westchester County, a suburb of New York City, and I was super-excited one night to discover that, according to the comic books, Professor Xavier's School for Gifted Youngsters was located near me. When I was nine years old, I would get on my bike nearly every weekend to ride around my neighborhood looking for the school. I was obsessed. I thought, if only I could locate it, I would find in that school a place where I finally fit in, a place where it was safe to be different, a place where I could discover and develop my own superpowers.

THE BOY WITH THE BROKEN BRAIN

In the real world, life was not very kind. It was around this time that my grandmother, who lived with us and helped raise me, started showing advanced signs of dementia. Watching someone you love lose their mind and memory is hard to describe. It was like losing her over and over until she passed. She was my world and, combined with my learning challenges, she is why I am so passionate about brain health and fitness.

Back in school, I was bullied and made fun of, and not just on the playground but in the classroom, too. I remember one day in elementary school a teacher, frustrated because I wasn't getting the lesson, pointed at me and said, "That's the boy with the broken brain." I was just crushed to realize that this was how she saw me—and that others probably saw me the same way.

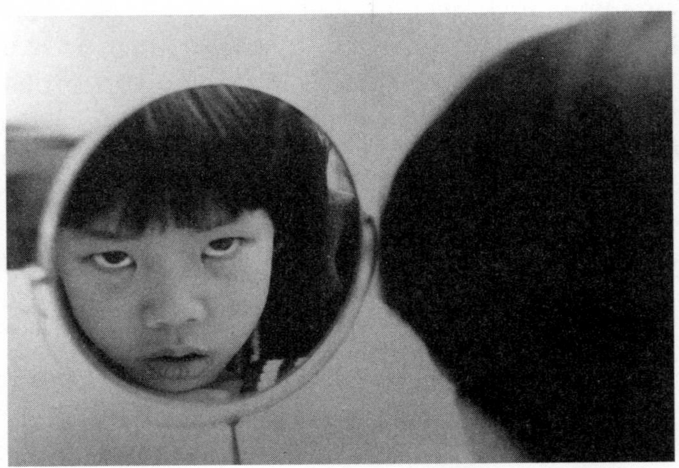

Often when you put a label on someone or something, you create a limit—the label becomes the limitation. Adults have to be very careful with their external words because these quickly become a child's internal words. That's what happened with me in that moment. Whenever I struggled to learn, did badly on a quiz, wasn't picked for a team in gym class, or fell behind my other classmates, I would tell myself it was because my brain was broken. How could I possibly expect to do as well as others did? I was damaged. My mind didn't work like everyone else's. Even when I studied much harder than my schoolmates, my grades never reflected the effort I was putting in.

I was too stubborn to give up and managed to move on from grade to grade, but I was hardly thriving. While I was advanced in math because of the help of a few of my academically talented friends, I was horrible at most of the other subjects, especially classes such as English, reading, foreign languages, and music. Then, in my freshman year of high school, things got to the point where I was at risk of failing English. My parents were called in by my teacher to discuss what I could do to muster a passing grade.

She offered an extra-credit project for me. I was to write a report comparing the lives and accomplishments of two geniuses: Leonardo da Vinci and Albert Einstein. She told me that if I did a good job on this report, she would be able to give me enough points to make sure I passed the class.

I considered this to be a huge opportunity, a chance to hit the reset button on what had been a difficult start to my high school career. I committed everything I had to writing the best report I possibly could. I spent hours and hours and hours at the library after school, trying to learn everything I could learn about these two brilliant minds while working on this paper. Interestingly, during that research I came across multiple mentions that Albert Einstein and Leonardo da Vinci each struggled with alleged learning difficulties.

After weeks of effort, I typed up the final report. I was so proud of what I'd done that I had the pages professionally bound. This report was a statement for me; it was the way I was going to announce to the world what I was capable of doing.

The day the report was due, I put it in my backpack, excited about handing it to my teacher and even more excited about the response I anticipated she would have to what I'd done. I planned to give it to her at the end of class, so I sat through whatever we were doing that day, trying to concentrate but constantly finding my thoughts flitting back to the look I expected to see on my teacher's face when I presented her with the report.

But then she threw me a curveball I was not prepared to hit. About halfway through the class period, the teacher ended her lesson and told the students that she had a surprise for them. She said that I had been working on an extra-credit report and that she would like me to present it to the class—now.

I had spent most of my school life trying to shrink so small that I wouldn't be called on in class; when you are the broken one, you don't feel like you have much to offer. I was beyond shy, and I didn't like to draw attention to myself. My superpower back then was being invisible. I was also deathly afraid of speaking in public.

I'm not exaggerating here. If you hooked me up to a heart monitor at that moment, I might have broken the machine. On top of this, I could barely breathe. There was simply no way I was going to be able to stand in front of everyone and talk to them about the work I'd done. So, I took the only option I saw available to me.

"I'm sorry; I didn't do it," I stuttered, just barely getting the words out of my mouth.

The expression of disappointment on my teacher's face—so different from the expression I'd fantasized earlier—was so profound that my heart nearly broke. But I just couldn't do what she wanted me to do. When class was over, after everyone had left, I threw my report in the garbage, and along with it a big part of my self-respect and worth.

YOU ARE CLOSER THAN YOU THINK

Somehow, in spite of all the troubles I had in school, I managed to get into a local university. I thought being a freshman in college meant a last opportunity to make a fresh start. I dreamt about making my family proud, and to showing the world (and, more importantly, myself) that I *did* have the potential to succeed. I was in a new environment. College professors taught differently than high school teachers did, and no one at this college had any preconceived notions about me. I worked my butt off, but I actually wound up doing even worse in my college classes than high school.

A few months into this, I started to face my reality. I couldn't see the point of wasting time and money that I did not have. I was ready to quit school altogether. I told a friend about my plans and he suggested that, before I made a decision, I go with him to visit his family for the weekend. He thought that getting me away from the campus might give me some perspective. When we arrived, his father showed me around their property before dinner. Along the way, he asked how school was going for me. It was the worst question anyone could ask me at the time, and I'm sure my response stunned him. I erupted into tears. Not holding-back-the-tears crying, but straight up bawling. I could see he was taken aback by this, but his innocent question had broken the dam holding back so many pent-up emotions.

I told him the whole "boy with the broken brain" story while he listened patiently. When I was finished, he looked me directly in the eyes.

"Jim, why are you in school?" he said. "What do you want to be? What do you want to do? What do you want to have? What do you want to share?"

I didn't have immediate answers to any of these questions because no one had ever asked me them before, but I felt as though I needed to answer them now. I started to speak, and he stopped me. He tore a couple of pieces of paper from his pocket diary and told me to write down my answers. (In this book, I'll show you how to ask questions to learn and achieve anything faster.)

I spent the next several minutes writing a bucket list. When I was finished, I began folding up the papers and preparing to put them in my pocket. But as I was doing so, my friend's father grabbed the pages out of my hand. I freaked out, because I didn't think what I'd written was going to be read by anyone else, especially this complete stranger. But he opened the pages and read while I stewed in my discomfort.

It seemed as though he took hours to read what I'd written, though I'm sure it was only a minute or two. When he finished, he said, "You're this close," holding the index fingers on his right and left hands about a foot apart, "to getting every single thing on that list."

That statement seemed absurd to me. I told him I couldn't crack this list if I had 10 lifetimes. But then he took his fingers and, without expanding the distance between them, placed one on each side of my head. The space he was describing was my brain.

"That's the key," he said. "Come with me; I have something to show you."

We walked back to the house where he took me to a room that I'd never seen before. It was filled wall-to-wall, floor-to-ceiling with books. Now remember, at that point in my life, I was not a fan of books; it was like being in a room full of snakes. But what made it even worse was that he started grabbing snakes from his shelves and handing them to me. I looked at the titles and realized these were biographies of incredible men and women throughout history, as well as some early personal-growth books such as *The Magic of Thinking Big, The Power of Positive Thinking,* and *Think and Grow Rich.*

"Jim, I want you to read one of these books a week."

My first thought was, *Have you not been listening to anything I've been saying?* I didn't ask this out loud, but I did respond: "I don't know how I could do that. You know, reading doesn't come easily to me, and I have so much schoolwork to do."

He held up a finger, saying, "Don't let school interfere with your education." I later learned he was paraphrasing a quote often attributed to Mark Twain.

"Look," I said. "I understand how reading these books would be really helpful, but I don't want to make any promises I can't keep."

He paused and then reached into his pocket, pulled out my bucket list, and started reading each one out loud.

There was something about hearing my dreams in another person's voice that messed with my mind and my soul something fierce. Truth be told, many of the things on the list were things I wanted to do for my family—things my parents could never afford or would never have done for themselves even if they could afford them. Hearing this read out loud moved me in ways I didn't think possible. It deeply tapped me into my drive and purpose. (We will unleash your motivation together in Part 3.) When he was finished, I told him I would do exactly what he suggested, though secretly I had no idea how I was going to accomplish that feat.

ASKING THE RIGHT QUESTION

I went back to school after the weekend, armed with the books he'd given me. On my desk were now two piles: one that I had to read for school, and one that I promised to read. The scale of what I'd agreed to registered with me. How was I going to make a dent in these piles when reading was such a labor for me? I was already struggling to get through the first pile—what was I going to do? Where would I get the time? So I didn't eat, I didn't sleep, I didn't exercise, I didn't watch television or spend time with friends. Instead, I practically lived at the library, until one night when I passed out from sheer exhaustion and fell down a flight of stairs, sustaining yet another head injury.

It wasn't until two days later that I woke up in the hospital. I thought I had died, and maybe a part of me wished that I had. It was truly a dark and low point in life. I was wasting away, my weight was down to 117 pounds, and I was so dehydrated that I was hooked up to IV bags.

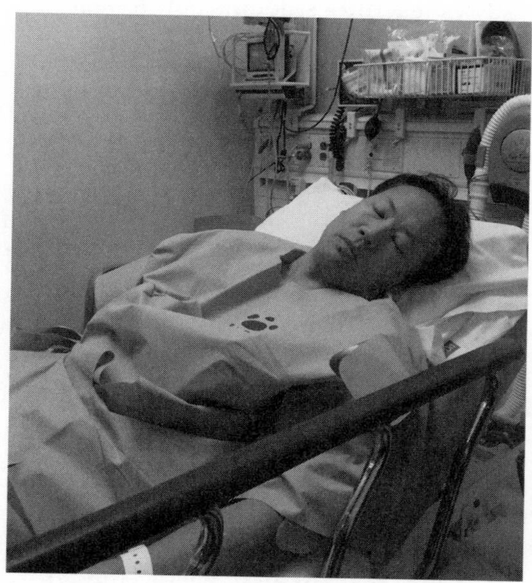

As miserable as I was, I said to myself, "There has to be a better way." At that moment, a nurse came into my room, carrying a mug of tea with a picture of Einstein on it, the very same subject of the book report that inspired me to dig deep and study back in grade school. The quote next to his image said, "No problem can be solved from the same level of consciousness that created it."

That's when it dawned on me: Maybe I was asking the wrong question. I started to wonder, what was my *real* problem? I knew I was a slow learner, but I had been thinking the same way about it for years. I realized that I was trying to solve my learning problems by thinking the way I'd been taught to think—to just work harder. But what if I could teach myself a better method to learn? What if I could learn in a way that was more efficient, effective, and even enjoyable? What if I could learn how to learn faster?

I committed in that very moment to finding that way, and with that commitment, my mindset began to shift.

I asked the nurse for a course bulletin and flipped through it, page by page. After a couple hundred pages, I could find nothing but classes on *what* to learn—Spanish, history, math, science—but there were no classes teaching students *how* to learn.

LEARNING HOW TO LEARN

When I got out of the hospital, I was so intrigued by the idea of learning how to learn that I set my studies aside and focused only on the books that my mentor gave me, as well as books I found on adult learning theory, multiple intelligence theory, neuroscience, personal growth, educational psychology, speed reading, and even ancient mnemonics (I wanted to know what older cultures did to pass on knowledge before they had external storage devices like the printing press and computers). I was obsessed to solve this riddle: How does my brain work, so I can work my brain?

About a couple months of deep immersion into my new self-directed studies, a light switch flipped on. My ability to focus was stronger. I started to understand new concepts because I was able to concentrate—I was no longer easily distracted. I could better recall information that I had studied weeks before with little difficulty. I had a new level of energy and curiosity. For the first time in my life, I could read and comprehend information in a fraction of the time that it used to take. My newfound competence gave me a sense of confidence that I'd never felt before. My daily life changed too—I was clear, I knew what to do to move myself forward, and I unlocked an empowering and sustainable sense of motivation. With these results, my mindset changed and I started to believe that anything was possible.

But I was also upset. It seemed to me all of my years of self-doubt and suffering could have been avoided if this critical method of meta learning (learning how to learn) had been taught in school. I remember teachers telling me constantly to study and concentrate harder. Telling a child to do things like "concentrate" is like telling them to play the ukulele; it's very difficult to do without ever being taught how.

And, following the hero's journey, I couldn't help but share the treasure and lessons I learned. I started tutoring these methods to other students. The turning point came when I worked with a freshman who wanted to learn how to read faster, boost comprehension, and retain the information she was studying. She worked diligently and achieved her goal of reading 30 books in 30 days. I knew how she did it—I taught her the method you'll learn in Chapter 14—but I wanted to know why. I discovered that her motivation was that her mother had been diagnosed with a terminal cancer, and she was determined to save her by studying books on health, wellness, and medicine. Months later, she called me, crying tears of joy, to tell me that her mother's cancer was in remission.

It was in that moment that I realized that if knowledge is power, then learning is our superpower. And our capacity to learn is limitless; we simply need to be shown how to access it. Seeing the way this woman's life was changed ignited in me a purpose, allowing me to recognize what became my life's mission: to teach the mindset, motivation, and methods to upgrade your brain and learn anything faster so you can unlock your exceptional life.

Over the course of more than two decades, I've developed a reliable and proven set of practical methods to enhance learning, many of which appear in this book. I have not only kept my promise to read a book a week, but continue to serve and support everyone from children labeled "learning disabled," to seniors with brain-aging challenges. Our team, dedicated to the memory of my grandmother, passionately supports Alzheimer's research. And we believe education is every child's birthright, funding the creation of schools around the world from Guatemala to Kenya, providing health care, clean water, and learning for children in need via amazing organizations such as WE Charity and Pencils of Promise. That's our mission—to build better brighter brains. We're leaving no brain behind.

I've taught these techniques to others with astonishing results, leading me to address more than 150,000 people in live audiences each year in every field imaginable, to serve as the brain coach to top personalities in sports and entertainment, to train at many of the world's leading companies and universities, to head a large accelerated learning online platform with students from 195 countries, and to host a top educational podcast called Kwik Brain, with tens of millions of downloads and to have my teachings receive hundreds of millions of video views. This book is filled with lessons and practical advice I've learned over the years, along with wisdom and resources from many of the guest experts who have been featured on our show.

I say all of this because, having dedicated my life to researching and teaching this subject, I know what's inside this book and, more importantly, I know what's inside you.

FINDING PROFESSOR X'S SCHOOL

There's a serendipitous coda to this story. As I mentioned, I regularly offer brain coaching to CEOs and their teams. A few years ago, Jim Gianopulos, then CEO and Chairman of 20th Century Fox, invited me to do a coaching session with his executive team. I went onto the film lot on a Friday morning and spent several hours with top staff members. They were particularly open to my message, and they instantly connected with the techniques.

When the session was over, Jim came up to me and said, "That was incredible. It was one of the very best training sessions we've ever held." I was delighted to hear this, of course. Who doesn't love positive feedback? Later, during a tour of the lot, my eye landed on a poster for the Wolverine movie, which was scheduled to come out later that year. I pointed to the poster and said, "I can't wait to see that film. I'm a huge fan."

"Oh, you like superheroes?" Jim said.

"Love 'em. The X-Men have played a major role in my life." I went on to tell him about my childhood brain injury, how comic books helped me learn to read, and my search for Professor X's school.

He smiled at me. "You know, we have another 30 days of shooting on the next X-Men movie in Montreal. Why don't you come along and spend a week on the set? The actors would love to work with you."

There was no way I was going to turn this down. I'd never been on a movie set before, and this wasn't just any movie set—it was an X-Men movie set.

The next morning, we got on the plane they called the *X-Jet*. The other passengers included most of the mutant cast, and I found myself sitting between Jennifer Lawrence and Halle Berry. This was turning out to be the best day ever.

On the plane and the next week on set, I got to share some of my brain tips for speed-reading scripts and for remembering lines with some of the extraordinary cast and crew. And guess what? The very first scene I got to see them shoot took place in Professor X's school—the very place I'd spent endless days imagining and searching for when I was a kid. It was such a surreal moment for me. What's one of your dreams? One that is ever present, like a splinter in your brain? Imagine it in vivid detail. Visualize it. Feel it. Believe it. And work daily for it.

Amazingly, that's not the best part of this story. When I got back from the trip, I came home to find a package waiting for me. It was huge, about the size of a large flat-screen TV. I opened the package and pulled out an enormous framed photograph of me with the entire X-Men cast. The photo had a note from the chairman, which read:

Jim, thank you so much for sharing your superpowers with all of us. I know you've been looking for your superhero school ever since you were a child. Here's your class photo.

See the actual full-color superhero photo at LimitlessBook.com/classphoto.

UNLIMITING TOGETHER

> **unlimiting**
>
> un·lim·it·ing *(noun)*
>
> The act or process of casting aside inaccurate and restrictive perceptions of one's potential and embracing the reality that, with the right mindset, motivation, and methods, there are no limitations.

For so much of my life, I allowed myself to be defined by my perceived restrictions. I'd gotten what I thought was a terrible break when I was a kid, and I was convinced that this had set the course for a compromised future. But, with the help of some key people, I came to discover that my perceived restrictions were not really restrictions at all. They were merely obstacles I needed to overcome or limitations I needed to unlearn. And when I did, what I could learn to be or do each day became limitless.

Becoming limitless is not just about accelerated learning, speed-reading, and having an incredible memory. Yes, you will learn how to do all of that and more. But being limitless is not about being perfect. It's about progressing beyond what you currently believe is possible. Just as you've learned limits from your family, culture, and life experiences, you can unlearn them. These constraints are only temporary obstacles that you can learn to overcome. What I have come to find over my years of working with people is that most everyone limits and shrinks their dreams to fit their current reality. We convince ourselves that the circumstances we are in, the beliefs we've accepted, and the path we are on is who we are and who we will always be. But there is another choice. You can learn to unlimit and expand your mindset, your motivation, and your methods to create a limitless life. When you do what others won't, you can live how others can't. By reading this book, you have taken an important step. Remember, one step in a better direction can completely change your destination.

The key when you are taking your steps is to have a map, a model of success. Armed with this, there is no trial or dragon you can't overcome. So here it is:

The Limitless Model

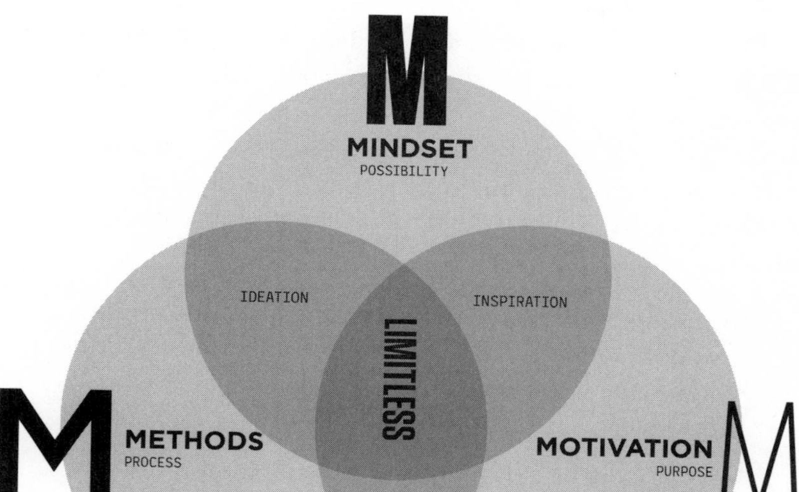

THE LIMITLESS MODEL

You can learn to be, do, have, and share with no constraints. I wrote this book to prove this to you. If you are not learning or living at your full potential, if there is a gap between your current reality and your desired reality, here's the reason: There is a limit that must be released and replaced in one of three areas:

- A limit in your Mindset—you entertain a low belief in yourself, your capabilities, what you deserve, or what is possible.

- A limit in your Motivation—you lack the drive, purpose, or energy to take action.
- A limit in your Methods—you were taught and are acting on a process that is not effective to create the results you desire.

This applies to an individual, a family, an organization. We all have our own unique story of struggles and strengths. Whatever your situation happens to be, here's the best part: You're not alone. I'm going to help you become limitless in your own way, within the three-part framework you're about to learn: Limitless Mindset, Limitless Motivation, and Limitless Methods. Let me break it down:

- Mindset (the WHAT): deeply held beliefs, attitudes, and assumptions we create about who we are, how the world works, what we are capable of and deserve, and what is possible.
- Motivation (the WHY): the purpose one has for taking action. The energy required for someone to behave in a particular way.
- Method (the HOW): a specific process for accomplishing something, especially an orderly, logical, or systematic way of instruction.

One other note about the diagram on the previous page. You'll see that where mindset crosses over with motivation, I have the word *inspiration*. You're inspired, but you don't know which methods to employ or where to channel your energy. Where motivation and method intersect, you have *implementation*. In this case, your results are going to be limited to what you feel you deserve, what you feel you are capable of, and what you believe is possible because you lack the proper mindset. Where mindset and method intersect, you have *ideation*. Your ambitions stay in your mind, because you lack the energy to do anything about them. Where all three intersect, you have the limitless state. You then have the fourth *I*, which is *integration*.

Throughout this book, you'll find exercises, studies, mental tools, and the results of exciting work being done both on the frontier of cognitive science and performance as well as ancient wisdom (for example, how ancient civilizations remembered generations of knowledge before external storage devices like the printing press). We'll approach the 3 M's in turn:

- In Part II, Limitless Mindset, you'll learn what is *possible* when you eradicate limiting beliefs.
- In Part III, Limitless Motivation, you'll discover why your *purpose* is your power and keys to unleash your drive and energy.
- In Part IV, Limitless Methods, you'll discover how to learn at your best with proven *processes*—the tools and techniques that will propel you forward toward the life you desire and deserve.

And, at the end of the book, I give you a 10-day plan to jump-start your progress toward a limitless week and a limitless life.

When you finish this book, you'll have the ability to be limitless in any area important to you, whether it's academic, health, career, relationships, or personal growth. Since I never truly got to study at the X-Men school, I created it for you in our online Kwik Learning Academy, where people of all ages from 195 nations train with us daily to unleash their mental superpowers. Consider *Limitless* your textbook. It would be an honor to be your Professor X, and I'm so excited that you've decided to take this journey with me. Class is now in session. And here's the best part; your timing could not be any better.

"We now accept the fact that learning is a lifelong process of keeping abreast of change. And the most pressing task is to teach people how to learn."

—PETER DRUCKER

2

WHY THIS MATTERS NOW

I'm a firm believer that we all have incredible superpowers that are waiting to be awakened. I'm not talking about the ability to fly, create iron-clad armor, or shoot lasers from your eyes, but real-life practical abilities like flying through books, iron-clad memory, laser focus, boundless creativity, clear thinking, mindfulness, superior mental attitude, and more. We are all superheroes in one way or another.

Just as every superhero has powers, so do they have arch nemeses. Enter the supervillain. Think the Joker to Batman, Lex Luthor to Superman. The villains we face may not look the same as they do in the movies, but they're still the bad guys—the ones you, as a superhero, need to vanquish and hold at bay. Modern-day supervillains get in our way and make life harder, keeping us from our potential. They hold us back and rob us of our productivity, prosperity, positivity, and peace of mind. And it's up to us to recognize and defeat them.

If you've ever read a comic book or watched a superhero movie, you know that supervillains are often born of unlikely places.

Take Harvey Dent, also known as Two-Face, for example. He starts out with the greatest of intentions—he's a prosecutor helping to uphold the law and put the bad guys in jail, and he's an ally of Batman. But through an act of revenge, Dent's face is scarred, and he turns angry, bitter, and vengeful. He becomes what he had spent his life fighting: a duplicitous criminal who gambles with his victims' futures. The good in him becomes twisted and used for sinister ends.

In the same way, the four supervillains of learning started out innocent—they are being fed by some of the greatest advancements that humankind has made in the last hundred years. They were given rise by technology. To be clear, technology is a vital part of progress and being limitless. It allows us to do everything from connecting to learning, making our lives that much more convenient. But it is possible that we consume digital technology at a rate that even its creators would find extreme. Much of the technology available to us today is so new that we don't know the level at which we need to control our interaction with it.

Through our educational platform Kwik Learning, we have students in 195 countries and have generated tens of millions of podcast downloads. Our community has expressed a growing concern about their overreliance on technology and they come to us to upgrade their brains to find relief from these "four horsemen" of our age: digital deluge, digital distraction, digital dementia, and digital deduction. It's important to note that overload, distraction, forgetfulness, and default thinking have been around for ages. While technology doesn't cause these conditions, it has great potential to amplify them. The benefits of the digital age are plentiful, but let's take a look at how the advances in technology that help you, can possibly also hinder you.

DIGITAL DELUGE

Do you have too much to process but not enough time? We're privileged to live in a world with so much unfettered access to information. In this age of connectivity, ignorance is a choice. Compared to the 15th century, we now consume as much data in a single day as an average person from the 1400s would have absorbed in an entire lifetime. Not so long ago, information moved glacially through word of mouth, or a newspaper, or a posted bulletin in a town square. Now we have so much access to information that it's taking a toll on our time and our quality of life. The average person consumes three times as much information as we did in the 1960s;[1] a 2015 report indicated that respondents spent eight hours a day consuming media.

In an NPR interview, *New York Times* tech reporter Matt Richtel said that after 20 years of glorifying technology as if all of it were good, "I think science is beginning to embrace the idea that some technology is Twinkies and some technology is Brussels sprouts. If we consume too much technology, just like if we consume too much food, it can have ill effects."[2]

In a University of California, San Francisco, study on the effect of downtime, researchers gave rats a new experience and measured their brain waves during and after the activity. Under most circumstances, a new experience will express new neural activity and new neurons in the brain—that is, if the rat is allowed to have downtime. With downtime, the neurons made their way from the gateway of memory to the rest of the brain, where long-term memory is stored. The rats were able to record memories of their experiences, which is the basis for learning.[3]

Doesn't that make you wonder what happens if you *don't* have downtime? There is a growing body of evidence that suggests that if we never let our mind wander or be bored for a moment, we pay a price—poor memory, mental fog, and fatigue.

As far back as the mid-1990s (when digital deluge was a fraction of the concern it is now), research was beginning to show that there were real health risks involved with navigating through an always-on world. A Reuters study, ominously titled "Dying for Information," showed that, "Two out of three respondents associated information overload with tension with colleagues and loss of job satisfaction; 42 percent attributed ill-health to this stress, 61 percent said that they have to cancel social activities as a result of information overload and 60 percent that they are frequently too tired for leisure activities." The study goes on to add, "Faced with an onslaught of information and information channels, they have become unable to develop simple routines for managing information."[4]

What's more, we also have to contend with the fact that the half-life of information has decreased. The half-life of information is the amount of time that passes before that information is replaced by newer or more accurate information. You can study to your heart's content; the information you process now will be outdated sooner than you think. "Facts" written in articles, books, and documentaries are based on strong evidence and accepted as truth. But then they are completely reversed when a new study comes out.

I don't need to tell you how completely inundated each of us is with digital details. Even when we try to go "off the grid," digital information somehow finds us. While I'm writing this, I've shut down all my devices. But I need to have access to the Internet for research purposes, and a handful of random notifications and updates still popped up on my computer (yes, I know I can turn these off as well, but you get my point).

In Chapter 12 (Study) and Chapter 14 (Speed Reading), you will discover practical ways to catch up, keep up, and get ahead of the digital deluge of information you must process each day.

KWIK START

Take a moment and schedule 30 minutes of white space in your calendar for this week. This is time to be spent away from technology, time dedicated to clear your mind, relax, and be creative.

DIGITAL DISTRACTION

Before mobile devices, we would say "brb" (be right back) all the time when we were online. We don't say it anymore. We no longer leave. We live here now. Because of our always-on, ever-connected devices, we're struggling to find connection when we're with friends and family, and we're struggling to stay focused at work. Most of us deal with some kind of work-life situation where we don't feel comfortable forgoing digital connection for large swaths of time every day. So we stay on the grid out of the fear that if we were unreachable, we would lose out.

The trouble is, we're wired to enjoy it. Each successive hit of dopamine we get from the likes we receive on social media, or from the texts we get from loved ones or friends, only reinforces our behavior. But those rewards are changing our brains. Instead of relaxing into the downtime that we might experience when waiting in line, waiting for a bus or an appointment, etc., we pull out our phones and train our distraction muscles. What happens when this is our constant way of being, when every loose moment is filled with shining stimulus?

Staying connected may make us feel more secure, but it doesn't make us happier. Ryan Dwyer, MA, of the University of British Columbia, led a study that showed how our digital habits are affecting our relationships. In one experiment, more than 300 adults and university students were asked to keep their phones on the table, easily accessible, while others were asked to put them on silent and keep them in a container on the table during a meal. Afterward, participants were asked to respond to a questionnaire that asked them about their feelings of connectedness, enjoyment, distraction, and boredom.

The survey also asked them to detail the amount of time they spent on their phone during the meal. Those whose phones were accessible used them more often . . . and they described themselves as feeling more distracted. They also enjoyed the dinner less than the diners who didn't have access to their phones. "Modern technology may be wonderful, but it can easily sidetrack us and take away from the special moments we have with friends and family in person," Dwyer says of the study.[5]

Just as few of us have learned how to learn, not many know how to process and filter the massive amount of information we are constantly seeing. We just multitask to get all of it in, and this doesn't serve us well. "Asking the brain to shift attention from one activity to another causes the prefrontal cortex and striatum to burn up oxygenated glucose, the same fuel they need to stay on task," notes neuroscientist Daniel J. Levitin in his book, *The*

Organized Mind: Thinking Straight in the Age of Information Overload. "And the kind of rapid, continual shifting we do with multitasking causes the brain to burn through fuel so quickly that we feel exhausted and disoriented after even a short time. We've literally depleted the nutrients in our brain. This leads to compromises in both cognitive and physical performance."[6]

From app notifications to message alerts, it's not just adults who deal with this. With the availability of technology and social pressure to be online and active on social media, children and teenagers experience the constant distraction, too.

In Chapter 11 (Focus), you will discover the keys to sustained concentration and focus development to learn and get things done.

KWIK START

Go to the notification settings of your phone and turn off all unnecessary and distracting pings and dings. Do this now.

DIGITAL DEMENTIA

When is the last time you had to remember someone's phone number? I'm dating myself here, but I'm part of a generation that, when you wanted to call your friend down the block, you needed to *know* their number. Can you still remember some of your best friends' numbers from childhood? What about the number of the person you talk or text with every day? You no longer have to, because your mobile remembers it for you. This is not to say anyone wants to or should memorize 200 phone numbers, but we've all but lost the ability to remember a new one, or a conversation we just had, the name of a new potential client, or something important we need to do.

Neuroscientist Manfred Spitzer uses the term *digital dementia* to describe how overuse of digital technology results in the breakdown of cognitive abilities. He argues that short-term memory pathways will start to deteriorate from underuse if we overuse technology. It's the same with GPS. Move to a new city and see how quickly you become reliant on GPS to tell you how to get around. Then notice how long it takes you to map new roads in your mind—probably much longer than when you were younger, but not because your brain isn't working as well. With tools like GPS, we don't give our minds the chance to work. We rely on technology to do the memorization for us.

This reliance may be hurting our long-term memory. Maria Wimber of the University of Birmingham told the BBC that the trend of looking up information prevents the build-up of long-term memories. In a study that examined the memory habits of 6,000 adults in the UK, France, Germany, Italy, Spain, Belgium, the Netherlands, and Luxembourg, Wimber and her team found that more than a third of respondents turned to their computer first to retrieve information. The UK came in the highest—more than half of the participants searched online first without trying to come up with the answer themselves.[7]

Why is this a big deal? Because such instant information can be easily and immediately forgotten. "Our brain appears to strengthen a memory each time we recall it, and at the same time forget irrelevant memories that are distracting us," said Dr. Wimber. Forcing yourself to recall information instead of relying on an outside source to supply it for you is a way of creating and strengthening a permanent memory. When you contrast that with the reality that most of us have a habit of constantly looking up information—maybe even the same information—without bothering to try to remember it, it seems we're doing ourselves harm.

Is relying on technology always bad? Many researchers disagree. The argument goes that by outsourcing some menial tasks like memorizing phone numbers or doing basic math or getting directions to a restaurant we've visited before, we're saving brain space for something that matters more to us. There's research that says our brains are more like a muscle, rather than a hard drive that fills up. That the more you use it, the stronger it gets, and the more it can store. The question is: Are we making those choices consciously, or are we acting out of unconscious habit?

Too often, we outsource our brains to our smart devices, and our smart devices are making us, well, a little bit stupid. Our brains are the ultimate adaptation machines, capable of seemingly endless levels of evolution. And yet we often forget to give it the exercise it needs. Just as there is a physical price to always relying on the technology of the elevator instead of taking the stairs, so is there a price for lazy mental muscles. Use it or lose it.

In Chapter 13 (Memory), I will show you simple tools and techniques to remember anything from names and speeches to languages, faster and easier.

KWIK START

Take a minute to exercise your memory: Memorize the phone number of someone you communicate with regularly.

DIGITAL DEDUCTION

"In a digital-first world, where millennials obtain all their answers to problems at the click of a mouse or swipe of a finger, the reliance on technology to solve every question confuses people's perception of their own knowledge and intelligence. And that reliance may well lead to overconfidence and poor decision-making," says Rony Zarom, founder of the video collaboration platform newrow.[8] The ubiquity of information about everything also means that there's a ubiquity of opinion about everything. If you want to know how to feel about a hot-button issue, you can just go online and collate the opinions of others. If you want to know the implications of an event or a trend, a quick online search will provide endless amounts of analysis. The upshot is that deduction—an amalgam of critical thinking, problem solving, and creativity that is an essential skill for being limitless—is becoming automated.

There's a certain amount of value to this, of course. Before the Internet, we were limited in our access to the opinions of others. In an ideal world, being able to get as many perspectives on a topic as possible would be enormously valuable in helping us to form our own opinions. Unfortunately, that's rarely how it plays out in the real world. Instead, we tend to identify a handful of sources with which we align and then give those sources extreme influence over our thinking and decision-making. In the process, the "muscles" we use to think critically and reason effectively are atrophying. We're letting technology do the deduction for us. And if technology is forming our deductions, then we are also ceding much of our problem-solving ability—something so important and something we will discuss at length later in this book.

Psychologist Jim Taylor defines thinking as, "The capacity to reflect, reason, and draw conclusions based on our experiences, knowledge, and insights. It's what makes us human and has enabled us to communicate, create, build, advance, and become civilized." He then goes on to caution that there is "a growing body of research that technology can be both beneficial and harmful to different ways in which children think."[9]

Patricia Marks Greenfield, Distinguished Professor of Psychology at UCLA, has been looking at this issue for more than a decade. In discussing the impact on education, she wrote, "What is the effect on learning if college students use their laptops to access the Internet during a classroom lecture? This was tested in a communication studies class where students were generally encouraged to use their laptops during lectures, in order to explore lecture topics in greater detail on the Internet and in library databases. Half of the students were allowed to keep their laptops open, while the other half (randomly assigned) had to close their laptops. Students in the closed laptop condition recalled significantly more material in a surprise quiz after class than did students in the open laptop condition."[10] Because they were engaging their minds in the lecture rather than looking for what the Internet already thought about the subject, they were much more responsive when it was time to reason for themselves. Greenfield analyzed another study that showed that college students who watched a news program without the crawl at the bottom of the screen remembered significantly more of what the anchors were discussing.

Playwright Richard Foreman fears that this reliance on the Internet to do much of our thinking is changing our very selves. "I come from a tradition of Western culture, in which the ideal (my ideal) was the complex, dense and 'cathedral-like' structure of the highly educated and articulate personality—a man or woman who carried inside themselves a personally constructed and unique version of the entire heritage of the West . . . . But today I see within us all (myself included) the replacement of complex inner density with a new kind of self-evolving under the pressure of information overload and the technology of the 'instantly available.'"[11]

Do you remember what it was like when you were approaching your teens and you first started formulating thoughts and opinions independent of your parents? My guess is that this experience was extremely liberating for you and that it might have even been the first time in your life when you truly felt like your own person. What had happened to you, of course, was that your critical faculties had become refined enough to allow you to regularly employ reason to navigate through life.

Why, then, would you want to turn this liberating skill over to a device? Think about it: How do you feel when someone tries to impose their thinking on you? If a family member, friend, or colleague came up to you and said, "Don't think about this; here's your opinion," you'd try to get away from that person as soon as you possibly could. Yet, when we immediately reach for the Internet to provide us with information, we're essentially inviting the same thing.

In Chapter 15, I will provide you with a powerful set of tools that will allow you to supercharge your thinking and expand your perspective on any topic or problem.

While these four horsemen are the ones we need to contend with most vociferously, there's another digital danger that is worthy of our attention. I call this *digital depression,* a result of the comparison culture that emerges when we let the highlight reels of the social media feeds of others cause us to perceive ourselves as less than. Now, I enjoy social media. I love staying connected with our community of students and podcast listeners and staying updated with the everyday lives of my family and friends. I appreciate it so much as not only a source of entertainment, but also education and empowerment. But I only recommend using it consciously, not mindlessly out of habit, and in a harmonious way so it doesn't highjack your productivity and peace of mind.

In the upcoming Part II: Limitless Mindset, I share ideas to mitigate these feelings of not being enough, as well as fears of looking bad or missing out. Those are the same limits that stand in the way of personal growth and learning. In Part III: Limitless Motivation, I will show you how to add, break, or change these habits.

Think about a decision you need to make. Schedule some time to work on that decision without the use of any digital devices.

KEEPING THE VILLAINS AT BAY

In the hero's journey, the heroes need villains just as much as villains need heroes. The challenges from trials and rivals make us grow and become better. The power and strength of the villain determines the necessary power and strength of the hero. If the villain was weak, there would be nothing to vanquish—and no need for the hero to rise to greatness. In my podcast interview with Simon Sinek, author of *The Infinite Game*, Simon refers to our "worthy rivals," those who help point out the personal weaknesses we need to address. That is where your opportunity lies.

As I mentioned, I love the light side of technology—how it can connect us, educate us, and empower us, make our lives easier. What we've just described are a few potential drawbacks of technology, which is an inherent part of all the good that it brings into our lives. Like fire, technology has changed the course of human history. However, fire can cook your food or burn your home down—it's all in how you use it. Like any tool, technology itself isn't good or bad, but we must consciously control how it's used. If we don't, then who becomes the tool? It's up to you to choose how you engage.

Which of the four digital villains do you believe are currently most disrupting your performance, productivity, and peace of mind? Take a moment and write the name of this villain down:

______________________________.

Conscious awareness is the first part to solving a problem.

"The human brain has 100 billion neurons, each neuron connected to 10,000 other neurons. Sitting on your shoulders is the most complicated object in the known universe."

—MICHIO KAKU

3

YOUR LIMITLESS BRAIN

You may be thinking, *Jim, I see what you mean about technology. I wouldn't want to live without it, but I do feel more overloaded, distracted, and forgetful than ever.* Here's the good news: You were born with the ultimate technology, the greatest superpower.

Let's take a moment to acknowledge just how extraordinary your brain is. It generates up to 70,000 thoughts per day. It races with the speed of the fastest race car. Like your fingerprints, it is uniquely yours—there aren't two brains in the universe exactly the same. It processes dramatically faster than any existing computer, and it has virtually infinite storage capacity. Even when damaged, it is capable of producing genius, and even if you only have half a brain, you can still be a fully functioning human being.

And remarkable stories about it abound. Like the one about the comatose patient who somehow developed a method of communication with his doctor. Or the woman who could recall important events *by date* going back as far as when she was 12 years old. Or the slacker who became a mathematical genius after suffering a concussion during a bar fight. None of this is science fiction or the product of a superhero comic. They're just examples of the extraordinary function built into that remarkable machine between your ears.

We take so much of that function for granted. Let's think about just what the average person has accomplished simply by being an "average" person. By the age of one, you learned how to walk, no simple task considering how many complex neurological and physiological processes are required. A year or so after that, you learned how to communicate through the use of words and language. You learned dozens of new words and their meanings on a daily basis and kept doing so all the way through school. And while you were learning to communicate, you were also learning to reason, to calculate, and to parse an endless number of complex concepts—and all of that was before you read a single page of a book or attended one class!

Our brains are what separate us from the rest of the animal kingdom. Think about it. We can't fly, we aren't particularly strong or fast, we can't climb with the dexterity of some animals, we can't breathe underwater. As far as most physical functions are concerned, we're just average. But because of the power of our brains, we are overwhelmingly Earth's most dominant species. By harnessing that incredible mental power, we have created ways to explore the ocean depths like a fish, move tons of weight like an elephant, and even fly like a bird. Yes, the brain is quite a gift.

The brain is so complex that we know more about our vast universe than we do about its workings, and we've learned more about it in the past decade than we'd previously learned over the course of human history . . . and we'll learn even more about it from the time this book goes to press to the time it hits the bookshelves. Our understanding of the brain is ever evolving, and we know that what we've learned about it is only a tiny fraction of what there is to be learned. But what we already know is staggering. So, let's take a journey through your limitless brain.

The brain is part of the central nervous system (CNS). Similar to the control tower at an airport, your brain acts as its control center, directing all the comings and goings of information, processes, and impulses. The brain has three major areas: the brain stem, the cerebellum, and the cerebral cortex (both the cerebellum and cerebral cortex start with *cere*, Latin for "wax," because of its waxy appearance). The brain is made of fat and water, weighs approximately three pounds, and facilitates incredible power and ability.[1]

The brain stem moderates the basic functions we need to live, such as breathing, maintaining a regular heart rate, impulses to eat or have sex, and our fight-or-flight responses. It is located at the top of your spine and the base of your skull, buried deep within the brain. At the back of the brain, the cerebellum is responsible for moderating movement and coordination. There's also increasing evidence that it plays a role in our decision-making.

The cerebral cortex is the largest part of our brain, where the majority of our complex thinking, short-term memory, and sensory stimulation take place. It is made up of the occipital, parietal, temporal, and frontal lobes. Our frontal lobes are where most of our thinking takes place: where logic and creativity derive.

The brain is split into two halves that are connected by the corpus callosum, which acts like a bundle of telephone wires between the lobes, sending messages back and forth. Right now, you have somewhere around 86 billion neurons (also called brain cells) firing and acting together in concert as you read these words and assimilate the information on these pages.[2] These neural signals are released into the brain and received by neurotransmitters, which then pass the message along to other neurotransmitters or stop the message altogether if that's the appropriate response.

We used to think that we reached our neurological peak in late adolescence, after which our brains never changed—other than to deteriorate. We now know that this is far from the truth. Our brains have the capacity for neuroplasticity, which means that it can be changed and shaped by our actions and by our environments. Your brain is always changing and molding itself to your surroundings and to the demands you place on it.

Because our brains are subject to the influence of our genes and environment, we each possess a brain that is entirely unique to us. They're like snowflakes; no two are alike. Each brain adapts to the needs of its owner. Let's look at someone raised in an environment that was full of stressors such as poverty, lack of access to food, or lack of safety. That person will have a very different brain structure than someone brought up in a very comfortable, affluent, well-cared-for setting. But before you jump to the conclusion that one environment is "better" than the other and breeds a better functioning brain, I challenge you to reconsider.

As I stated earlier, the brain is capable of being molded and shaped, meaning that at any point anyone can decide to change the way their brain functions. While it's easy to assume that the individual who grew up in a more stressful, unsupportive environment may not wind up reaching their full potential due to their brain's development under those circumstances, growing evidence suggests those people are able to thrive and reach new levels of success due to the mindset they are forced to develop in such a situation. Based on the number of successful people who overcame troubled upbringings, it may be that a difficult childhood or challenging upbringing breeds resilience among other attributes that lead to success.

UNDERSTANDING NEUROPLASTICITY

What can we learn from the brains of London taxicab drivers?

This is the question neuroscientist Eleanor Maguire of University College London posed as she considered the vast amount of information held in the brains of the city's cab drivers, appropriately called "The Knowledge." To earn their licenses, applicants traveled by moped through a specific section of the city—a 10-kilometer radius of Charing Cross station—for three to four years, memorizing the maze of 25,000 streets within as well as the thousands of attractions they supported. Even after this intense study, only about 50 percent of applicants pass the series of licensing exams. Perhaps, thought Maguire, those successful had larger than average hippocampi.

Maguire and her colleagues discovered that London taxi drivers did indeed have "more gray matter in their posterior hippocampi than people who were similar in age, education, and intelligence who did not drive taxis. In other words, taxi drivers had plumper memory centers than their peers. It seemed that the longer someone had been driving a taxi, the larger his hippocampus, as though the brain expanded to accommodate the cognitive demands of navigating London's streets."[3]

The London Taxi Cab Study provides a compelling example of the brain's neuroplasticity, or ability to reorganize and transform itself as it is exposed to learning and new experiences. Having to constantly learn new routes in the city forced the taxi cab drivers' brains to create new neural pathways. These pathways changed the structure and size of the brain, an amazing example of the limitless brain at work.

Neuroplasticity, also referred to as brain plasticity, means that every time you learn something new, your brain makes a new synaptic connection. And each time this happens, your brain physically changes–it upgrades its hardware to reflect a new level of the mind.

Neuroplasticity is dependent on the ability of our neurons to grow and make connections with other neurons in other parts of the brain. It works by making new connections and strengthening (or weakening, as the case may be) old ties.[4]

Our brain is malleable. We have the incredible ability to change its structure and organization over time by forming new neural pathways as we experience, learn something new, and adapt. Neuroplasticity helps explain how anything is possible. Researchers hold that all brains are flexible in that the complex webs of connected neurons can be rewired to form new connections. Sometimes, that means the brain compensates for something it has lost, as when one hemisphere learns to function for both. Just as there are people who have suffered strokes and have been able to rebuild and regain their brain functions, those that procrastinate, think excessive negative thoughts, or can't stop eating junk food may also rewire and change their behaviors and transform their lives.

If learning is making new connections, then remembering is maintaining and sustaining those connections. When we struggle with memory or experience memory impairment, we are likely experiencing a disconnection between neurons. In learning, when you fail to remember something, view it as a failure to make a connection between what you've learned and what you already know, and with how you will use it in life.

For example, if you feel that something you've learned is valuable in the moment, but that you'll never use it again, you are unlikely to create a memory of it. Similarly, if you learn something but have no higher reasoning as to why it's important to you or how it applies to your life or work, then it's likely that your brain will not retain the information. It's totally normal to have a memory lapse—we're human, not robots. But if we respond to this lapse in memory with the attitude that "I have a bad memory," or "I'm not smart enough to remember this," then we negatively affect our ability to learn and grow. In other words, the belief we might develop in response to forgetting does far more damage than the lapse in memory. That kind of self-talk reinforces a limiting belief, rather than acknowledging the mistake and reacquiring the information.

What does this mean for learning? Plasticity means that you can mold and shape your brain to suit your desires. That something like your memory is trainable—when you know how to help your brain receive, encode, process, and consolidate information. It means that with a few simple changes to something like your environment, your food, or your exercise, you can dramatically change the way your brain functions. I will share these energy tips in detail in Chapter 8.

Here's the bottom line: Plasticity means that your learning, and indeed your life, is not fixed. You can be, do, have, and share anything when you optimize and rewire your brain. There are no limitations when you align and apply the right mindset, motivation, and methods.

YOUR SECOND BRAIN

My students tell me after they learn about the vastness of their brain, they have a whole new sense of worth, that their self-esteem grows overnight. Here's more good news: You are not limited to just one brain, you have a second—your gut. Have you ever had a "gut feeling"? That moment when you just knew? If you've ever "gone with your gut" to make a decision or felt "butterflies in your stomach," did you ever wonder why that was? Hidden in the walls of the digestive system, this "brain in your gut" is revolutionizing medicine's understanding of the links between digestion, mood, health, and even the way you think.

Scientists call this little brain the enteric nervous system (ENS). And it's not so little. The ENS is two thin layers of more than 100 million nerve cells lining your gastrointestinal tract from esophagus to rectum. Science is only beginning to understand the brain-gut axis and how it affects our brains, our moods, and our behavior. You may hear it referred to as the "brain-gut connection." In the last decade, we've discovered that the gut has an outsize effect on the way our brains function. One can liken it to the way a tree functions. The roots in the ground are drawing up vital nutrients and water from the soil as well as communicating with other plants. Those nutrients are then brought up into the body of the tree, fortifying and building the trunk, and giving the tree what it needs to sprout new leaves each spring, which in turn gather light, another energy source.

In the same way, the nutrients we take in are absorbed through our intestines. We rely on those nutrients to fuel our brains. While

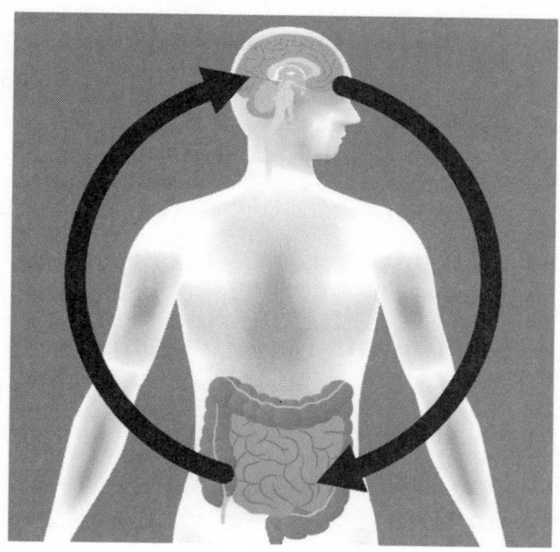

our brains take up very little of our total body weight, they use 20 percent of the energy we take in, so nutrients make a huge difference in the way our brains function on a day-to-day basis.

The gut is lined with more than a hundred million nerve cells, and it makes up part of the ENS. When a baby grows in the womb, the ENS and the CNS develop from the same tissue and remain connected via the vagus nerve. In many ways, the two systems mirror each other in structure. They also both use many of the same neurotransmitters to function, including serotonin, dopamine, and acetylcholine. As with CNS, we used to believe that we are each born with a certain amount of cells—and that's it. But like the brain, we now know the ENS makes new neurons throughout adulthood and can be repaired when damaged.[5] The gut is made up of these neurons as well as a network of bacteria that form the microbiome, and as with the brain, each of us has our own unique microbiome.

What's more, these nerve cells operate through startlingly similar pathways as the brain. In 2010, neuroscientist Diego Bohórquez of Duke University discovered that the enteroendocrine cells of the gut had "footlike protrusions" that resembled the synapses that neurons use to communicate. This caused Bohórquez to wonder if these cells could "talk" to the brain using signals similar to the way neurons do. He hypothesized that if this were happening, they would have to be using the vagus nerve, which connects the gut and the brain stem.[6] After further testing, they discovered that the cells do in fact use the vagus nerve to take up messages and send them to the brain, faster than could be done via the bloodstream.

TEAM EFFORT

The connection between the brain and the gut is still being explored, but it seems that they function in very similar ways and that they function in tandem. The little brain in conjunction with the big one partly determines our mental state. When you have a gut feeling that something isn't right, or conversely that you should follow a hunch, it's not just superstition—your gut has its own way of interpreting events and giving your brain signals. Furthermore, when you feed your gut with subpar food, you're also feeding your brain with subpar fuel.

Right now, your gut is digesting the food you just ate and sending that fuel to your brain. At the same time, a part of your brain is taking in the feel of the pages under your fingertips (or your e-reader, if that's your preference), sensing the comfort of the chair supporting you, and monitoring the environment around you to make sure you're safe. Another part of your brain is taking in the smells of the environment, maybe coffee, or perfume, or the scent of the book's pages. Another part of your brain is absorbing the word-symbols on the page of this book and turning them into meaning, which is then processed and stored in short-term memory, where it will then be sent to long-term memory (under the right conditions, which we'll get to in a moment).

All of this is to say that you have the ultimate superpower between your ears. You also have the ability to hone that superpower and make it greater—or to let it falter and decay. You get to decide what kind of environment your superpower lives in: one that supports your mission in life, or one that distracts you from your greatest dreams.

THE ELUSIVE OBVIOUS

Given that we have this tremendous power of our minds available to us, why are we struggling? If your brain is indeed so magnificent, why are overload, distraction, forgetfulness, and feelings of inadequacy affecting us so much? How do we reconcile the fact that we have so much potential but have days where we can't remember a simple name or think our way out of a paper bag? The answer is so simple, it's almost the elusive obvious: We were not taught how.

Give a person an idea, and you enrich their day. Teach a person how to learn, and they can enrich their entire life.

School is a great place to learn. There, we're taught what to learn, what to think, and what to remember. But there are few if any classes on *how* to learn, *how* to think, and *how* to remember.

In his seminal book on education, *Creative Schools*, Sir Ken Robinson says, "One of my deepest concerns is that while education systems around the world are being reformed, many of these reforms are being driven by political and commercial interests that misunderstand how real people learn and how great schools actually work. As a result, they are damaging the prospects of countless young people. Sooner or later, for better or for worse, they will affect you or someone you know."[7]

My guess is that they have *already* affected you and everyone close to you. As you already know, my own experience with the education system was a complicated one, and I acknowledge that my circumstances were unusual. In reality, though, even if I'd

"The only way to win is to learn faster than anyone else."

—ERIC RIES

never had that fateful head trauma in kindergarten, I would probably have gotten much less out of my school education than was ideal. That's because very few schools anywhere in the world have incorporated learning how to learn into their curriculums. They'll fill us with information. They'll expose us to great works of literature and to figures who changed the course of civilization. They will test us—sometimes endlessly—to determine whether we can repeat back what they've taught us. But they won't get underneath all of this to teach us how to teach ourselves, to make enriching our minds, discovering new concepts, and truly absorbing what we learn fundamental to our everyday lives.

This is not about placing the blame on the teachers who work hard to teach our children. In my opinion, teachers are some of the most caring, compassionate, and capable human beings in our society. In fact, my mother became a teacher after my brain injury because I was struggling so much and she wanted to help me and others like me. The problem lies in the outdated system in which teachers work. If Rip Van Winkle woke up from decades of slumber, the only thing he would recognize today are classrooms, because they have evolved so little. Education hasn't changed enough to prepare us for the world we live in today. In a era of autonomously driven electric cars and vehicles capable of taking us to Mars, our education system is the equivalent of a horse and carriage.

And then there's the matter that how we earn our livings is changing profoundly and increasingly rapidly. Automation and artificial intelligence (A.I.) are affecting the future of work, and

I'm not speaking only about factories where laborers are being replaced by robots. In addition, many of us are facing the need to switch from the structure of an office job to the volatility of the gig economy. And jobs that few of us might have imagined even five years ago have gained traction, while others are emerging this very moment that will affect the workplace in the coming years.

All of this points us in the same direction: We must take charge of our own learning. If schools tell us what to learn, but not *how* to learn, then we need to do the rest of the work ourselves. If digital overload threatens to hijack our brains, then we need to use what we know about learning to reset the ground rules. If the workplace is evolving with so much rapidity that we can never be sure of what work will mean to us tomorrow, then only by taking complete control of our learning can we truly be prepared for an unknowable future.

TURN ON THE POWER

A quick, often-told story: One day at a power plant, everything comes to an abrupt halt. All of the machines go offline. The silence is deafening. The people running the plant are frantic and after hours and hours, none of the workers can track down the problem. The head of operations is desperate at this point, so he calls the best local help he can find.

The expert technician arrives and glances around the facility. He goes to one of the numerous beams among all the electrical boxes, opens one of them, and stares at the various screws and wires inside. He turns one screw, and, like magic, everything starts working again and the plant comes back to life.

The head of operations is *so* relieved. He thanks the technician and asks him what he owes him. The technician says, "$10,000." The head of operations is shocked. "What do you mean, $10,000? You were here for a few minutes. You turned one single screw. Anyone could have done that. I need an itemized bill, please."

The technician reaches into his pocket, pulls out a notepad, scribbles a few seconds, and hands the other man the bill. The head of operations reads it and immediately pays him. The bill read: "Turning screw: $1. Knowing which screw to turn: $9,999."

What's the lesson of the story? It's not that you have a screw loose. The story illustrates two things.

The first is how much added value a limitless mind can offer you and others. We've entered an expert economy in which brain power trumps brute strength. Where what you have between your ears is your greatest wealth-creating asset. There are those who know and those who don't know. And that applied knowledge is not just power, it's profit. Your ability to think, solve problems, make the right decisions, create, innovate, and imagine is how we add value. The faster you can learn, the faster you can earn.

And that takes us to the second lesson. That one screw made all the difference. I've mentored and coached some amazing minds, and you don't have to be a genius to see that genius leaves clues. One of those patterns is that elite mental performers filter and focus for those handful of "screws" that make all the difference and turn everything else on. This book is filled with many of the behaviors, tools, and strategies I've discovered to give you the maximum results and rewards for your effort.

The world is throwing more challenges at you than ever before, and there's every indication that those challenges will continue to increase. At the same time, there is more to be gained from having a finely tuned brain than ever before, and you know now that you have more than enough potential to meet any challenge. But it's going to require taking control of your learning.

It may seem as if it would take superhuman capabilities to keep up with the demands of our current reality. But you already have a hidden superpower: your brain. You may not be able to shoot webs from your hands, but you have something far better, the neural webs in your head. That superpower plant of a network between your ears is your greatest gift and greatest advantage. All we have to do is upgrade your brain the same way you upgrade your phone. How do you install new software into your brain? One of my favorite ways is what you're doing right now. It's called reading.

"I not only use all

the brains that I have,

but all that

I can borrow."

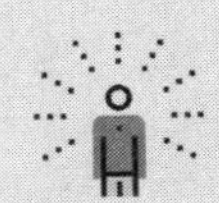

—WOODROW WILSON

4

HOW TO READ AND REMEMBER THIS (AND ANY) BOOK

Your time is one of your greatest assets. It's the one thing you can't get back.

As your brain coach, I want you to get the greatest results and return on your attention, so here are some recommendations on how to get the most out of this book. You can apply this advice toward practically anything you want to learn and read.

Let's start with a question: Have you ever read something only to forget it the next day?

You are not alone. Psychologists refer to this as the "forgetting curve." It is the mathematical formula that describes the rate at which information is forgotten after it is initially learned. Research suggests humans forget approximately 50 percent of what they learn within an hour, and an average of 70 percent within 24 hours.[1]

Below are a handful of recommendations that will help you stay ahead of the curve. Later, I will share advanced strategies to accelerate your learning and retention in the sections on study, speed-reading, and memory improvement.

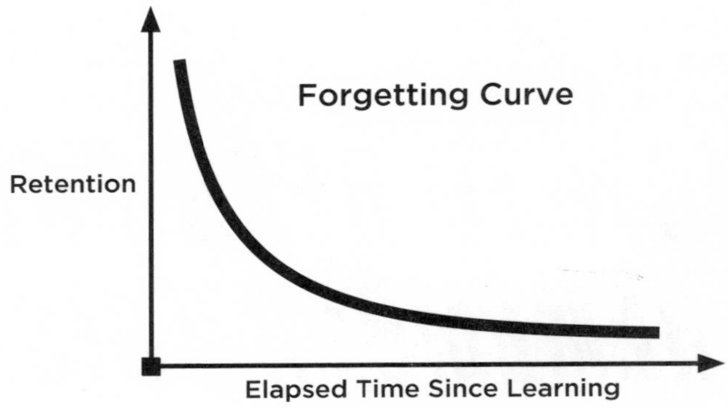

Research suggests that our natural ability to concentrate wanes between 10 to 40 minutes. If we spend any longer on a given task, we get diminishing returns on our investment of time because our attention starts to wander. For that reason, I suggest you use the Pomodoro technique, a productivity method developed by Francesco Cirillo based on the idea that the optimal time for a task is 25 minutes, followed by a 5-minute break.[2] Each 25-minute chunk is called a "Pomodoro." As you read this book, I suggest that you read for one Pomodoro and then take a 5-minute brain break before continuing.

When it comes to learning, the Pomodoro technique works for reasons related to memory, specifically the effect of primacy and recency.

The effect of primacy is that you're more likely to remember what you learn in the beginning of a learning session, a class, a presentation, or even a social interaction. If you go to a party, you might meet 30 strangers. You're most likely to remember the first few people that you meet (unless you've been trained to remember names with my method, which I'll teach you later in this book).

The effect of recency is that you're also likely to remember the last thing you learned (more recent). At the same party, this means that you'll remember the names of the last few people you met.

We've all procrastinated before a test and then, the night before the exam, sat down to "cram" as much as possible without any breaks. Primacy and recency are just two of the (many) reasons cram sessions don't work. But by taking breaks, you create more beginnings and endings, and you retain far more of what you're learning.

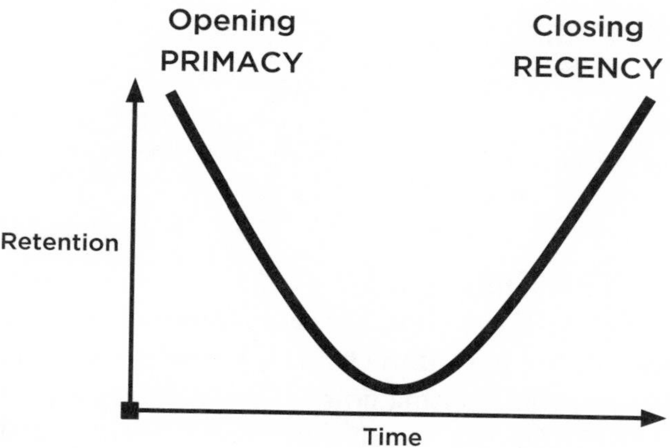

If you sit down to read a book over the course of two hours without taking any breaks, you might remember the first 20 minutes of what you read, then maybe you'll experience a dip around the 30-minute mark, and then you're likely to remember the end of what you read. This means the lull in between, with no breaks for assimilation or thinking through what you just read, results in a dead space for learning. So, take this book one Pomodoro at a time so you get the most out of what you read. If you still choose to cram, you'll learn helpful methods in the book to retain the "in-between" information.

Did you know that the very act of reading this book will make you smarter? I realize that's a big claim, but I'm completely convinced that it's true. On one level, it's going to teach you to be smarter through the tools and tactics I share here. But on another level, when you actively read it, you'll form pictures in your mind, and you'll make connections between what you know and what you're learning. You will think about how this applies to your current life, and you will imagine how you can use the knowledge you're taking in. It promotes neuroplasticity. Oliver Wendell Holmes said, "Every now and then a man's mind is stretched by a new idea or sensation, and never shrinks back to its former dimensions."[3] When you read any book, you have the opportunity to stretch the range of your mind, and it will never be the same.

KWIK START

Set a timer for 25 minutes right now and concentrate on what you're reading in this book for that amount of time. When your alarm goes off, bookmark this book and close it. Then write down what you learned within that 25-minute period.

USE THE FASTER METHOD

To get the most out of this book, here is a simple method for learning anything quickly. I call it the FASTER Method, and I want you to use this as you read, starting now.

The acronym FASTER stands for: Forget, Act, State, Teach, Enter, Review. Here's the breakdown:

F is for Forget

The key to laser focus is to remove or forget that which distracts you. There are three things you want to forget (at least temporarily). The first is what you already know. When learning something new, we tend to assume we understand more than we do about that subject. What we think we know about the topic can stand in the way of our ability to absorb new information. One of the reasons children learn rapidly is because they are empty vessels; they know they don't know. Some people who claim to have twenty years of experience have one year of experience that they've repeated twenty times. To learn beyond your present sense of restraints, I want you to temporarily suspend what you already know or think you know about the topic and approach it with what Zen philosophy calls "a beginner's mind." Remember that your mind is like a parachute—it only works when it's open.

The second thing is to forget what's not urgent or important. Contrary to popular belief, your brain doesn't multitask (more on this later). If you're not fully present, it will be difficult for you to learn when your focus is split.

KWIK START

As you are reading this book, when your mind inevitably wanders into something else—and that something else is important but not urgent—don't try to not think of it. What you resist persists. Instead, keep a notebook close by to capture that thought or idea by writing it down. You can thus release it temporarily, to be addressed after the task at hand is complete.

And finally, forget about your limitations. These are the preconceived notions you believe about yourself, such as that your memory isn't good or that you're a slow learner. Suspend (at least temporarily) what you believe is possible. I know this may sound difficult but keep an open mind to what you can do. After all, since you are reading this book, some part of you deep down must believe there's more to life than what you've already demonstrated. Do your best to keep your self-talk positive. Remember this: If you fight for your limitations, you get to keep them. Your capabilities aren't fixed, and it's possible to learn anything.

A is for Act

Traditional education has trained many people that learning is a passive experience. You sit quietly in class, you don't talk to your neighbor, and you consume the information. But learning is *not* a spectator sport. The human brain does not learn as much by consumption as it does by creation. Knowing that, I want you to ask yourself how you can become more active in your learning. Take notes. Do all the Kwik Start exercises. Download the Kwik Brain app to test and train your limitless abilities. Go to the resource page at www.LimitlessBook.com/resources for additional free tools. I recommend you highlight key ideas, but don't become one of those highlight junkies who make every page glow in the dark. If you make everything important, then nothing becomes important. The more active you are, the better, faster, and more you will learn.

What is *one* thing you will do to make reading this book a more active experience? Write it down here: ______________________

____

S is for State

All learning is state-dependent. Your state is a current snapshot of your emotions. It is highly influenced by your thoughts (psychology) and the physical condition of your body (physiology). Your feelings or lack thereof about a subject in a specific situation affect the learning process and ultimately the results. In fact, when you tie a feeling to information, the information becomes more memorable. To prove this, I'm guessing there's a song, fragrance, or food that can take you back to your childhood. Information times emotion helps create long-term memories. The opposite is also true. What was the predominant emotional state you felt back in school? When I ask audiences this question, most people in the room shout out "boredom!" In all likelihood, you can relate to this.

If your emotional energy at school was low, it's no wonder you forgot the periodic table. But, when you take control of your state of mind and body, you can shift your experience of learning from boredom to excitement, curiosity, and even fun. To achieve this, you might try shifting the way your body moves in a learning environment or piquing different moods before you sit down to learn. Change your posture or the depth of your breathing. Sit or stand the way you would if you were totally energized and excited for what was coming. Get excited about how you will benefit from what you are about to learn and what you will do with your new knowledge. Remember, all learning is state-dependent. Consciously choose states of joy, fascination, and curiosity.

KWIK START

How motivated, energized, and focused are you at this moment? Rate your current state on a scale of 1 to 10. What is *one* thing you will do right now to increase that number?

T is for Teach

If you want to cut your learning curve dramatically, learn with the intention of teaching the information to someone else. Think about it: If you know you have to give a presentation on what you learn, you will approach how you learn the topic with the intention of mastering it well enough to explain it to someone else. You will pay closer attention. Your notes might be more detailed. And you might even ask better questions. When you teach something, you get to learn it twice: once on your own, and then again through educating another person.

Learning isn't always solo; it can be social. You may enjoy this book more if you invite someone else to learn with you. Buy a copy for a friend, or, even better, start a Limitless Book Club that meets weekly so you can discuss the ideas and concepts in this book. You'll enjoy learning more when you're making memories with a friend or group of friends. Working with someone else will not only help you stay accountable, but it will give you someone to practice this method with.

KWIK START

Find a learning buddy to read this book with and hold each other accountable. Name that person (or persons) here: ____________

____

E is for Enter

What is the simplest and most powerful personal performance tool? Your calendar. We enter important things on our schedule: work meetings, parent-teacher gatherings, dentist appointments, taking Fluffy to the vet, and so on. Do you know what a lot of people don't schedule? Their personal growth and development. If it's not on your calendar, there's a good chance it's not getting done. It's too easy for the day to slip by with you "forgetting" to work out your body and brain.

KWIK START

Take out your calendar and enter your Limitless readings for the next seven days. Label these LIMITLESS ME, GENIUS TIME, BRAIN TRAINING, CONVERSATIONS WITH JIM, or anything else provocative enough to guarantee that you'll keep this date on your calendar.

R is for Review

One of the best ways to reduce the effects of the forgetting curve is to actively recall what you learned with spaced repetition. You are better able to retain information by reviewing in multiple spread-out sessions. Going over the material at intervals increases our brain's ability to remember it. To leverage this principle, before you begin your reading session take a moment, if only a few minutes, to actively retrieve what you learned the session before. Your brain will give greater value to the reviewed material and prime your mind for what's to come.

KWIK START

Before each reading, take a few minutes to talk about or write what you remember from the previous reading.

CHOOSE WISELY

The French philosopher Jean-Paul Sartre noted that, "Life is C between B and D," meaning that the life we live is the choices we make between the "B" of birth and the "D" of death. The profound simplicity of that statement is particularly relevant to the journey we're engaged with here. Being limitless is a choice, and that choice is entirely yours, regardless of your circumstances. You can choose to give up this power, but why would you when you

"This is your last chance. After this, there is no turning back. You take the blue pill—the story ends, you wake up in your bed and believe whatever you want to believe. You take the red pill—you stay in Wonderland, and I show you how deep the rabbit hole goes. Remember: all I'm offering is the truth. Nothing more."

—MORPHEUS

know that you can truly live a life without barriers? But choosing is an active thing, and the time to make this choice is right now.

So, I want you to resolve and commit. Most people are sincerely interested in doing something that they know they *should* do. But they don't do it, because they consider it a preference not a promise. There's tremendous power in making a real resolution. I want you to write down your commitment to complete this book. When we write something down, we're more likely to do what we promise.

Opposite, I've included a commitment page for you to fill out. If you want extra points, take a photo of your signed promise, then post it on social media. This public resolution will help you stay accountable. Tag me @JimKwik #LimitlessBook so we can cheer you on!

THE QUESTIONS ARE THE ANSWER

Have you ever read a page in a book, arrived at the end, and could not recall what you just read? You may even reread it, only to forget it again. I don't want you to experience this while you are reading this book, so why do you think it happens? The answer is, you're not asking the right questions. Questions, in fact, are the answer.

Every second, your senses gather up to 11 million bits of information from the world around you. Obviously, if you tried to interpret and decipher all of them at once, you'd be immediately overwhelmed. That's why the brain is primarily a deletion device; it's designed to keep information out. The conscious mind typically processes only 50 bits per second.

What makes it through the filter is determined by the part of the brain called the reticular activating system, or RAS for short. The RAS is responsible for a number of functions, including sleep and behavior modification. It also acts as the gatekeeper of information through a process called habituation, which allows the brain to ignore meaningless and repetitive stimuli and remain sensitive to other inputs.

One of the ways to guide the RAS are the questions we ask ourselves. These tell that part of our brain what is important to us.

Let's take my younger sister's birthday as an example. Years ago, my sister kept sending me postcards, pictures, and e-mails of

I, ______________________________, commit to reading this book in 10- to 25-minute increments until it is finished.

I commit to focusing by forgetting my prior understanding, distractions, and limiting beliefs of what is possible.

I commit to being active in the process. I will do all the Kwik Start exercises, take notes, highlight, and practice asking myself relevant questions as I read.

I commit to manage my state of being as I read, checking in regularly with my energy levels and being proactive in adjusting my motivation as needed.

I commit to teaching what I learn to others, so we may all benefit.

I commit to entering my reading time in my calendar, because if it's in my schedule I will do it.

I commit to review what I have already learned so I can remember it better before moving on to something new.

And finally, I commit that even if I "mess up" with any of the above, I won't beat myself up. I'll get back at it and do my best.

Yes! I am ready to be LIMITLESS!

Signed,

______________________________ Date: ____________

“The one real object of education is to leave a person in the condition of continually asking questions.”

—BISHOP MANDELL CREIGHTON

pug dogs. You know, the ones with the mushy faces and the bulgy eyes. They're very docile; you can dress them up as ballerinas and they won't care. Of course, I wondered why she was sending me photos of pugs—and then I remembered her birthday was coming up, and it became evident she was leaving clues because she wanted one.

Later that day, I was checking out at the health food store, and I looked over at the other checkout line. To my surprise, I saw a woman carrying her pug over her shoulder. *Wow, I haven't seen one of one of those in a long time—what are the chances of that?* I thought. The next day I went running in my neighborhood, and there was someone walking six pugs.

The question is, where did the pugs come from? Did they just magically appear? Of course not. They were always there. But in the flood of stimuli, I had never paid attention to them before. Once pugs broke through my awareness, I started seeing them all over the place. Have you had an experience like this? Maybe it was a specific kind of car or outfit that "magically" began appearing everywhere.

In an interview with media personality Jeannie Mai, we compared this effect to how your favorite social media platform starts showing you more posts based on past expressed interest. The site you're on knows this because of what you clicked, liked, or watched before. Your RAS is like that site's algorithm. It shows you more of what you express interest in, and it hides the things you don't engage in.

So often the answers we want are there, but we're not asking the right questions to shine a spotlight on them. Instead, we're asking useless questions or worse, questions that are disempowering. Why am I not smart enough? Why am I not good enough? Why can't I lose weight? Why can't I find the person I'm meant to be with? We ask such negative questions, and then those questions give us evidence—or pugs—as answers. The human mind is always generalizing in order to make sense of the world. Here, there, and everywhere, we can find evidence to confirm our beliefs.

Thinking is a process of reasoning through something, during which we ask and answer questions. You may be asking, is that true? See, you had to ask a question. While we have tens of thousands of thoughts a day, we have one, maybe two dominant questions we ask more than others. As you can imagine, these questions direct our focus, which directs how we feel, and how we consequently spend our lives. As a thought experiment, imagine someone whose most frequent question is, "How do I get people to like me?" You don't know their age, career, or what they look like. But you know more than you probably realize. What do you imagine their personality is like? You don't need to know much to guess that they're a people pleaser, they're indirect in expressing their needs, and they're not authentic about how they feel or think in any given moment. Someone who is constantly asking themselves how to get people to like them can never truly be their true self because they will always be molding themselves to the preferences of the people around them, even if they're not aware of it. You know all this information, and you only know one question they ask themselves. What do you think is your dominant question?

YOUR DOMINANT QUESTION

When I felt my brain was broken, I loved to escape into the world of superheroes, comic books, Dungeons and Dragons. The world of fantasy helped me forget my pain. I decided that the superpower that would be best for me was invisibility, and my dominant question became, "How do I stay invisible?" Instead of being seen, I was always watching everyone else, wondering what everyone's life was like. I wondered why this person was so popular, and that person was so happy, or what made another person so smart. I was suffering all the time, so as I watched people and learned from the world around me, my dominant question changed to, "How do I make this better?" I wanted to solve this riddle: "How does my mind work so I can work my mind?" The more and more I asked these new questions, the more answers I got. This book is the result of two decades of asking empowering questions.

"He who

asks questions

cannot avoid

the answers."

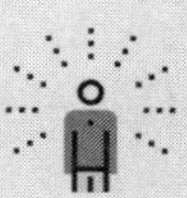

—CAMEROON PROVERB

I first met Will Smith at Quincy Jones's 80th birthday party. After hearing about my traumatic brain injury, he invited me to be his guest at the premiere of the film *Concussion,* a movie about the concerns of football-related head trauma. (I'll talk about brain protection in an upcoming chapter.) Eventually, Will booked me to come to Toronto to spend time with him for a week on set. He was shooting a superhero film, so you can imagine that I was in my glory.

What was interesting to me was the cast and crew were working each night, from 6 P.M. to 6 A.M., outside in the dead of winter. Not all Hollywood is glitz and glam; there's a lot of hurrying up just to wait on set. During a break, Will and I discovered a few of his dominant questions, one of which is "How do I make this moment even more magical?" While we were waiting for Will's next scene to shoot, his family and friends were huddled in tents watching the other actors work. At 3 A.M., while I'm sure everyone was cold and tired, we got to see his dominant question in action. He was bringing everyone hot cocoa, cracking jokes to make us smile, and actively playing host when he could have been resting. He was indeed making the moment even more magical. The result of this question directed his focus and his behavior, and completely changed the experience for everyone.

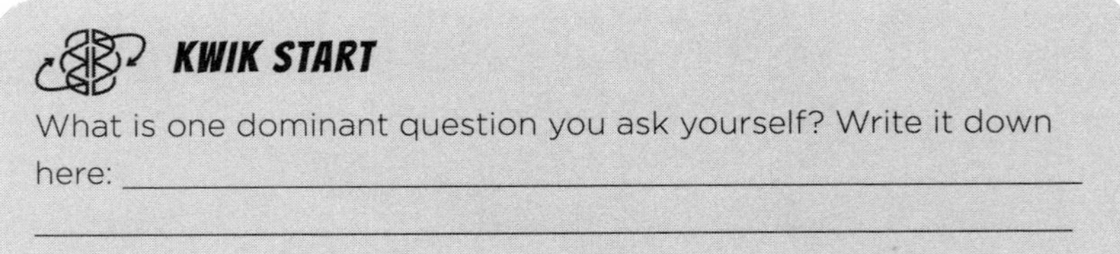

KWIK START

What is one dominant question you ask yourself? Write it down here: ________________________________

____

PREPARE YOUR MIND

Questions direct your focus, so they play into everything in life—even reading comprehension. Because people typically don't ask enough questions when they read, they compromise their focus, understanding, and retention. If you prep your mind with the right kinds of questions before you read, you'll see answers (pug dogs) everywhere. For that reason, I place specific key questions throughout the book.

To start you off, here are the three dominant questions to ask on our journey together. They will help you to take action on what you learn and turn the knowledge into power.

- How can I use this?
- Why must I use this?
- When will I use this?

KWIK START

These are your three magic questions: How can I use this? Why must I use this? When will I use this? They will help you integrate the knowledge from this book into your head, heart, and hands. Ingrain them. Write these questions down where you can see them—on your desk or in your phone.

Instead of passively reading, consider these questions as you take in the knowledge in this book. Remember, questions are the answer. At the beginning of every chapter for the rest of the book, you will find a series of questions that are designed to prime your focus as you read. Study the questions before you read each chapter, and you'll be better prepared to understand and remember what you learn.

Along with the questions, do the "Kwik Start" exercises seeded in strategic places throughout the book. They are specific activities designed to train you to take immediate action in your learning and life. Most of these can be done in one or two minutes. Remember the power of neuroplasticity: Every time you answer a question and do a new activity, you rewire your brain. I also conclude each chapter with exercises to do before you move on to the next section, to really set these lessons into practice.

"Everybody is a genius.
But if you judge
a fish by its ability
to climb a tree,
it will live its whole life
believing that
it is stupid."

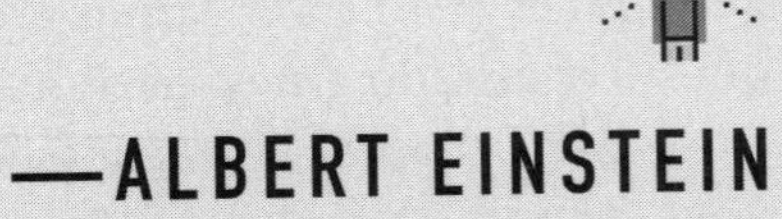

—ALBERT EINSTEIN

PART II

LIMITLESS MINDSET

THE WHAT

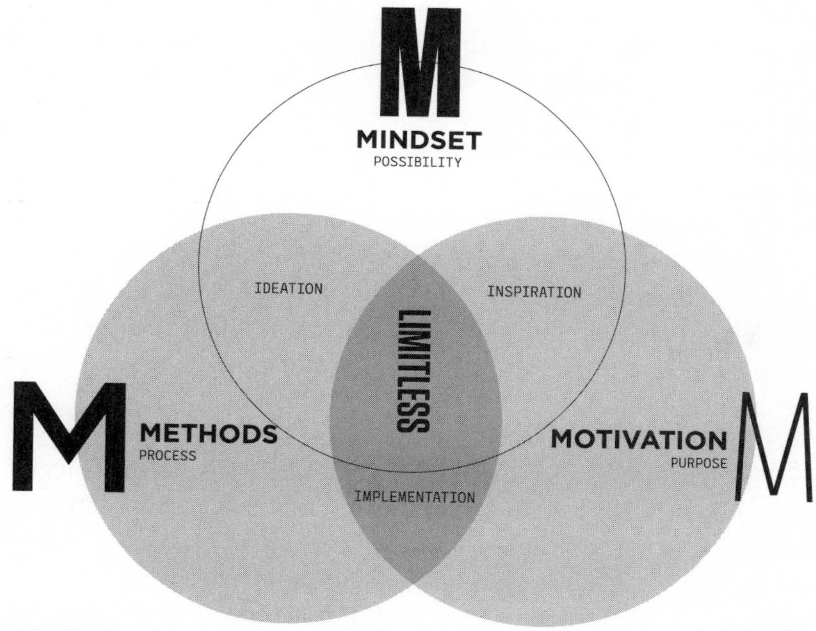

mindset

mind·set *(noun)*

The deeply held beliefs, attitudes, and assumptions we create about who we are, how the world works, what we are capable of and deserve, and what is possible.

The first element of the three-part Limitless Model is Mindset, which is the mental attitude or disposition that predetermines a person's responses to and interpretations of situations. Mindset is made up of beliefs, assumptions, and attitudes we hold about ourselves and the world around us. All behavior is driven by belief, so before we address how to learn, we must first address the underlying beliefs we hold about what is possible.

We're not born with pre-installed mindsets about what we're capable of achieving—we learn these fixed and limited ways of thinking from the people in our lives and the culture we experience growing up.

Think of a young elephant tied to a stake in the ground. When it's a baby, the elephant isn't strong enough to pull the stake up, so it eventually stops trying because it learns the effort is futile. As the elephant grows, it gains more than enough power and strength to pull out the stake, but it remains tied up by something as inconsequential as a rope and a flimsy piece of metal because of what it learned as a baby. In psychology, it's called learned helplessness.

Most of us behave like that elephant. At some point, we had an experience that gave us an impression of what we're capable of, and our belief about our potential has been set ever since. But just as helplessness is learned, it's just as possible to learn to be limitless. In this section, you're going to learn about the seven lies we've been taught about our potential and how to replace them with new beliefs.

I use the term LIE intentionally. In this case, LIE is an acronym for Limited Idea Entertained. If you are like the vast majority of people out there, you are entertaining ideas about yourself that define you as something less than what you truly have the potential to achieve. You're giving these ideas energy and allowing them to take residence in your mind, but they're really nothing but BS (in this case, an abbreviation for Belief Systems). Over the coming chapters, you will discover where these lies come from, how they imprison you, and what you can do about it. And keep asking yourself this question: How many of my perceived constraints are nothing more than LIEs and BS? I think you're going to be stunned with the answers, and that these answers are going to be liberating.

A quick story before we get going. One of the most cherished friendships of my life was the one I shared with Stan Lee. As you know, Stan's Marvel creations helped me through some of the biggest challenges of my life when I was younger, and they continue to be a nonstop source of inspiration to this day. My conversations with Stan were always engaging and very often illuminating.

I remember one such conversation when we were in a car together on our way to a dinner. Stan looked resplendent in his suit with a bold Spiderman tie, and I was inspired to ask him something I'd always wanted to ask.

"Stan, you've created so many great characters over the years, like the Avengers and X-Men," I said. "Who's your favorite character?"

He didn't even hesitate a second.

"Iron Man," he said. "And who's yours?"

I pointed to his tie. "That would be Spiderman."

Stan nodded and said, "With great power comes great responsibility."

"That's so true, Stan. And the opposite is also true: with great responsibility comes great power."

He seemed to like that, which tickled me to no end. But while I'd never phrased it that way before, I realized that I was voicing one of the key tenets of the limitless mindset. When we take responsibility for something, we are imbued with great power to make things better.

That's what a limitless mindset is all about. Our background and circumstances may have influenced who we are, but we must be accountable for who we become. It's about understanding that we are responsible for our assumptions and attitudes. And when you accept that all of your potential is entirely within your control, then the power of that potential grows dramatically.

So, superhero, let's get started on unlimiting your mindset. As Stan would say, "Excelsior!"

"It ain't what you
don't know that
gets you into trouble.
It's what you
know for sure
that just ain't so."

—MARK TWAIN

5

THE SPELL OF BELIEF SYSTEMS

Why do your beliefs have such an effect on your life?

Why do limiting beliefs keep you from your goals?

How do you reject limiting beliefs?

Grab some imaginary popcorn, because we're going to take a quick side trip to the movies. The scene goes like this:

A bridge is about to collapse because a supervillain has weakened the supports to the point where the entire thing is going to go crumbling into the river. As the bridge creaks and teeters, our superhero learns about the crisis and races to the scene. She's the only person with the strength to avert catastrophe and save hundreds of lives.

Our superhero is less than 10 seconds from the bridge now. But as she gets closer, a voice in her head reminds her of the time she face-planted while doing a somersault in elementary school. A couple of seconds later, she recalls her father telling her that it would be best if she set her sights low for her future. With the bridge in sight, another vision emerges in front of her: her former best friend ridiculing her for her delusions of grandeur.

Rubble from the bridge topples into the water. The creaking gets louder. The screams of dozens and dozens fill the air.

And our superhero, overwhelmed with doubt, sits down by the side of the road, covers her face with her hands, and drowns in self-pity.

Wait . . . what?

You've never seen that scene in a superhero movie, right? There are some reasons for that. One is that it would be a terrible story. Another is that, regardless of the darkness in their pasts or the moral conflicts they might be facing, superheroes don't become true superheroes by giving in to limiting beliefs. Superman doesn't think that, maybe on a good day, he might be able to leap a tall building or, maybe, you know, a couple of stories at least. Tony Stark doesn't think, "This Iron Man suit is probably going to fail me at the worst possible time because I'm inherently a screw-up." Captain Marvel doesn't break through our atmosphere and suddenly start thinking, "I'm not sure I have the emotional capacity to fly solo through space." They have superpowers, and any sense of restriction be damned.

And you know what? You have superpowers too. How do you realize them? You begin with your mindset.

FINDING MY ROGER BANNISTER

When I was a kid, maybe 9 or 10 years old, we had a big family reunion. There were a couple dozen of us around a huge table in a big, busy restaurant. It was a Saturday night, so the place was packed, with the waitstaff ping-ponging from table to table as quickly as they could.

A few minutes after we all gathered, our waitress came over to take our order. As you can imagine, this was a lengthy process. About halfway through, the waitress came around to ask me what I wanted to eat and drink. It was then that I realized that she hadn't been writing down anything my relatives had ordered. I found this extremely curious. There was something like 25 of us, and I'd seen her serving other customers, so I knew we weren't her only table. How was she possibly going to remember everything we'd ordered? I told her what I wanted and then watched her carefully as she made her way around the rest of the table.

I did not have a high level of confidence that my meal was going to remotely resemble what I'd requested. Even at that age, I had a healthy amount of skepticism. Not because I was a negative person or because I didn't have faith in people, but rather that I needed to *see* anything out of the ordinary before I *believed* it was possible. In this case, I figured that, at best, the waitress would get most of our orders correct, but she'd wind up putting them down in the wrong places, and we'd find ourselves trading plates all across the table.

Well, first our drinks came, and everyone got exactly what they wanted, even the cousin who wanted no ice in her Coke and another who'd requested that her drink come with a twist of lemon, a twist of lime, and two cherries. *Okay,* I thought, *that was pretty good. But there's a lot more to come.* A few minutes later, the salads came out, and again everything was perfect. The people who wanted their dressing on the side got it that way, the people who wanted their dressing tossed with their salads got that, and everyone got the dressing they'd asked to get. My skepticism was being tested. And then the main courses were delivered. Not one mistake—and there were some crazy special requests. Everything was cooked the way we wanted, and all of the side dishes were the right ones.

I dove into my meal at that point, but I couldn't stop thinking about what the waitress had accomplished. At this age, I'd only just begun to read competently, and my brain injury had caused me all kinds of learning challenges. And yet here was someone who had shown me that our brains are capable of far more than I would have imagined.

That waitress was my Roger Bannister. Bannister was a track star in the 1950s. In the early years of Bannister's career, it was widely assumed that it was physically impossible for an athlete to run a mile in less than 4 minutes. The feeling was that our bodies would break down from the effort before the time could be achieved. Then, on May 6, 1954, Bannister ran a mile in 3 minutes and 59.4

seconds, proving that the 4-minute barrier was indeed breakable. What is most interesting to me is that less than two months later someone broke Bannister's record, and then that record was broken, and then that one. The times have been dropping ever since.

What Bannister did was show that this barrier wasn't in fact a barrier at all. That was what this waitress showed me. Through her, I saw that what I'd perceived my brain's capacity to be was so much less than what it really was. As you know, I continued to struggle with learning for many years, but from the moment of that dinner I had a model for what was possible.

The waitress in this way was limitless. She demonstrated something in front of me that I would never in a million years have thought was possible. I never got to know her, but I'm forever grateful because what she did for me personally was to permanently change my perceptions of my own restrictions. She altered my mindset. It was impossible for me to buy into the notion that I could expect to accomplish only a modest amount with my brain when I knew that others could achieve so much more. I just needed to find a method.

I'm going to share much of that method with you in this book. At its core is one fundamental concept: unlimiting. The key to making yourself limitless is unlearning false assumptions. So often, we don't accomplish something because we've convinced ourselves that we can't do it. Let's go back to Roger Bannister for a moment. Every day before May 6, 1954, people were absolutely certain that a sub-four-minute mile was beyond the range of human capabilities. Forty-six days after Bannister did it, someone else beat his time, and more than 1,400 racers have followed them. Running a mile in less than four minutes is still an extraordinary feat—but it is not an impossible feat. Once that "barrier" was broken, many achieved it.

So, how do you face down limiting beliefs?

WHAT LIMITING BELIEFS DO TO US

Limiting beliefs are often revealed in our self-talk, that inner conversation that focuses on what you're convinced you *can't* do rather than what you already excel at and what you're going to continue to achieve today and into the future. How often do you stop yourself from attempting to do something or from pursuing a dream because that voice convinces you that it is beyond your reach? If this sounds like you, you are very far from alone, but you're also not doing yourself any favors.

"We come into this world not knowing if life is hard or easy, if money is scarce or abundant, if we're important or unimportant. We look at two people who know everything: our parents,"[1] said belief change expert Shelly Lefkoe in our podcast interview. Parents are our first teachers, and although they probably meant us no harm, we still come away from our childhoods with the limiting beliefs they unconsciously instilled in us.

Limiting beliefs can stop you in your tracks even when you're doing something at which you normally excel. Have you ever had the experience of being in a pressure situation where you need to do something that typically comes easily to you—writing a memo or doing a quick calculation, for example—but the intensity causes you to doubt yourself so much that you fail at this task? That's a limiting belief setting you back. If you could just get out of your head, you'd have no trouble getting the job done, but your inner voice confounds you.

Now, take that situation and extend it to an entire segment of your life. Your career aspirations, perhaps, or your ability to make friends. If your limiting beliefs are in control, you could find yourself mired in underachievement, either wondering why you never really get ahead or convinced that you don't deserve it.

Alexis, who cofounded Kwik Learning with me, struggled with learning as a child much like I did, but for very different reasons. She was born in South Korea to entrepreneurial parents who struggled in business. They didn't have a lot of money, but always worked hard to make ends meet. While she had a roof over her head, her family of four lived in a one-room basement in Korea. Their second business had just failed when they received a letter from the United States saying their visa application had been approved—they had filed seven years earlier. On the verge of desperation, her family thought this was a new chance, so they borrowed the equivalent of $2,000 and left for America.

Alexis didn't know a word of English when she arrived. It was total culture shock—she didn't know what was being said around her, and the cultural norms were entirely different. Her parents didn't speak English either, so they were all struggling to understand their new world.

Alexis enrolled in school near her new home. She was a shy and introverted student, and, because she didn't know the language, she often sat alone at the lunch table or ate in a bathroom stall just to avoid feeling like an outcast.

It took Alexis six years to be able to truly understand English, and both the kids and the teachers in her school didn't understand why she struggled for so long. After a couple of years, classmates started to criticize her for being a slow learner. "What's wrong with you?" "Are you stupid? "You're weird," were phrases she heard frequently as a child.

Her difficulties in school even extended to physical education, the one area where she ostensibly didn't need to use many words. She remembers sitting on the bleachers repeatedly copying out the words, "I will bring my gym clothes to class." But she had no idea what she was writing, and no one managed to communicate to her that she needed to bring a change of clothing.

By the time she was in her early twenties, Alexis had a hard time reading a book from front to back. She battled with her internal voices whenever she attempted to learn. One overarching voice constantly criticized and doubted her abilities, while another small voice questioned that critic. Something inside her couldn't fully accept the notion that she was "dumb." Her parents worked hard to give her a second chance, and she couldn't let them down. While there were moments where she felt she wasn't good enough to do anything special in her life, there were also moments where she was sure there had to be more to life than merely accepting her circumstances.

If Alexis allowed those external voices to shape her reality, then it would've stopped her in her tracks. She wouldn't have searched for solutions to her problems. Instead, she looked for answers by observing and learning from others. She started wondering what they were doing differently to find success and happiness. She wanted to know if it was sheer luck and genius, or if there was a method behind it. In her quest to learn how to be successful, she ended up in one of my early classes. She wasn't sure what she was getting into, but knew she wanted something different for herself—she needed to feel a sense of hope.

On day one, we covered memory. It was eight hours of intense training, but at the end of the session, Alexis felt refreshed and even excited about what she was learning. "How else can I use my brain?" she wondered. For the first time in her life, she didn't feel slow and she felt excited about learning.

Day two was all about speed reading. She wasn't initially excited about this because of her previous challenges. But when Alexis learned the smart reading habits and went through the speed-reading exercises, a lightbulb turned on. She suddenly saw the potential—and even the fun—of reading. She realized she was not too slow or stupid to understand; she was just never shown how to learn and use the super-computer between her ears. As she experienced the power of learning, the years of negative self-talk and limiting beliefs took a backseat in her mind.

After that class, Alexis read a complete book for the first time and was blown away by how much she understood, how much she remembered, and how much she liked the experience.

It was a huge turning point in her life. She went from a limited mindset, believing that "things are the way they are," to knowing that she could change and shape her mind to reach her goals. For the first time in her life, she began to believe in herself and imagine what might be possible.

Today, Alexis doesn't shy away from learning something new. She doesn't feel inadequate if she doesn't know something. She goes out to find answers and applies them. Out of her passion for learning, she also started Kwik Learning Online with me to share the transformation she experienced with others in every country in the world.

In their book *Mequilibrium*, authors Jan Bruce, Dr. Andrew Shatté, and Dr. Adam Perlman call these kinds of beliefs "iceberg beliefs" because of how many of them lie beneath the surface of our subconscious. "Iceberg beliefs are deeply rooted and powerful, and they fuel our emotions," they say in the book. "The more entrenched an iceberg is, the more havoc it wreaks on your life. . . creating your schedule chaos, getting in the way of successfully sticking to a diet, or holding you back from seizing opportunities."

And, perhaps most significantly, they say, "If we get a handle on our icebergs, we gain an *enormous* amount of control over our feelings and our lives. Melt an iceberg and all the downstream events it causes get washed away as well."[2]

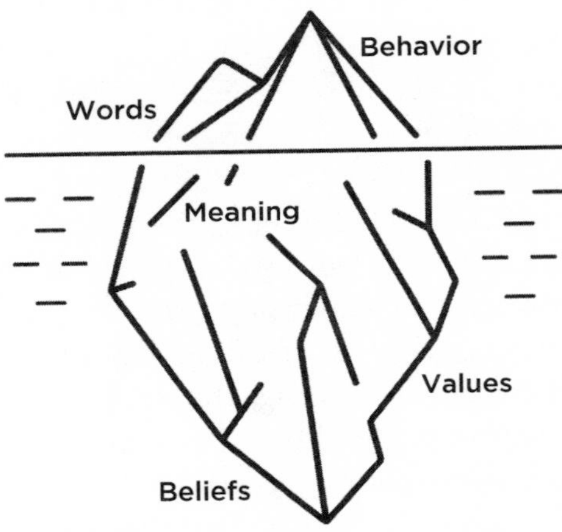

Dr. Jennice Vilhauer, director of Emory University's Adult Outpatient Psychotherapy Program in the Department of Psychiatry and Behavioral Science in the School of Medicine, implores us to come face-to-face with our inner critic, "the voice in your head that judges you, doubts you, belittles you, and constantly tells you that you are not good enough. It says negative hurtful things to you—things that you would never even dream of saying to anyone else. *I am such an idiot; I am a phony; I never do anything right; I will never succeed.*"

She adds: "The inner critic isn't harmless. It inhibits you, limits you, and stops you from pursuing the life you truly want to live. It robs you of peace of mind and emotional well-being and, if left unchecked long enough, it can even lead to serious mental health problems like depression or anxiety."[3]

Let's revisit our failed superhero from the beginning of this chapter. She certainly had the motivation to save the day. And she certainly had the methods to save the day. But what she didn't have was the mindset. Her inner critic convinced her that she wasn't good enough, so she sat on the sidelines feeling sorry for herself instead of taking care of business. Certainly, one takeaway from this story is that our failed superhero blew it. She flopped at a critical time because she couldn't get out of her own head.

But there's another hugely important component to this story: our superhero had everything inside of her to succeed. If only she'd been able to prevail over the beliefs that were holding her back, her extraordinary talents would have shone through.

That's how important it is to conquer your limiting beliefs.

WHAT IF I TOLD YOU THAT YOU WERE A GENIUS?

When you think of geniuses, who are the first people that come to mind? I'm guessing Einstein and Shakespeare are on your short-list. Others might include Stephen Hawking, Neil DeGrasse Tyson, Marie Curie, or Ruth Bader Ginsburg. These names pop into many people's heads because each of them was extraordinary in the kinds of intelligence we tend to equate with genius. But was Roger Federer on your list? How about J. Lo? Or Oprah? Or Gandhi? Or you?

It wouldn't be surprising if you didn't include the latter names on your list. Most of us tend to equate genius with one particular measurement of intelligence: IQ. People with outsize IQs are geniuses, and people with lesser IQs can be good or even great at something, but they aren't considered geniuses.

If this sounds like your kind of thinking, you're far from alone in defining genius far, far too narrowly. I would even take this to the point of suggesting that most people define genius in this way. But there are two problems with that. One is that it prevents you from appreciating the genius a wide variety of people hold. The other is that it might prevent you from identifying the genius in yourself.

There are multiple forms of genius. Various experts differ on the number, but it is commonly agreed that genius expresses itself in one of four manners. Here's a way of looking at it that has been around for thousands of years:

- **Dynamo genius:** Those who express their genius through creativity and ideas. Shakespeare was a dynamo genius because of his brilliance at inventing stories that told us so much about ourselves. Galileo was a dynamo genius because of the way he could see things that others couldn't see when he looked up at the skies. Dynamo geniuses are those we most commonly think of when we think of geniuses.
- **Blaze genius:** Those whose genius becomes clear through their interaction with others. Oprah Winfrey is a blaze genius because of her extraordinary ability to connect with the hearts, minds, and souls of a wide range of individuals. Malala Yousafzai's blaze genius expresses itself through her ability to make her story relatable to people all around the globe. Blaze geniuses tend to be master communicators.
- **Tempo genius:** Those whose genius expresses itself through their ability to see the big picture and stay the course. Nelson Mandela was a tempo genius because he was capable of seeing the wisdom of his vision even in the face of overwhelming odds. Mother Teresa's tempo genius allowed her to imagine better circumstances for those around her even at the darkest times. Tempo geniuses tend to understand the long view in ways that most of those around them cannot.
- **Steel genius:** Those who are brilliant at sweating the small stuff and doing something with the details that others missed or couldn't envision. Sergey Brin used his genius at seeing the potential of large amounts of data to co-found Google. If you read the book *Moneyball,* then you know that Billy Beane and his staff redefined baseball through their genius at crunching data. Steel geniuses love getting all the information they can get and have a vision for doing something with that information that most others miss.

KWIK START

What would you say is your genius? Write it down here: ________
____

There's a very good chance that your own genius is a combination of two or more of these. Very few of us are only data people or are only adept at being empathetic. But what's important for you to understand here is that genius extends far beyond your ability to excel at academics or recite the periodic table on command—and that you have genius inside of you.

If you find that last statement surprising, you might want to go back and reread some of the earlier chapters in this book. Making yourself limitless is all about unleashing your innate genius. Maybe you aren't the dynamo of Shakespeare or the blaze of Oprah, but there is some combination of genius inside of you that is either waiting to express itself or waiting to express itself *more*. The key is letting it free.

IT ISN'T ONLY IN YOUR HEAD

Before I give you some tools to help you shift toward a more positive mindset, let's just talk for a minute about how important positive thinking is. There are clear connections between positive thinking and physical health. In a Johns Hopkins study, Dr. Lisa Yanek found that "positive people from the general population were 13 percent less likely than their negative counterparts to have a heart attack or other coronary event."[4]

Meanwhile, the Mayo Clinic notes that "The positive thinking that usually comes with optimism is a key part of effective stress management. And effective stress management is associated with many health benefits."

They note that these benefits include:

- Increased life span
- Lower rates of depression
- Lower levels of distress

- Greater resistance to the common cold
- Better psychological and physical well-being
- Better cardiovascular health and reduced risk of death from cardiovascular disease
- Better coping skills during hardships and times of stress[5]

REFRAMING LIMITING BELIEFS

There's a metaphor I've always found useful when helping people to move away from limiting beliefs. I tell them that the difference between limiting beliefs and a limitless mindset is like the difference between a thermometer and a thermostat. A thermometer has only one function: to react to the environment. It reads the temperature and nothing more. This is similar to how people commonly react to limiting beliefs. They read their sense of restriction, react in a constrained way to that, and conduct their lives in a limited way.

On the other hand, a thermostat gauges the environment and makes the environment react to it. If a thermostat notices that a room is too cold or too hot, it changes the environment to fit the ideal for which it is set. Similarly, if you encounter external or internal attempts to put constraints on you, you can act like a thermostat to reject those limiting beliefs and create an environment that aligns with your most ambitious goals.

So, how do you minimize limiting beliefs and develop a superhero mindset? To me, there are three keys.

Key 1: Name Your Limiting Beliefs

You've seen some examples here of limiting beliefs, but there are many more where those came from (and we'll go over the seven most prevalent limiting beliefs on learning in a moment). They might have to do with your talents, your character, your relationships, your education, or anything else that leads to internal whispers that you can't be what you want to be. Start paying attention right now to every time you tell yourself that you're incapable, even if you think that this particular thing might not be consequential in your life.

For example, maybe you tell yourself that you're terrible at telling jokes. Perhaps this isn't a big deal to you, because being a good joke-teller isn't a personal aspiration. But you might also be telling yourself that you don't think you're entertaining, or good company, or an enjoyable companion; and that kind of self-talk can ultimately cause you to double-clutch when you're in an important social situation or when you need to speak in front of a group. So, listen carefully every time you find yourself using phrases like "I can't," "I'm not," or "I don't." You're sending messages to yourself that are affecting how you think about your life in general, even if what you're beating yourself up over is something specific and seemingly not important to how you define yourself.

At the same time, try also to identify the origin of this sort of self-talk. Limiting beliefs often start in childhood. That doesn't automatically mean that your family is their only source. Early social settings can cause limiting beliefs, as can early experiences with education. Some might take hold simply because something didn't go well for you the first few times you tried it as a kid.

Being aware of how you're holding yourself back with your self-talk and spending some time to get to the source of these beliefs is extremely liberating, because once you're aware, you can begin to realize that these aren't *facts* about you, but rather *opinions*. And there's a very good chance that those opinions are wrong.

Once you identify the voices in your head that are focusing on what you can't do, start talking back to them. When you find yourself thinking, "I always screw up this sort of thing," counter with, "Just because I haven't always been good at this in the past doesn't mean that I can't be great at it now. Keep your opinions to yourself."

Key 2: Get to the Facts

One of the fundamental tyrannies of limiting beliefs is that, in so many cases, they're just plain wrong. Are you *really* terrible at speaking in public? Are you *really* bad at leading a group? Are you *really* the least interesting person in the room wherever you are? What's the evidence to support that? How many times have you actually been in these situations, and what have the results been?

"Life has

no limitations,

except the ones

you make."

—LES BROWN

One of the most pernicious things about limiting beliefs is that they play so heavily on our emotions. When you come up against a limiting belief, you're likely to find those beliefs warring—and usually winning—against your rational self. But how much of this self-talk has a basis in reality? Think about your experiences speaking in public (an extraordinarily common fear, by the way). Rather than focusing on how you felt in these instances, consider how things went. Were you booed off the stage? Did people come up to you afterward to laugh at you and tell you how awful you were? Did your boss sit you down the next day to say that you might want to consider a career where you never had to utter a word?

I'm guessing none of these things happened. Instead, it's likely that your audience felt connected to what you were saying. If it was in a professional setting, maybe they were taking notes, and you almost certainly taught them something. Does this mean that your next speech should be at TED? Of course not. But it definitely means that you're likely much better at conveying information to a group than that voice in your head is telling you that you are.

And then there's this question to ask: How much of my perceived poor performance was because my self-talk just wouldn't leave me alone? This is a real issue for many people. They'll be in the middle of doing something in which they lack confidence, and the inner critic will become so distracting that they can't focus on what they are doing . . . and therefore don't do it very well. This is one of the reasons why it's so important to learn to face down and quiet your limiting beliefs. The better you are at this, the better you'll be at keeping down distractions during your biggest growth challenges.

So, when you're examining the facts behind your limiting beliefs, be sure to consider two things: whether there is in reality any evidence to prove that you are truly hampered in this area and whether even that evidence was tainted by the noise in your head.

Key 3: Create a New Belief

Now that you've given your limiting beliefs a name and now that you've carefully examined the reality of those beliefs, it's time to take the most essential step—to generate a new belief that is both truer than the LIEs you've been accepting and beneficial to the limitless you that you are creating.

You're going to see this process at work in the next chapter, but let's take it for a spin right now. Let's say that one of your limiting beliefs is that you always come up short at the most important moments in your life. Having identified that as a limiting belief, you've then taken the step of examining the facts. What you realize is that, while you have occasionally succumbed to nervousness in pressure-packed moments, very few of these instances have been disastrous for you and, upon examination, you can think of several times when you "came through in the clutch." In fact, now that you really think about it, you've succeeded way more often than you've faltered.

So, now it's time to create a new belief. In this case, your new belief would be that no one triumphs at the most critical juncture 100 percent of the time, but that you should be proud of yourself for how many times you've performed at your best when the pressure was highest. This new belief completely supplants the old belief, is fully supported by the facts, and gives you a much healthier mindset the next time a critical situation comes along.

I have one more tool for you to use here. I've spoken to many experts over the years, and the conversation often comes back to the same thing: as long as you believe that your inner critic is the voice of the true you, the wisest you, it's always going to guide you. Many of us even use phrases like, "I know myself, and . . ." before announcing a limiting belief.

But if you can create a separate persona for your inner critic—one that is different from the true you—you'll be considerably more successful at quieting it. This can be enormously helpful and you can have fun with it at the same time. Give your inner critic a preposterous name and outrageous physical attributes. Make it cartoonish and unworthy of even a B-grade movie. Mock it for its rigid dedication to negativity. Roll your eyes when it pops into your head. The better you become at distinguishing this voice from the real you, the better you'll be at preventing limiting beliefs from getting in your way.

THE POSSIBILITIES BECOME LIMITLESS

Now that you know how to conquer your limiting beliefs, you can start to bring your positive mindset to bear on your quest to become limitless. That might sound like an audacious plan, but there's lots of evidence to support the connection between mindset and accomplishment.

One of my podcast guests, James Clear, the *New York Times* best-selling author of *Atomic Habits* who you will meet again later in this book, wrote about a study performed by Dr. Barbara Fredrickson, a positive psychology researcher at the University of North Carolina. He prefaced their conversation by underscoring what negative emotions do to us, using the example of encountering a tiger in the forest. "Researchers have long known that negative emotions program your brain to do a specific action," he noted. "When that tiger crosses your path, for example, you run. The rest of the world doesn't matter. You are focused entirely on the tiger, the fear it creates, and how you can get away from it."[6] The point that Clear is making is that negative emotions drive us to narrow the range of what we are capable of doing. It's all about getting away from the (metaphorical) tiger, and nothing else matters. If we let negative emotions (such as limiting beliefs) control us, we're regularly operating in survival mode and therefore confined to a reduced range of possibilities.

What Dr. Fredrickson discovered is that a positive mindset leads to precisely the opposite result. She created an experiment where participants were divided into five groups and presented with film clips. The first group saw clips that elicited joy. The second saw clips that elicited contentment. The third saw clips that generated fear and the fourth clips that generated anger. The fifth group was the control group.

After they'd seen the clips, the participants were asked to imagine similar situations to what they just saw and how they would react to these situations. They were then asked to fill out a form that had 20 prompts that began with, "I would like to." The people who experienced fear and anger wrote the fewest responses, while those who experienced joy and contentment listed far more than even the control group. "In other words," Clear noted, "when you are experiencing positive emotions like joy, contentment, and love, you will see more possibilities in your life."[7]

What's also essential to note is that the benefits of a positive mindset extend well beyond the experience of a positive emotion. Clear offers this example:

> A child who runs around outside, swinging on branches and playing with friends, develops the ability to move athletically (physical skills), the ability to play with others and communicate with a team (social skills), and the ability to explore and examine the world around them (creative skills). In this way, the positive emotions of play and joy prompt the child to build skills that are useful and valuable in everyday life. . . . The happiness that promoted the exploration and creation of new skills has long since ended, but the skills themselves live on.[8]

Fredrickson refers to this as the "broaden and build" theory because positive emotions *broaden* your sense of possibilities and open your mind, which in turn allows you to *build* new skills and resources that can provide value in other areas of your life.

> The theory, together with the research reviewed here, suggests that positive emotions: (i) broaden people's attention and thinking; (ii) undo lingering negative emotional arousal; (iii) fuel psychological resilience; (iv) build consequential personal resources; (v) trigger upward spirals towards greater well-being in the future; and (vi) seed human flourishing. The theory also carries an important prescriptive message. People should cultivate positive emotions in their own lives and in the lives of those around them, not just because doing so makes them feel good in the moment, but also because doing so transforms people for the better and sets them on paths toward flourishing and healthy longevity.[9]

The new mindset that comes from silencing your inner critic presents you with a world of possibility. When you're surging with positive emotions, you're seeing—and seizing on—opportunities you might never have noticed before. And with a high sense of motivation (and, really, how could you not be motivated by this?) and the right methods, you're well on the road to becoming virtually limitless.

BEFORE WE MOVE ON

To learn faster, we must transcend the narrow definition of what we believe is possible for ourselves. In the following pages, you'll learn about the seven learning lies that are the most common limiting beliefs that hold people back. I've seen students and clients cling to these beliefs throughout my decades of teaching people how to learn. These restrictions are the only real barrier you face. After all, people can't learn to read faster if they believe it isn't possible. They can't learn to memorize things more efficiently if they keep telling themselves they have a bad memory. Everything else falls into place once you snap out of the trance of these so-called "limitations." By tackling these lies, you'll be tackling the core blocks that keep you from being limitless. Here are a few things to try before going on to the next chapter.

- Think of a time when you saw someone accomplish something that truly impressed you. Now think about what personal inspiration you can draw from that.
- Reimagine your inner critic. Change the attributes of this voice in your head so you begin to give it less credence.
- Face down one limiting belief right now. What do you regularly tell yourself you *can't* do? Find the evidence that shows you that this belief isn't true.

“There is one grand lie—that we are limited. The only limits we have are the limits we believe.”

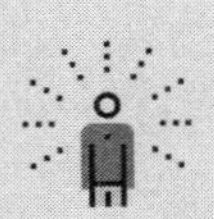

—WAYNE DYER

6

THE 7 LIES OF LEARNING

What are the most limiting myths you tell yourself?

How can you overcome the debilitating effect of these myths?

How can you turn these limiting beliefs into positive ones?

You're being lied to. Constantly. Sometimes by yourself. We are all subject to an endless stream of misinformation about our constraints to our capabilities, and we receive this information so often that most of us have no other choice than to believe it. The problem is that these messages directly oppose your quest to become limitless. These limited ideas entertained (LIEs) in our mind can stall us or steer us in a direction we don't want. So, let's bring seven to light, examine them for what they are, and replace them with something better.

LIE NO. 1: INTELLIGENCE IS FIXED

On the surface, it looked like Rae was a pretty positive person—she ran her own business, she had a thriving social network, and she loved being around people with big ideas who could imagine possibilities that most of us wouldn't dream of.

When Rae had a daughter, she realized that perhaps she wasn't as positive as she thought she was. A different kind of mindset started to show up in very subtle ways, as these things do. First it was in the way she reacted to some of the things her little girl did. Rae tended to think that "that's just the way she is," instead of believing that she could have an effect on the way her daughter behaved. When her partner tried to teach their daughter new things, Rae noticed she felt a subtle discomfort, as if she wanted to protect her daughter from disappointment if she wasn't able to learn what she was being taught. She became aware of the constant thought that her daughter was "too young to learn that."

One day, her partner looked at her and said, "Do you think she can't learn, that she's never going to improve from where she is?" The answer was of course not—she loved her daughter, and the little girl was bright and curious and learning something new every day. The opposite was obviously true . . . and yet, Rae was aware that there was some belief buried deep inside her that whispered, "No, she is the way she is." Rae was struggling with a fixed mindset about her daughter's intelligence.

These beliefs are incredibly subtle. Few of us consciously think about our restrictions or the restrictions we believe others have. But it leaks out in places that deeply affect our happiness—in our work, in our home life, and with our children. If we believe that it's not possible to improve, then in reality it won't be possible to improve. It's extremely difficult to accomplish something when you don't believe it can be done in the first place.

Carol Dweck, a professor of psychology at Stanford University, describes the difference between a fixed and a growth mindset:

> In a fixed mindset, students believe their basic abilities, their intelligence, their talents, are just fixed traits. They have a certain amount and that's that, and then their goal becomes to look smart all the time and never look dumb. In a growth mindset, students understand that their talents and abilities can be developed through effort,

> good teaching and persistence. They don't necessarily think everyone's the same or anyone can be Einstein, but they believe everyone can get smarter if they work at it.[1]

Like Rae, most of us don't think about whether we have a fixed or a growth mindset. Most of us have carried on thinking in the same patterns that our family did, without even knowing it. As subtle as this is, the adoption of one or the other deeply affects the way we approach life. With the fixed mindset, things are the way they are—we are powerless to change them. With the growth mindset, we have the ability to improve anything.

If Rae thinks, even on a very subtle level, that her daughter can't improve or grow, what does she do instead of teaching her? Probably a number of things—placating, giving time-outs, diverting attention. All of those work to alleviate the stress of the moment, but they don't contribute to her child's growth. In the same way, if as adults we believe that we don't have the capacity to learn, what do we do instead of taking the responsibility to teach ourselves what we want or need to know? We tell ourselves it isn't necessary, we make excuses, we blame other people or circumstances, and then we distract ourselves with things that make us feel good.

The genesis of this limiting belief is likely one that you either don't remember or that came from your early years. And it has a deep effect on the way you view intelligence and your capacity to learn. IQ scores and testing were created in the early 1900s to better assess which students would experience the most difficulty in school. French psychologist Alfred Binet and his student Theodore Simon were some of the first scientists to come up with a test that measured intelligence after they were commissioned to do so for the French government.[2] They were able to devise a test that took into consideration age as it related to competency. They were also lauded for the fact that the test was easily adaptable to other languages and cultures.[3]

More than 100 years later, it's still hotly debated whether these tests have the ability to measure intelligence, which is the ability to acquire and assimilate knowledge and information. Interestingly, Binet himself was not happy with the way his test was used because it didn't measure creativity or emotional intelligence.[4] Furthermore, our cultural understanding of these tests means we give these scores undue weight. We tend to think of IQ scores as a fixed reflection of our intelligence, but this isn't the case. The IQ test actually measures current academic capabilities, not innate intelligence.[5] To this day, IQ tests still don't measure creativity or practical intelligence (which you can think of as "street smarts"), and they certainly don't measure emotional intelligence[6]—all three of which are increasingly more important in the workplace and in life.

The important distinction here is to remember the difference between test scores and your ability to learn. "Those who claim that IQ is fixed for life are in fact referring to our IQ test scores, which are relatively stable—not to our intelligence levels, which are constantly increasing," says Bryan Roche of the National University of Ireland.[7]

David Shenk furthers this idea in his book, *The Genius in All of Us*. He writes that everyone has the potential for genius, or at the very least, greatness. But the reason we prefer to believe that we're either a genius or we're not, or that we're either talented or not, is because it relieves us from the responsibility of taking control of our own life. "A belief in inborn gifts and limits is much gentler on the psyche: The reason you aren't a great opera singer is because you can't be one. That's simply the way you were wired. Thinking of talent as innate makes our world more manageable, more comfortable. It relieves a person of the burden of expectation."[8]

Your intelligence is not only malleable but dependent on your ability to cultivate a growth mindset. Start looking at your attitude. Listen to the way you talk; a fixed mindset usually shows up in your language. Maybe you say to yourself, "I'm not good at reading." This kind of statement implies that you believe this is a fixed situation and that your skills can't be improved. Instead, try saying something like "This is something I'm not good at *yet*." This shift in language can be applied to anything you want to improve.

Test scores do not determine your future. They don't determine what you're capable of learning and accomplishing. Take your education into your own hands.

Here's the truth: It's not how smart you are; it's how you are smart. There are multiple types of intelligence (more on this later). Like so many things, intelligence is a combination of attitudes and actions, and is dependent on context.

New belief: Intelligence is fluid.

LIE NO. 2: WE ONLY USE 10 PERCENT OF OUR BRAINS

We've all heard this myth. Some of us heard it for the first time in a classroom, some of us heard it from a friend. Some of us heard it through the media—maybe a documentary, a TV show, or a movie. This myth is usually used in the context of highlighting longed-for possibilities: If only we could access the rest of our brains, what could we accomplish?

The story has been traced to a number of different sources, but as so often happens in the shaping of public opinion, it's likely built on by successive events. Some attribute it to author and philosopher William James, who wrote in *The Energies of Men* that "We are making use of only a small part of our possible mental and physical resources."[9] It could have originated with the work of Pierre Flourens, a French physicist famous for his discoveries in the late 1800s about how the brain and the nervous system work and work together.

The myth could also be related to the work of Dr. Karl Lashley in the 1920s; when Lashley removed parts of rats' cerebral cortex, an area responsible for higher order cognitive processing, he found the rats could still relearn some tasks. This led him to hypothesize —incorrectly—that whole parts of the brain were not necessarily being used.[10] Some blame the earliest neuroimages from PET and fMRI scans, which showed bright blotches on a screen with simplified explanations like "This is what your brain does when you pick something up." These images typically showed just one portion of the brain lighting up, leading the layperson to conclude that we only use a small portion of our brains at one time.[11]

This assumption has also been perpetuated in countless ads and movies over the last hundred years. The adaption of the book *The Dark Fields*, which was produced as *Limitless* in 2011, says we use 20 percent of our brain function; the 2014 movie *Lucy* claimed we use 10 percent at any given time. In 2017, an episode of *Black Mirror*, a show known for its research and well-thought-through use of facts and statistics, touted the myth, saying, "even on a good day, we only use 40 percent of our brain capacity." All of these storylines were focused on the idea of unlocking our greatest, albeit hidden, potential.

Needless to say, this myth is pervasive, and yet it's not true.

In a succinct NPR segment, the host plays a clip of Morgan Freeman posing, in his dramatic bass voice, the what-if scenario upon which *Lucy* is based: "What if there was a way of accessing 100 percent of our brain? What might we be capable of?"

Neuroscientist David Eagleman gives a pointed response: "We would be capable of exactly what we're doing now, which is to say, we do use a hundred percent of our brain."[12]

Countless evidence backs this up—too much of it to include it all here—but Barry Beyerstein, a professor of psychology at Simon Fraser University in British Columbia, described some of the major scientific discoveries that refute this myth, which I've paraphrased here:[13]

- Studies of damaged brains show that there is no single area of the brain that can sustain damage without a loss of ability, contrary to earlier theories. Brain scans have shown that all brain areas are active, no matter what the activity. Even while we sleep, all parts of our brains show activity.
- Our brains are energy-hogs. The brain takes up only 2 percent of space by weight, and yet accounts for 20 percent of energy consumption, more than any other organ. We wouldn't need such an incredible amount of energy for an organ that functioned at 40 percent or less.
- Scientists have also determined that the brain's regions have distinct functions that work together. After extensively mapping the brain over decades, they've concluded that there are no functionless areas of the brain.

- Finally, as we've learned, the brain uses a process called synaptic pruning. If we didn't use a large portion of our brains, we would expect to see large areas of degeneration (we don't—unless brain diseases are present).[14]

To sum up, this myth just isn't true. In an interview with *Scientific American*, neurologist Barry Gordon from Johns Hopkins School of Medicine in Baltimore, said that the idea is "so wrong it is almost laughable."[15]

Here's the truth: What I want you to take from this is that you have all the power of your brain available to you now. The utopia that each of these movies and TV shows depicts is already possible for you. While we use all of our brain, some people use their brain better than others. Just as most people use 100 percent of their body, there are some bodies that are faster, stronger, more flexible, and more energized than others. The key is to learn how to use your brain as efficiently and effectively as you possibly can—and by the end of this book, you'll have the tools to do so.

New belief: I am learning to use my whole brain in the best way possible.

LIE NO. 3: MISTAKES ARE FAILURES

When we hear the name Einstein, we think of brilliance and intellectual feats the likes of which most of us believe we'll never accomplish. The nearly synonymous relationship is well deserved; Einstein did more to further the scientific field in general and physics in particular than any other scientist of our time. His discoveries have made possible some of our most important modern-day technology.

With such an illustrious reputation, it would be easy to assume Einstein rarely made mistakes—but that is not the case. To begin with, his development was described as "slow," and he was considered to be a below-average student.[16] It was apparent from an early age that his way of thinking and learning was different from the rest of the students in his class. He liked working out the more complicated problems in math, for example, but wasn't very good at the "easy" problems.[17]

Later on in his career, Einstein made simple mathematical mistakes that appeared in some of his most important work. His numerous mistakes include seven major gaffes on each version of his theory of relativity, mistakes in clock synchronization related to his experiments, and many mistakes in the math and physics calculations used to determine the viscosity of liquids.[18]

Was Einstein considered a failure because of his mistakes? Hardly. Most importantly he didn't let his mistakes stop him. He kept experimenting and making contributions to his field. He is famously quoted as having said, "A person who never made a mistake never tried anything new." What's more, no one remembers him for his mistakes—we only remember him for his contributions.

So, why do we fear mistakes so much? It could be ingrained—as school children, we were judged on our mistakes, and the number of them on any given test determined whether we passed or failed. If we were called on in class and said the wrong answer, most of us were usually too embarrassed to raise our hands again. Unfortunately, mistakes are not often used as a tool for learning; they are used as a way of measuring one's capabilities. Make too many mistakes and you fail your test or your class.

We need to change that. Too many of us don't come close to our capacities because we are too afraid of making a mistake. Instead of looking at mistakes as proof of failure, take them as proof that you are trying.

Beth Comstock, former vice chair of General Electric, and her team learned this when the company had to scrap a new line of products in which it had invested. Comstock, author of *Imagine It Forward: Courage, Creativity, and the Power of Change,* often speaks on the ever-growing demand on businesses and the people within them to adapt and change faster.[19] She reflects on how she and her team were able to look at the mistakes they made not as a failure, but as major learning lessons that led to the development of a new line that moved the company forward.[20] Instead of dwelling on the mistakes, they asked themselves what they learned.

Here's the truth: Mistakes don't mean failure. Mistakes are a sign that you are trying something new. You might think you have to be perfect, but life is not about comparing yourself to anyone else; it's about measuring yourself compared to who you were yesterday. When you learn from your mistakes, they have the power to turn you into something better than you were before.

Also, remember that you are not your mistakes. Making a mistake doesn't mean anything about you as a person. It's easy to jump to the conclusion that you're inherently worthless, but you make mistakes; mistakes don't make you. Place them under your feet and use them as stepping stones to rise to the next level. It's not how we make mistakes, but how we deal with them that defines us.

New belief: There is no such thing as failure. Only failure to learn.

LIE NO. 4: KNOWLEDGE IS POWER

We've all heard the phrase "knowledge is power," usually as a reason for learning, as if knowledge alone will give us power. You might have also heard this phrase used with the opposite intent: as a reason to withhold information or knowledge from another person, say, in a negotiation.

Although the phrase "knowledge is power" is commonly attributed to Sir Francis Bacon, the first known use of the exact wording was not penned until Thomas Hobbes, who acted as secretary to Bacon in his younger years, used the phrase *scientia potentia est,* Latin for "knowledge is power," in *Leviathan* in 1651. He then expanded on the idea in *De Corpore* in 1655. Unfortunately, Hobbes's original sentiments have been cut short over the years. In the original, Hobbes says: "The end of knowledge is power; and the use of theorems is for the construction of problems; and, lastly, the scope of all speculation is the *performing of some action, or thing to be done.*" [Emphasis added.][21]

Put another way, knowledge is important, but it is "the performing of some action" that is required to make it powerful. This is where we get stuck as a culture. As discussed, we're deluged with information on a daily basis. We have more access to knowledge than we have ever had in the history of humankind, and yet this glut of information makes it more and more difficult to act.

I used to believe this myth. When I was the "boy with the broken brain," I wanted nothing more than to be able to learn like the rest of the kids in my classroom. But once I was able to do that, I quickly realized that possession of knowledge wasn't going to differentiate me from the people around me—it was how I used my knowledge that would.

Here's the truth: Knowledge is not power. It only has the potential to be power. You can read this book and learn everything in it, but if you don't take it and apply the knowledge, it will be useless. All the books, podcasts, seminars, online programs, and inspiring social media posts in the world won't work until you put your knowledge into action.

It's easy to talk about what we learn, but I want to challenge you not to talk about it, but to show what you learned. It's better well done than well said. Don't promise, prove. Your results will speak for themselves.

New belief: Knowledge × Action = Power

LIE NO. 5: LEARNING NEW THINGS IS VERY DIFFICULT

When we hear the word *learning*, we usually think of school. Few of us have fond memories of school. Even if we did well academically, school is typically a place associated with the growing pains of youth, where we felt romantic love for the first time (and probably rejection), and where we experienced crushing boredom. For those of us who struggled in school, the added emotions of shame, doubt, and the ever-present feeling that we're too dumb to learn anything colors the word. It's no wonder that when we think of learning, we think of difficulty and strife.

Carol Greider is an American molecular biologist who won the Nobel Prize in 2009 for her part in discovering how telomeres change with age, which has an enormous potential for how we understand and treat cancer.[22] Greider has the distinction of being a Bloomberg Distinguished Professor and a Daniel Nathans Professor, and she is the director of molecular biology and genetics at John Hopkins University. With such an illustrious career, one would assume that Greider whizzed through school, but such was not the case.

"When I was in elementary school, I was considered a poor speller and somebody who couldn't sound out words, so I was taken into remedial classes," recalls Greider. "I remember having a tutor come down and take me out of class and bring me to a different room. It certainly felt like I wasn't as good as the other kids."[23]

It turned out she had dyslexia, a learning disability that affects parts of the brain that process language. Those who struggle with dyslexia have problems identifying speech sounds and relating them to letters and words, which results in difficulty reading and sometimes speaking.[24] Greider felt stupid and describes the situation as hard to overcome, but she didn't give up.

> I kept thinking of ways to compensate. I learned to memorize things very well because I just couldn't spell words. So later when I got to take classes like chemistry and anatomy where I had to memorize things, it turned out I was very good at that. I never planned a career. I had these blinders on that got me through a lot of things that might have been obstacles. I just went forward. It's a skill that I had early on that must have been adaptive.[25]

Even though school was hard at first, she found other ways to make up for her disability, and because of her ability to adapt, she became the kind of problem-solver who could not only learn but could contribute to research that changed the way we view cancer. Learning was hard for her, but she figured out how to work around her disability. After all, it's not how smart you are, but how you are smart. Because Greider had to problem-solve her way through learning, she now has a career that is having an impact on the world.

The truth is that learning won't always be easy, but the effort pays dividends. In fact, learning should be at least a little uncomfortable; otherwise you're mostly reinforcing what you already know. If you've ever tried to cut wood with a dull blade, you know that it takes far more time and energy to accomplish the task than it should. In much the same way, lacking motivation or having inadequate methods will slow you down and make you feel as if learning is too hard (and we'll show you how to address those issues later in this book).

The key is taking small, simple steps. Think about a stonecutter. The stonecutter may sit there and hammer away at his block of stone for what feels like an eternity, making only small chips and dents here and there. But in one moment, the stone will crack open. Was it the one time that did it? No—it was all the sustained effort that prepared the stone to split.

Approach your learning like a stonecutter. It will require you to cultivate patience, to have a positive attitude, and to be adaptive to your own needs. If you are the kind of learner who does best with a book in your hands, that's fantastic. But if you already know that doesn't work for you, why keep trying the same thing? Look for other ways to learn that do work for you.

Know that it won't be hard, but it will require effort—though perhaps not as much as you think. The key is consistency. You must have the patience to consistently come back at it again and again. When you do, you will not only reap the rewards of your hard-earned knowledge, but you'll be a better person for having cultivated the tenacity to keep trying.

Here's the truth: Sometimes it *is* hard to learn new things. What's more accurate is to understand that learning is a set of methods, a process that can certainly be easier when you know how to learn.

New belief: When you learn new ways how to learn, the challenge of learning new things can be fun, easier, and more enjoyable.

LIE NO. 6: THE CRITICISM OF OTHER PEOPLE MATTERS

Years ago I was a keynote speaker at an event hosted by Deepak Chopra. After my presentation, I sat down in the audience to watch the rest of the programming. To my surprise, a tall figure approached and loomed over me, and I looked up to see one of my favorite actors, Jim Carrey.

What followed was a deep conversation in the lobby about creativity. At one point he said, "Jim, I'm working on *Dumb and Dumber 2*, and I need to get really smart to be dumb and dumber."

A few weeks later, we spent a day together at his home. During one of our breaks, while making guacamole (one of my favorite brain foods) in the kitchen, I asked, "Why do you do what you do? You're such a unique actor, and you're a little bit extreme on camera." Jim said, "I act that way because I want to give the people who are watching permission to be themselves. The biggest travesty in the world is people preventing and limiting themselves from expressing who they really are because they're afraid of what other people think." This sentiment comes close to a religion for Jim; he calls it "freeing people from concern." He elaborated on this during a commencement address at Maharishi International University:

> The purpose of my life had always been to free people from concern. . . . How will you serve the world? What do they need that your talent can provide? That's all you have to figure out. . . . The effect you have on others is the most valuable currency there is. Everything you gain in life will rot and fall apart, and all that will be left of you is what was in your heart.[26]

The fastest learners on the planet are children, and that's partly because they don't care what others think of them. They have no shame around failing. They will fall 300 times and get up 300 times in the course of learning to walk, and don't feel embarrassed; they just know they want to walk. As we get older, we have a harder time staying this open. We might take a singing lesson, or maybe a coding class, and if we hit a flat note or make a mistake as we learn, we shrink or stop.

Part of being limitless is learning to let go of the fear of criticism from other people. History is littered with examples of those who overcame the negative opinions of the people around them. The Wright brothers accomplished their incredible feat of making a machine fly through the air—and initially received virtually no acclaim for it. When they returned home from their inaugural flight on December 17, 1903, they were not met with brass bands and cigars and streamers. They were met with doubt.

Their biographer, Fred Kelly, wrote that the neighbors had a hard time believing what had happened. Said one: "I know you boys are truthful and if you say you flew through the air in the machine, I believe you. But then, down there on the Carolina coast, you had special conditions to help you. Of course, you couldn't do it anywhere else."[27]

Hardly the enthusiastic response one would expect, right?

The papers and media didn't report on their accomplishment, either. According to Kelly, noted scientists of the time had already explained why man couldn't fly, so no newspaper reporter was willing to report on the story for fear of being humiliated.[28] No editor wanted to print a story that directly refuted a respected scientist's proclamations that flying was not scientifically possible. The lack of public recognition didn't faze the Wright brothers. They knew they had more work to do and set about perfecting their flying machine, which eventually did earn the recognition that it deserved.

Most of us fear the opinions of other people when we simply think about trying something new. What the Wright's story shows is that public imagination is woefully underwhelming, and people have a hard time reconciling what they believe is possible with what is actually happening.

Here's the truth: Creating the life you want can be scary. But you know what's scarier? Regret. One day we will take our final breaths and not one of other people's opinions or your fears will matter. What will matter is how we lived. Don't take criticism from someone you wouldn't take advice from. People will doubt you and criticize you no matter what you do. You will never know your true potential until you break the unfair judgements you place on yourself. Don't allow other people's opinions and expectations to run or ruin your life.

New belief: It's not your job to like, love, or respect me. It's mine.

LIE NO. 7: GENIUS IS BORN

Bruce Lee is known today as a film star, philosopher, and one of the most accomplished martial arts fighters in the history of the sport. And yet, given his background, you wouldn't have pegged him as a future icon if you were under the assumption that genius is born.

Lee's family moved from San Francisco to Hong Kong shortly after he was born.[29] Not long after they arrived, Hong Kong was occupied by Japan, making it a politically and socially tumultuous place to grow up. As a young man, Lee was faced with the difficulty of being the ultimate outsider. He was not purely Chinese, so the students in his classes made fun of him. He also wasn't British like other kids in his private school, so he was frequently taunted for being "oriental." The feeling of tension was ever-present for him—so he turned to fighting to battle his way through.[30] Fighting began to define him. His grades were low, and he fought so often in school that he transferred to a different primary school.

When Lee was 13, he met his teacher Yip Man, who taught him Wing Chun. He was accepted into this famous teacher's school and began to learn this style of Kung Fu. Not unlike the rest of his education, he was still taunted by the Chinese children who felt he was not enough like them to be "allowed" to learn the technique. He constantly had to prove himself and his abilities, and his fighting spilled over into the streets. This internal tension, coupled with Hong Kong's slide into gang violence, led to Lee fighting far more often than learning. He developed a reputation for being street-tough through his willingness and propensity for battle.

After one particularly bad street fight, a high-ranking police officer approached Lee's parents and told them their son would be arrested. The boy he had beat up the night before was the son of this police officer. Lee's father quickly arranged for Lee to go back to America; after all, he still had citizenship. So, off Lee went with $100 in his pocket. "Like most Chinese kids who had just gotten off the boat, my first job was washing and bussing dishes,"[31] said Lee in a later interview. He worked to support himself with odd jobs and eventually started teaching martial arts.

Lee wasn't just talented—he was also willing to teach other people, and he accepted everyone who came to him as a student, regardless of their race or background. This soon ruffled the feathers of the Chinese community in Oakland, who felt that these techniques should not be taught to anyone who wasn't Chinese. Eventually, he was forced to defend his right to teach. The Chinese traditionalists challenged him to a fight, saying that if he won, he could keep his school. But if he lost, he would be forced to shut it down and stop teaching to people outside of their ethnic group.

Lee's style was different from any one form of martial arts. When he was still living in Hong Kong, he took dancing lessons, and in 1957 he was so good he won the cha-cha championship. He added the movements he learned in dance to his fighting techniques. Where other fighters took a mostly solitary stance with their feet, he kept his moving constantly, which fueled his ability to adapt to his opponent's moves. Lee did this with everything he learned later in life. Eventually, his style incorporated not only Wing Chun, but boxing, fencing, and dancing.

It was a major turning point—the old vanguard against the new. Lee's wife Linda was eight months pregnant at the time, and she remembers the scene vividly, almost comically. She recalls it took three minutes for Lee to get his opponent down to the ground; before this take-down, the opponent had run around the room, trying to get away from Lee.

After the fight, Linda found Lee with his head in his hands, despite his victory. He told her that his training didn't prepare him for this kind of a battle. As she describes it, this was the beginning of the evolution to his own way of martial arts.

After this battle, Lee no longer tried to fit his knowledge and teachings into one box and discarded most of his original training. He openly took influences from areas of fighting outside of Wing Chun and Kung Fu, using them to form a philosophy of martial arts. In a later interview, he said, "I do not believe in styles anymore. I do not believe there is such a thing as the Chinese way of fighting, Japanese way of fighting."[32] Instead, Lee's approach focused on fighting as a way of ultimate self-expression. "When people come to me to learn, they're not coming to me to learn to defend themselves. They want to learn to express themselves through movement, anger, or determination." He believed that the individual is more important than any style or system.

No one remembers Lee for his academic endeavors. Lee is remembered for his tenacity, his ability to defeat his opponents, his philosophy, and for the way he managed to break out of the box of orthodox thinking and bring different styles of fighting together to create an entirely new philosophy. So was he a natural genius, someone born to achieve outsize physical, mental, and philosophical feats?

In *The Talent Code*, author Daniel Coyle delves into whether talent is innate or whether it can be developed. He argues "greatness isn't born, it's grown." Through deep practice, ignition, and master coaching, anyone can develop a talent so deep that it looks like genius.[33]

Bruce Lee's daughter Shannon spoke at our annual conference about her father's approach to memory and learning. She said that, by the time Lee was a film star and notable teacher, he had already achieved thousands upon thousands of hours of deep practice, at least in part because of his early days in fighting on the streets. Later in life, Lee didn't master the famous one-inch punch in a day. That alone took years of hard repetition and practice. Lee continued to train and condition himself even with a back injury—it was a daily commitment. Ignition is the motivation, the fuel to do what you do. It seems Lee's initial fuel was the tension he felt as a Chinese American in a place that didn't accept him as either. Later, his ignition seems to have been his drive for ultimate self-expression. And finally, Lee had training from a master teacher, Yip Man, who himself was trained by several master teachers from the time he was a child. When Lee became his student, he had been teaching Kung Fu for decades.

Lee's talent was born of a confluence of experiences and circumstances that served him well, although they may have defeated someone else. How many of us would look at a young child with a propensity for fighting and poor grades and predict that he would become a master teacher and philosopher?

Here's the truth: Genius leaves clues. There is always a method behind what looks like magic.

New belief: Genius is not born; it's made through deep practice.

KWIK START

How many of the LIEs described above did you believe in before reading this book? Are there any other ones you would add? Write them down now: ______________________________

____

____

BEFORE WE MOVE ON

Understanding that these commonly held limiting beliefs are nothing more than myths is an essential part of becoming limitless. When you convince yourself that any of these are true, you're giving yourself an unnecessary burden to carry around. While these seven are among the most common, keep your radar up for any "conventional wisdom" that has the effect of putting constraints on your potential and examine that wisdom very carefully. In most cases, you're going to find that such constraints don't apply to anyone willing to push beyond them. Before going to the next chapter, give these things a try:

- Take a good look at some of the mistakes you've made. Have you let these define you? How have your feelings about these mistakes changed after reading this chapter?
- Find a way to put something you've recently learned (even today) into action. Notice the difference it makes when you turn knowledge into power.
- Think about a situation where you allowed the opinions of others to sway your actions. How would you approach that same situation differently if the only opinion that mattered was yours? Get my 4Gs to a limitless mindset, including more strategies for replacing limited beliefs, at LimitlessBook.com/resources.

"Culture is nourished by human motivation—a limitless resource that can sometimes be underestimated."

—LYNNE DOUGHTIE

PART III

LIMITLESS MOTIVATION

THE WHY

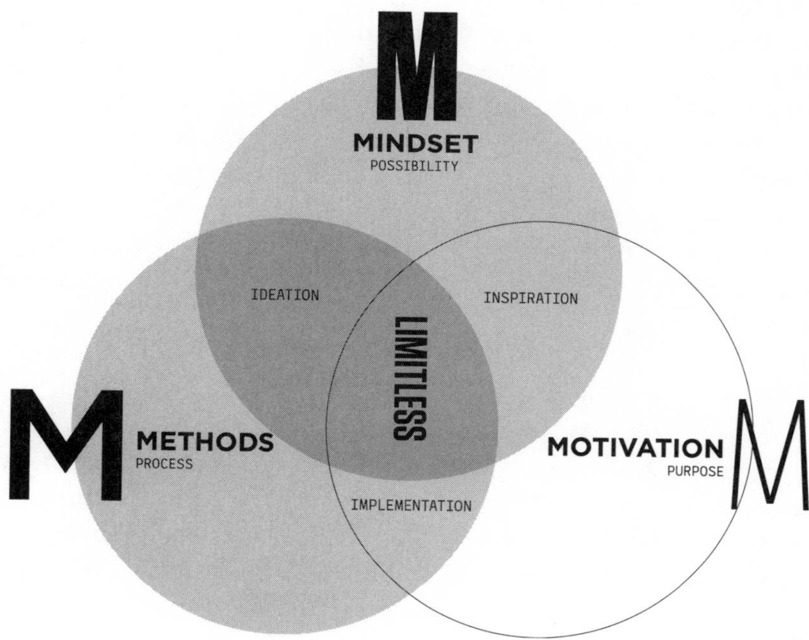

motivation

mo·ti·va·tion *(noun)*

The purpose one has for taking action. The energy required for someone to behave in a particular way.

In the movie *Limitless*, writer Eddie Morra was completely unmotivated, unfocused, and had no energy. When he popped the pill that made him suddenly take action, his life drastically changed for the better because he was able to make things happen.

Let's unlimit a few LIEs commonly held around motivation. Contrary to popular belief, like your mindset, motivation is not fixed. No one has a set level of motivation. And when people say they are unmotivated, it's not completely true. They could have a high level of motivation to stay in bed and watch television.

Motivation also doesn't mean you must enjoy something that you need to do. My friend, entrepreneur Tom Bilyeu, hates working out, but he has a clear and compelling reason to do so, so he does it every morning. I really don't like taking cold showers, but I do it daily (I'll explain why in Chapter 8).

Finally, motivation is not something you wake up with or not. We put ourselves in a trance when we say, "I don't have any motivation." Motivation is not something you have; it's something you do. And it's entirely sustainable. Unlike a warm bath, it's not something that you experience for a moment and then lose unless you heat it up again. Motivation isn't derived from a seminar that temporarily pumps you up. It's a process. And since it's a strategy, you have control over it and can create it consistently by following the right recipe.

Here's the formula: Motivation = Purpose × Energy × S^3

When you combine purpose, energy, and small simple steps (S^3), you get sustainable motivation. And the ultimate form of motivation is the state of flow. Think about it as energy management. Creating it, investing it, and not wasting it. A clear purpose or reason gives you energy. Practices you employ will cultivate energy for your brain and the rest of your body, and small simple steps require little energy.

In this section, we'll talk about how to cultivate powerful sustainable motivation around learning and life that lasts. We'll achieve this by getting clear on your purpose, fostering the mental and physical energy that will sustain you, and establishing small simple steps. And tapping flow states.

Purpose drives us to act, and our purpose must be clear enough that we know why we're acting and what we're hoping to gain. Generating sufficient energy is vital—if you're tired or sleepy, or if your brain is foggy, then you won't have the fuel to take action. Small simple steps take minimal effort and keep you from being paralyzed with overwhelm. And finally, finding flow is the ultimate boon to motivation.

“Reasons reap results.”

—JIM KWIK

7

PURPOSE

How do certain defining phrases determine who you are?

How do your values define you?

What does your sense of purpose say about who you are?

For the longest time, my kryptonite was lack of sleep. Sleep has never been easy for me. As a kid for years I was pulling regular all-nighters, studying long hours trying to compensate for my learning challenges. I developed bad sleeping problems. I was always tired at school, but I would plow through the fatigue anyway because I had a strong desire to work hard and make my family proud. My purpose and reasons were super-clear, so I was plenty motivated. Even after I learned accelerated learning skills at age 18 and I no longer had to put in crazy hours, my sleeplessness continued into adulthood and has grown steadily worse—two to four hours total of very interrupted sleep for about 20 years.

The longer you go without sleep, the harder it becomes to maintain a sense of reality—or motivation, for that matter. Lack of sleep compromises all of your cognitive skills, your focus, your memory, and your overall brain health. A common contributing factor for depression and many mood disorders is lack of sleep. I can attest to the dark places I've found myself in as a result of lack of sleep. My intense speaking and global travel schedule certainly did not help; one year I was on the road for 235 days. Time zones, jet lag, unfamiliar stale hotel rooms, you get the picture. And my brain was feeling it; just imagine a memory expert forgetting what city he is waking up in.

This puzzled me, because as a long-time meditation student, my mind was not ruminating or racing at night; it was as calm as could be. It was only a handful of years ago, when I ended up hospitalized from multiple nights without rest, that I participated in an overnight sleep study and was diagnosed with severe obstructive sleep apnea, a physical disorder where evidently I stopped breathing more than 200 times each and every night.

Today, after multiple treatments, I'm happy to say my sleep is worlds better. Once I was able to fix the physical obstruction with surgery, I was then able to optimize my sleep with a number of tools I will cover in Chapter 8.

During my most difficult moments, I've asked myself why I continue to do what I do. Why struggle when I could easily tell myself I don't have the energy for this? As a child, my purpose and motivation (motive for taking action) was to compensate for my lack of talent with hard work, to prove to myself I was capable. But once I'd leveled up my learning, why did I continue to work so hard—despite being exhausted, sleep-deprived, and an extreme introvert—to make speech after speech, video after video, podcast after podcast? It's the same thing that drove me as a child: I have clear and definite purpose. I don't want anyone to struggle and suffer the way I did. The mission that drives me is to unlock better, brighter brains.

Often our greatest struggles lead to our greatest strengths. My two biggest challenges as a child were learning and public speaking. Life has a sense of humor because I spend most of my life public speaking on learning. I couldn't read, and now I teach people from all over the world how to read better. I struggled to understand my brain, and now I speak in front of audiences of thousands to help them understand the amazing tool they possess. I've learned there is a gift in most challenges. In the same way, decades of lack of sleep has given me two very important lessons.

First, it's forced me to live everything in this book. I wouldn't be able to perform at the level I do without the tools I've learned, so I've doubled down on everything I teach. I rarely have to prepare for a speech, because I use these skills every single day. I live them. It's who I am.

Second, I've had to become really clear on my purpose, my identity, my values, and my reasons for doing what I do every day. When you don't sleep, and you have a very limited amount of energy and focus, you don't waste it. You prioritize and get crystal clear about your commitments and why you are making them. All of those choices have led to inexhaustible motivation. That's what we'll talk about in this chapter.

START WITH WHY

Among my favorite books is *Start with Why* by Simon Sinek, who I've interviewed multiple times on my show. He often stresses the importance of being able to convey to others *why* you do *what* you do. If, Sinek explains, you can articulate the belief that is driving you (your why), people will want what you are offering. Or, as he so often says: "People don't buy *what* you do, they buy *why* you do it, so it follows that if you don't know *why* you do *what* you do, how will anyone else?"

There's a reason why the second of the magic questions is, "Why must I use this?". (Do you recall the other two questions?) For most children, their favorite word is *why,* which they're asking all the time. Do you know why it was important to memorize the periodic table or historic dates? If you don't, you probably don't remember them. We hear the words *purpose* and *goals* used frequently in business, but do we really know what they mean and how they are the same or different? A goal is the point one wishes to achieve. A purpose is the reason one aims at to achieve a goal.

Whether your goal is to read a book a week, learn another language, get in shape, or just leave the office on time to see your family, these are all things that you need to achieve. But how do you do this? One of the popular ways is setting SMART goals. Yes, this is an acronym:

- **S is for Specific**: Your goal should be well defined. Don't say you want to be rich; say you want to make a certain amount of money.
- **M is for Measurable**: If you can't measure your goal, you can't manage it. Getting fit isn't measurable—running a six-minute mile is.
- **A is for Actionable**: You wouldn't drive to a new town without asking for directions. Develop the action steps to achieve your goal.
- **R is for Realistic**: If you're living in your parents' basement, it's hard to become a millionaire. Your goals should challenge and stretch you, but not so much that you give up on them.
- **T is for Time-based**: The phrase, "A goal is a dream with a deadline" comes to mind. Setting a time to complete your goal makes you that much more likely to reach it.

The challenge for many people is that this process, while logical, is very heady. To get your goals out of your head and into your hands, make sure they fit with your emotions—with your HEART:

- **H is for Healthy**: How can you make sure your goals support your greater well-being? Your goals should contribute to your mental, physical, and emotional health.
- **E is for Enduring**: Your goals should inspire and sustain you during the difficult times when you want to quit.
- **A is for Alluring**: You shouldn't always have to push yourself to work on your goals. They should be so exciting, enticing, and engaging that you're pulled toward them.
- **R is for Relevant**: Don't set a goal without knowing why you're setting it. Ideally, your goals should relate to a

challenge you're having, your life's purpose, or your core values.

- **T is for Truth:** Don't set a goal just because your neighbor is doing it or your parents expect it of you. Make sure your goal is something you want, something that remains true to you. If your goal isn't true to you, you're far more likely to procrastinate and sabotage yourself.

ON PURPOSE AND PASSION

Knowing your purpose in life helps you live with integrity. People who know their purpose in life know who they are, what they are, and why they are. And when you know yourself, it becomes easier to live a life that's true to your core values.

Your life purpose consists of the central motivating aims of your life—the reasons you get up in the morning. Purpose can guide life decisions, influence behavior, shape goals, offer a sense of direction, and create meaning. For me, my life purpose is to create a world of better, brighter brains.

The English language is rife with words that get used interchangeably, as if they mean the same thing. Let's take the words *nice* and *kind*, for example. These two words are often used in the same way, but their roots reveal a different story. The origin of *nice* comes from the Latin word *nescius*, which means "ignorant." *Kind*, on the other hand, is of Germanic origin and is related to the word *kin*. The original sense of the word was "nature, the natural order," and "innate character, form, or condition." It morphed from the sense of "feeling of relatives with one another," and became a word that meant "friendly, deliberately doing good to others."[1]

Passion and purpose are in the same camp—they're often confused with one another. Both concepts are discussed all over the Internet, in motivational books, in TED talks. It's easy to feel as if you must be lacking if you don't feel a burning passion or purpose in your life. In my experience, however, passion and purpose are not the same thing; instead, one leads to the other.

Finding your passion is not about choosing the right path or finding the perfect professional destiny. It's about experimenting to see what ignites your joy. Passion comes when we rediscover our authentic, alive self, the one who has been muted and buried beneath a pile of other people's expectations. There is not a single right path to be discovered or revealed. Instead, I believe that when we exchange a fixed mindset for a growth mindset, as we discussed in Chapter 6 in the section on myths, we learn that interests can be developed through experience, investment, and struggle.

Furthermore, different passions can be cultivated simultaneously. You don't have to choose one over the other when you're exploring. Finding your passion is like finding true love, in that you have to go out on many dates to get to the perfect match. Once you find that special person, it doesn't just magically "work," because it takes effort to build a relationship. Finding your passion is no different—it takes experimentation to see what clicks for you, and it takes effort.

To sum it up, passion is what lights you up inside. My passion to learn was born out of such a struggle that it became a major part of my life's identity.

KWIK START

What are your current passions? List three here: ______________

____

____

____

____

Purpose, however, is about how you relate to other people. Purpose is what you're here to share with the world. It's how you use your passion. When you get down to it, we all have the same purpose: to help other people through our passion. The greatest task we have in life is to share the knowledge and skills we accumulate. It doesn't have to be more complex than that.

Your passion might be underwater basket weaving, but your purpose is to share underwater basket weaving with other people. My passion is learning, and my purpose is to teach other people to learn. This is so deeply ingrained that I don't have to force myself to do it—it comes naturally. I wake up ready, motivated, and excited to help people learn.

Podcast guest Jonathan Fields, founder of the Good Life Project, believes that we will naturally have many passions over the course of our lives. Because you will change, the medium through which you express your passions will change, too. He believes that if you define yourself by one very specific passion and your life changes in a way that doesn't allow you to pursue that passion any longer, you might feel lost. The key is finding the underlying meaning in your passions to find a new way of channeling your expression.

KWIK START

Do you know your life's purpose? Even if you don't yet, write down a little bit about what it could be: ____________________

____

____

____

____

WHO DO YOU THINK YOU ARE?

What often isn't discussed in the quest for motivation is identity —who you are . . . and who you *think* you are at your core. They say the two most powerful words in the English language are the shortest: "I am." Whatever you put after those two words determines your destiny.

Let's say you want to stop smoking. Maybe you've had a few warnings from your doctor, and you're finally coming around to the idea that you should quit. If you identify as a smoker and regularly say, "I am a smoker," it's going to be difficult to quit until you dismantle that identity. When you say you are defined by a particular action, you are essentially priming yourself to identify with and justify a certain behavior.

This is so integral to behavior change that it can't be overstated. A fascinating study out of Stanford University showed the effects of priming on participants. Researcher Christopher Bryan separated participants into two groups. The first group responded to a questionnaire that included phrases like "to vote" and questions like "How important is it to you to vote?" The second group's questionnaire had slightly altered questions, like "How important is it to you to *be a voter* [emphasis added]?"[2] The participants were also asked whether they planned to vote in the upcoming elections. Later, researchers used public voting records to confirm whether the participants had voted or not. Bryan and his team found that the participants whose survey included personally identifying statements like "voter" were 13 percent more likely to vote than those who were simply asked about the likelihood that they would vote.[3]

When you consciously decide to identify with the habit or goal you want to create or achieve, or consciously un-identify with a habit you no longer want, you will experience enormous power. If you've been telling yourself all of your life that you are a slow learner, or that you can't learn, you might start telling yourself "I am a fast and efficient learner" instead. The highest drive we have is to act consistently with how we perceive ourselves—it is one of the most powerful forces in the universe. Use it to your benefit.

KWIK START

Take 60 seconds and, stream of consciousness, fill these lines with "I am" statements. ____________________________________

____

____

____

____

____

A HIERARCHY OF VALUES

Next, we need to consider our values. You can set up the most well-thought-out habits, but if your values are not in alignment with the ultimate goal, you're not going to do it. For example, someone who wants to remember people's names should value relationships and their connection to other people. Your behavior has to support your values in some way, or there is no drive for it.

Our values have a hierarchy to them. If I asked you what's most important to you in life, you might tell me family is one of your core values. I would then ask what family does for you. For me, it provides love. For you, it might provide belonging. The important distinction here is that family is a *means value*—a means to an end. The *end value* is actually love or belonging. When we look at our values, we can determine whether the value we've stated is an end or whether it evokes something else.

Values need to be prioritized. My values are love, growth, contribution, and adventure, in that order. Each value builds on and contributes to the next. One's values tend to not change from year to year unless you experience life conditions that change them—such as having a kid, losing a loved one, or ending a relationship, to name just a few.

When we're unaware of our values and the values of the people closest to us, it creates a space for conflict to arise; discord usually results from values conflicting. Let's say your values include adventure and freedom. If your partner values safety and security, it's no surprise that you'll often be at odds. It's not that one set of values is right and the other is wrong—it's that they aren't in alignment. Or let's say both of you highly value respect, but what you consider to be respectful or disrespectful differs. There's still room for disagreement unless you've talked about what constitutes respect.

FINDING YOUR REASONS

When it comes to doing anything in life, reasons reap rewards. My story is evidence that feeling good is not required to feel motivated. If I waited until that day, I would have stopped teaching others to learn better when my sleeping problems escalated. And besides, how many times have we felt good on a given day and still not done what we said we would do? You could feel amazing and still get nothing done if your reasons for doing so are not strong enough.

Reasons that are tied to your purpose, identity, and values will sufficiently motivate you to act, even in the face of all of the daily obstacles that life puts in your way. The healthy 70-year-old doesn't go to the gym at 4:35 A.M. because he likes it—he goes because maintaining his health so he can continue to be with his family is motivation enough to him, even though he would much rather sleep in. The good student doesn't pick up her textbook because she's in a good mood. She does it because she wants to ace that test so she has the best chances of landing the internship that will lead to her dream job.

It's likely that there's a good reason behind every task you need to accomplish, even the unpleasant ones. You don't love making dinner, but you want your family to eat well and you understand the dangers of overreliance on take-out and fast food. You're uncomfortable giving speeches, but you know that your team is relying on you to rally the whole organization behind your project at the conference. You find economics daunting and a little boring, but you need the class to get your marketing degree, and you can't wait to put your marketing skills to work in the real world.

If you're struggling to find motivation to learn, or to accomplish anything else in your life, there is a good chance you haven't uncovered the *why* of the task. Consider your passion, your desired identity, and your values: How can they create the basis for your reasons? You already know that you're much more likely to remember something when you're motivated to remember it. Conversely, if you don't find any motivation in knowing someone's name, you're going to forget it as soon as you move on to your next conversation. Let's say your passion is to help people forge better relationships, you identify as a connector, and one of your values is love. Your reasons for learning to remember names could be simple to find: "I want to learn to remember names so that I can better connect with people in my community and help foster a stronger network of people I care about."

Right now, stop and consider three reasons that you want to learn better. Your reasons should be concrete, like: "I want to learn Spanish so that I can finally speak to my father-in-law," or "I want to learn American history so I can help my kid learn better in school," or "I want to learn how to research better so I can finish my business plan and find an investor for my company." Write them down here:

____

____

____

____

____

Having reasons has helped me become crystal clear when it comes to commitments. A big part of self-love is being protective of your time and energy. Setting boundaries around your time, emotions, mental health, and space is incredibly vital at any time, but especially when you don't sleep. When you lack any necessary fuel, such as sleep or food, your resources aren't as abundant as they are at other times, so protecting what you have becomes very important. When I make decisions, everything is either a heaven yes or heaven no (just trying to keep it clean here). If I don't feel completely aligned with something, I don't do it, because I don't have the energy to spare. And I can honestly say that I don't suffer from FOMO (fear of missing out). In the last few weeks I've been invited to a handful of social and work gatherings but declined because I'm clear about my purpose and motivation in spending time writing this book. I'd love for you to join me in celebrating JOMO—the joy of missing out.

Most of us feel tired and fatigued these days. I believe that's because we feel like we need to say "yes" to every opportunity, invite, or request that comes our way. While it's great to be open-minded and consider options, when you say yes to something, you need to be careful that you're not inadvertently saying no to yourself and your own needs.

WHAT DO YOU HAVE TO LOSE?

What is motivation? Motivation is a set of emotions (painful and pleasurable) that act as the fuel for our actions. Where does it come from? Motivation comes from purpose, fully feeling and associating with the consequences of our actions (or inactions).

Let's do an exercise. Write down all the *disadvantages* you have to face if you do not learn to use the material in this book. What will it cost you right now and in the future? For example, you could write, "I will have to keep studying hard and settle for the same mediocre grades or job." Or, "I won't be able to spend time with my loved ones," or "I won't get that raise." The key is to make sure you feel the emotions. Don't make this an intellectual thing. We make decisions based on how we feel. Really feel the pain that you will have if you don't do something about it. This is the only way for you to make a change last and to get you to follow through.

Pain can be your teacher, if you use it and not let it use you. Use pain to drive you to make things happen. If you are honest, you may write something like: "I will have to settle for a job I hate, make very little money, have no free time for myself or anyone else, and I will have to put up with it for the rest of my life, bored and frustrated." This will get you to do something about it! Do this now:

____

____

____

____

____

Now, here is the more exciting part. Write down all of the *benefits* and *advantages* you will receive from learning the skills and techniques in this book. Make a list of things that will really get you excited and motivated. For instance: "I'll be able to ace my tests, have more time to be with family, start that business, and learn new languages to travel the world." Or, "I will have more free time to exercise and get healthy, to go away for spring break, and to spend more time with my boy/girlfriend!" Or maybe something simple like, "I will finally have some free time to just get caught up and relax!"

Again, make sure your reasons are compelling enough to be backed with real emotion. You must really get yourself to see and feel the benefits of learning this material. Do this now:

____

____

____

____

____

TYING IT ALL TOGETHER

Now, let's apply all of this to learning. As you move through this "Motivation" section of the book, I want you to consider where learning fits into your passion, identity, values, and reasons.

It was not until I was an adult that I found my passion and purpose. Through my struggle to learn, I developed a love of learning because it helped me become unlimited, and my purpose is teaching other people to learn so they can unlimit themselves.

As a kid, I forced myself to study, trying to rise to the level of average. I had a lot of identity issues to resolve; I was the boy with the broken brain, and I believed that I was stupid. I had to change the way I saw myself and give up the identity that kept me locked into being unable to learn. Instead of saying "I am broken," I had to say, "I am a learner."

As for values, as I mentioned earlier I value growth and adventure. For me, learning falls under both of these, because it contributes directly to my growth and it gives me a sense of adventure, especially when I learn something novel and challenging. There's no ambiguity here; learning directly contributes to the fulfillment of my values.

Every single one of my reasons keeps me motivated so that I can help more people learn. As any author knows, writing a book is a challenge. But my reason for writing this book—to teach my methods to a wider audience around the world that may not have access to my online courses—has kept me going.

If you're trying to force motivation, but you haven't addressed these invisible, limiting identities, you won't get very far. When you feel stuck, come back to the way your goal fits into your values, and then ask yourself what needs to be brought back into alignment.

Going back to the previous chapter's list of the seven lies that hold you back, perhaps the eighth lie is that you *have* motivation—that you wake up and feel motivated every day. The reality is that you *do* motivation. Ultimately, motivation is a set of habits and routines, guided by your values and your identity, that you carry out every day.

BEFORE WE MOVE ON

Finding your passion is about giving yourself novelty and putting yourself in a new environment to see what lights you up. It's difficult to do that if you feel limited or if you're self-conscious about looking bad, so let that go and enjoy the experience. Those initial moments of discomfort just might lead you to an entirely new passion and purpose in life. Here are a few things to try before moving on to the next chapter:

- Write down a list of your most common "I am" statements. How do you feel about the ways in which these statements define you?

- Create a list of the things you value the most. Now prioritize that list and think about how this aligns with your definition of yourself.
- Get into the habit of asking the question "why" before you do anything.

"You see, when

you give your body

the best possible fuel,

you have more energy,

you're stronger,

you think

more quickly."

—MICHELLE OBAMA

8

ENERGY

How do you make sure your brain is as healthy and energized as it can be?

What should I make sure to have in my diet if I want my brain to be at its strongest?

How do I consistently get a good night's sleep?

You have a clear purpose for doing something, and you've broken down the project or goal into small, simple steps. Does that guarantee sustainable, limitless motivation?

For example, even if you have a reason to read daily and have a plan to read for just five minutes a day, what can keep you from doing so is fatigue. Mental and physical vitality is the fuel needed to drive your actions. We know the importance of time management. Well, motivation is all about energy management and optimization.

Here are my 10 recommendations for generating limitless brain energy. For each tip, please rate, on a scale of 1 to 10, how much attention you are putting into that specific area. You may be surprised by your answers.

1. A GOOD BRAIN DIET

Resiliency expert Dr. Eva Selhub often likens the brain to a high-performance vehicle. "Like an expensive car," she writes, "your brain functions best when it gets only premium fuel. Eating high-quality foods that contain lots of vitamins, minerals, and antioxidants nourishes the brain and protects it from oxidative stress—the 'waste' (free radicals) produced when the body uses oxygen, which can damage cells."[1] She goes on to note that when your brain is forced to run on inferior fuel, it can't possibly do everything it was built to do. Refined sugar, for example, contributes to impaired brain function, leads to inflammation, and can even cause depression (something you might want to consider the next time you reach for a tub of ice cream to contend with a tough day).

In my podcast interviews with Dr. Lisa Mosconi, neuroscientist, integrative nutritionist, and author of *Brain Food* and *The XX Brain,* she explains why the dietary needs of the brain are different from those of other organs. "The human brain requires 45 distinct nutrients to function best. While most of these nutrients are created by the brain itself, the rest are imported from our diet."[2]

Since we know for sure that there's a direct connection between a good diet and a healthy brain, it's essential that you feed your brain with the best food nature has to offer. On the page opposite, you'll see a list of my top 10 favorite brain foods. (For a quick video on how to memorize this list, go to www.LimitlessBook.com/resources.) If you're the kind of person who hates hearing you need to eat your vegetables, employing this list might require a bit of an adjustment. But there's some good news, because there's evidence to show that your brain runs very well with a little bit of dark chocolate in the mix. Remember, what you eat matters, especially for your gray matter.

What are your favorite brain foods? How can you incorporate one more into your daily diet?

THE TOP 10 BRAIN FOODS

Avocados: They provide monounsaturated fat, which helps to maintain healthy blood flow.

Blueberries: They protect your brain from oxidative stress and reduce the effects of brain aging. There have also been studies that show they can help with memory.

Broccoli: A great source of vitamin K, which is known to improve cognitive function and memory.

Dark chocolate: This helps your focus and your concentration and stimulates endorphins. Chocolate also has flavonoids, which have been shown to improve cognitive function. The darker here the better, as the darkest chocolate has the least sugar, and we've already talked about how sugar is something to eat sparingly.

Eggs: They provide memory-improving and brain-boosting choline.

Green leafy vegetables: These are good sources of vitamin E, which reduces the effects of brain aging, and folate, which has been shown to improve memory.

Salmon, Sardines, Caviar: They're rich in omega-3 essential fatty acids, which help reduce the effects of brain aging.

Turmeric: It helps reduce inflammation and boost antioxidant levels while also improving your brain's oxygen intake. There's also some indication that turmeric helps reduce cognitive decay.

Walnuts: These nuts provide high levels of antioxidants and vitamin E that protect your neurons and protect against brain aging. They also contain high levels of zinc and magnesium, which are really good for your mood.

Water: Your brain is about 80 percent water. Dehydration can cause brain fog, fatigue, and slower reaction and thinking speed. Studies show that well-hydrated people score better on brainpower tests.

I met Mona Sharma when she was featured on Facebook's Red Table Talk as the nutritionist for Will Smith and his family, alongside Dr. Mark Hyman. She shared with me how "the foods we eat can have a big impact on our energy, the quality of our health, and the function of our brains. Focusing on key ingredients like good quality omega-3 rich fats, vegetables loaded with antioxidants and phytonutrients, and spices to enhance our digestion and focus, and can support both short- and long-term brain function." Here's a sample day of some of her go-to recipes to optimize brain power and vitality:

MORNING BRAIN TONIC

Serves 2

Ingredients:

- **2-inch piece of ginger, peeled and cut into slices**
- **2-inch piece of turmeric, peeled and cut into slices (note: this will stain, so watch clothes and countertops)**
- **4 cups filtered water**
- **organic green tea (loose or plastic-free tea bags for 2 servings)**
- **½ organic lemon, juiced**
- **Dash of black pepper**
- **Raw honey (optional)**

Place the turmeric, ginger, and water into a small saucepan.

Bring to a slow simmer on medium-high heat. Add the green tea and simmer for at least 5 minutes.

Remove from the heat. Add the lemon juice, dash of black pepper, and honey (if using).

Strain and serve hot. Avoid eating for 20 minutes after drinking this tonic.

Note: You can also make a large batch of the tonic mix ahead of time. Simply add a larger quantity of turmeric, ginger, and lemon to a juicer. Place this juice into the fridge, covered tightly with a lid, for up to 7 days. When serving, just add to hot water and green tea.

MORNING MAGIC SMOOTHIE

Serves 1

Ingredients:

- ½ cup frozen wild blueberries
- ½ cup chopped jicama (peel removed)
- Big handful of organic spinach (you can add more, too!)
- 2 tablespoons hemp seeds
- 1 teaspoon MCT oil
- 1 teaspoon organic spirulina powder
- ½ cup unsweetened coconut water
- ½ cup unsweetened almond milk
- Ice (optional)

Add all ingredients to a blender, blend, and start your day with brain and body fuel!

BRAIN BOOST SALAD

Serves 2

For the salad:

- 2 cups organic arugula
- 2 cups organic spinach
- ¼ cup pomegranate seeds
- ¼ cup raw walnuts, chopped
- 1 avocado, sliced
- 4 organic eggs, boiled then sliced when cool (if vegan, replace eggs with 2 tablespoons hemp seeds and 1 tablespoon pumpkin seeds)

For the dressing:

- 3 tablespoons raw apple cider vinegar
- ¼ cup extra virgin olive oil
- ½ lemon squeezed
- 1 tablespoon raw honey
- ¼ teaspoon Himalayan sea salt
- 2 tsp black sesame seeds (for garnish)

Place all salad dressing ingredients (except sesame seeds) into a bowl or mixing container and blend/shake well. Set aside.

Add the arugula, spinach, pomegranate seeds, and walnuts to a large salad bowl.

Pour salad dressing on top of the salad and mix together.

Transfer the mixed salad onto two plates. Top each salad with ½ sliced avocado and 2 sliced eggs. Garnish with sesame seeds. Enjoy!

EASY ROASTED SALMON & BROCCOLI WITH SWISS CHARD

Serves 2

Ingredients:

- 2 tablespoons of fresh lemon juice
- 2 teaspoon of chopped garlic
- 5 tablespoons extra virgin olive oil, divided
- 2 salmon fillets, preferably wild not farmed (4 to 6 ounces each)
- 2 to 4 slices of lemon
- 1 large head of organic broccoli, chopped into bite-sized florets (3 to 4 cups)
- 2 teaspoons Himalayan sea salt, divided
- 1 small shallot, finely chopped
- 1 small bunch organic Swiss chard or rainbow chard, finely chopped
- 1 teaspoon organic mustard seed powder

Line a large sheet pan with parchment paper and preheat the oven to 400 degrees F.

Mix the lemon juice, chopped garlic, and 2 tablespoons olive oil in a small bowl.

Lay the salmon down in the middle of the sheet pan and pour the lemon–garlic–olive oil mixture on top of each fillet evenly. Then place the lemon slices on top of each fillet.

Mix the broccoli florets, 2 tablespoons olive oil, and 1 teaspoon sea salt together in a large bowl. Place the mixture around each salmon fillet on the sheet pan.

Place in the preheated oven and bake for 20 minutes.

While the salmon and broccoli are baking, heat the remaining 1 tablespoon olive oil on low heat in a skillet. Add the chopped shallot, stirring often until clear and cooked. Add the Swiss chard with 2 tablespoons water to the skillet and cook for 3 to 5 minutes, stirring occasionally until the chard is softened. Remove from heat.

Add the salmon, broccoli, and chard to two serving plates. Sprinkle the broccoli with mustard seed powder to boost anti-inflammatory benefits. Serve and enjoy!

COCOA-CINNAMON-GINGER "HOT CHOCOLATE"

Serves 2

Ingredients:

- 4 cups unsweetened almond or coconut milk
- 2-inch ginger piece, peeled and sliced lengthwise
- 3 tablespoons unsweetened raw organic cocoa powder
- 1 teaspoon organic cinnamon powder
- 1 to 2 tablespoons coconut sugar (sweeten as desired)
- ½ teaspoon vanilla extract
- Small pinch of sea salt
- 2 cinnamon sticks, as garnish

Heat the almond milk and ginger slices in a medium saucepan over medium-high heat, stirring occasionally. Bring to a gentle simmer.

Add the cocoa powder, cinnamon, coconut sugar, vanilla, and sea salt and whisk until dissolved.

Bring to a gentle simmer once again before removing from the heat. Pour into two mugs, using a strainer to prevent the ginger from going into the cups. Add one cinnamon stick to each mug and enjoy!

Note: This drink can be served cooled during the summer months. Also, if serving as a dessert, add one dollop of coconut cream and blend for a sweeter, frothier taste.

2. BRAIN NUTRIENTS

As we've discussed, diet affects brain function. But what if you aren't able, because of your schedule or lifestyle, to regularly eat a rich brain-food diet? Research has shown that particular nutrients have a direct effect on your cognitive ability. I always prefer getting my nutrients from real, whole, organic foods. Talk to your qualified health practitioner to learn what you might be deficient in.

In my podcast episode with Max Lugavere, author of *Genius Foods,* we discussed the benefits of supplementing with phospholipid DHA—your brain uses this to create healthy cell membranes.[3] This is important because our cell membranes form all the receptors involved in mood, executive functioning, attention, and memory. B vitamins have been shown to improve women's memories. Curcumin, the nutrient found in turmeric, can forestall cognitive decay. You can get a list of nutrients and their effect on the brain from the National Institutes of Health website.[4]

There are natural sources for all of these nutrients, but getting all of them into your diet might not fit your lifestyle or your palate. The good news is that supplements are readily available for all of these (though not all supplements are created equal; make sure to do some research). You can also combine these with the brain foods discussed in this chapter to give your brain the fuel it needs. For a list and links to my favorite brain supplements, go to www.LimitlessBook.com/resources.

3. EXERCISE

"Exercise changes the brain in ways that protect memory and thinking skills," writes Heidi Godman, the executive editor of the *Harvard Health Letter*. "In a study done at the University of British Columbia, researchers found that regular aerobic exercise, the kind that gets your heart and your sweat glands pumping, appears to boost the size of the hippocampus, the brain area involved in verbal memory and learning."[5]

I can almost hear some of you complaining or making excuses as you read that last paragraph: Exercise is boring. You don't have time for it. You can't afford a gym membership. But the simple fact is that exercise is enormously valuable if you want to unshackle your brain. Think about it: When you're active and moving, you feel sharper, right? Some of us even *need* to move around in order to get our brains operating at top efficiency. That's because there's a direct correlation between exercise and brain function. And you don't need to become an Olympic athlete in order to keep your brain sharp. There's lots of evidence to show that even 10 minutes of aerobic exercise a day can have enormous benefits.

As your body moves, your brain grooves. Check out a few of my favorite exercise videos at www.LimitlessBook.com/resources.

KWIK START

Set your phone alarm to remind yourself to move for a few minutes every hour.

4. KILLING ANTS

Dr. Daniel Amen, a clinical neuroscientist, author of the bestseller *Change Your Brain, Change Your Life,* and a frequent guest of ours, came home one night after a particularly bad day at the office dealing with suicide risks, angst-ridden teens, and dysfunctional couples to find thousands of ants in his kitchen. "It was gross," he wrote. "As I started to clean them up, the acronym came to me. I thought of my patients from that day—like my infested kitchen, my patients' brains were also infested by the negative thoughts that were robbing them of their joy and stealing their happiness. The next day, I brought a can of ant spray to work as a visual aid and have been working diligently ever since to help my patients eradicate their ANTs."[6]

ANTs are "automatic negative thoughts" and, if you're like most people, you place limitations on yourself in the form of these thoughts at least some of the time. Maybe you tell yourself that you aren't smart enough to learn a skill that you'd really like to have. Or perhaps you repeat on an endless loop how pushing yourself to accomplish something is only going to lead to disappointment.

ANTs are everywhere, and there isn't enough ant spray in the world to get rid of all of them. But eliminating them from your life is an essential part of unlimiting your brain. The reason for this is simple: If you fight for your limitations, you get to keep them. If you regularly tell yourself that you can't do something, or that you're too old to do something, or that you don't have the smarts to do something, you won't do that thing. Only when you move on from this kind of destructive self-talk can you truly accomplish what you want to accomplish.

What is your biggest ANT? What could you replace it with?

5. A CLEAN ENVIRONMENT

A 2018 piece in the medical journal *The Lancet* identified that "air pollution might cause 30 percent of all strokes and thus might be one of the leading contributors of the global stroke burden." It went on: "Given the strong association between stroke, vascular risk factors, and dementia, the suggested link between air pollution and dementia is to be expected."[7] The air you breathe is critical to the way your brain functions. If you've ever been stuck in a room with a smoker, you know how hard it is to even think while you're breathing that toxic air. Conversely, if you're hiking in the mountains and take a deep breath from the crisp, clean atmosphere, you can feel your senses thriving.

If you live in a factory town or a big city with pollutants everywhere, there isn't a lot you can do about the air around you. Fortunately, there are devices available to clean the air in your home and in your office, and you can make an increased effort to get to cleaner spaces more frequently.

A clean environment goes beyond air quality. Removing clutter and distractions from your surroundings will make you feel lighter and improve your ability to focus, so take time to Marie Kondo your mind and remove any unnecessary stuff.

KWIK START

What is one thing you can do today to clean your environment?

6. A POSITIVE PEER GROUP

Your brain potential is not just related to your biological networks or your neurological networks; it is also related to your social networks. Who you spend time with is who you become. Motivational speaker Jim Rohn says that you are the average of the five people you spend the most time with. Whether you believe that or not, I don't think any of us can disagree with the notion that the people around us have a meaningful influence on our lives. A recent Temple University study showed that people (specifically teenagers in this study) act differently when they are alone than they do when they are with others. In reporting on the study for *The New York Times*, Tara Parker-Pope said that "Dr. Steinberg [one of the authors of the study] notes that the brain system involved in reward processing is also involved in the processing of social information, explaining why peers can have such a pronounced effect on decision making."[8]

Because of this influence, those you spend time with have a genuine effect on brain function. Certainly, they affect your self-talk, as most of us tie at least a part of our beliefs to the beliefs others have about us. But they can affect everything from what you eat to how much you exercise, to even how much sleep you get. There are lots of books out there dedicated to helping you distinguish people who are good for you from people who are not, but for the purposes of this chapter, just take a few minutes to think about who your peers are, how much influence they have on your life, and how this affects your desire to unlimit yourself.

KWIK START

Who is someone you need to spend more time with? Reach out and make a date with that person now.

7. BRAIN PROTECTION

This probably goes without saying, but protecting your brain is critical if you're going to make the most of your brain. You have only one brain. If you were given only one car to use for the rest of your life, how well would you treat that car? You would take care of it as if your life depended on it. Accidents are unavoidable, but putting yourself in situations where brain injury is less likely improves your chances of avoiding the worst. Hard-contact or extreme sports are not ideal if you want to make the most of this precious asset. Driving 20 miles an hour over the speed limit all the time on your motorcycle isn't advisable, either. If you love these things too much to give them up, at the very least take as many precautions and use as many safety tools as you can.

8. NEW LEARNING

One of the most important things you can do for the health of your brain is to keep learning. We are all capable of expanding the capacities of our brains, even as we get older, which we discussed when we talked about neuroplasticity in Chapter 3.

What this means is that, as long as we keep learning, we continue to create new pathways in our brains. We keep our brains plastic and supple, capable of processing new information in relevant ways. This is especially true if we give ourselves genuine challenges in our learning. Attempting to master a new skill, to discover a new language, to embrace parts of your culture or the cultures of others that are new to you all keep those neurons firing and creating new pathways. By increasing the ways you use your brain, you increase the capabilities of your brain.

KWIK START

Create an ongoing "To Learn" list. What are some things on that list? Write two down here: ______________________________

____

____

____

9. STRESS MANAGEMENT

We all experience some level of stress in our everyday lives, sometimes a great deal of stress. Whenever we experience stress, a hormone known as cortisol is released to alleviate the physical rigors of stress on our bodies. If this happens occasionally, it's not a problem, but if it happens with great regularity, the buildup of cortisol in our brains can lead it to cease functioning properly.

But there's more. "There is evidence that chronic (persistent) stress may actually rewire your brain," says a piece on the Harvard Health Blog. "Scientists have learned that animals that experience prolonged stress have less activity in the parts of their brain that handle higher-order tasks—for example, the prefrontal cortex—and more activity in the primitive parts of their brain that are focused on survival, such as the amygdala. It's much like what would happen if you exercised one part of your body and not another. The part that was activated more often would become stronger, and the part that got less attention would get weaker. This is what appears to happen in the brain when it is under continuous stress: it essentially builds up the part of the brain designed to handle threats, and the part of the brain tasked with more complex thought takes a back seat."[9]

With such clear evidence that stress can be debilitating to your brain, finding ways to reduce or avoid stress becomes critical. I'm going to offer a number of suggestions in this area over the course of this book.

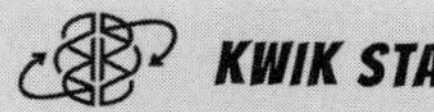

KWIK START

What is your favorite thing to do to cope with stress? When was the last time you did it?

10. SLEEP

If you want better focus, you need to get good sleep. If you want to be a clearer thinker, you need to get good sleep. If you want to make better decisions or have a better memory, you need to get good sleep. According to the National Institutes of Health:

> Quality sleep—and getting enough of it at the right times—is as essential to survival as food and water. Without sleep you can't form or maintain the pathways in your brain that let you learn and create new memories, and it's harder to concentrate and respond quickly. Sleep is important to a number of brain functions, including how nerve cells (neurons) communicate with each other. In fact, your brain and body stay remarkably active while you sleep. Recent findings suggest that sleep plays a housekeeping role that removes toxins in your brain that build up while you are awake.[10]

The takeaway: getting enough sleep—and getting enough *quality* sleep—is essential if you're going to make the most of your brain.

Sleep Is Not a Choice

I know there are lots of people out there who say they don't need a lot of sleep, or that they don't have time for sleep, or even consider it a point of pride that their lives are so full of activity that they "have no choice" but to sacrifice sleep. That's a mistake, and, if you're one of these people, it's something I want you to reconsider right now.

"Sleep is crucial to overall health and daily functioning," writes Dr. Jean Kim, a psychiatrist and a clinical assistant professor of psychiatry at George Washington University. "Increasing evidence has tied lack of sleep to a host of mental and physical disorders, including increased depression, irritability, impulsivity, cardiovascular disease, and more. One study noted that sleep actually functions as a sort of laundry cycle for the brain, where during sleep, blood vessels (and lymphatic channels) in the brain hyperperfuse and flush out metabolic buildup from the day and remove neurotoxins and distribute components that enhance cellular repair."[11]

In his TED talk about sleep, Dr. Jeff Iliff of Oregon Health and Science University takes the "laundry cycle" metaphor even further. He notes that, while we're awake, the brain is so busy doing other things that it doesn't have the capacity to clean itself of waste. The buildup of this waste, amyloid-beta, is now being linked to the development of Alzheimer's disease.

"When the brain is awake and is at its most busy, it puts off clearing away the waste from the spaces between its cells until later, and then, when it goes to sleep and doesn't have to be as busy, it shifts into a kind of cleaning mode to clear away the waste from the spaces between its cells, the waste that's accumulated throughout the day."[12]

A little later in the talk, Iliff warns against doing something that so many of us do: sacrificing sleep until we get a chance to catch up. "Like our housework, it's a dirty and a thankless job, but it's also important. In your house, if you stop cleaning your kitchen for a month, your home will become completely unlivable very quickly. But in the brain, the consequences of falling behind may be much greater than the embarrassment of dirty countertops, because when it comes to cleaning the brain, it is the very health and function of the mind and the body that's at stake, which is why understanding these very basic housekeeping functions of the brain today may be critical for preventing and treating diseases of the mind tomorrow."[13]

So, if you're one of the many people who have convinced themselves that there's a level of nobility in getting by with minimal sleep, it's time to revise your thinking. There's simply too much to gain from a good night's sleep (including what you can learn from your dreams).

Getting through the Night

It's one thing to say you're going to get a good night's sleep. It's another thing entirely to accomplish it. About a quarter of all Americans experience some level of insomnia every year.[14]

There is, however, very strong evidence connecting exercise to sleep, even among chronic insomnia sufferers. A study performed by Dr. Kathryn J. Reid and others found that aerobic exercise had strong positive results on a group of participants who'd previously regularly encountered sleep problems. "Results from this study indicate that a sixteen-week program of moderate intensity aerobic physical activity plus sleep hygiene education is effective in improving self-reported sleep quality, mood, and quality of life in older adults with chronic insomnia," the authors wrote. "These results highlight the potential of structured physical activity programs to improve the effectiveness of standard behavioral approaches for the treatment of insomnia, particularly in a sedentary older adult population."[15]

A group at Northwestern University's Feinberg School of Medicine built upon this study by drilling down on the data gleaned and then studying the interconnection between exercise and sleep. What they found is important to consider: exercise is not a magic pill. If you're having trouble sleeping, you can't solve the problem with one session at the gym. They found that, even after two months, the effects of exercise on sleep were minimal. But by the end of the 16-week study, the results were considerable, with participants getting as much as an hour-and-a-quarter extra sleep per night.[16]

So, there's a clear connection between exercise and sleep, but you're going to need to give it time. But, given the overall benefits of exercise on your health, committing to an exercise routine is always a good idea, even if you won't feel the benefits on your sleep right away.

There are varying ideas about how much exercise is necessary to affect sleep, but a commonly stated amount is 2.5 hours a week of aerobic exercise, coupled with some resistance work. "Brisk walking, light biking, elliptical machine, anything that increases your heart rate so that you can still talk while exercising but have to catch your breath every few sentences or so, is considered moderate exercise," recommends Dr. Christopher E. Kline of the University of Pittsburgh.[17]

Giving Your Mind a Break

One of the many reasons why people have trouble sleeping, is not being able to get your mind to turn off. We've all been there: You have a huge meeting coming up, or something disruptive (either positive or negative) happened during the day, or you got a phone call just before bedtime that got you riled up. Your head hits the pillow, but you might as well be running laps around your house because your mind is busy with this inciting event. You wind up lying there for hours, and sleep seems as unapproachable as Everest.

Fortunately, you have a tool available to you at all times that can help you deal with this: meditation. The benefits of meditation are numerous (and there are many, many books out there that detail them), including everything from boosting immune function to decreasing anxiety to actually increasing your gray matter. One of those many benefits is helping with insomnia.

In a study performed by Dr. David S. Black and others, a group of older adults with sleep problems were introduced to mindfulness meditation through six two-hour sessions. By the end of these sessions, this group showed meaningful improvement with insomnia.[18]

If meditation seems foreign to you (and, if that's the case, you're in the vast majority, as less than 15 percent of Americans meditate),[19] it's likely because you've heard that meditation is difficult or that it requires you to completely blank your mind. Ariel Garten, creator of Muse, a headband that assists in meditation, clarifies that it isn't about emptying your mind, but rather, "training your mind to be aware in the present moment."[20]

She told me that you can choose any time and any place to meditate and that you can feel the benefits from it with as little as three minutes spent with eyes closed, taking deep breaths and then releasing those breaths, counting as you go. Another tool she advocates is focused attention, a super-simple process of placing all your attention on your breathing. When your mind wanders from your breathing (as it invariably will), just notice this and bring it back. This technique promises to demystify meditation for anyone who thinks you need to be a Zen master to get anything out of it. Few of us are capable of locking our focus on one thing for an extended period, so it's good to know refocusing is equally valuable.

When you regain your attention on your breathing, Garten says, "you're exerting an important skill—you're learning to observe your thinking. You're not caught up in your thoughts, but you're in a process of observing that you're thinking. You begin to recognize that you can have control over your thoughts and that you can choose what you are thinking."[21]

Meditation can improve your sleep, even with these simple methods. My meditation coach, Emily Fletcher, author of *Stress Less, Accomplish More* has a unique process called Ziva Meditation. You can watch a full video of us going through her process by going to LimitlessBook.com/resources and we will walk you through it.

KWIK START

What is your top sleep tip? Write it here: ______________________

____

____

BEFORE WE MOVE ON

Fueling your brain is fundamental to becoming limitless, and we have lots more to get to in order to make this happen. But first, let's stop and focus on a few things from this chapter:

- Put a shopping list together for all the brain foods you don't currently have in your home. I realize that not all of these foods are going to be compatible with your palate, but really try to include as many as you can. Then take this list with you to the store.
- Spend some time identifying your ANTs. What limitations are you placing on yourself? Give yourself a few minutes with this. What are you telling yourself you can't do? Write this down.
- Think about how you'd like to expand your learning. What have you always wanted to master that you haven't found the time to master? Is it a different language? Computer coding? A new sales or marketing technique? What can you do to fit that into your life right now?

- Use one of the tools we talked about here to improve the amount and quality of your sleep. Keep track of this for at least a week.

- I made two videos for you on how to easily memorize the top 10 brain foods and my 10 brain energizing recommendations. Go to www.LimitlessBook.com/resources to watch.

"We first make
our habits,
and then our habits
make us."

—JOHN DRYDEN

9

SMALL SIMPLE STEPS

What is the smallest simple step I can take now?

How do we start good habits or end bad ones?

What daily routine will help me become limitless?

You have a reason or purpose to do something. You have the necessary energy to do it. What is missing?

A small simple step (S^3). The tiniest action you can take to get you closer to your goal. One that requires minimal effort or energy. Over time, these become habits. That's the reason I've filled this book with the small simple steps called Kwik Starts.

Back in the 1920s, a Russian psychologist, Bluma Zeigarnik, was sitting in a Viennese restaurant when she noticed that the waiters swirling around her in the busy eatery were highly efficient at remembering customer orders while they were in process but tended to forget who had what as soon as the orders were filled.

Intrigued by this, she ran a study where she had people perform simple tasks while they were sometimes interrupted. Afterward, she queried participants about which tasks they remembered and which they did not, finding that those who'd been interrupted were twice as likely to remember the things they'd been doing when they'd been interrupted than the things they'd been able to complete without interruption. She came to the conclusion—subsequently known as the Zeigarnik effect—that uncompleted tasks created a level of tension that keeps that task at the front of our minds until it is completed.

In all likelihood, you're familiar with this tension from your experience with procrastination. When you have something you know you need to do and you keep putting it off, it weighs on you, even making it more difficult to do anything else well as long as this task goes uncompleted. What you need to do seems hard, or it seems like less fun than the other things you could be doing, or it's going to be uncomfortable, or you've simply convinced yourself that you have plenty of time to get to it later. We still struggle to complete tasks when we are clear on our vision for our lives and know who we want to become. Why is it still so hard to act, even when we have sustained motivation?

One of the most significant reasons that people fail to act is that we feel overwhelmed by what we need to do. A project or a chore might seem so big and time-consuming that you can't imagine how you're ever going to get it done. We look at the project in its entirety and immediately feel that the task at hand is too big, so we shut down or put it off. "Incomplete tasks and procrastinating often lead to frequent and unhelpful thought patterns," says psychologist Hadassah Lipszyc. "These thoughts can impact on sleep, trigger anxiety symptoms, and further impact on a person's mental and emotional resources."[1]

BE KIND TO YOURSELF

If you struggle to get something done with some amount of regularity, there's a good chance that you feel guilty about this and you beat yourself up over it. It's likely you give yourself a much harder time about it than is helpful. We already know that unfinished tasks create tension in your brain. If you layer guilt and shame on top of this, you're making it even harder to get a task done, and you're making yourself miserable.

"Feeling guilty when you're away from work, when you aren't in a position to do anything about it, is not helpful, and can be painful," writes Dr. Art Markman, a professor of psychology and marketing at University of Texas, Austin. "It will make you feel worse about your job in general and spoil time that you could be spending with friends, family, or engaging in an enjoyable activity. Shame, though, is a different story. There is evidence that people will explicitly procrastinate to avoid shame. Feeling shame about work you have not completed is likely to make the problem worse, not better, making it an emotion that is almost never helpful."[2]

Feeling bad about your lack of progress is likely to make it more difficult for you to stop procrastinating. So, give yourself a break. Beating yourself up isn't going to improve anything, and, since you're reading this book now, you're already taking steps to avoid procrastinating in the future.

In my experience, the best way to deal with this is to find a way to break the task into bite-size pieces, which lead to habits that lead toward success. Circling back to the Zeigarnik effect, every time you complete one of these smaller tasks, you get to take that weight off your mind. And as each of these subtasks is finished, you're that much closer to completing the task overall.

TAKE BABY STEPS

Podcast guest Dr. B. J. Fogg, the founder and director of the Behavior Design Lab at Stanford University and the author of *Tiny Habits,* has been studying human behavior for more than two decades. What he's learned is that only three things can change a person's behavior long term. One is to have an epiphany, which very few people can summon on demand. Another is to change your environment, which is possible for nearly everyone, but not necessarily feasible at any given time. The third is to, as Dr. Fogg puts it, "take baby steps."[3]

I like the way this story illustrates the principle of small, simple steps:

> A King was watching a great magician perform his act. The crowd was enthralled and so was the King. At the end, the audience roared with approval. And the King said, "What a gift this man has. A God-given talent."

> But a wise counsellor said to the King, "My Lord, genius is made, not born. This magician's skill is the result of discipline and practice. These talents have been learned and honed over time with determination and discipline."
>
> The King was troubled by this message. The counsellor's challenge had spoiled his pleasure in the magician's arts. "Limited and spiteful man. How dare you criticize a true genius. As I said, you either have it or you don't. And you most certainly don't."
>
> The King turned to his bodyguard and said, "Throw this man into the deepest dungeon." And, he added for the counselor's benefit, "So you won't be lonely, you can have two of your kind to keep you company. You shall have two piglets as cellmates."
>
> From the very first day of his imprisonment, the wise counselor practiced running up the steps of his cell to the prison door carrying in each hand a piglet. As the days turned into weeks, and the weeks into months, the piglets steadily grew into sturdy boars. And with every day of practice the wise counselor increased his power and strength.
>
> One day the King remembered the wise counselor and was curious to see how imprisonment had humbled him. He had the wise counselor summoned.
>
> When the prisoner appeared, he was a man of powerful physique, carrying a boar on each arm. The King exclaimed, "What a gift this man has. A God-given talent."
>
> The wise counselor replied, "My Lord, genius is made, not born. My skill is the result of discipline and practice. These talents have been learned and honed over time with determination and discipline."[4]

One of the only things that is likely to change your behavior is to make incremental progress. You really don't want to make dinner? Make something simple for your family to snack on while you cook dinner later. You're having trouble writing that big speech for next month's conference? Just write the keynote to the speech now. You're overwhelmed by the amount of reading you need to do for your economics class? Set a goal for yourself of reading the first chapter. Like the wise counselor, you must take it one step at a time, one day at a time.

What you'll notice in all of these scenarios is two things. One is that they present you with something achievable—a win on the way to reaching the championship of getting this job done. The other is that they all put you in a situation where you're likely to get even more accomplished. You're already in the kitchen now, so you might as well finish making dinner. You've gotten through the keynote and you're on a roll, so maybe it makes sense to draft some more pages. The first chapter of your economics text wasn't nearly as dry as it seemed from the outside, and you already have the book open; you can handle a few more chapters.

By breaking a task that you're procrastinating about into smaller pieces, the path to getting it done becomes clear.

The best way to deal with the tension between what you want and what you've done so far to achieve it is to remember what the Zeigarnik effect teaches us. You're not going to be able to ease your mind about this task until you complete it, so get yourself moving toward completion. Start somewhere. Anywhere. Even if you don't have the energy or the motivation to get the entire thing done, get started on getting it done. You'll be thankful for the relief.

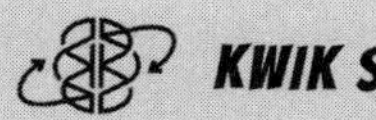

KWIK START

Think about an important task you've been putting off. What is it? How can you break it down into simpler steps that you can do each day?

ON AUTOPILOT

Small simple steps repeated lead to habits. Our habits are a core part of who we are. Various studies have shown that somewhere between 40 and 50 percent of what we do every day is the product of a habit. That means that half of our lives is governed by what scientists term *automaticity*. This percentage might sound high to you—it certainly did to me the first time I heard it—but consider how many things you do every day without really thinking

"As you step into your limitless self, you might be confronted with old habits and patterns that are not necessarily based in truth. These old ways of being show up because you have repeated many of them thousands of times."

—DEBBIE FORD

about them. You brush your teeth without thinking about it. You check your phone at predictable intervals. You drive to the office and don't particularly recall how you got there. You zip up your jacket, get a glass out of the cupboard, and click on the TV remote automatically.

This, of course, is essential to how we conduct our lives. Could you imagine how overwhelming it would be if you had to think about *every single thing* you did? If even brushing your teeth required some conscious level of calculation, you'd be exhausted by 10 in the morning.

"Without habit loops, our brains would shut down, overwhelmed by the minutiae of daily life," writes Charles Duhigg in his best-selling book, *The Power of Habit.* "People whose basal ganglia are damaged by injury or disease often become mentally paralyzed. They have trouble performing basic activities, such as opening a door or deciding what to eat. They lose the ability to ignore insignificant details—one study, for example, found that patients with basal ganglia injuries couldn't recognize facial expressions, including fear and disgust, because they were perpetually uncertain about which part of the face to focus on."[5]

James Clear, author of the best-selling book *Atomic Habits,* says, "The habits you repeat (or don't repeat) every day largely determine your health, wealth, and happiness. Knowing how to change your habits means knowing how to confidently own and manage your days, focus on the behaviors that have the highest impact, and reverse-engineer the life you want."[6]

"All habits serve you in some way," Clear told me. "As you go through life, you face a variety of problems. You need to tie your shoe; your brain is automating the solution to that problem. That's what a habit is. It's the solution to a recurring problem that you face throughout life, one that you've employed so many times that you can do it without thinking. If the solution doesn't work anymore, then your brain will update it."[7]

Clear identifies the habit loop as having four components: a cue, a craving, a response, and a reward. Using the example of turning on a light when you enter a room, the cue is walking into the room and finding it dark. The craving is feeling that there would be some value in the room not being dark. The response is flipping on the light switch, and the reward is that the room is no longer dark.[8] You can apply this loop to any of your habits, such as getting your mail when you come home from work. The cue is reaching your driveway or front door at the end of the day. The craving is hoping there's something in the mailbox. The response is going to the mailbox to find out. And the reward is getting the mail out of your mailbox. You probably didn't think about any of this until you actually had the mail in your hands.

The Habit Loop

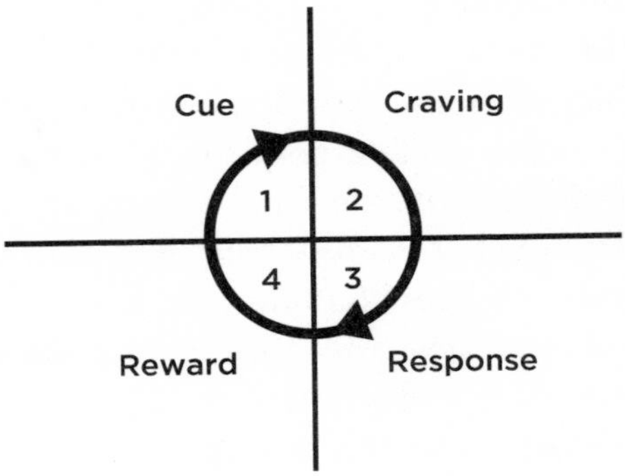

Cue
Craving
1
2
4
3
Reward
Response

Creating habits to automate essential parts of our lives is a fundamental streamlining technique that we do largely unconsciously, often to our benefit. Of course, we also automate all kinds of things that we'd probably be much better off not turning into habits. I'm sure you know some version of this. Perhaps a cue is walking past your kitchen pantry. The craving comes from the knowledge that your favorite chips are in the pantry, and your innate desire to eat them. The response is that you go into the pantry, open the bag of chips, and take out a big handful. And the reward is crunchy, salty, fatty deliciousness . . . that doesn't benefit your health in any way. Our negative habits operate with the same level of automaticity as our healthy ones. Those chips are in your stomach before you've even had the opportunity to register that you were stuffing them in your mouth.

Now, because you're in the process of becoming limitless, you know that perpetuating negative behaviors is a drain on your superpowers. So, how do you break bad habits and, just as importantly, how do you create new habits that will help you?

GETTING IN THE HABIT

Before we get to this, let's talk for a moment about how long it takes to form a habit. In a study for University College London, Phillippa Lally, Cornelia H. M. van Jaarsveld, Henry W. W. Potts, and Jane Wardle took participants through the process of developing a new healthy eating, drinking, or exercise habit, such as drinking water with lunch or jogging before dinner. They were asked to perform this new behavior based on specific situational cues every day for 84 days. "For the majority of participants," they wrote, "automaticity increased steadily over the days of the study, supporting the assumption that repeating a behavior in a consistent setting increases automaticity." By the end of the study, they'd found that it took an average of 66 days for the new behavior to become a habit, though it took individual participants as little as 18 days and as many as 254.[9]

It is also widely assumed that breaking a bad habit isn't about ending that habit, but rather about replacing it with a different, more constructive, habit. Dr. Elliot Berkman, director of the Social and Affective Neuroscience Laboratory at the University of Oregon, notes, "It's much easier to start doing something new than to stop doing something habitual without a replacement behavior. That's one reason why smoking cessation aids such as nicotine gum or inhalers tend to be more effective than the nicotine patch."[10]

So, if the process of starting a new habit, such as setting aside time to read every day, is fundamentally the same as the process of ending a negative habit, such as grabbing those chips every time you pass the pantry, how does it work?

As with so many of the things we've discussed in this book, motivation plays a key role. Speaking specifically about the effort to break habits, Dr. Thomas G. Plante, adjunct clinical professor of the Department of Psychiatry and Behavioral Sciences at Stanford

"Habit is either the best of servants or the worst of masters."

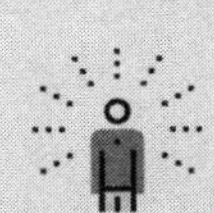

—NATHANIEL EMMONS

University School of Medicine, said, "It depends on how much you really want to break the habit. Many people are ambivalent. They want to lose weight, but they like the foods they eat. They want to reduce their alcohol consumption but love their happy hour. They want to stop picking their nails, but it reduces stress for them. So, one important issue is how strongly you really want to break the habit in question. Second, how established is the problem habit? It is easier to break a new habit than an old one. Third, what are the consequences of not breaking the habit? Will a partner leave you? Will you lose a job? Will you get sick? Will something really bad happen if you don't change?"[11]

Dr. B. J. Fogg created the Fogg Behavior Model to identify the circumstances that need to be present for behavior change to occur. "For a target behavior to happen," he notes, "a person must have sufficient motivation, sufficient ability, and an effective prompt. All three factors must be present at the same instant for the behavior to occur."[12] In other words, you need three things in place in order to develop a habit: You need the desire to do it, since it is exceedingly difficult to make habitual anything you really don't want to do; you need the skills to do it, since it's nearly impossible to make a habit out of anything you don't have the capacity to accomplish; and you need something to get the habit loop started (what James Clear and others refer to as "the cue"). Let's look at each element in turn:

Motivation

We've talked about motivation already, but it's worth revisiting the subject here to see it from Fogg's perspective. Fogg identifies three key motivators:

1. **Pleasure/pain**: This is the most immediate motivator. In this case, the behavior has a nearly immediate payoff, positive or negative. "I believe pleasure/pain is a primitive response," says Fogg, "and it functions adaptively in hunger, sex, and other activities related to self-preservation and propagation of our genes."[13]

2. Hope/fear: Unlike the immediacy of the previous motivator, this one is all about anticipation. When you're hopeful, you're anticipating something good happening; when you're fearful, you're anticipating the opposite. "This dimension is at times more powerful than pleasure/pain, as is evidenced in everyday behavior," Fogg notes. "For example, in some situations, people will accept pain (a flu shot) in order to overcome fear (anticipation of getting the flu).[14]

3. Social acceptance/rejection: Humans have always desired to be accepted by their peers, dating back to the time when being ostracized could mean a death sentence, and this remains an extremely strong motivator. "The power of social motivation is likely hardwired into us and perhaps all other creatures that historically depended on living in groups to survive."[15]

Ability

Fogg equates ability with simplicity, noting that when something is simple for us, we are considerably more likely to do it. He defines six categories of simplicity:

1. Time: We only perceive something to be simple if we have the time available to perform the function.

2. Money: Similarly, if something stretches our financial resources, we do not consider it simple.

3. Physical effort: We consider things that are physically easy for us to be simple.

4. Brain cycles: Simple things don't tax our thinking, and we shy away from things that require us to think too hard.

5. Social deviance: This goes back to the acceptance motivation. A simple act fits into societal norms.

6. Nonroutine: How far something is out of one's normal routine will define its level of simplicity.

Prompts

Finally, Fogg notes three types of prompts:

1. **Spark:** A spark is a type of prompt that immediately leads to a form of motivation. For example, if opening your e-mail leads to a level of fear over what you might find there, you're likely to adopt a habit that will change that fear.
2. **Facilitator:** This type of prompt works when motivation is high, but ability is low. For example, if you want to use a certain kind of software on your computer but are tech-averse, a tool that makes that software easier for you to use is likely to cause you to adopt this behavior.
3. **Signal:** In some cases, you'll have both high motivation and high ability. The only other thing you need to make a behavior a habit is some kind of reminder or signal. If you love making brain smoothies, all you need is to walk into your kitchen in the morning and see the blender to prompt you to make one.

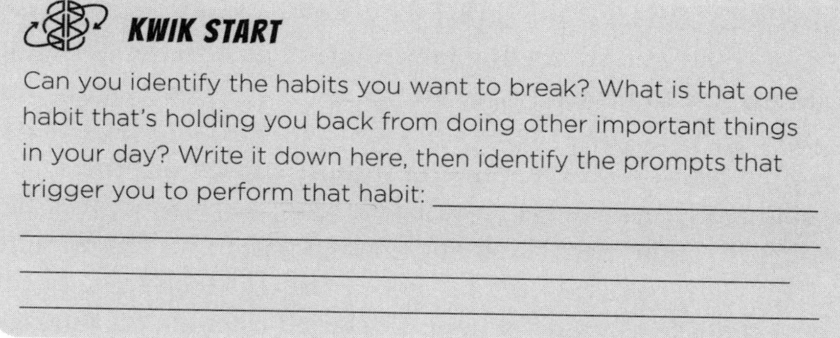

KWIK START

Can you identify the habits you want to break? What is that one habit that's holding you back from doing other important things in your day? Write it down here, then identify the prompts that trigger you to perform that habit: ______________________________
____
____
____

CREATING A NEW HABIT

The Fogg Behavior Model shows us everything that needs to be in place for a particular behavior to become a habit. We know that making habits of behaviors we consider good for us is important to our growth, and we also know that the key to breaking bad habits is to replace them with more constructive ones. But how do you make something a habit? Just remember WIN:

- **W is for Want:** Make sure you really want it. It's nearly impossible to turn something into a habit if you don't want to do that thing. Does one of the motivators in the Fogg Model apply to the habit you're trying to adopt? If not, is there something close to this habit that might accomplish something similar for you?
- **I is for Innate:** Does the new habit you're trying to adopt align well with your innate abilities? Remember that you're unlikely to make something a habit when it is consistently difficult for you to perform. If the habit you're trying to adopt is something that you're good at or you know you can be good at, you're well on your way.
- **N is for Now:** Create a prompt for yourself that encourages you to perform the new habit now. This can be anything from a reminder on your phone to placing something in your office that makes you remember to set aside time to do what you're setting out to do.

GROWING YOUR LIFE ONE HABIT AT A TIME

In case you're still wondering how much of an effect establishing good habits can have on your life, let me share a story about one of our clients. Xiang suffered from schizophrenia and depression. He often heard voices telling him to hurt himself or others, and he endured several stints in psychiatric wards because of this. After finding the right medication and emerging from his latest round of treatment, he discovered my podcast and learned some of the tactics that I teach in my school. He started listening on a regular basis and participated in the Kwik Challenge, a series of exercises I take people through to introduce novelty to their thinking and therefore keep their brains tuned for learning.

At first, this was hard for Xiang, but he focused on doing just two particular challenges: brushing his teeth with his opposite hand and taking a cold shower every morning. He increased his time under the cold water by one minute each week and, in doing so, discovered that being able to do something hard, like standing under freezing cold water for several minutes each morning, made him realize that there were areas in his life in which he was fighting for his limitations. Building from these Kwik Challenge experiences, he started applying what he was learning about habits and behavior change to other areas.

Xiang's life improved dramatically. He took his driver's license test and passed. He changed his diet, cut out sugary drinks, and started taking a five-minute jog in the park every morning. He started reading books—the first being *Mindset* by Carol Dweck—and as he read, he listened to baroque music to pace his reading and distract himself from hallucinations. It took him a month to finish the book, but when he did, he felt a sense of confidence he had never had before. Trips to the library became a regular thing. Xiang has even taken his learning to the next level and enrolled in computer science classes at a local college. And the best part is that he now believes he is a lifelong learner.

You may think that because of all your past failed attempts to change your habits and routines you're doomed to failure forever. Xiang's story shows that by changing just one or two small habits in your day, incredible progress can follow. Something as simple as brushing your teeth with the opposite hand can be the start to an entirely new way of life.

ESTABLISHING A MORNING ROUTINE

Why is your morning routine so important? I strongly believe that if you jump-start your day by jump-starting your brain with a series of simple activities, you have a huge advantage. In addition, if you set up winning routines early in the day, you can benefit from what Tony Robbins calls "the science of momentum": the notion that once you set accomplishment in motion, you can keep it in motion with much less effort than if you were trying to accomplish something from a standing start.

I have a carefully developed morning routine to help me win the day that involves priming my mind. I don't do every single one of these things every day, especially when I'm traveling, but I always do most of them, and I know for certain that it gets me mentally prepared and poised for performance, productivity, and positivity from the minute I get up.

Let me walk you through a typical morning.

Before I even get out of bed, I spend some time reflecting on my dreams. Dreams are an expression of the work your subconscious is doing while you're sleeping, and there's gold to be mined from them. Many geniuses throughout history have regularly accessed and often gleaned their best ideas and made their greatest discoveries from their dreams. Mary Shelley came up with the idea for *Frankenstein* in her dreams. A dream was the source of Paul McCartney's "Yesterday," and Einstein's theory of relativity.

So, the first thing I do every morning, even before lifting my head from the pillow, is think back on my dreams to see if there's an idea or a perception or a new way of looking at something that can be useful to what I'm trying to accomplish. I know that some of you have trouble recalling your dreams, so I'm going to provide you with a quick mnemonic technique designed to help you do so. Just think of the word DREAMS:

- **D is for Decide**: The night before, make a conscious decision that you're going to recall your dreams. If you set the intention, your chances improve dramatically.
- **R is for Record**: Keep a pen and paper by your bedside, or even have a recording app readily available on your phone. As soon as you wake up, record any lingering remembrance of your dreams.
- **E is for Eyes**: Keep your eyes closed right after you awaken. Dreams can disappear within minutes, and if you keep your eyes closed, this will help you reflect.
- **A is for Affirm**: Before you go to sleep, affirm that you are going to remember your dreams, because affirmation is a critical tool in accomplishment.
- **M is for Manage**: For lots of reasons but specifically here for the sake of remembering your dreams, it's important to manage your sleep and establish good sleep routines.

- **S is for Share:** Talk about your dreams with others. When you do so, you bring them more and more to the surface, and you develop the routine of tapping into your dreams so you can discuss them later.

The first thing I do after I get out of bed is make the bed. This is a success habit, my first accomplishment of the day. It's an easy win, and it has the added advantage of making my bedtime more pleasant, because it's always nicer to return that night to a bed that is made. It's why, in the military, they train you to make your bed first thing in the morning, because it sets you up to be excellent at everything you do.

After that, I have a tall glass of water. Hydration is so important first thing in the morning because our bodies lose a lot of water while we sleep through the simple act of breathing. Remember: Our brains are approximately 75 percent water, so if we're going to fire up our brains, we need to be well hydrated. I also have a glass of celery juice, which boosts the immune system, helps flush toxins from the liver, and helps restore the adrenal glands (hat tip to Anthony William, the Medical Medium, for this idea). Right after this, I'll take my probiotics to make sure my second brain is getting what it needs.

Then I brush my teeth with my opposite hand. I do this to train my brain to do difficult things, because it stimulates a different part of your brain, and because it forces me to be present. I can't be doing other things in order to do this well.

Then I do a three-minute workout. This is not my full workout, but I want to get my heart rate up first thing in the morning, as it helps with sleep and weight management, and with oxygenation to the brain.

Once I'm finished with that, I take a cold shower. I'm sure some of you will cringe at the idea of starting the day pummeling yourself with cold water, but cold therapies of this type do a great job of resetting the nervous system and have the added benefit of helping manage any inflammation.

When I'm out of the shower, I go through a series of breathing exercises to fully oxygenate my body. Then I do about 20 minutes of meditation to give me a clear mind as I enter the day. The process I use, Ziva Meditation, was developed by my meditation coach, Emily Fletcher, a three-step process that involves mindfulness, meditation, and manifestation. To watch a video of it, go to www.LimitlessBook.com/resources.

Next, I make my "brain tea," a combination of gotu kola, ginkgo, lion's mane, MCT oil, and a few other things. Then I'll sit down to spend some time journaling, getting my first thoughts of the day down on the page. My goal in any given day is to accomplish three things for work and three things personally, and I set this agenda now. I follow this with about a half hour of reading. I set a goal to read a minimum of one book a week and making this a part of my morning routine to keep me on course.

Finally, I drink my "brain smoothie," a combination of many of the brain foods we discussed earlier in this chapter (no salmon here, in case you were wondering).

Now, admittedly, this routine requires a good deal of time. As I mentioned, I can't get to all of it every day, and I can appreciate if it seems like more than you can handle, particularly if you need to get others started on their day. But if your goal in reading this book is upgrading your brain, then some variation on a morning routine of this type is an integral part of the process. Here are the keys:

- Check in on your dreams before you get out of bed. There's so much gold to mine here, so I strongly recommend that you not skip this step.
- Get yourself hydrated and oxygenated.
- Nourish yourself with some of the brain foods mentioned in this chapter.
- Set a plan for the day.

If you do at least these four things, you'll be well on your way to revving up your brain to operate at a high-octane level. Build as many of these things into the start of your day as you can. The most important thing is having a productive morning routine. I can't stress enough how much of an impact getting your day off to the right start has on how the day goes for you overall.

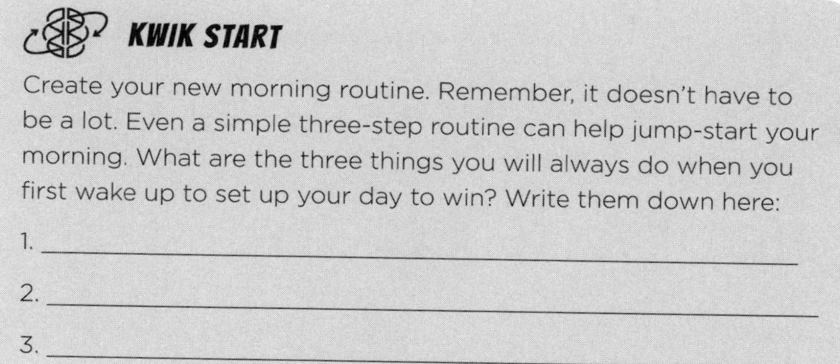

KWIK START

Create your new morning routine. Remember, it doesn't have to be a lot. Even a simple three-step routine can help jump-start your morning. What are the three things you will always do when you first wake up to set up your day to win? Write them down here:

1. ______________________________

2. ______________________________

3. ______________________________

BEFORE WE MOVE ON

None of us would be able to live without habits, of course, but consciously working to bring constructive new habits into your life and to replace bad habits with better ones will take your superpowers to a new level. Before you move on to the next chapter, here are a few things to do:

- Bolster your understanding of the habit loop by thinking about the four components of some of your most common habits, like making your breakfast or taking the dog for a walk. What's the cue, the craving, the response, and the reward for each of these?
- Spend a few minutes thinking about a habit that you'd love to replace with a more constructive one. Using the Fogg Behavioral Model, what new behavior can you adopt that fits neatly into the model?
- Walk yourself through the process of starting a valuable new habit using WIN.

"To put it another way:

flow is the

telephone booth

where Clark Kent

changes clothes,

the place from

where Superman

emerges."

—STEVEN KOTLER

FLOW

Why is flow so important to becoming limitless?

How do I achieve a flow state?

What are the key enemies of flow?

I'm sure there have been times when you were so completely caught up in what you were doing that everything else disappeared and it just felt like the most natural thing you've ever done. Time probably melted away for you during these experiences. People regularly tell me about focusing so deeply on what they were doing that they had no idea that afternoon had become night or that they'd missed multiple meals in the process.

This experience is flow.

In his groundbreaking book, *Flow: The Psychology of Optimal Experience*, psychologist Mihaly Csikszentmihalyi describes *flow* as "the state in which people are so involved in an activity that nothing else seems to matter; the experience itself is so enjoyable that people will do it even at great cost, for the sheer sake of doing it." To Csikszentmihalyi, flow is an expression of "optimal experience."[1]

Dr. Csikszentmihalyi describes flow as having eight characteristics:[2]

1. Absolute concentration
2. Total focus on goals
3. The sense that time is either speeding up or slowing down
4. A feeling of reward from the experience
5. A sense of effortlessness
6. The experience is challenging, but not overly so
7. Your actions almost seem to be happening on their own
8. You feel comfort with what you are doing

As you've likely experienced yourself, being in a flow state dramatically boosts your productivity. Reports have suggested that flow can make you as much as five times more productive. The people at McKinsey have even imagined a workforce where flow is commonplace:

> When we ask executives during the peak-performance exercise how much more productive they were at their peak than they were on average, for example, we get a range of answers, but the most common at senior levels is an increase of five times. Most report that they and their employees are in the zone at work less than 10 percent of the time, though some claim to experience these feelings as much as 50 percent of it. If employees working in a high-IQ, high-EQ, and high-MQ environment are five times more productive at their peak than they are on average, consider what even a relatively modest 20-percentage-point increase in peak time would yield in overall workplace productivity —it would almost double.[3]

WINNING WITH FLOW

Patrick, a member of our community, struggled constantly with ADHD and an inability to focus. It had been a problem for him throughout his life. He was easily distracted, or, in the reverse, he was hyperfocused to the detriment of everything and everyone around him. He even experienced this during his Brazilian jujitsu tournaments. He had difficulty deciding which technique to use with opponents and felt as though he was trying to use every move at once, even though many of them weren't appropriate for the situation. His inability to focus affected his work, his family life, and his favorite sport, and he felt a high level of stress nearly all the time.

Then one day he started listening to episodes of my podcast, where he heard about the stages of flow (which we will get to in a moment), as well as several other high-performance habits. Patrick applied what he was learning to his everyday life and saw immediate results. He was finally able to identify and understand what he was struggling with, and he immersed himself in his pursuits more fully than ever before. Finding flow was the key.

In his next tournament, Patrick was able to release his intense focus and take his mind off the problems that had distracted him in the past. He found his flow quickly . . . and felt like he was in *The Matrix*; he could see his opponent's moves coming before they happened. Even better, he was able to find flow in other areas of his life too. The better he did in his martial arts tournaments, the better he did in life. Patrick finally felt a release from the stress that dogged him endlessly, at last believing that he could let go and enjoy his life more.

THE FOUR STAGES OF FLOW

The flow state has a predictable arc to it. Our podcast guest, Steven Kotler, founder of the Flow Research Collective and the author of *The Rise of Superman,* has identified the four stages of flow:[4]

Stage 1: Struggle

This is when you're digging deep to access whatever it is that you need to reach the flow state. It could be a workout regimen, extensive research, an intense bout of brainstorming, or anything else that you are focusing on. Warning: This often feels like a struggle and, in fact, the opposite of flow.

Stage 2: Relaxation

This is the break you take before fully diving into flow. It is an essential step, as it keeps you from burning out over the struggle you've just been through. This break—a walk, some breathing, anything that helps you relax—is decidedly different from a distraction such as moving on to another task or checking sports scores.

Stage 3: Flow

This is the stage that Kotler describes as "the superman experience." This is that flow state that hopefully you've experienced at various points in your life, where you're doing your absolute best work and it almost seems to be happening automatically.

Stage 4: Consolidation

In this final stage you pull together everything you accomplished during the flow stage. Often, this is accompanied by feeling somewhat let down. All kinds of positive chemicals have been running through your brain while you're in flow, and now that high is ending. But another cycle can be waiting just around the corner.

Kotler believes that finding flow is the "source code" of motivation. When you find flow, you get "maybe the most potent dose of reward chemistry" your brain can give you—which is the reason he believes flow is the most addictive state on Earth. Once we start to feel flow in an experience, we are motivated to do what it takes to get more. But it's a circular relationship—if you have motivation to accomplish a task but you have no flow, you will eventually burn out. Motivation and flow need to work together, and they must be coupled with a solid recovery protocol, like good sleep and nutrition.

Have you ever experienced the flow state? Where were you? What were you doing? How did it feel? What did you achieve at the end of it? Visualize that state. Even if you can't visualize, imagine that you can.

FINDING FLOW

If you're going to become limitless, you're going to want to get yourself into a flow state as often as possible. So how do you do this? I can offer five ways:

1. Eliminate Distractions

Earlier, we talked about the importance of keeping distractions to a minimum. If you're going to find yourself in a flow state, eliminating distractions is absolutely essential. It can take you up to 20 minutes to reconnect with what you're doing after you've been distracted from doing it. How are you ever going to get into the flow if you're constantly rebooting because a text drew away your attention, or because you just wanted to make a quick check of social media before you got back to work? So, put everything else aside and concentrate completely on what you're doing.

2. Give Yourself Enough Time

Make sure you have a block of time set aside to get into flow. It's commonly believed that, when conditions are right, it takes about 15 minutes to achieve a flow state and that you don't really hit your peak for closer to 45 minutes. Clearing out only half an hour or so isn't going to allow you to accomplish much. Plan to set aside at least 90 minutes, and ideally a full two hours.

3. Do Something You Love

When we think of flow, we tend to think of people achieving at extremely high levels: the athlete perfecting her game, the musician crafting the ideal guitar solo, the writer quickly putting words down on the page as though taking dictation rather than creating. What's common among all of these people is that they are doing something that matters to them a great deal. They wouldn't be satisfied with only being moderately competent, as they aren't performing a task with which they have a casual relationship. They're doing things they love.

I've been talking to people about flow for decades, and I don't think I've ever heard someone mention being in a flow state about something they were doing only to pass the time. It's like the difference between driving an old junker and driving a brand-new Aston Martin. Both might get you to the office, but you're only likely to really get into the driving experience with one of them. If you find certain annoyances in something you're doing, or if you find it to be dull much of the time, these negatives are going to prevent you from truly getting into the flow.

4. Have Clear Goals

One of the most efficient flow preventers is a lack of clarity. If you don't know what you're trying to accomplish, it's likely that casting around for a mission will keep flow at bay. A novelist friend of mine separates the plotting of his novels from the actual writing for precisely this reason. For him, plotting is an arduous task with lots of fits and starts, whereas he takes tremendous pleasure in choosing the right words for his stories and making his characters come alive. By plotting ahead of time, he knows exactly what he's going to write about on any given day and regularly finds himself disappearing into the flow of his work for hours at a stretch.

So, once you've carved out the time, give yourself a clear purpose for how you are going to use that time. If you set yourself on a mission at the outset, and it is something that you're excited about achieving, you're likely to find yourself deeply immersed in that mission.

5. Challenge Yourself . . . A Little

When I talk to people about flow, I consistently hear that they are most likely to achieve flow when they're doing something that is *a little bit* of a challenge. In other words, they're outside of their comfort zone, but not way outside of it. The logic here is clear. If you do something that you can do with both hands tied behind your back, you're probably going to become bored fairly quickly, and boredom and flow are incompatible.

On the other hand, if you do something that you find extremely difficult, you're likely to become frustrated, and that frustration is going to keep flow from happening. But if you do something that you love that also has a moderate level of challenge to it—trying to hit a baseball to just one part of the field, trying a new form of tuning on your guitar, or writing from the perspective of a new character, for example—this level of challenge is likely to keep the task exciting for you and therefore engage you deeply.

CONQUERING THE ENEMIES OF FLOW

Training yourself to achieve flow regularly and even in multiple sessions in the same day will have you performing like a superhero. But we all know that superheroes are constantly challenged by supervillains, and a number of them are lurking around every corner, stalking your flow and trying to extinguish it. Here are the four supervillains you need to keep at bay if your flow is going to thrive:

1. Multitasking

We've talked about this before, even in this chapter, but it bears repeating. Being a "master multitasker" is not synonymous with being limitless. In fact, research repeatedly shows that people who multitask are considerably less productive than those who focus on one task at a time. Given what you now know about flow, it should be obvious that multitasking is the mortal enemy of this feeling. You're never going get into the flow state to craft that epic solo or create that jaw-dropping presentation if you're also checking in with colleagues, sending off a quick note to a friend, and reading your company e-mail. The only way to vanquish the supervillain Multitask is to ignore him completely. Clear your schedule of everything else and get into the flow.

2. Stress

This is a particularly deadly supervillain and one that sometimes requires a monumental battle to defeat. If you have lots of outside stressors in your life—deadlines, relationship issues, family problems, worries about your job security, etc.—they're likely to sneak up on you at any given moment. I'm sure you've had the experience of thinking about something entirely different when you're suddenly ambushed by an anxious reminder that you're facing some troubles at home. Once that thought is in your head, any opportunities for flow are crushed. Defeating this supervillain requires two expert moves. The first is to look the supervillain in the eye before you start and ask yourself if there's anything that you *absolutely must* deal with before you can get into flow. If the answer is yes, address that first. But in all likelihood, the answer will be no. It isn't that the stressors aren't real, but they often don't need your immediate attention, and they aren't going to be worse two hours from now. If that's the case, contend with this supervillain by putting up your force field. Make your space impenetrable by outside stressors so you can concentrate completely on the task at hand.

3. Fear of Failure

"Perfectionism reduces creativity and innovation," writes Hara Estroff Marano, editor at large and the former editor in chief of *Psychology Today*. "It is a steady source of negative emotions; rather than reaching toward something positive, those in its grip are focused on the very thing they most want to avoid—negative evaluation. Perfectionism, then, is an endless report card; it keeps people completely self-absorbed, engaged in perpetual self-evaluation—reaping relentless frustration and doomed to anxiety and depression."[5] If you go into a task with the belief that you absolutely must perform this task perfectly and that failure will be devastating, you're going to be so focused on not failing that you'll never get into a state where you can truly excel.

Remember earlier when we talked about how one of the ideal conditions for flow is pushing yourself just a little outside of your comfort zone? When you do this, you increase the odds that you're not going to get everything right the first time. If you allow the supervillain of perfectionism to master you at this point, your flow will be forfeited. To best this villain, you need to convince yourself that lack of perfection is not only okay but is a clear sign that you're pushing yourself in ways that you must.

4. Lack of Conviction

Nearly as devilish a supervillain as perfectionism is a lack of belief in what you're doing. "The brain perceives uncertainty as a threat, which sparks the release of cortisol, a stress hormone that disrupts memory, depresses the immune system, and increases the risk of high blood pressure and depression," writes Travis Bradberry, president of TalentSmart.[6]

If you don't believe you're going to accomplish anything of importance, you'll guarantee that will be the outcome. If you go into a task doubting your ability to complete it, ask yourself these questions: Do I have the necessary skills to do this? Do I have all the information I need to do this? Do I have enough passion for this project to do this? If the answer to any of these is no, set the task aside until you can answer each of these questions in the affirmative. But if the answer to all three of these questions is yes, take this supervillain down and get into the flow.

BEFORE WE MOVE ON

The flow experience is one of the greatest highs any of us will ever experience. It is also fundamental to becoming limitless. By this point, you should have a better sense of what flow is and how to get there. Before we move on, take a little time to try out the following:

- Reflect on a few times you've been in the flow. What were you doing? What was consistent about those experiences? How can you get back there more often?
- Take out your calendar and find a spot in the next few days where you can carve out 90 minutes to two hours. This needs to be a time when you can free yourself of all distractions. Now, what are you going to do with that time to dramatically boost your productivity?
- How often do you go into a project with one of the supervillains we talked about in this chapter stalking you? What can you do *right now* to defeat that supervillain before going into your next project?

"The illiterate of the 21st century will not be those who cannot read and write, but those who cannot learn, unlearn, and relearn."

—ALVIN TOFFLER

PART IV

LIMITLESS METHODS

THE HOW

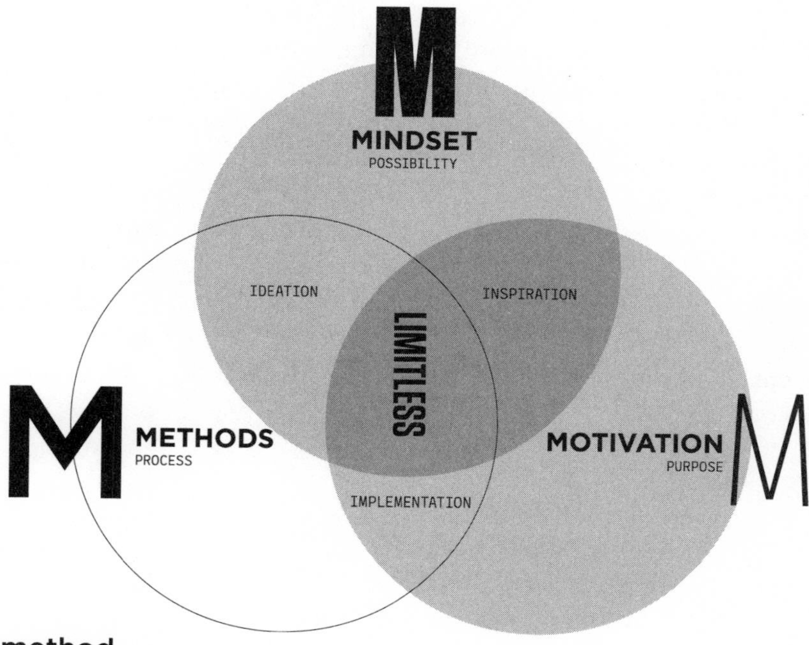

method

meth·od *(noun)*

A specific process for accomplishing something, especially an orderly, logical, or systematic way of instruction.

By this point, you've discovered how to unleash two of the elements necessary to become limitless. You've learned how to approach every day with a productive mindset, and you've learned how to do so with an optimal level of motivation. But there's one more *M* that differentiates limitless people from those who are encumbered by their limitations: method.

Methods are the procedures or processes for accomplishing something. In this context, method is the process of learning how to learn, also called meta learning. When we go through the education system, we are taught very antiquated and inefficient ways of learning, such as sub-vocalization and rote memorization. As I mentioned at the start of this book, when I was struggling as "the boy with the broken brain," I wasn't incapable of learning; history has shown that. But I wasn't succeeding at learning in the way I was being taught. It wasn't until I mastered a new way of learning—a method you will see over the course of the coming chapters—that I could finally use my brain to excel.

In this section, you're going to learn the science of accelerated learning and meta learning in five areas: focus, study, memory, speed reading, and thinking. These are the five flagship programs that we teach to individuals and organizations at Kwik Learning. Take special note of the lead-in questions at the start of these chapters, and make sure to try out all the exercises I've included. Once you start using these tools, I think you'll find yourself using them all the time—and I think you'll be amazed at what they unlock for you.

"Whenever you want to achieve something, keep your eyes open, concentrate, and make sure you know exactly what it is you want. No one can hit their target with their eyes closed."

—PAULO COELHO

11

FOCUS

What can I learn from what I'm like when I'm most focused?

How can I increase my ability to concentrate?

How do I limit my distractions and calm my busy mind?

What's the difference between someone performing at superhero levels and someone failing to ever discover their superpowers? In many cases, it's a matter of focus. I'm sure you've had numerous times in your life when you've really locked in on a task. Maybe it was writing a report that mattered a great deal to you. Maybe it was having a session with a mentor you love. Maybe it was attacking a bowl of your favorite ice cream. How did you do with these tasks? In all likelihood, you crushed them, writing one of the best reports of your life, learning huge amounts from your mentor, and devouring that ice cream like it was the last dessert in the world. This happened because you were able to train your focus on the task at hand, get right on that task, and not let anything distract you from that task. So why do most of us have only so much ability to maintain focus? Simply, I think it's because we were never taught to do so. Certainly, I don't recall having a focus class when I was in elementary school.

Do you remember when you were a kid and you went outside on a sunny day with a magnifying glass? How cool was it to hover the glass over a leaf, see an intensely bright spot appear on the leaf, and then watch as the leaf started to smoke and burn? What you were able to do was focus a greater level of the sun's intensity on that leaf. And where the bright spot appeared, things were at their hottest. Interestingly, when we talk about someone being intelligent, we often call them "bright." Going back to our magnifying glass analogy, maybe what we're really saying isn't that this person is much more intelligent than most other people; maybe that person is just more focused.

Focus allows us to train our brain power on a particular task to burn through that task. It's amazing what we can accomplish when we're focused. Conversely, when we're less focused, we're less likely to accomplish what we truly want to do because we're just not as committed—both emotionally and physically—to doing it. The primary enemy to focus is distraction.

Rate your current level of concentration from 0 to 10. Now rate your desire to increase this level. Your concentration is like a muscle. You can train to become stronger with practice.

PRACTICING CONCENTRATION

"Concentration is at the crux of all human success and endeavor," Hindu priest, entrepreneur, and former monk Dandapani told me during one of my podcasts. "If you can't concentrate, you can't manifest."[1] What Dandapani is saying is that concentration is a critical component of anything you want to accomplish. But, like so many other things we've discussed already, we've never really been taught *how* to concentrate. Sure, our parents and our teachers might have implored us to concentrate harder, maybe even criticizing our lack of focus with a question such as, "Why can't you just concentrate?" But the simple answer to that is that most of us never learned how.

Dandapani points out that concentration is like a muscle that gets stronger the more you exercise it. "Concentration is something you can learn and something you can practice to get better at," he said.[2] However, what most of us practice instead is distraction. We allow our minds to jump from thought to thought, often using technology to help us practice distraction until we're experts at it—and we should be, because we often get a dozen or more hours of practice a day. Just imagine what it would be like if we practiced concentration for even a fraction of that time.

Dandapani has a remarkably clear way of looking at this. "I define concentration as my ability to keep my awareness on one thing for an extended period of time. Every time my concentration drifts, I use my will power to bring my awareness back."[3]

Most of us think of lack of concentration as a function of our mind bouncing from place to place. Dandapani has a different—and more helpful—metaphor. To him, it isn't your mind that's moving; it's your awareness. He sees awareness as a glowing ball of light that moves to different parts of your mind. In order to excel at concentration, you need to make yourself keep that ball of light trained on one spot in your mind for an extended period. This won't be easy at first, but a conscious effort to exercise your will power in this way is likely to lead to impressive results.

You can work on this during nearly any pursuit. If you're having a conversation with someone, make a concerted effort to pay attention to nothing other than that conversation. If you notice your awareness drifting away from the conversation, refocus your glowing ball of light. If you're reading a report for work, train your eyes on the words as though nothing else exists. Again, if you notice the light of your awareness beginning to shine on something else, bring that ball back to the report. If you make the commitment to practice concentration an hour or so a day, it will soon become second nature.

Whenever possible, try to do one thing at a time. We've talked a bit about multitasking already, but for now just remember that multitasking is a grossly inefficient way to get anything done. If at all feasible, allow yourself to do whatever you're doing to the exclusion of everything else. If you're on the phone, don't scroll through social media at the same time. If you're making breakfast, don't also work on your to-do list for the day. By doing one thing at a time, your concentration "muscle" will become incredibly strong, and your focus will reach limitless levels.

Another key to boosting your concentration is de-cluttering your environment. A Princeton University study found that, "Multiple stimuli present in the visual field at the same time compete for neural representation by mutually suppressing their evoked activity throughout the visual cortex, providing a neural correlate for the limited processing capacity of the visual system."[4] In layperson's terms, what this means is that physical clutter in your surroundings competes for your attention, which results in decreased performance and increased anxiety and stress levels.

So, if you want to become a master at concentration, divest yourself of the potential for distraction whenever concentration is critical. If you're working on your computer, shut down every application and every open tab other than the ones you absolutely need to perform the task at hand. Limit the number of items in your physical workspace as well. While I think many of us consider a desk piled with books, magazines, papers, pictures of our kids, and souvenirs from our vacations to be cozy or even the sign of an active mind, every single one of those items creates a pull away from your concentration. Family heirlooms are wonderful, and you already know how I feel about books. Just limit the number of these things that share residence with the place where you need to be most productive.

CALMING YOUR BUSY MIND

Unlimiting your focus requires more than just getting to the tasks at hand. As we've already discussed, focus requires an ability to set aside distractions and give all your attention to what you're doing. But is that even possible anymore? Most of us are working on multiple devices at the same time, often with multiple applications running on each of those devices. We have meetings to attend, e-mails and texts to answer, social media statuses to update, and multiple projects in play. Yet, precisely because of this, it's more important than ever to find ways to bring calm to your mind.

You might not even realize it, but all the input you're getting on any given day is causing you a considerable amount of stress. If you're like many people, you might even think of this as a positive thing, because it means that you're busy, and by being busy, you're making a meaningful contribution to the world. While this might be true, it is *in spite* of this anxiety rather than because of it.

"Anxious thoughts can overwhelm you, making it difficult to make decisions and take action to deal with whatever issue bothers you" writes psychologist Melanie Greenberg, Ph.D., author of *The Stress-Proof Brain*. "Anxiety can also lead to overthinking, which makes you more anxious, which leads to more overthinking, and so on. How can you get out of this vicious cycle? Repressing anxious thoughts won't work; they will just pop up again, sometimes with more intensity."[5]

Juliet Funt is the CEO of the consulting firm WhiteSpace at Work. She describes *whitespace* as "the thinking time, the strategic pause that's in between the busyness."[6] When she was on my podcast, Juliet called whitespace "the oxygen that allows everything else to catch fire."

What both Greenberg and Funt are identifying is the need for all of us to have more time when our minds aren't cluttered. It's obvious how doing this will positively affect our mental health. But what's less obvious is how it will also dramatically improve our focus and our productivity. Some interesting studies in neuroscience underscore this, showing us how distraction is actually changing our brains. One, from University College London, compared the brains of heavy media multitaskers with those of light media multitaskers and found that the anterior cingulate cortex (ACC), which is involved in focus, was smaller among the former group. Conversely, a study at the Max Planck Institute found that, among people going through training exercises to increase attention, their ACCs grew thicker.[7]

And distractions can be a serious time sink. A study from University of California, Irvine, shows how distractions can really disrupt your day. "You have to completely shift your thinking, it takes you a while to get into it and it takes you a while to get back and remember where you were," said Gloria Mark, lead author of the study. "We found about 82 percent of all interrupted work is resumed on the same day. But here's the bad news—it takes an average of 23 minutes and 15 seconds to get back to the task."[8] That's more than 20 minutes every time you're distracted—and how often are you distracted every day?

Tools like meditation, yoga, and certain martial arts can be tremendously valuable in helping you calm your busy mind. But if you're in the middle of the day and can't afford to get away for more than a few minutes, there are still some things you can do. Three important ones are:

1. Breathe

We've already talked about the value of taking deep cleansing breaths as part of your morning routine. But doing the same thing is valuable whenever you need to re-center yourself. Holistic health expert Andrew Weil, M.D., developed a breathing tool that he calls the 4–7–8 Method. It works like this:

- Exhale completely through your mouth, making a whoosh sound.
- Close your mouth and inhale quietly through your nose to a mental count of 4.
- Hold your breath for a count of 7.
- Exhale completely through your mouth, making a whoosh sound to a count of 8.

This is one breath. Now inhale again and repeat the cycle three more times for a total of four breaths.[9]

2. Do Something That Has Been Causing You Stress

This goes back to what we talked about earlier regarding procrastination. As we now all know (thanks to Bluma Zeigarnik), things weighing on our minds are going to continue weighing on our minds until we deal with them. If you're having trouble focusing or if your mind is operating on a dozen planes at the same time, it's very possible the reason this is happening is because there's something that you need to do that you've been avoiding doing. If that's the case, do a little 4–7–8 breathing, deal with the stressful task, and then you can get back to everything else you want to do with increased focus.

What is that one important thing that you're avoiding that is affecting your focus?

3. Schedule Time for Distractions

It might be a challenge for you to turn off your phone and your e-mail when you need to focus, but if you can convince yourself to do these things, great. They're relatively easy to do. What's likely to be considerably harder is to avoid letting worries and obligations get in the way of whatever you're trying to accomplish in that moment. There's a reason you're seeing these things as worries or obligations, and that makes them much harder to push out of your mind. Addressing one of your concerns head-on, as we just discussed, is one way to deal with this, but there are going to be situations where that's simply not possible. Instead, what if you set aside a specific time in your schedule to move these worries and obligations to the forefront of your mind? Simply saying, "I'll worry about that later" isn't likely to keep that worry from creeping back 20 minutes from now. But saying, "I'll worry about that at 4:15" very well might.

Schedule your next distraction time.

BEFORE WE MOVE ON

Unlimiting your focus is a key to unleashing your superpowers. When your mind is truly focused, when you're completely throwing yourself at a task, you achieve at levels that are impossible when you're distracted or divided in your thoughts. Before we move on from this chapter, let's try a few things:

- Take a good look at your to-do list and identify the thing (or things) on it that is likely to invade your thoughts until you get it done. Formulate a plan for dealing with that task using some of the antiprocrastination tools you now have.
- Do something right now that changes your productivity environment so you can do a better job of staying on task.
- Practice a technique for calming your busy mind. Does it work for you? If so, commit to using it regularly.

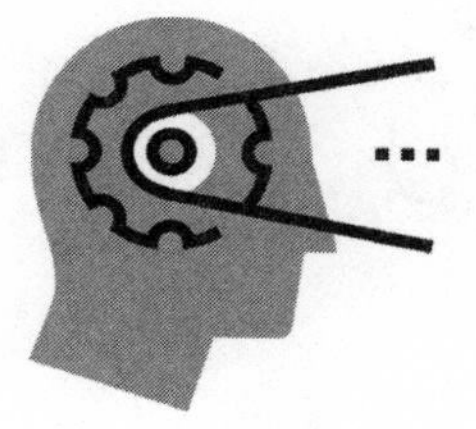

"Nothing has such a power to broaden the mind as the ability to investigate systematically."

—MARCUS AURELIUS

12

STUDY

If I'm going to be a lifelong student, how can I optimize my study time?

Is cramming the best way to learn something?

How do I become a better note-taker?

One Friday night, after a very busy workweek, I received a call. The person on the other end of the phone told me that we had a common friend and that this friend had suggested he reach out to me.

"Sure, how can I help you?" I said.

For the first 30 seconds of our call, this man had seemed entirely calm. But with that question, his voice became more animated.

"You've gotta help me, please. My speaker can't make it out tomorrow because of an emergency. He was supposed to give our keynote."

I told him that I was sorry to hear about his predicament but that I didn't take speaking assignments on the spur of the moment. I usually booked speaking gigs six months in advance, and I always gave myself time to prepare for them.

That didn't deter this caller. He said that our mutual friend had raved about speeches he'd seen me give and that if anyone could deliver a strong presentation on short notice it was me.

"Please save me," he said with even more emotion in his voice.

This guy's plight was starting to get to me. I happened to be free on Saturday, and the conference he was throwing was in Manhattan, where I lived. I decided to ask him the topic of the keynote. When he told me, I stared at the phone as though the caller were speaking to me in an alien language.

"Why are you calling me about this?" I said. "I know nothing about that topic."

"Yes, but the speaker who canceled has a book."

"I'm not sure how that matters."

The caller responded so quickly that it was clear he'd already prepared this argument. "I've heard you're a speed reader. I was thinking you could come in a little early, study the book, and then give the speech."

This scenario was so completely outlandish that I did the only thing I could do under the circumstances: I took the engagement. How could I turn down a challenge like that? We agreed on the particulars, he told me a bit more about the audience to whom I'd be speaking, and then I hung up, asking myself what just happened.

I got to the conference center the next morning at 10 A.M. The man who'd called the night before handed me a copy of the book and set me up in a quiet room. I was to deliver the keynote at 1 P.M. Over the next three hours, I read the book, made a ton of notes, and laid out the basic parameters of the presentation I was about to give. I then went up on stage and gave a keynote that turned out to be the most highly rated talk of the conference. I was exhausted, but I have to admit that the entire experience was quite the rush.

You are unlikely to ever find yourself in a situation like this. But as outrageous as the caller's request had been, I knew I could do this, because with competence comes confidence. I'm not saying this to to impress you; I'm saying it to express to you what's possible. To illustrate to you how any sense of constraint fades when you've learned how to absorb a subject in a sitting, remember what you've learned, have the ability to highlight the most essential points, and have an understanding of how people learn—in other words, many of the things we're discussing in this book.

I never would have been able to deliver that particular keynote if I hadn't been a quick study. And just like the other skills we've been addressing here, this isn't an ability you either do or don't have. Instead, it's an ability you've either cultivated or haven't. You can learn how to unlimit your studies. And when you do, it'll be a superpower you'll employ the rest of your life.

KWIK START

Think about a topic or subject you'd like to learn this month. How would you go about studying this topic? What's your current approach or process?

THE FOUR LEVELS OF COMPETENCE

Since the sixties, psychologists have noted that there are four levels of competence or learning. The first, known as "unconscious incompetence," is when you don't know what you don't know. For example, you might not even be aware of the fact that something like speed-reading exists. So, you're also not aware that you're currently not capable of doing it.

In the next level, known as "conscious incompetence," you're aware of what you don't know. For example, you're aware that people have learned to read and comprehend much faster through speed-reading techniques, but you yourself have not had any training in this area, nor do you understand what tools are necessary to become a speed-reader.

The third level is "conscious competence." What this means is that you're aware of a skill and have the capacity to perform that skill, but only when you actively put your mind to it. You can do it, but it takes work. Continuing with speed-reading, this would be akin to speed-reading successfully, but only when you focus on employing a speed-reading technique. Similarly at this stage for other activities, like typing or driving, you can do it, but it requires your conscious attention.

The fourth level—the one any lifelong learner is seeking—is "unconscious competence." In this case, you know how to perform a skill, and it's second nature to you. With speed-reading, you would reach the point of unconscious competence when this simply becomes the way you read. You're not *making* yourself read faster; you're just doing so. You are typing or driving without your deliberate attention.

Now the key to get from conscious competence to unconscious competence is obvious. It's practice. Practice makes progress.

While the model psychologists use ends there, I would add a fifth level: true mastery. This is a step beyond unconscious competence to where it's second nature to perform a skill at an elite level. This is the level of being limitless. And if you're going to be a master, you're going to need to study like a superhero.

HOW TO STUDY BETTER

Why are most of us restrained in our ability to study? Most people do not know how to study effectively, because they were never taught. Many people naturally assume they already know how to learn. The challenge is that most of the techniques you use now are old and ineffective. Many of them date back hundreds of years.

We now live in a highly competitive information age where information is everywhere. Yet we are still using the same methods to absorb and process it all. Today, our requirements for learning are much different. But most of us were taught that studying was all about reviewing material over and over and over so we could spit it back out during a test. We're going to talk in a moment about why cramming is such a bad idea but suffice it to say, the process is far from optimal.

The most successful people in the world are lifelong students. That means they're continuously learning new skills, keeping up with the latest in their chosen fields, and staying apprised of what other fields might be able to offer to them. As we discussed earlier in this book, there are enormous benefits to spending a lifetime learning, so if you're going to approach your goal of being a limitless learner, you're going to want to make study a part of your entire life.

This is something that James, one of our students, discovered —although it took a little time. James struggled with his education and, after high school, he spent three years working at a liquor store even though he'd always dreamed of becoming a successful businessman. He realized that, in order to fulfill his dream, he was going to have to go to college but, he told me, "It was like pulling teeth. I eventually got my accounting degree, then got into an accounting firm, and then went into banking. But for the longest time, I couldn't build up to being a wealth manager. I got into an analyst position, and that required a lot of learning, a lot of studying, and I was just barely getting by. I had the people skills and I had the discipline, but the studying part was really hard for me. A lot of the designations I have now, I failed the tests a few times before I got those designations. When it was time to take my CFP exam while I was working, it just became so burdensome."

James was six weeks away from his big test—a test that normally requires 12 weeks of study—when he learned about my speed-reading program. This allowed him to turn the corner, improving his studies, helping him "keep my brain healthy through the whole process of intensively studying," and providing him with a big boost on the day of the test.

James got his CFP designation, and this allowed him to get a new position where he works directly with clients as a wealth manager. He continues to use his newly refined learning skills while going through the vast number of prospectuses he needs to read and understand.

James could easily have allowed restrictions to stop him in his tracks. Instead, he learned to unlimit his old ways of studying to overcome the obstacle in his career.

BUT WHAT ABOUT CRAMMING?

The all-nighter is an age-old study tradition that many people continue long after their school days are over. Much of this is due to procrastination and putting off the work that needs to be done for that big test or that big presentation. But many people also believe that cramming is their most effective form of preparation. Chances are good, however, that it is not.

"In reality, cramming is associated with emotional, mental and physical impairments that reduce the body's ability to cope with its environment," wrote journalist Ralph Heibutzki in the *Seattle Post-Intelligencer.* He cited a Harvard Medical School study that indicates that cramming leads to many unwanted side-effects, including impaired mental function.[1]

In addition, cramming usually requires forgoing all or at least much of one's normal amount of sleep, and this can wind up undermining the very purpose of cramming. UCLA professor of psychiatry Andrew J. Fuligni coauthored a study on cramming and came away with a clear connection between this by-product of cramming and the expected results. "No one is suggesting that students shouldn't study," he said, "but an adequate amount of sleep is also critical for academic success. These results are consistent with emerging research suggesting that sleep deprivation impedes learning."[2]

In working with students of all ages, I have learned that cramming is rarely as useful as we would like it to be. Concentrating on one subject for many, many hours makes it less likely that you're going to retain the information. Earlier, we talked about the effect of primacy and recency on memory. If you tend to remember the first thing and the most recent thing best, cramming a huge amount of information between that first and most recent thing is only going to lead to your having more things that you forget. We'll talk about a better alternative in a moment.

Whether you're a high school junior taking five AP classes with the goal of gaining acceptance to a top college or a corporate head faced with the need to stay on top of your rapidly changing industry, you're likely facing two challenges simultaneously: a mountain of information to scale, and little time in which to scale it. If this is you, you're going to want to make sure you're studying as efficiently as you can. Over my years of helping people to learn faster and study better, here are seven of my favorite simple habits to unlimit your studies.

Habit 1: Employ Active Recall

Active recall is a process through which you review material and then immediately check to determine how much of it you've remembered. This allows you to draw the distinction between simple recognition (familiarity with the words on the page) and recollection (making the material an active part of your memory).

"Most students do not realize how important it is to force themselves to recall," writes neurologist Dr. William Klemm of Texas A&M University. "In part, this is because they are conditioned by multiple-choice tests to recall passively, that is recognize when a correct answer is presented, as opposed to generating the correct answer in the first place. Studies of student learning practices reveal how important to memory formation it is to retrieve information you are trying to memorize."[3]

To employ active recall, do this:

- Review the material you are studying.
- Then close the book, turn off the video or lecture, and write down or recite everything you remember from what you just reviewed.
- Now, look at the material again. How much did you remember?

Make sure you have enough study time to allow yourself to go through this process multiple times. As Klemm points out, the studies showed that "optimal learning occurred when an initial learning session included repeated study and forced-recall testing of all items at least four times in a row."[4] This leads me to the next important habit to adopt.

Habit 2: Employ Spaced Repetition

As discussed earlier in this chapter, cramming has many downsides. While it is natural to procrastinate, leaving yourself in situations where you need to study a tremendous amount of material all at once makes it likely that you aren't going to learn that material at all. The reason is that trying to work that way puts us in direct opposition to the way our brains work.

Alternatively, if you space out your reviews of the material, focusing more heavily on information that you haven't retained in the past, you're using your brain to the best of its abilities. "Spaced repetition is simple but highly effective because it deliberately hacks the way your brain works," agrees James Gupta, CEO of the online learning platform Synap. "It forces learning to be effortful and, like muscles, the brain responds to that stimulus by strengthening the connections between nerve cells. By spacing the intervals out, you're further exercising these connections each time. It produces long-term, durable retention of knowledge and, in my experience, once people start using it, they swear by it."[5]

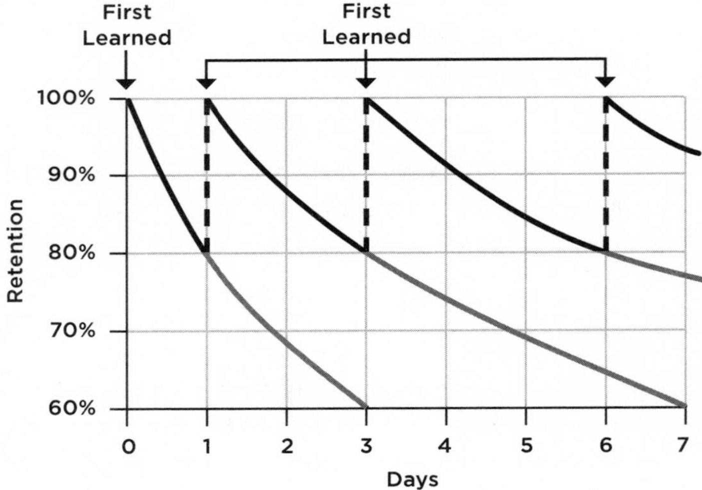

Spaced repetition seems to work most effectively when you can review the material at similar intervals. This is why it's important to give yourself enough time. Perhaps you perform the review once in the morning and again right before dinner for four days in a row, and then move on to other material you need to study at similar intervals. Use this technique in concert with active recall.

Review the material, test yourself on what you remember, then take a break before coming back to this particular material.

Habit 3: Manage the State You're In

As we talked about earlier in this book, the state you're in when you perform any activity will have the greatest impact on your success. For example, if you had a really bad day and were asked to give a presentation for your job or take a test, you most likely would not perform to the best of your ability. This is because your state of mind did not promote optimal performance. On the other hand, if you're feeling great, when the same opportunity arises, you would definitely produce better results. The more positive and resourceful your state, the greater the results you'll produce. Studying is no different.

Your posture also controls the state of your mind. Sit as if you're about to learn the most crucial life-changing information. Did you just have to move? If you did, then notice how you feel more focused after you've changed your posture. When you sit straight, it also facilitates breathing and the circulation of necessary oxygen to your brain and the rest of your body. If you are slumped over, it could stifle the breathing process and make you tired.

KWIK START

While you are sitting in a chair, slump over, look down, take short breaths, and put a frown on your face. Do this now. How motivated do you feel to achieve success? How productive do you think you are in this state? This is the posture a lot of students take while studying. Is it any wonder they dislike studying and have to work hard to achieve bare minimum results? Now sit up straight and smile. How much better do you feel?

Habit 4: Use Your Sense of Smell

I'm sure something like this has happened to you: You walk into a room and discover the air filled with a particular scent. Maybe it's the smell of a specific spice baking in the oven. That scent immediately sends you back to a day with a childhood friend when she made a joke that was so funny that milk came out of your nose. Why would the smell of that spice trigger that memory? Because that smell was in the air when the event that you're remembering happened, and smells are especially effective at bringing memories to the forefront of our brains. The scent of rosemary has been shown to improve memory. Peppermint and lemon promotes concentration.

"The answer is likely due to brain anatomy," writes Jordan Gaines Lewis, postdoctoral researcher at Penn State College of Medicine. "Incoming smells are first processed by the olfactory bulb, which starts inside the nose and runs along the bottom of the brain. The olfactory bulb has direct connections to two brain areas that are strongly implicated in emotion and memory: the amygdala and hippocampus. Interestingly, visual, auditory (sound), and tactile (touch) information do not pass through these brain areas. This may be why olfaction, more than any other sense, is so successful at triggering emotions and memories."[6]

What this shows us is that smell is an enormously important, yet underused, memory tool. If a particular scent can rocket us back to our childhoods, a different scent can be used to accelerate our recall. If you're studying for a big test, put a bit of a particular essential oil on your wrist while you're studying and then make sure you do the same thing before you take the test. If you do the same thing in preparing for a big meeting, the results should be similar. Obviously, you want to take other people into consideration, so you don't want to douse yourself with the scent, but just a touch is enough to heighten your recall.

Habit 5: Music for the Mind

Think about how you did some of your earliest learning. Did you, like so many people, memorize the alphabet through a song? Or perhaps you know how a bill gets through Congress because *Schoolhouse Rock* sang it to you. Parents have probably been teaching toddlers basic concepts through music for as long as music has been around. They do it because it works, and it works because there is strong science behind it.

Numerous studies link music to learning. The arousal-and-mood hypothesis, introduced by Dr. E. Glenn Schellenberg, identifies a connection between music and mood and the subsequent connection between mood and learning, suggesting that music can put us in conditions that improve our ability to learn.[7]

Baroque music seems to have some particularly valuable qualities. "Music stabilizes mental, physical and emotional rhythms to attain a state of deep concentration and focus in which large amounts of content information can be processed and learned," states music and learning expert Chris Boyd Brewer. "Baroque music, such as that composed by Bach, Handel or Telemann that is 50 to 80 beats per minute creates an atmosphere of focus that leads students into deep concentration in the alpha brain wave state. Learning vocabulary, memorizing facts, or reading to this music is highly effective."[8]

There's no similar evidence that the results would be the same with, say, rap or K-pop, but because one's reaction to music is such a personal thing, it's possible that this music would work for you as well. But since streaming music is so ubiquitous, I'd recommend adding a baroque playlist as background to your study sessions. Amazon Music, Apple Music, and Spotify all have baroque playlists and, if you wanted to explore further, each have classical music playlists (comprised largely of baroque music) that have been specifically compiled for the purpose of studying.

Habit 6: Listen with Your Whole Brain

If you are going to unlimit your learning, you're going to want to make sure your listening skills are fully tuned up. There's a very strong connection between listening and learning, and more than a quarter of us are auditory learners, meaning that the primary way in which we learn is through hearing something.[9]

Listening is critical to learning, and we spend a large percentage of our waking time listening. But most of us are not particularly good at it. "Plenty of studies examine this phenomenon," write Bob Sullivan and Hugh Thompson in their book *The Plateau Effect*. "While listening is the core of most of our communications—the average adult listens nearly twice as much as he or she talks—most people stink at it. Here's one typical result. Test takers were asked to sit through a 10-minute oral presentation and, later, to describe its content. Half of adults can't do it even moments after the talk, and 48 hours later, fully 75 percent of listeners can't recall the subject matter."[10]

One of the reasons we don't listen well is that we tend not to apply all our brainpower to the exercise. Sullivan and Thompson, who conducted a study with Carnegie Mellon University on the nature of digital distractions, point out that "the human brain has the capacity to digest as much as 400 words per minute of information. But even a speaker from New York City talks at around 125 words per minute. That means three-quarters of your brain could very well be doing something else while someone is speaking to you."[11]

To help alleviate this problem, I've devised a tool that will help you listen with your whole brain. Just remember the acronym HEAR:

- **H is for Halt:** In all likelihood, as you're listening to someone else speak, there will be other things going on in the same space. Maybe there are people milling about. Maybe your phone is chirping, telling you that you've just received a text. Maybe there's music playing in the room or a television in the background. Meanwhile, you're thinking about your to-do list, your next meeting, or what you're going to have for dinner that night. Do everything you can to tune all of this out and to be completely present with whomever you're listening to. Remember that listening involves more than just the words a person is saying; vocal inflection, body language, facial expressions, and more create additional context and provide additional information. You can absorb all of this only if you halt everything else.
- **E is for Empathy:** If you can imagine yourself in the speaker's shoes, you're likely to learn more from this listening experience than if you do it dispassionately.

Trying to understand where the speaker is coming from and why brings additional substance to what they might be saying and allows you to feel it from their perspective.

- **A is for Anticipate:** Engage in the experience with a sense of anticipation. Remember that learning is state-dependent and that what you can learn from this speaker will become a long-term memory if you attach emotion to it. Your enthusiasm for what you're hearing will greatly increase your potential of truly hearing it.
- **R is for Review:** If you have the opportunity to directly engage with the speaker, do so. Ask clarifying questions or maybe even for a point to be repeated. If you're in the position to take notes, do so. And afterward, reflect on what the speaker said. Paraphrase it in your mind and imagine yourself teaching it to someone else. Doing so will solidify it in your mind.

Habit 7: Take Note of Taking Notes

Studying under the best conditions will likely improve your retention considerably. And, both in preparation for your studies and in concert with your studies, upgrading your note-taking ability is invaluable.

The ultimate advantage of taking notes is that they customize the information you need to retain to your vocabulary and your mode of thinking. At their best, notes allow you to organize and process information in a way that makes it most likely that you can use this information afterward.

But many people take notes ineffectively. Common pitfalls include concentrating so heavily on writing notes that you're not actually listening to the information, trying to write down every single thing you hear, and writing notes in such a way that they won't be helpful to you a day later. It's easy to avoid all of these pitfalls once you are aware of them, so let's put a plan together for upgrading your note-taking ability.

First off, be sure that you understand the purpose for taking these notes. For example, the goal of taking notes in a midsemester lecture might be very different from the notes you take in the review class before a big final. Similarly, what you're trying to accomplish with the notes you take in a weekly meeting with your team is likely to be different from the notes you take in the week leading up to a major client presentation.

By being clear on your intention with your notes, you are able to distinguish between information that is relevant to you and information that is not. I have a friend who is a writer and insists on transcribing every interview he does even though it would be more time-efficient to have a transcription service do it for him. The reason, he says, is that by doing it himself he only transcribes the parts of the interview that he knows he's going to be able to use, therefore eliminating the possibility that these quotes will get lost among all the other conversation that might not be relevant to the book he's writing. What he's left with is nearly pure content. Likewise, if you take notes with a goal in mind, every note you take will have relevance.

Once you're clear on your goals, take an active approach to note-taking. Listen with the intention of getting exactly what you need, and write your notes in ways that will benefit your recall later. If you're going to use abbreviations and shortcuts, use ones that are familiar to you. The last thing you want is for your own notes to be indecipherable to you later.

Equally important is making sure that you use your own words wherever possible. As noted earlier, one of the key pitfalls to effective note-taking is trying to record *everything*. There are two obvious downsides to this. One is that it is impossible to write as quickly as most people speak. On average, people handwrite 10 to 12 words a minute, and the average speaker speaks at around 100 words a minute. Even if you were typing your notes (which I don't recommend; more on this shortly), you'd probably only be able to get down about half of what the speaker was saying.

But there's an even more fundamental downside: If you're copying what someone is saying verbatim, you're probably not processing any of it. That means that, at the most essential moment of learning, you're utilizing most of your brain to the task of taking dictation. When you use your own words in your notes, you begin to process the information, and that greatly enhances learning.

And while we're on the subject of writing, I'd recommend handwriting your notes. Even if you're using a tablet computer to store your notes, use an electronic pen to do so. For one thing, there are readily available programs that can convert your handwriting to text for later organization. But most importantly, writing by hand requires you to start processing the material immediately, and that has proven to be more effective.

"The present research suggests that even when laptops are used solely to take notes, they may still be impairing learning because their use results in shallower processing," write Pam A. Mueller and Daniel M. Oppenheimer in their study on this topic. "We found that students who took notes on laptops performed worse on conceptual questions than students who took notes longhand. We show that whereas taking more notes can be beneficial, laptop note takers' tendency to transcribe lectures verbatim rather than processing information and reframing it in their own words is detrimental to learning."[12]

Most importantly, make sure you are really listening. You're not there as a secretary; you're there as someone who is receiving information for later use. Therefore, it is important to actually hear what others are saying. Take note of what's being emphasized. Make sure you're understanding the points the speaker is making and, if the opportunity is available, ask questions. This can only happen if you're devoting at least as much attention to the information being delivered as you are to your recording of that information.

While you're taking notes, use a method that I call "capture and create." On the left side of the paper, you're capturing, you're taking notes; on the right side, you're creating, you're making notes. You're writing your impression of what you're capturing. How can I use this? Why must I use this? When will I use this?

After your note-taking session is over, review your notes immediately. This will help you retain the information much more effectively than if you don't read your notes for days. As an added benefit, you'll be able to supplement your notes with anything you might have missed while taking them, because the information will still be fresh in your mind.

A TIP FOR UPGRADING YOUR NOTE-TAKING

If you want to make sure you're always getting the most from your note-taking, remember the mnemonic TIP:

- **T is for Think:** Before you begin any session where you're going to be taking notes, think about what you're hoping to retain most from this session. This will help you filter the high-value information from the information that is less relevant to your goal.
- **I is for Identify:** Listen carefully to the information being presented and identify what is most important in the context of your goal. Remember that attempting to write down everything is going to make it impossible to process the information at the time and will probably make studying harder. Identify what you need the most and write that down.
- **P is for Prioritize:** As you review your notes after the presentation, prioritize the information that is most valuable to you, perhaps adding additional notes as necessary to make the priority information clearer or making an outline to highlight key points.

BEFORE WE MOVE ON

If you acknowledge that unlimiting yourself means being a student for life, then how you go about your studies is vitally important. Before we move on to the next chapter, let's try a few things:

- Take your active recall out for a spin. Introduce yourself to some new material and immediately assess how much of it you retained.
- Find a music playlist that works for you. There are many of them available, and the right music is likely

to enhance your ability to absorb information, so take some time to find one that you like. Maybe you'll even want to have it in the background while you read the rest of this book.

- Try out your new note-taking tools. Maybe go through this chapter again and take notes about it. Or watch a TED talk and take notes on that instead. Use the skills you've learned here to upgrade this experience.

"If we all did
the things we are
capable of doing,
we would
literally astound
ourselves."

—THOMAS EDISON

13

MEMORY

What can I do to improve my memory right away?

How do I keep a big chunk of information in my memory?

How can I easily access this information when I need it?

A few years back, I walked into our office early in the morning, before anyone else had come in. The phone started ringing, so I went to answer it. Immediately, a woman's effusive voice sang out from the other end.

"I love you, I love you, I love you!"

Trust me that this was not a common response I received to answering a call.

"Whoa," I said. "Who is this?"

"It's Anne. I took your course." She then quickly declared, "I found it!"

Okay, she had me. "What did you find?"

"I don't know what it is, but I've been doing all of these exercises you've been teaching, and I've started to remember things. Even when I'm not using the strategy, I'm remembering names and conversations."

So, she hadn't answered that question, either. I realized I was just going to have to let her tell her story the way she wanted to tell it. Over the next few minutes, I learned that a few years earlier she'd been given a family heirloom from her grandmother. It was a necklace that had been passed down from generation to generation, and her grandmother skipped over her own daughter and her three older sisters to bequeath the necklace to her. Anne was extremely honored to receive this gift and vowed to be careful with it. There was only one problem: She'd been so concerned about keeping the necklace safe that she'd hidden it somewhere that she couldn't remember. When she realized she didn't know where the necklace was, she started searching, but to no avail. This led to monumental levels of angst and an enormous amount of guilt compounded by her family.

After three years, she'd come to the conclusion that she'd either misplaced the heirloom forever or that someone had stolen it. Then, at 2 A.M. the morning of this call, she woke up out of a dead sleep. She went down two flights of stairs to her basement, ran over to the boiler, moved behind it, and reached into a crevasse there. She pulled out the necklace and nearly died from the relief.

"That's an amazing story, congratulations," I said to her. "I'm curious, though. I didn't teach you how to find misplaced items. That's not one of the things we've covered in our classes."

"Yes, but you did something way more valuable. I don't know what it is, but for the past few weeks I'm just remembering all kinds of things. Not just in the present, but stuff I hadn't thought about for years.

"Jim, thank you for giving me my brain back."

What Anne was illustrating through her excitement is something I've been sharing with people for a long time. Yes, your brain is an organ. But it acts like a muscle. And it most significantly resembles a muscle in that it's a use-it-or-lose-it device. Our brains stay fit only when we make a concerted effort to keep them fit. If we fail to keep our brains in shape—either through laziness or being overly dependent on technology to do our thinking for us or by failing to challenge ourselves with new learning—it becomes "flabby." Think about it this way: If you have your arm in a sling for six months, you don't come away with a stronger arm. In fact, after you take the arm out of a sling, you're likely to have very little function at all. Your brain is the same way. If you don't exercise it regularly, it might not be at its best when you need it the most. But if you make the effort to keep your brain in top shape, you'll discover that it's always ready to do superhero-level work for you, just as it did for this caller.

YOU CAN ALWAYS RELY ON MOM

Memory is arguably the most important part of the learning process. If you could not remember, then you could not learn anything. There is no knowledge without memory. But why do most people have less-than-ideal memory skills? I think it's because of the way we were taught to memorize things, which was usually through rote memorization. To this day, most schools teach students to memorize by repeating a fact or a quote until it is temporarily burned in, even though people tend to forget this information as soon as they no longer need it and this type of memory rarely leads to mastery of the material being memorized.

Your memory is also one of your greatest assets. It supports you in every area of your life. I challenge you to do anything without utilizing your memory. If you did not have a memory, life would be extremely challenging, to say the least. Imagine waking up each day and forgetting everything you ever knew. You would have to teach yourself how to get out of bed, how to get dressed, how to brush your teeth, how to eat your breakfast, and how to drive a car. That would be quite inconvenient. Luckily you were born with a great memory; you just need to be shown how to use it.

KWIK START

How would you rate your memory right now? What aspects would you like to improve? Take our memory assessment at www.LimitlessBook.com/resources to understand more.

If you're going to perform a major upgrade on your brain, you're going to want to unlimit your memory, as memory is such a fundamental part of most brain function. Since that's the case, let me reassure you with a very important fact: There's no such thing as a good memory or a bad memory; there is only a trained memory and an untrained memory. If you have trouble remembering people's names, making presentations without notes, or even finding your car keys in the morning, it's extremely unlikely that this is because you're incapable of doing these things. Instead, you just haven't gotten the training.

Joshua Foer is proof positive that memory can be trained. In 2005, Joshua was a journalist who had taken on the assignment of writing about the little-known world of mental athletes. Fascinated by what he saw in elite memorization contests, he wanted to discover more about the participants. To his surprise, he learned that almost every participant he interviewed described themselves as having a poor or average memory before they learned and practiced the principles of memorization. Now they were competing at the highest levels of these contests.

It dawned on Foer that there were no restrictions to memory and that memory can be trained just like athletic skill. He began to practice what he learned. One year later, he returned to the U.S.A. Memory Championship but this time as a competitor. The day of the event, we had lunch together between competitions and marveled at the fact that often what appears to be genius can actually be learned. Later that day, Foer placed number one and took home the trophy. He went on to write the groundbreaking book *Moonwalking with Einstein: The Art and Science of Remembering Everything.*

Why is memory so important if you're going to unlimit yourself? Because your memory serves as the foundation for every action you take now and every one you will take in the future. Imagine what it would be like if your computer had very little storage or had inconsistent access to what it had stored. Most functions would be nearly impossible to perform—you'd start to write an e-mail message, and your computer might or might not have the addressee among your contacts and might or might not remember how to send the message after you'd written it—and the ones that it did perform would take excruciatingly long while your computer figured out how to do it.

While I've likened our brains to supercomputers, we all know that they're so much more than that. Perhaps the most significant difference is our ability to reason, to consider the facts or the situation in front of us, and to act, innovate, or navigate through circumstances based on those facts and situations. The process of reasoning requires us to shift through our rich store of memories, using tools that have proven useful in the past to make informed and productive decisions.

"It is impossible to think creatively into the future without a sense of what is known," writes Dr. Eve Marder, professor of neuroscience at Brandeis University. "We commonly say that we are looking for interdisciplinary and synthetic thinkers who can make connections between disparate fields and see new paths for discovery. I cannot imagine finding those creative leaders for the future among the legions of students who forget everything they have learned because they can 'just look it up.' How does one know what to look up if one has forgotten so much?"[1]

Dr. William R. Klemm, who we met in Chapter 12, gives us five reasons why improving memory is essential:

1. **Memorization is discipline for the mind.** Much needed in an age when so many minds are lazy, distracted, have little to think about, or think sloppily. Memorization helps train the mind to focus and be industrious.
2. **No, you can't always "Google it."** Sometimes you don't have access to the Internet. And not everything of importance is on the web (and a great deal of irrelevant trash will accompany any search). Nor is looking up material helpful under such situations as when you learn to use a foreign language, must write or speak extemporaneously, or wish to be an expert.
3. **Memorization creates the repertoire of what we think about.** Nobody can think in a vacuum of information. To be an expert in any field requires knowledge that you already have.
4. **We think with the ideas held in working memory, which can only be accessed at high speed from the brain's stored memory.**

Understanding is nourished by the information you hold in working memory as you think. Without such knowledge, we have a mind full of mush.

5. **The exercise of the memory develops learning and memory schema that promote improved ability to learn.** The more you remember, the more you *can* learn.[2]

I want to emphasize this last point. It's not accurate that your memory works like a container, cup, or hard drive in that once it's full of data no more can fit. It's more like a muscle in that the more you train it, the stronger it gets and the more you can store.

In this chapter, we're going to discuss some tools and techniques designed to train your memory. You will be applying basic principles of the mind and developing your memory in such a way that will make learning (remembering) more natural, easy, and fun. The most fundamental of these, though, is this: always remember MOM, a mnemonic device I created to kick up your memory instantly:

- **M is for Motivation**: The simple fact is that we are considerably more likely to remember things that we are motivated to remember. If someone says to you, "Hey, remember our call tomorrow," you may or may not remember that you've scheduled a call with that person. If instead he says, "Hey, if you remember our call tomorrow, I'll give you $5,000," you will definitely remember that you've scheduled the call. You are overwhelmingly more likely to remember something when you have a strong motivation to do so. So, if you want to train yourself to have a stronger memory, give yourself a stronger motivation to do so. Reasons reap results, so make remembering personal. If you can convince yourself that there's value in retaining a memory, there's a good chance that you will.
- **O is for Observation**: How often do you forget someone's name as soon as you hear it? The reason is likely that you weren't entirely paying attention when you heard

that name. Maybe you were looking around the room to see who else you knew. Maybe you were still thinking about a conversation you'd just had. For whatever reason, you weren't entirely present. Most of the time, when we fail to remember something, the issue isn't *retention* but rather *attention*. If you're serious about boosting your memory, condition yourself to be truly present in any situation where you want to remember something.

- **M is for Methods**: Over the course of this chapter, I'm going to provide you with a set of tools that you'll be able to use when you want to remember something. Make sure you're always carrying these around in your mental toolkit, and be sure to employ them to the point where they become second nature.

THE MORE MEMORABLE BAKER

The chances of remembering something increase dramatically if people can attach a reference point to the thing they are trying to remember. A number of years ago, after a study testing peoples' ability to put names to faces, researcher Gillian Cohen coined the name for what came to be known as the Baker/baker Paradox. In the study, participants were shown photographs of faces, offered the names and various details about the people in the photographs, and then asked to later recall the names. The study showed that people had far more trouble remembering last names than they did occupations, even when the last name and the occupation was the same word. So, for example, it turned out to be significantly easier for a participant to remember that someone was a baker than that their last name was Baker.

Let's go back to Joshua Foer a moment for an explanation:

> When you hear that the man in the photo is a baker, that fact gets embedded in a whole network of ideas about what it means to be a baker: He cooks bread, he wears a big white hat, he smells good when he comes home from work.

> The name Baker, on the other hand, is tethered only to a memory of the person's face. That link is tenuous, and should it dissolve, the name will float off irretrievably into the netherworld of lost memories. But when it comes to the man's profession, there are multiple strings to reel the memory back in.
>
> Even if you don't at first remember that the man is a baker, perhaps you get some vague sense of breadiness about him or see some association between his face and a big white hat, or maybe you conjure up a memory of your own neighborhood bakery. There are any number of knots in that tangle of associations that can be traced back to his profession.[3]

What the Baker/baker Paradox illustrates for us is that creating associations for ourselves is likely to boost our memories dramatically. The exercises on the following pages are tools along these lines that I have found particularly effective.

RECALLING A GREAT DEAL OF INFORMATION

One of the things I do regularly when I'm speaking to large groups is ask audience members to throw out a group of random words—somewhere between thirty and a hundred—that I will then repeat, backward and forward. It never fails to get an awed reaction from the crowd, but that isn't what I'm looking for. Instead, I do this to get across a key point: that everyone has the capacity to do the same thing.

We've already talked about the importance of memory in performing nearly all brain functions. If you're going to unlimit your brain and therefore unlimit yourself, you need to unlimit your memory. This means training your memory to the point where it can retain a great deal of information and allow you easy access to that information. What I do on stage with the list of a hundred words might have the immediate impact of a parlor trick, but how I trained myself to do this is through a technique that anyone can use to remember and access lots of information. Maybe in your case it's the specifications for your entire line of products. Or maybe it's a long string of mathematical formulas. Maybe it's the directions to all the stops on your swim-practice carpool. Whatever it is, this tool can help.

For the sake of this exercise, let's talk about how to memorize a list of words. The technique will be the same regardless, but it'll be easier to explain it to you if we can focus on a particular thing.

Below we have provided you with a list of simple words. Your assignment is to memorize them in the order they are given. Spend no more than 30 seconds looking at the list, then flip the page over. Good luck!

Fire Hydrant	Diamond
Balloon	Knight
Battery	Ox
Barrel	Toothpaste
Board	Sign

What was the method you used to remember this list? Did you repeat the words in your head over and over? For instance, were you saying to yourself "fire hydrant, balloon, battery, fire hydrant, balloon, battery, fire hydrant, balloon, battery, barrel, etc." Did you find that you needed to repeatedly say the words over and over again, until they stayed in your head? Did you try to see the words as pictures in your mind? Most people use one or a combination of the first two methods described. The process of repeatedly saying or writing information down to remember it is called repetition learning, otherwise known as rote learning.

You may have used rote learning in the second grade to remember your multiplication tables. You would say to yourself "seven times seven is forty-nine, seven times seven is forty-nine, seven times seven . . . ." Or you may have written it out "7 × 7 = 49, 7 × 7 = 49, 7 × 7 = 49," and would continue to fill up your sheet of paper. This is also most likely the method you used in elementary school to learn how to spell. Your teacher may have asked you to spell a word like *chair* 50 times on a piece of paper. What was happening was your natural learning ability was being stifled.

You bored your mind continually with this method until it finally gave up and said *You win! For the 100th time, Columbus landed in 1492, just no more of this chanting!*

Most people find rote learning to be a very tedious and boring process. It taxes your mind and is extremely ineffective for remembering most things. We know that as much as 85 percent of the information you take the time to remember in this fashion is lost in only 48 hours. That is why some students find the need to cram, because they know that the material will be lost in a very short period of time.

ELEMENTARY LEARNING

One of the reasons rote learning is inefficient is because it only involves a small part of your brain. You're using a more analytical part of your brain to process information and store what you need to learn. By implementing rote learning, you only engage part of your mind and an even smaller portion of your potential.

In the traditional education system, you probably learned this way in such topics as:

- **History**: "Calvin Coolidge was the 30th president of the United States, Coolidge 30, 30 Coolidge . . ."
- **Chemistry**: "Glucose C6H12O6, Glucose C6H12O6, Glucose C6H12O6 . . ."
- **French**: "*Comment allez-vous* means 'how are you?' *Comment allez-vous* means 'how are you?' *Comment allez-vous* is 'how are you?' . . ."

The list goes on and on and on and on. The question you must ask yourself now: "Is the way I learned in elementary school the best method for me to learn today?" The answer is most likely no. In school, they taught you the three Rs: reading, 'riting, and 'rithmatic (too bad spelling wasn't one of them). I always thought the fourth R should have been recall. Your requirements for learning have changed a lot over the years. Repetition learning had some decent results when you were younger, but in today's world, it will leave you drowning in information and mental fatigue. (Note: The word *rote* literally means "an unthinking repetition or mechanical memorization.")

In this section I'm going to show you the skills to remember more effectively than you ever thought possible. These skills will help you to replace the feeling of hoping you'll remember with the feeling of confidence in knowing that the information you possess will be available, whenever you need it.

Now, take a minute and, without looking back, try to recall the list in the order it was presented. Write down as much as you can remember. Take a minute and do this now.

____

____

____

How did you do? If you are like most people, you probably were able to retain a few of the words on the list.

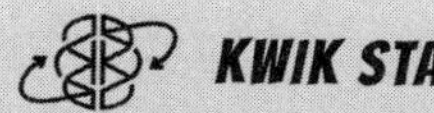

KWIK START

Now let's try something else. Take a minute and stretch. Take a few deep breaths. Clear your mind and relax more with every breath that leaves your body. Just take a moment and relax. When you are done, continue.

Next, make sure you are comfortable and imagine you're standing next to a giant fire hydrant, the biggest one you've ever seen. Now, attach a bunch of balloons on top of the fire hydrant. There are so many balloons that it takes the hydrant out of the ground so it floats up high in the sky. Then suddenly it is hit with a load of batteries and explodes. The batteries are being launched into the sky in large barrels. The barrels are being thrown up with a wooden board like a seesaw. The board is being balanced by a large diamond, a big brilliant sparkling stone. Then a knight in shining armor takes the diamond and runs away. He's quickly stopped by an ox. The only way to get through is to brush the teeth of the ox with toothpaste. The ox moves aside and reveals a big neon sign with the word *Congratulations* on it, and then there is a huge explosion.

Now take a minute, close your eyes and review this little story. You may read the story again if you need to. Do this now before continuing.

Without looking back, write the story down.

As you may be aware, we turned your list into a story. Now go through the story in your mind and list as many of the words as you can remember. Check your answers and write down the number you got correct.

How did you perform the second time? If you are like most students, you were able to recall more of the words than you did previously. The amazing thing is that once you start training your memory in this way, you can use this tool to memorize vast amounts of information. I've used this technique to help actors learn all their lines in a script, to help students memorize the periodic table, and to help salespeople speak about a product with a level of granularity that made it seem as though they'd engineered the item themselves. Remember that there's no such thing as a good memory or a bad memory, only a trained memory or an untrained memory. Employing this tool regularly will give you the kind of training that you can access in all kinds of situations.

YOUR ACTIVE FOCUS IN MEMORY

This is a very important concept: Most people approach learning as a passive activity. They encounter information in books, notes, or lectures and if the material is absorbed, great! But if it is not, they feel that there is nothing they can do. This passive outlook is the hit-or-miss approach. It holds that if the information sticks, it's more a result of luck and repetition than focus and skill. By taking

"The secret of a good memory is attention, and attention to a subject depends upon our interest to it. We rarely forget that which has made a deep impression on our minds."

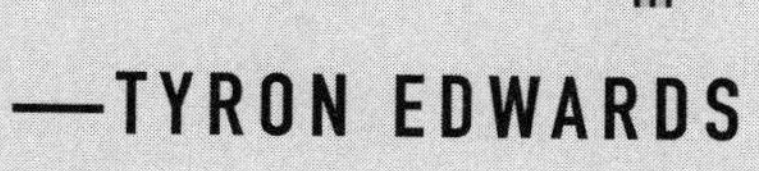

—TYRON EDWARDS

a more active approach to learning, you will have greater results and the satisfaction that comes from involvement and personal awareness. Learning passively is weak; active learning is strong.

Visualization

Your visual memory is very powerful. By seeing the pictures a story paints and not just the words that represent those pictures, you create a stronger means by which to remember. Thinking is done through the use of pictures. Do this now: Think of your bed. What did you visualize? Maybe you saw a queen-size mattress, with a wooden headboard, navy-blue sheets, and giant pillows. You probably did not see the words *navy-blue sheets* and *giant pillows* in your mind; you saw pictures of them. This is how your mind thinks. If you doubt this, then ask yourself, do you frequently find yourself dreaming in words? Probably not. Remember a picture is worth a thousand words!

Association

This is the key to memory and all of learning: In order to learn any new piece of information, it must be associated with something you already know.

This is worth repeating. To remember any new piece of information, you must associate it with something you already know. You have done this all your life; you just might not have been aware of it. Here's a simple test. What comes to your mind when you think of a cherry? Perhaps red, sweet, fruit, pie, round, seeds, etc. These are words and pictures that you have learned to link to a cherry. You associated something you knew to something you did not know. You use association to ride a bike, eat your food, have a conversation, and to learn to do anything. In the same way, by making a story out of the words on your list, you associated them consciously, for easier recall. Your mind is constantly making countless associations every minute, most of them without your conscious awareness. This is how you learn. Do you have a song that reminds you of a special person? That memory is an association. Do you have a smell that reminds you of a time in

"All thought is a
feat of association:
having what's
in front of you
bring up something
in your mind that you
almost didn't know
you knew."

—ROBERT FROST

your childhood? That memory is an association. Why not use this information and make associations consciously to learn more effectively?

Emotion

Adding emotion makes something memorable. Information by itself is forgettable, but information combined with emotion becomes a long-term memory. When we add emotions to something, we make it adventurous, we make it action-filled, we make it humorous, and we're much more likely to remember it.

Location

We are really good at recalling places because as hunter-gatherers, we didn't need to remember numbers and words, but we needed to remember where things were. We needed to know where the clean water was, where the fertile soil was, where the food was. If you can associate something with a place, you're more likely to remember it.

These are some of the keys to having a great memory; the rest of this chapter will be dedicated to showing you specific techniques and applications you can use in different situations. If you did not have much luck with the memory story, don't worry. This is understandable, you may just need a little practice. Most people have not used their imaginations since they were children. You may want to review the story a few times as it will be a good workout for your creative mind. Do this now.

Notice that you can also go through the story backward; the associations can give you the list in any order. Practice this and see for yourself.

You should be truly amazed. For most people, using rote methods, it takes anywhere from 10 to 30 minutes to memorize this list and with only very temporary results. However, you'll find that this story, which took you no more than a minute to learn, will be available for you to recall days or even weeks from now without reviewing it once. This is the power of working smart and not hard. This is the power of your imagination. This is the power of your mind. Let's try it again.

A KWIK MEMORY EXERCISE

Ask a friend to give you a list of 10 random words. Or you can make a list yourself: To make this as random as possible, grab the nearest piece of printed media available to you, whether it's a book, a newspaper, a magazine, or a flyer from your local supermarket. Use the first substantive words in the first 10 paragraphs you see (in other words, don't use things like *I, the, when,* etc.), making sure not to use any word more than once. Write these down.

Now flip over the paper you wrote these words on and try to write the list again, in order. Check what you wrote against the original list. How did you do? You probably didn't remember all 10, but you probably didn't forget all 10, either. That's instructive, because genius leaves clues, by which I mean that your innate intelligence teaches you about your intelligence. There was a method that allowed you to memorize what you did, and you can access that to move to the next step.

Tell yourself out loud which of the words you remembered and why you think you remembered those words. Doing so will help you to understand how you memorize things. For example, there's a good chance that you remembered the first word and the last word. This is that common phenomenon we discussed back in Chapter 4 known as primacy and recency, where people tend to remember the first thing as well as the most recent thing they heard in any given situation. Which other words did you remember? Do these words have anything in common, such as that they all start with the same letter or they're all action words? What does this tell you? Were the other words you memorized organized in any way? Did they evoke any kind of emotion in you? Was there something unique about any of the words you remembered?

What you've likely learned by this point is that the words you were able to remember on your first pass had certain qualities about them. The words you didn't remember failed to have any quality that resonated with you. So, let's create a process where every word has a memorable quality.

- Tell yourself a story using these 10 words, moving from one word to the next. You're not trying to win a literary competition with this story, and it doesn't matter if the story makes much sense. What's important is that you provide some kind of imaginative detail for all the words on your list (for example, if one of your words is *outside,* imagine that you're in a vast field) and that you "link" your words in the story in the order in which they appear on your list by creating an image for each. Remember, the more emotional and exaggerated they are, the better you will recall.

- Now, on a separate piece of paper, write down the list again, using the story you created to remind you of the words and of the order in which they appeared. How did you do this time? In all likelihood, you did better, though there's a good chance you still didn't get all of them.
- Now write down the list again (not looking at any previous versions of the list you created), but this time write it down backward. You'll need to access the story you invented in a different way in order to do this, but this is really going to help lock these words down for you.

At this point, you've probably memorized most if not all the words on your list. At the same time, you're likely wondering how this is going to help you remember all the details in a presentation you're giving.

DELIVERING A GREAT DEAL OF INFORMATION WITHOUT NOTES

As we've discussed, your memory is fundamental to nearly everything you do. There's really no way to unlimit yourself without having a well-trained memory, because memory governs your ability to reason, to calculate possible outcomes, and to serve as a resource to others. And sometimes you just need to be able to deliver a significant amount of information to a person or a group of people at once. This might take the form of delivering a report to your board, giving a speech to an assemblage, sharing your expertise in a subject in front of your class, or any number of other situations. And in many of these cases, it's critical that you be able to do this without having any notes in front of you, because the notes would suggest that you are less well versed in the material than you should be.

I've been teaching business executives, students, actors, and others a time-honored technique for making their presentations without notes. And when I say time-honored, I mean this quite literally. The method I teach and that I'm going to share with you now is a version of the loci method, something that has been around for more than 2,500 years.

The legend behind the loci method is that the Greek poet Simonides of Ceos survived a building collapse that killed all others in attendance. When officials tried to identify the victims, Simonides was the only person who could help them, because he remembered who the victims were based on where they were standing at the time of the collapse. In the process, Simonides created a memory tool that is as effective today as it was in 500 B.C.

Loci is the plural version of the word *locus,* which means "a particular point or place." The loci method, then, is a memory tool that aligns the things you want to remember with specific points or places that you know well. Here's how I teach it:

- Identify the 10 major talking points from your presentation. These can be keywords or phrases or perhaps quotations that you want to incorporate. They should not, however, be multiple paragraphs long, as that will make this process cumbersome and your presentation feel stiff and overly rehearsed. The assumption here is that you know your topic well and that you have some facility with the material. This method is designed to help bring each of the key points to the forefront of your mind when you need them.
- Now imagine a place that you know well. This can be a part of your home, a street that you walk often, a nearby

park, or anything else with which you have a great deal of familiarity and that you can easily recall vividly.

- Now consider a path through that location. If it's a room in your house, for example, imagine walking into that room and traveling through it. Identify 10 spots in this room that you can quickly see in your mind. Maybe one is the lamp in the corner that you see as you enter the room. Perhaps another is the chair just to the left of that lamp. The next might be the side table next to that chair, and so on. Make this path as procedural as possible. Zig-zagging around the space is likely to be less productive. Just see yourself walking through this space clockwise noticing what you always notice as you pass each item.
- Once you've picked out your 10 locations, assign a major talking point to each of these locations. Be sure to make the order of your talking points match the order in which you walk through the room. For example, using the room we just described, if the first thing you want to say is the keynote message to your entire presentation, assign that to the lamp. If the next major talking point is an essential product detail or a key historical fact, assign that to the chair, and so on.
- Now practice your presentation, using your walk through the location as a tool for remembering each of the primary messages in the presentation. Each component of the presentation should come to you as you need it.

As with all tools, this memory tool might require some time for you to become expert at it, but it will likely begin to help you immediately. With practice you should find it possible for you to access large chunks of information without referring to your notes. Your recall will improve dramatically, and your speeches and reports will seem more natural. You can employ this approach whenever you need to memorize in bulk.

BONUS TOOL 1: A QUICK WAY TO REMEMBER EVERYONE'S NAME

As we discussed earlier, failure to remember something like the name of a person you've just met is often a case of your not being attentive in that moment. Remembering MOM can be enormously helpful in that regard. But I also have a technique specifically geared to helping people remember names that you might find useful. The mnemonic here is BE SUAVE:

- **B is for Believe:** Believing that you're going to be able to do this is the essential first step. If you try hard enough to convince yourself that you can't remember names, you'll succeed.
- **E is for Exercise:** As with the other tools in this book, doing this is going to take some practice, but you should be able to become very good at this very quickly.
- **S is for Say it:** When you hear a person's name for the first time, say it back. This will both confirm that you heard the name correctly and offer you the opportunity to hear the name twice.
- **U is for Use it:** During the course of your conversation with this person, use their name. This will help lock it in.
- **A is for Ask:** Ask where a person's name came from. This would be a bit odd if you were asking about a name like "Jim," but it's particularly helpful when meeting someone with a less-common name.
- **V is for Visualization:** Vision is an incredibly powerful memory tool, as we already saw with the loci method. Try to attach an image to a person's name. For example, if you meet someone named Mary, you can imagine that person wearing a wedding veil on the day she gets married.
- **E is for End:** When you part ways with that person, end your conversation by saying the person's name.

BONUS TOOL 2: A QUICK WAY TO REMEMBER VOCABULARY AND LANGUAGES

Vocabulary is one of the cornerstones of learning. To remember the meaning of words is easy; just use the very same systems you have been using. One of the most powerful concepts is word substitution. You already know how to do this, you just now have a name or a vocabulary term for it. Word substitution is the process of turning intangible (hard to picture) information into an image that is more concrete and easy to visualize.

Here are some examples of word substitutions:

- Nitrogen can be a knight
- Monroe can be a man rowing
- Washington can be by a washing machine
- Armstrong can be by a strong arm

The main idea behind word substitution is coming up with a picture (or series of linked pictures) that sounds similar enough to remind you of the original word. This abstract word, idea, or concept that was once so difficult to understand is now not so foreign. By creating a picture of the word, you now have something more tangible, something you can see. Remember that we tend to remember that which we create. Some more examples:

- Cytology, *the study of cells.* You see a towel with a huge "G" (cytology) on it. You have always wanted one, so you take it, and you are thrown in a jail cell. Or you sigh, looking at your toe, in a low G (sigh toe low G), but this is not allowed and you are put in a cell and forced to study. Even though this is thoroughly bizarre, it is very memorable, and it works!
- Lenient, *compassionate, gentle.* Picture a leaning ant (an ant leaning). The ant is leaning on a clean wall and getting it dirty. His mother, instead of being angry, is compassionate and gentle.

This system can be used for practically anything, including learning foreign languages, which works the same way as remembering vocabulary. In fact, some of the vocabulary words you encounter in English might as well be in another language! For example:

- *Très bien* (French), which sounds like tray bean, means "very good." Picture yourself babysitting and rewarding the child a silver tray with a giant bean on it. The child was very good.
- *Facile* (French), which sounds like face eel, means "easy." Picture a friend challenging you to hold an eel close to your face; you do it and say, "That's easy!"
- *Travailler* (French), which sounds like traveler, means "to work." Picture a traveler coming up to you and inviting you on a vacation, but you can't go because you have to work.
- *Escargot* (French), which sounds like scar go, means "snail." Picture a snail getting into an S-car (car shaped like an *S*) and making the car go.
- *Merci* (French), which sounds like mare sea, means "thank you." Picture yourself saving a mare from drowning in the sea. She then says "thank you."
- *Aprender* (Spanish), which sounds like a blender, means "to learn." Picture yourself taking your books and putting them in a blender.
- *Escuela* (Spanish), which sounds like S-quail, means "school." Picture a quail with a giant superman *S* on its chest going to your school.
- *Ayuda* (Spanish), which sounds like are-you-the, means "help." Picture yourself drowning (in need of help) and someone comes to rescue you and asks, "Are you the person drowning?"

- *Mando* (Spanish), which sounds like man (or moon) doe, means "to command." Picture a man commanding a doe to jump to the moon.
- *Estrada* (Spanish), which sounds like extra day, means "road or highway." Picture yourself going on vacation and being stuck in traffic for an extra day on the highway.

Try these Spanish terms on your own:

- *Desventaja* (handicap)
- *Pelo* (hair)
- *Bolso* (handbag)
- *Dinero* (money)
- *Leer* (read)

I've used these examples to better introduce you to the basics. Build upon them and understand their significance. You can use these skills for practically anything. These systems are both flexible and universal. For example, if you want to remember whether a word is masculine or feminine, simply add the picture of a top hat for masculine words and a dress for feminine words. There are no rules, so be creative and outrageous, and have fun with them!

STACK IT

To learn new vocabulary or foreign-language words, combine the strategy above with methods that you've already learned from our chapter on study. For example, we talked about spaced repetition. That would be extremely valuable in this application. We talked about using music. Baroque music is very effective at helping to learn languages. The study techniques already in your toolkit will serve a bold new purpose here.

BEFORE WE MOVE ON

I hope you can see now that having a well-trained memory is an essential part of unlimiting yourself. When your memory is finely tuned, you're exponentially stronger than if you're trying to get by with an untrained memory. This book covers the foundation to jump-start your memory. Visit www.LimitlessBook.com/resources to get the three-part memory training videos as my gift to you. Before we move on to the next chapter, try a few things:

- Think about ways to provide yourself with greater motivation to remember. Simply thinking it would be nice to have a better memory is probably not enough.
- Consider ways in which you can try to be less influenced by distractions when you're in a situation where remembering something might be important. I'm going to give you some tools to help with this later in this book, but what can you do right now to help you focus more?
- Take each of the tools I've provided in this chapter out for a spin. There's a good chance you'll see a noticeable difference in your memory right away.

"The man who does not read good books has no advantage over the man who can't read them!"

—MARK TWAIN

14

SPEED READING

Why is it so important to read?

How do I increase my reading focus and comprehension?

How can I get more out of every reading experience?

What do Oprah Winfrey, Thomas Edison, John F. Kennedy, and Bill Gates all have in common? They were all great readers. Leaders are readers.

Welcome to the age of data. Never in history has there been such an information surplus. More information has been produced in the past few decades than in the previous few thousand years. According to Eric Schmidt, the former CEO of Google, "There were 5 Exabytes of information created between the dawn of civilization through 2003, but that much information is now created every 2 days." And it's only getting faster and faster. All of this information makes today's age extremely competitive. Those people who can keep up with the latest information will have the competitive edge needed to succeed, not only academically and professionally, but in other key areas of life as well.

Studies show that there is a direct relationship between your ability to read and your success in life. Skilled readers enjoy better jobs, higher incomes, and greater opportunities for success in all realms of life. Think about this: If you have average reading skills, then you have the same understanding that most people have. That doesn't give you much of a competitive advantage, does it?

Unfortunately, for most people reading is regarded as a boring task, something very time-consuming and tedious. Have you ever gone through a page in a book and found yourself asking, "What on earth did I just read?" If the answer is yes, you are not alone.

We've talked before about the challenges I faced early in my college career. As you know, those challenges were so great for me that I seriously considered quitting school altogether. But as I rose to the task of reading a book every week in addition to the reading I needed to do for my classes, I started to make considerable progress with my learning. I didn't realize how much progress I'd made, though, until one surprising day.

Growing up, I've always tried to keep myself out of the spotlight. I was a shy kid, and I felt more comfortable blending into the scenery than being front and center. That continued when I went away to school. Big classes held in lecture halls were especially appealing to me, because I could sit in the corner and avoid being noticed.

I was in one such classroom one day along with a few hundred other students. Up front, the professor was lecturing to us and using an overhead projector to show images. At one point, he put some text up on the projector, and I instantly burst into laughter. This was an entirely natural reaction for me; the quote was funny. But it was otherwise completely quiet in the hall, which caused a huge number of people to swivel their heads in my direction. I'm guessing most of these people would never have been able to identify me as one of their classmates before this moment.

I was hugely embarrassed. I'd made so much effort to be invisible, and now it was as though I'd stormed the stage to draw attention to myself. I was blushing so hard that I thought my face was going to combust, and I shrank back as far as I could.

Then several seconds later, others in the hall started laughing. At first, I thought they were laughing at me, but as more joined them, I looked out and noticed that they weren't staring at me at all; they were reading the text. And that's when I realized the source of my embarrassment: I'd read the words so much faster than my classmates that I'd reacted to it way sooner than everyone else. I'd known I improved the speed at which I read and the level at which I comprehended it, but until that moment I had no idea how rare but learnable an ability it was.

While still feeling a bit awkward about my unintended outburst, I left that class buoyed by the understanding that my learning had risen to an entirely new level. Due to the techniques I'd taught myself, reading had become one of my superpowers, paving the way to enormous breakthroughs in my learning. While I vowed not to laugh so loudly in the future, I walked out of that lecture hall with an incredible sense of excitement about learning and about discovering the other superpowers that were just emerging.

HOW READING MAKES YOUR BRAIN LIMITLESS

Any plan to make your learning limitless needs to include reading. Just as memory is foundational to nearly all brain function, reading is foundational to nearly all learning. If anyone tells you that they don't read, they're essentially saying, "I've stopped trying to learn." Yes, you can learn something from watching videos, listening to podcasts, or going to the movies. Even the silliest network sitcom is likely to teach you *something*. But it is nearly impossible to make learning a dynamic and renewable part of your life without a dedicated approach to reading. Here's why this is true:

- **Reading kicks your brain into gear.** When you read, you're using your brain for many functions at once—which is a vigorous and rewarding workout. As Dr. Ken Pugh, president and director of research at Haskins Laboratories, points out, "Parts of the brain that have evolved for other functions—such as vision, language, and associative learning—connect in a specific neural circuit for reading, which is very challenging. A sentence is shorthand for a lot of information that must be inferred by the brain."[1] In other words, reading gives you an incomparable level of mental exercise, and the brain is always a "muscle" that gets stronger the more you challenge it.

- **Reading improves your memory.** Because you're giving your brain such a great workout when you read, your brain functions at a higher level. One significant benefit of this is with regard to memory. In a study conducted by Dr. Robert S. Wilson at Rush University Medical Center in Chicago, reading was shown to have a meaningful effect on memory decline. "We shouldn't underestimate the effects of everyday activities, such as reading and writing, on our children, ourselves, and our parents or grandparents," he noted. "Our study suggests that exercising your brain by taking part in activities such as these across a person's lifetime, from childhood through old age, is important for brain health in old age."[2]
- **Reading improves your focus.** One of the things we do when we sit down with a book or even spend some dedicated time with a newspaper is train our focus on this one thing. Unlike when we browse the Internet or click through YouTube, when we're reading, we usually give the vast majority of our attention to what we're reading. This practice makes it easier to apply the same level of focus to other tasks.
- **Reading improves your vocabulary.** Some people just sound smarter. How do you react when you encounter one of these people? In all likelihood, you offer them increased respect and even a certain level of deference. People who sound smart tend to have access to and a facility with a wider vocabulary than the average person. Reading allows you to build vocabulary organically. The more you read, the more you are exposed to an expanded range of language and the use of that language in a variety of contexts. And because reading is such a superior focusing tool, you're absorbing a great deal of this, and it will be accessible to you as you need it.
- **Reading improves your imagination.** If you were ever given a story prompt at school or at work, you know that it is often easier to think creatively when using a tool to get

started. Reading is essentially one story prompt after another. "What would it be like to be in this person's shoes?" "How can I use this technique to be more productive?" "What am I going to do first, once Jim Kwik helps me become limitless?" A great imagination helps you see more possibilities in your life, and reading keeps your imagination on high alert.

- **Reading improves understanding.** Learning comes in many forms, and learning as a success tool has many elements. And while agile thinking and mastery of skills are critical to success, empathy and understanding can't be overlooked. Reading exposes you to lives you'd never known before, experiences you'd never imagined, and modes of thinking far different from your own. All of this builds both your empathy for others and your understanding of how the world works beyond yourself.

KWIK START

If you can read faster with greater comprehension and enjoyment, what books would you start reading this month? Create a list of three books you want to start reading.

READING SELF-ASSESSMENT

The first thing you must do is discover your present reading speed, also known as your base rate. This reading rate is measured in words per minute. In order to measure it, you will need an easy reading novel, a pencil, and a timer. Then do the following:

1. Set an alarm to go off in two minutes.
2. Read at a comfortable speed and stop when the alarm goes off (put a mark where you left off).
3. Count the total number of words in three regular lines, and divide that number by three. This is the average number of words per line.

4. Count the number of lines you just read (only count those lines that at least make it halfway across the page)
5. Multiply the number of words per line by the number of lines you just read (multiply your answers from steps 3 and 4).
6. Divide this number by two (because you read for two minutes) and this is your words per minute. Do this now. It is critical to have this exercise completed before moving on. Write it down here:

   What is your current reading speed? __________ words per minute

The average person's reading speed can usually be found somewhere between 150 to 250 words per minute. This range varies with the difficulty of the material. If you are reading much below 100 words per minute, the material may be too difficult or you may want to seek remedial help (the skills you learn here will still be of great value).

Let's say a person reads at 200 words per minute. This person reads and studies for four hours a day. A person who reads at 400 words per minute (twice as fast) needs only to study for half as much time. A faster reader saves at least two hours each day.

If you can save two hours each day, what would you do with this extra time? Take a moment to write down how you would spend those extra two hours daily.

CHALLENGES TO READING

People either don't read or choose to read very little for a variety of reasons. You work long hours, and you're exhausted at the end of the day. It's easier to be entertained passively (through television, film, music, etc.) than to engage in the activity required to read. If you're going to work for your entertainment, you'd rather be playing a videogame. I hear you, but if you've absorbed the benefits I just listed above, you know that you need to fit some time into your day—every day—to read.

Another key reason why people don't read is that they find it a laborious process. It can take them five minutes to get through a single page in a book, making the idea of reading a 300-page book akin to walking from New York to Georgia. People tend to read slowly for a few reasons. One is that they stopped learning to read relatively early—maybe second or third grade—and their reading level (and, more importantly, their reading technique) never increased much beyond this, even as they continued to learn in spite of this constraint. The other is that they don't allow themselves to focus when they're reading. They're listening for the kids, half-watching television, checking e-mail every few minutes, and so on. They therefore find themselves reading the same paragraph over and over again, because they're not focused enough to comprehend what they're reading.

There are a couple of primary reasons why people read slowly. Your reading efficiency is made up of two main parts: Your reading rate (speed) and reading comprehension (understanding). Before we look at various ways to increase your reading efficiency, we first need to look at three of the barriers and obstacles that prevent us from reading more quickly.

1. Regression

Has this ever happened to you? Have you ever read a line in a book and found yourself rereading that same line again? Or do you ever find yourself "wander reading" (going back mindlessly and rereading words)? *Regression* is a term used to describe the tendency that your eyes have to go back and reread certain words. Almost everyone does it to some degree, and most of the time it is done subconsciously. By doing so, people believe they will increase their comprehension, but usually they hamper it. By regressing, or back-skipping, it is very easy to lose the meaning and essence of your reading. Regression seriously disrupts the reading process as well as slows down reading speed.

2. Outdated Skills

Reading is not so much a measure of intelligence as it is a skill and with any skill, it can be learned and improved. When was the last time you took a class called reading? For most, it was back in the 4th or 5th grade. And if you're like most people, your reading skill is probably still the same as it was back then. Here's the challenge: Has the amount and difficulty of what you're reading changed since? The complexity of material has likely increased dramatically, yet our reading skill has remained the same.

3. Subvocalization

Subvocalization is a fancy word for your inner voice. Do you notice a voice inside that is saying the words as you read this? Hopefully, it's your own voice. Subvocalization limits your reading speed to only a couple hundred words per minute. That means your reading speed is limited to your talking speed, not your thinking speed. In reality, your mind can read a lot faster.

Where did subvocalization come from? It occurred, for most people, when you were first learning to read. Then it was necessary for you to read out loud so that your teacher knew you were doing it correctly. Do you remember when you would have to get into a circle with the other children and you each took turns reading aloud? For a lot of us, this was a very stressful event. There was a lot of pressure on you to say the word properly. How you pronounced the word was very important. It was then that your brain made the association: If I want to understand a word when I am reading, I must be able to correctly say it.

Later on, you were told to no longer read aloud, but rather silently, to yourself. This is when you internalized that "reading voice," and most of us have been doing it ever since. In essence, you believe if you don't hear the words, then you won't understand the words. This is not the case.

Here's an example: We know that President John F. Kennedy was a very fast reader, reading somewhere between 500 and 1200 words per minute. He brought speed-reading instructors to train his staff. He also gave speeches at approximately 250 words per minute. Clearly, when he was reading, there were a lot of words he wasn't saying in his mind. It is not necessary to say the words in order to understand them.

Take a moment and think about a specific car, yours or someone else's. What does it look like? What color is it? Do this now.

What was it that you thought about? You might have said, "It is blue, has four tires, and brown leather seats." Question: Did the words *blue, tires,* or *leather* appear in your mind, or did you picture a car with all of these things? For most of us, our minds think primarily in images, and not words. As we discussed in the previous chapter on memory, words are just a tool we use to communicate our thoughts or pictures.

As you are reading, you can greatly increase both your speed and comprehension by visualizing the material. It is not necessary to "say" all of the words, as it takes too much time, just as you don't read and say "period, comma, question mark," when you see them in a sentence. You wouldn't read a sentence like this: "I just bought some avocados comma blueberries comma and broccoli period." You understand that punctuation marks are just symbols that represent various meanings.

Words are symbols as well. You've seen 95 percent of the words you read before. You don't need to pronounce those words, just as you don't need to pronounce filler words like *because, this,* or *the*. You know them by sight, not by sound. It is the meaning of what the word represents that is important. And the meaning is usually better described and remembered in the form of pictures. Understanding this concept is the first step in reducing subvocalization.

READING MISCONCEPTIONS

Myth 1: Faster Readers Don't Comprehend Well

This is a rumor spread around by slow readers, and it is not true. In fact, faster readers often have better comprehension than slower readers. Here's an analogy: When you're taking a slow drive down a quiet street, you can be doing many things. You may be listening to the radio, drinking a green juice, waving to a neighbor, and singing your favorite song. Your attention is not in any one place; it just flows and wanders.

But imagine you're driving pedal to the metal down a racetrack taking hairpin turns. Do you have more focus or less? I would bet that you are very focused on what is in front, behind, and ahead of you. You're not thinking about your dry cleaning. The same holds true for reading. The key to better reading comprehension is focus and concentration. But some people read so slowly that they completely bore their own minds. A bored mind doesn't concentrate well. Your mind can handle vast amounts of information, and yet most people as they read feed it one . . . word . . . at . . . a . . . time. This is starving the brain.

If your mind ever wanders and daydreams, this could be the reason. If you don't give your brain the stimulus it needs, it'll seek entertainment elsewhere in the form of distraction. You may find yourself wondering what you'll have for dinner, what to wear on your date tomorrow, or listening to a conversation out in the hall. We've asked before about reading a page or a paragraph and not remembering what you've just read. It may be because you read so slowly that you bored your brain and it simply lost interest. Or, you may be using reading as a sedative and you fall asleep. By reading faster, you keep your mind stimulated, find yourself more focused, and have better comprehension.

Myth 2: It's Harder and Takes More Effort to Read Fast

Reading faster requires *less* effort, primarily because trained readers tend not to back-skip as much as slower readers. Slow readers stop at words, reread them, go to another word, regress to a previous one, and so on, and this continues throughout their reading. This takes a lot more effort and is extremely draining and boring. Faster readers go through words much easier and in a lot less time. This makes them more efficient because they put in less time, and get more out of the process!

Myth 3: Faster Readers Can't Appreciate Reading

This is not true either. You don't have to study the individual brushstrokes of a work of art in order to appreciate it. Likewise, you do not have to study each and every word in a book, to realize its value. One of the best things about being a trained reader is flexibility. Faster readers have the option of speeding through boring/nonessential material and slowing down or even rereading the exciting/important information. Flexibility is power. Faster readers appreciate reading most material because they know it will not take all day.

VISUAL PACER: GIVE YOUR READING THE FINGER

You were probably told as a child not to use your finger to point to the words when you're reading. The traditional belief is that doing so will slow down your reading. But as children know naturally, using your finger as a guide keeps your eyes focused and prevents them from wandering. Using your finger to read actually increases your reading speed because your eye is attracted to motion.

It is one thing to know this intellectually; it's another for you to experience it. Let's practice using your finger by rereading what you used for your assessment earlier (page 241). Start from the beginning and use your finger to track the words. End where you originally left off. Do not worry about comprehension and don't time this because it is just practice. The purpose of this exercise is for you to become familiar with using your finger while reading.

When you are done, set the alarm for two minutes. Start from where you ended during your first assessment. Continue reading until the alarm goes off. Figure out your new reading rate (based on the original formula), and write it down here:

My new reading rate is _______________ words per minute.

Studies show that the use of the finger while reading can increase your reading rate anywhere from 25 percent to 100 percent. The more you practice using this technique, the better your results will be. It may be a little awkward at first, just like it was when you first learned how to drive, but be patient and remember that it always takes more effort to sharpen your skills first than it does to bulldoze your way through learning later.

Reading with your finger also introduces another one of your senses, the sense of touch, into the learning process. Much as your sense of smell and sense of taste are closely tied, your sense of sight and sense of touch are also very closely linked. Have you ever tried to show something new to a child? The child's natural instinct is to want to touch the object.

Using your finger also dramatically decreases regression, and is one of the reasons why your reading speed increases with this practice. Your eyes are naturally attracted to motion, so by moving your finger forward, your eyes are much less likely to regress backward.

Practice reading with your finger, this tool alone will significantly increase your speed and comprehension and will revolutionize your learning. If your finger gets tired, practice using your whole arm, moving it back and forth. It's a bigger muscle and will not tire as easily.

HOW TO READ EVEN FASTER

Here are some more tools that will help you to become an accelerated reader:

1. Reading Is Like Exercising

When you go to work out, you cannot expect your muscles to grow if you pamper them. You need to push your muscles to where they are a little uncomfortable in order for them to grow. The same applies to reading. If you push yourself to read faster, your "reading muscles" will become stronger, and what was once hard, becomes easy. You can read faster, simply by training yourself to read faster. Those of you who run know this. When you are running on a treadmill, if you practice regularly, you can watch yourself run at faster and faster levels. The levels that were once hard become easy a week later, because you have pushed yourself to a higher degree of excellence.

To increase your speed, even more, try this exercise: You will need an easy-reading novel, a pencil, and a watch or timer:

1. Read comfortably (using your finger or a visual pacer) for 4 minutes. Set the alarm to go off in 4 minutes and read as you normally would read. Mark the line when your alarm goes off. This is going to be your "finish line."
2. Now set your alarm for 3 minutes. The goal here is to reach the finish line before your alarm goes off. Then

read (using your finger) until the line in step 1 in 3 minutes.

3. Set your alarm for 2 minutes. Don't worry about comprehension. Try to get to the finish line before your alarm goes off in 2 minutes. Use a visual pacer and go through it line by line. Have your eyes follow your finger as fast as possible.
4. Final stretch. Set your timer for 1 minute. Do your best to get to the finish line in one minute. Do not skip any line, and don't worry about comprehension right now.
5. Now breathe. Set your timer for 2 minutes. Start from your finish line to read a new section. Read at a comfortable rate with comprehension. Count the number of lines you read, multiply by the number of words per line, then divide this number by two. This is your new reading rate. Write it here: ________ words per minute.

How did that feel? By doing this exercise, you will notice that your rate has increased. Here's an analogy: If you are driving on the highway at 65 mph, and then slow down to 40 mph for some mild traffic, you will notice quite a bit of difference. This is because you are used to driving at a higher speed. But in reality, you are not going very slowly, because it is all relative.

The same principle applies to reading. If you push yourself to read two or three times faster than what you are used to, when you finally decrease your rate to a comfortable speed, your original rate feels slow.

You want to practice this 4-minute exercise at least once a day until you reach a level that you are pleased and satisfied with. Schedule your reading. Just as with exercising, you cannot expect to work out only one time and be done for life. You must read on a regular basis, otherwise your reading muscles will grow weak.

2. Expand Your Peripheral Vision

Your peripheral vision is the span of letters or words that your eyes can see in a single glance. By increasing your peripheral vision, you will be able to see and take in more words at a time. Most people were taught to read only one word at a time. But in fact, you are capable of reading more than that.

When you first learned to read, you were taught that letters made up larger structures, called words. As a child, you would sound out a word by its letters. For example, the word *report* would be broken down into letters so that you could understand it, *R-E-P-O-R-T.* Now that you are older, you are not as aware of the letters as you are reading, you see the larger units, known as words.

One of the reasons why people have a limited reading speed is because they read one word at a time. But if you put the word *card* at the end of the *report,* you get *REPORT CARD.* These two words have their own distinct meanings, but your mind sees them as one unit. Just as your mind is capable of seeing these two words together, it is also capable of seeing groups of words at the same time. By doing so, you will take your reading speed to even greater heights. Just as you see the words and not the individual letters, skilled readers see groups of words (or ideas) and not the individual words. On page 252 are additional tips that you can use to condition yourself to "see" more.

3. Counting

By using the exercises I've outlined, the challenge of subvocalization will begin to decrease. The process of reading faster naturally makes it more difficult to say all the words, even inside your head. When you have passed a certain rate (about 300 to 350 words per minute), it will be impossible to subvocalize all the words. As you hit this threshold, your brain will begin to make the shift from saying the words to seeing them more as images. Reading a book will be more like watching a movie.

Counting is another tool you can use to drown out this inner voice. The process is deceptively simple: count out loud as you are reading, "one, two, three . . ." and so on. You'll find it is very difficult to count out loud and talk inside (subvocalize) at the same time. Doing this process conditions you to subvocalize less, allowing you to see the words rather than say them, thus leading to better speed and comprehension.

People tend to remember and understand what they *see,* more than what they *hear.* This makes sense, as most people can recall someone's face they see, more than the name they hear. By practicing these other exercises, your reading speed will improve because you are no longer saying every word. Initially, you may be a little confused (and your comprehension may even decrease), but in a very short time, your mind will grow bored of counting and will eventually stop. With practice, your comprehension will soon increase and expand because you will be able to more fully see and understand the material.

SUCCESS STORIES

I could fill an entire book with speed-reading success stories from students, and we post them regularly on social media. Here's one we received today. Sarah was a very slow reader, had difficulty focusing, and felt it impossible to remember names and events. After years of struggle in this arena, she was convinced that there was very little chance she'd ever be capable of improving her reading ability or her ability to study.

In my programs, I make it a point to reassure my students that we are not aiming for perfection but for progress, and this resonated with Sarah. She realized she had been looking for complicated solutions, but that the tools and techniques we teach—which are easy to ignore or overlook because they are simple—were the best to use. She decided to show up with dedication and do her best, no matter what doubts she might have.

The results speak for themselves; Sarah's reading speed is now three times faster—she went from reading 253 words per minute to 838 words per minute. She starts her day by reading, which starts each morning with positive momentum and makes her feel like she's already achieved something for the day.

Lou, another student, also experienced a profound difference in his reading ability once he learned a technique that could truly help him. Lou excelled at high-level left-brained topics such as engineering and math and obtained a bachelor of science in electrical engineering. But he struggled in every single English class he ever took. Throughout his school years, he had enormous

ADDITIONAL READING TIPS.

- Hold your book upright. If the book is flat on your desk, you may be doing one of two things, either

    1. looking at the print at an angle versus directly, thus putting unnecessary strain on your eyes, or

    2. you will be slouched over in order to see the print clearly, and this (as you know) disrupts the flow of oxygen through your body and makes you feel tired.

- Read for only 20 to 25 minutes at a time. Remember the primacy and recency effect. Also, if your eyes ever get tired or feel strained, take a break. Close your eyes and let them rest.

- Make reading a habit. Those who have reached a high degree of success in life are almost always avid readers. Great readers read often. The key is to make reading a habit. Give yourself this gift.

trouble understanding the words he was reading and comprehending the lessons behind them. In fact, he's convinced that he graduated only because his teachers gave him undeserved Cs out of sympathy.

When he was 35, Lou began to take lessons to learn how to read. These were helpful, but he still found himself at a second-grade reading level after four years of work. This was a vast improvement from where he had been, but it wasn't nearly what he wanted, and he continued to be frustrated with his inability to master words and concepts. A big part of the problem was that he had been trying to learn by rote memorization—reading the same passages over and over in the hope that he would absorb what he was reading. But he consistently found himself having learned nothing by the end of the page.

While he had made significant progress, finding programs was the key for Lou. As our memory program taught him how to absorb the material he was reading, he began to take a little more time to visualize words as he read them, and he used his left hand as a pacer to help stimulate the right side of his brain. Finally, for the first time, he found himself reading books and understanding them.

KWIK START

Block out at least 15 minutes each day for reading and put it in your calendar like an important appointment. Commit to making reading part of your daily habit.

BEFORE WE MOVE ON

Unlimiting your reading and learning will offer you an unparalleled level of freedom. People who make the most of their capacity to learn find themselves experiencing the world with a sense of mastery and with the confidence that no task or challenge will intimidate them. Visit www.LimitlessBook.com/resources and put what you learned here into practice. You can watch an hour speed-reading masterclass where I walk you through these methods. Before we get to the next chapter, try a few things:

- Identify a current reading habit that you'd like to change. Any transformation requires you to acknowledge what's holding you back and notice when it shows up during your practice.
- Practice reading with a visual pacer each day. Schedule your reading, for even 10 minutes each day, to build your "reading muscle."
- Make a list of the books you would like to read this month and write down what can change in your life when you finish reading them.
- Take my speed-reading online masterclass (free) at www.jimkwik.com/reading.

"Thinking is the hardest work there is, which is the probable reason why so few people engage in it."

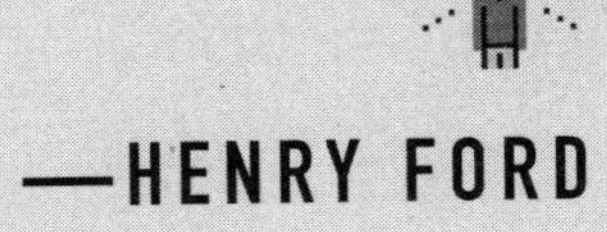

—HENRY FORD

15

THINKING

Why is it important to think from a variety of perspectives?

What are the various ways people use their intelligence?

What kinds of superpowers can you harness by thinking differently?

Accomplishing something big often requires new approaches to thinking. An observation usually attributed to Albert Einstein posits, "We can't solve problems by using the same kind of thinking we used when we created them." And this of course makes perfect sense. So often, we adopt a particular perspective at work, in our home lives, and in our studies, and that outlook effectively walls out any approach that doesn't fit into that viewpoint. But there are two key problems with that. One is that all perspectives should be challenged on a regular basis to confirm that they are still viable. For example, so often when a company goes out of business, it's later shown that it was so completely mired in one approach to the marketplace that it wasn't capable of seeing that the audience they were targeting was no longer as responsive as they once were. The second problem a fixed perspective faces is that challenges are often the product of a particular type of thinking, and the answer can be found only by bringing a fresh approach to the table.

Why do most of us have a restricted range of thinking? I think the answer is the same as it was when we were discussing focus: because we somehow missed out on "thinking class" when we were in school. Fortunately, it's never too late to attend that class, and I'm going to enroll you in it right now.

THE THINKING HATS

Dr. Edward de Bono devised the concept of the "six thinking hats" as a tool for getting out of whatever rut of thinking one might be mired in.[1] Regularly used to help groups problem-solve in a more productive way, it is easily adaptable by any individuals hoping to keep their thinking fresh. The core notion is to separate thinking into six distinctly defined functions by progressively donning a series of metaphorical hats:

- You put on a **white hat** when you're in information-gathering mode. At this point, your focus is on collecting details and getting all the facts you'll need to address whatever issue you're trying to address. To help you remember this, think of a white lab coat.
- You switch to a **yellow hat** to bring optimism to your thinking. Here, you're trying to identify the positives in any problem or challenge you're facing, highlighting the value inherently in place. As your memory tip here, think of the yellow sun.
- Next, you'll wear a **black hat** to pivot from looking at the good side of the challenge to facing its difficulties and pitfalls. This is where you'll come face to face with the consequences of failing to successfully address a problem. Memory tip: Think about a judge's robe.
- Once you've done that, don your **red hat** to allow emotion to come into play. This is the point where you can let your feelings about the problem come to the surface, and maybe even express fears. This is also

where you can allow speculation and intuition to enter into the conversation. To remember this, think about a red heart.

- Now it's time for the **green hat**. When you're wearing this hat, you're in creativity mode. You've looked at the problem analytically and you've looked at it emotionally. Now ask yourself, what new ideas can you bring to what you already know about the problem? How can you come at it in a way you haven't considered before? Memory tip: Think about green grass.
- Finally, wear the **blue hat** to be in management mode, and make sure you've addressed your agenda productively and gone through the process in a way that benefits from all the other hats you've worn. Often, organizations will start with the blue hat to set goals for a meeting and then put it on again at the end. Even if you're using the six hats by yourself, this is something you might want to consider. To remember this, think about blue skies.

The De Bono approach to problem-solving is an ingenious and elegantly organized method for getting the most from your thinking. At its core, it is a neatly defined way of looking at an issue from all sides. First, you make sure you're clear on what you need to address. Then, you determine that you have all the facts in front of you. Next, you make sure you're dealing with the issue with a positive perspective. Then, you get real about the challenges you're facing, and allow yourself to feel what you're feeling about it. After this, you allow yourself to attack the problem from perspectives you might not have considered before, letting your imagination run free. And then you circle back to make sure you've addressed what you set out to address during this session.

Look at how many different ways you've used your brain for this one task. You've been analytical, you've been emotional, and you've been creative. You've explored the sunny side and the dark side. And you've almost certainly attacked the issue with tools you don't automatically use every single day (though you might from now on). Einstein would be proud of you.

KWIK START

Think of a problem you need to be solved right now. It can be anything from "How can I get that job," to "How can I communicate better with my family?" Use the Six Thinking Hats model to run through the different perspectives of looking at the problem you're trying to solve.

HOW ARE YOU SMART?

Why is it important for us to have tools to help us think in different ways? Because people usually have a dominant way of using their intelligence. Dr. Howard Gardner, professor of cognition and education at the Harvard Graduate School of Education, has studied intelligence extensively and has identified eight distinct forms of intelligence:[2]

1. **Spatial**: This is someone who usually thinks from the perspective of the space around them. Airline pilots tend to be spatial thinkers, but so do people who excel at playing chess, as both require an innate understanding of how things fit into space. The artist Claude Monet comes to mind as another example because of his remarkable use of space in his paintings.
2. **Bodily-Kinesthetic**: Someone with a dominance of this form of intelligence uses their body as a form of expression or problem-solving. Gymnasts have refined bodily-kinesthetic intelligence, as do drummers. The first name that jumps into my head when I think of this form of intelligence is Venus Williams, who expressed her genius with her body on a tennis court in ways that very few ever have.
3. **Musical**: This is a person with a strong "sensitivity to rhythm, pitch, meter, tone, melody and timbre."[3] Musicians obviously have a dominance in musical

intelligence, but you'll also find it in poets, who often use meter and rhythm as effectively as they use words. My poster child for musical intelligence is Wolfgang Amadeus Mozart.

4. **Linguistic**: Someone with a dominance in linguistic intelligence is particularly attuned to all the implications of words, not just their strict dictionary definition. Writers of course have this trait, but so do great orators and lawyers. The first person I think of with linguistic intelligence is William Shakespeare.
5. **Logical-Mathematical**: This is a strength in seeing the "logical relations among actions or symbols."[4] Mathematicians find themselves very comfortable seeing or seeking the connections between different numbers. Scientists likewise draw connections between physical objects or the forces acting on objects. Our friend Albert Einstein immediately leaps to mind as a prime example.
6. **Interpersonal**: Someone with a dominance in interpersonal intelligence has a deep innate ability to connect with other people and a rich understanding of how others might be feeling at any given moment. Therapists tend to have strong interpersonal intelligence, as do schoolteachers. When I think of interpersonal intelligence, I think of Oprah Winfrey, because of her amazing ability to relate to whomever she is speaking with.
7. **Intrapersonal**: If you have dominance in intrapersonal intelligence, you have a particularly refined sense of what is going on inside of you. People with strong intrapersonal intelligence do a great job of "taking their own temperature." They're in touch with their feelings, they know what triggers them, and they have a good sense of how to manage this. If you know someone who is cool under even difficult circumstances, it's likely that this person has strong intrapersonal intelligence. Mahatma Gandhi is an exemplar of this form of genius.

8. **Naturalistic:** This kind of intelligence expresses itself in an ability to see the world of nature in all its complexities. Where you might see a field of flowers, someone with this dominance will see four different kinds of tulips, a couple of varieties of lavender, and a rare grass that you just thought was a weed. Zoologists tend to have a dominance in naturalistic intelligence, as do landscape architects. The first person with this trait who comes to my mind is the remarkable primatologist Jane Goodall.

Do you see yourself in one of these descriptions? There's a good chance you'll relate to more than one, because people rarely have only one form of intelligence. It's likely you have a dominance in one or two, and there may be a couple of others that you employ with some regularity. At the same time, you'll almost certainly find some on the list that you use rarely, if at all.

But all of these forms of intelligence identify successful ways of operating in the world, and any one of them might come into play when you're facing a particular task or problem. Awareness of all eight, and considering each while wearing your six thinking hats, is a remarkably effective way to unlimit your thinking.

WHAT IS YOUR LEARNING STYLE?

Just as types of intelligence vary from person to person, the way one learns varies. The VAK learning styles model has been in use since the 1920s and is useful in showing you how you prefer to learn new things:

- **V is for Visual,** meaning that you tend to learn through illustrations, charts, video, and other visual media.
- **A is for Auditory,** meaning that you find yourself most comfortable learning by listening, either to a lecture, a discussion, a podcast, an audiobook, etc.
- **K is for Kinesthetic,** meaning that you prefer to learn via physical interaction. Kinesthetic learners tend to gain more from taking a hands-on approach to learning.[5]

“The life which
is unexamined
is not worth
living.”

—PLATO

Here's a quick quiz you can take to give you a sense of what kind of learner you are:

1. When you don't quite understand or remember something:

a. It doesn't ring a bell or resonate
b. It seems hazy or unclear
c. You can't get a handle on it or feel it

2. You are about to give a friend directions to your home. Would you:

a. Draw a map on paper?
b. Tell her the directions?
c. Pick her up in your car?

3. You are staying in a hotel and have a rental car. You would like to visit a friend whose address you do not know. Would you like them to:

a. Draw you a map?
b. Tell you directions?
c. Pick you up in their car?

4. Learning technical material is easiest for you when:

a. Someone explains the ideas to you
b. You visualize the concepts and see the whole picture
c. You can learn by doing or get a feel for the ideas

5. You are going to cook a dessert as a special treat for your family. Do you:

a. Cook something familiar?
b. Look through a cookbook for ideas?
c. Ask for the advice of others?

6. You are about to purchase a new sound system. Other than the price, what would most influence your decision?

a. A friend speaking about it
b. How it makes you feel
c. Its distinctive look or appearance

7. Recall a time in your life when you learned how to do something like playing a new board game. Try to avoid choosing a very physical skill like riding a bike. How did you learn best? By:

a. Looking at the directions, pictures, diagrams, or charts
b. Listening to somebody explain it
c. Doing it

8. Which of these games to you prefer?

a. Pictionary
b. 20 Questions
c. Charades

9. You are about to learn how to use a new program on a computer. Would you:

a. Read the instructions?
b. Call a friend and ask questions about it?
c. Turn it on and learn by experimentation?

10. You most easily are aware of and notice:

a. The quality of music from a sound system
b. If colors, shapes, or patterns clash
c. If clothes feel uncomfortable

11. You are not sure whether a word should be spelled "separate" or "seperate." Do you:

a. See the word in your mind and choose the best way it looks?
b. Sound it out?
c. Write down both versions?

12. A new movie has arrived in town. What would most influence your decision to go or not go?

a. Friends/family talking about it
b. You have an intuition or sense about it
c. You saw a preview of it

13. You most easily remember directions when you:

a. Repeat them to yourself as you hear them
b. Visualize them
c. Intuitively sense how to get there

14. Do you prefer a teacher or trainer who likes to use:

a. Handouts, flow diagrams, charts, and visuals?
b. Field trips, experiments, and applications?
c. Discussions, guest speakers, and conversations?

15. Once you completely understand a new idea:

a. It is now concrete, or you have a feel for it
b. You have it loud and clear
c. You can envision it

16. You make decisions best when you rely on:

a. Your gut instinct
b. What looks clearest to you
c. What sounds best to you

17. At a party, you are most interested in people who

a. Are interesting and articulate speakers
b. Convey a warm and relaxing feeling
c. Radiate a visual beauty

Once you've written down your answers, use this key to see which type of learning comes most naturally to you:

1: a (A) b (V) c (K),	**7:** a (V) b (A) c (K),	**13:** a (A) b (V) c (K),
2: a (V) b (A) c (K),	**8:** a (V) b (A) c (K),	**14:** a (V) b (K) c (A),
3: a (V) b (A) c (K),	**9:** a (V) b (A) c (K),	**15:** a (K) b (A) c (V),
4: a (A) b (V) c (K),	**10:** a (A) b (V) c (K),	**16:** a (K) b (V) c (A),
5: a (K) b (V) c (A),	**11:** a (V) b (A) c (K),	**17:** a (A) b (K) c (V)
6: a (A) b (K) c (V),	**12:** a (A) b (K) c (V),	

Your answers will give you a good sense of the kind of learner you are. In all likelihood, you'll be some mix of audio (A), visual (V), and kinesthetic (K). But you might see a real dominance in one of these, and that can prove to be extremely useful as you embark on unlimiting your thinking, as you can make a conscious effort to bring the others into the mix.

MENTAL MODELS

Mental models are constructs for thinking that help us make sense of the world around us. Think of them as shortcuts. For example, we've all heard of the economic mental model of supply and demand. You're probably familiar with the idea that supply is representative of the amount of something available within a market, whether that's a service, product, or commodity. When that is juxtaposed against the demand for that item, value is determined, and that often dictates the price of the item. This model is a quick way to understand what's happening in a market. It's not always accurate and doesn't explain every factor involved, but it serves as a simple way of evaluating the price or value of an item.

Mental models train your mind to think; after all, you don't rise to the level of your expectations, you fall to the level of your training. Models can act as shortcuts that save you valuable energy and time when you're evaluating an idea, making a decision, or problem-solving.

In the following pages, I'm including some of my favorite mental models for faster and sharper decision-making and for creative problem-solving.

Decision-Making: The 40/70 Rule

One of the greatest barriers to quick decision-making is the ever-present feeling that we don't have enough information to make the "right" decision. Colin Powell, former secretary of state, addresses this with his 40/70 rule.[6] His rule is to never make a decision with less than 40 percent of the information you are likely to get, and to gather no more than 70 percent of the information available. According to Powell, anything less than 40 percent and you're just guessing. Anything more than 70 percent and you're stalling over making the decision. Of course, this means you need to be comfortable with the possibility that you're going to be wrong, which is necessary in any case.

"When you have about seventy percent of all the information, you probably ought to decide, because you may lose an opportunity. My own experience is that you get as much information as you can and then you pay attention to your intuition, to your informed instinct. Sometimes what my analytical mind says to me is not what I'll do," Powell said.[7]

Productivity: Create a Not-to-Do List

This one might seem counterintuitive, but sometimes it's just as important to know what *not* to do as what to do. This tactic is used best for directing your attention to the essentials and avoiding what doesn't matter in the moment.

Often at the beginning of a project, or even just a packed day, it can feel overwhelming to decide what to concentrate on. The power of the not-to-do list is that you decide from the very beginning what you will definitely put aside. When we write down our list of tasks for the day, we usually don't prioritize, nor do we assign a value to these tasks. It's easy for a conventional to-do list to become a catchall for all the things we know we have to do that day, instead of the things that must be done first, for the most value.

Lest you think that the not-to-do list is filled with things like participating in social media, let's work out exactly how you should compile this list:

- First, write down tasks that might be important but can't be done because of outside circumstances. Maybe you're waiting for an e-mail from someone else, or you're waiting for a colleague to finish their portion of a project.
- Next, include tasks that you think need to be done but that don't add value to your life; you might also think of these as busywork. You might ask yourself if you can delegate or hire someone else to do them. You can also

ask if anyone but you will notice whether the task is left undone. The idea here is that your time is best spent on tasks that will move your life and goals forward.

- Then include current and ongoing tasks that don't benefit from additional attention. This might include systems that are already set up, such as making the kids' lunches or having a brief meeting with your team at the start of the work day. These are part of your routine and shouldn't be clogging your to-do list on a daily basis.
- Last, include urgent tasks that are often to-do lists given to us by other people, such as getting some background research on a project or making follow-up calls. These are tasks that might be necessary to do but perhaps don't need to be done by you.[8]

When you're finished with your don't-do list, it should read like an anti-menu, a list of items that aren't available for your time. You will then be able to easily identify what will actually move you forward and do those activities instead.

KWIK START

Do this right now. Take a moment to create your *not*-to-do list for today. What are the things you need to avoid today to focus and achieve your goals? Be specific and check off that list by not doing it.

Problem-Solving: Study Your Errors

When we take the time to study the mistakes we make, especially those that have a lasting effect on our lives, we turn every mistake into a learning opportunity. Use this model to evaluate what went wrong so you can get a better result next time.

- First, get clear on what did or didn't happen. Often, we confuse cause with correlation, so be sure you understand what happened and what led to the mistake or error.

- Next, ask yourself why those mistakes happened. Look for the deeper layers behind the incident. You might ask "why" until you've run out of layers to question.
- Then ask how you can best avoid the same mistakes in the future. If some of the factors that caused the error are out of your control, ask how you can prevent causes that can't be eliminated.
- Finally, using what you've gleaned from this exercise, determine how you can create the best conditions to support your desired outcomes in the future.[9]

To help illustrate this strategy, let's imagine this scenario: the fundraising project you orchestrated for your child's school greatly underperformed your expectations. First, you need to be clear on what happened. Did you and your team fail to inspire people to give, or did the donors fail to show up? In this case, let's assume that the donors were available, but they didn't give as much as you anticipated or sometimes didn't give at all.

Now, you need to ask yourself why. Did it have something to do with the way you presented the need? Did it have something to do with the time of year? Did it have something to do with the economy? Remember that your answer here might lead to additional questions. In the scenario we're playing out, let's determine that you decide that you might not have emphasized the importance of this campaign, because there'd been a fundraiser at the school only two months prior and you didn't want to appear pushy, and that your being overly polite caused potential donors to think the cause wasn't critical.

So, how do you avoid this in the future? You decide that the next time you run the campaign, you're going to do it earlier in the school year and, regardless of the proximity of any other fundraiser, you're going to go out of your way to stress the value and importance of this one and why donors need to open up their checkbooks. The upshot of this is that you realize that you need to improve the way you send out the message about your campaign, and you determine to take a class on this so you will be much better prepared when next year's campaign comes along.

Strategy: Second-Order Thinking

Most of us think about the consequences of our actions, but few of us think even two steps beyond the immediate effects our actions will have on our lives. Let's consider Ryan Holiday's book, *Conspiracy*, which describes how entrepreneur Peter Thiel planned and executed a takedown of one of America's most prolific (and disliked) online magazines, *Gawker*.[10] Thiel's desire to confront *Gawker* was born after the mag outed him as gay. But he did not act immediately. Over the course of 10 years, he and a team strategically made one move after the next based on a plan they had devised to destroy *Gawker* for good. Regardless of what you think about Thiel's actions, they were definitely not the product of impulsive thinking. This is an example of second-order thinking, the ability to think strategically through a series of events.

This model is simple and yet not always easy. To use second-order thinking when considering future actions:

- Always ask yourself, "And then what?"
- Think in increments of time. What do the consequences look like in five days? Five months? Five years?
- Draw out the possible courses of action you might take using columns to organize consequences.[11]

First-order thinking is easy, but it's second-order thinking that allows us to go deeper through time and consequences. Best of all, it allows us to see what others can't see.

TAKING GIANT LEAPS

Moving forward incrementally is a significant sign of progress. Every step you can take in the process of becoming limitless is a step in the right direction. But what if you could move your genius forward *exponentially*? After all, if we take 30 normal steps forward, we'll wind up somewhere down the street. But if we took 30 exponential steps, we'd circle the Earth more than two dozen times. That's the kind of thinking advocated by Naveen Jain, winner of the Albert Einstein Technology Medal and founder of some of the most innovative companies in the world, including Moon Express (the first private company to be authorized to land on the moon), World Innovation Institute, iNome, TalentWise, Intelius, and Infospace.

"Exponential thinking is when you start to see things from a different mindset," Jain told me. "It's not about thinking outside the box; it's about thinking in a completely different box."[12] This is where normal genius begins to border on limitless genius. As Jain explains, linear thinking (the kind of thinking most of us employ) causes us to look at a problem and seek a solution. We might come at the problem from a number of angles. We might put on different hats to address the problem in ways that stretch our thinking. And we might even come up with a solution that addresses the problem effectively and moves us forward. That's all meaningful progress.

But what if we looked at the root cause of the problem and solved that instead? This would lead to exponential progress, world-changing progress. Jain uses as an example the lack of fresh water in many parts of the world. One could attempt to tackle that problem from a number of viewpoints, including finding ways to improve filtration and creating systems for moving fresh water from places where it was abundant to places where it was scarce. But what if instead you identified that, among the various causes for fresh-water scarcity, the biggest is that so much fresh water is being used for agriculture rather than drinking? You would attempt to solve the problem in an entirely different way. What if you could use significantly less water for agriculture, perhaps through some combination of aeroponics, aquaponics, or other techniques currently being experimented with or not yet invented? This would result in such an abundance of fresh water that the original problem would become eminently solvable. That's exponential thinking at work, and the value of it is obvious.

When Jain started his company Viome, his goal was to attack the pervasive nature of chronic illness, which he sees as underlying the world's health crisis. Understanding that every individual's immune system is different and therefore how each person processes the foods they consume can vary greatly, he and his team developed a tool for analyzing an individual's gut microbiome so a person can "Get to the bottom of what foods are right for your body and discover how optimizing the activity of your gut can dramatically improve the condition of your health."[13] As I write this, they're in the process of collecting information from a huge number of users, data that will lead to powerful recommendations for every individual who employs the tool.

Naveen Jain operates at the grandest of scales. He's a successful entrepreneur who has never started two companies in the same industry, and one of his operating principles is that creating a billion-dollar company is *simply* a matter of solving a $10-billion problem. Now, most of us don't think on such a massive scale, but you can still use exponential thinking to exercise your mind and unlimit your personal genius. To learn more about Viome and watch my interview with Naveen Jain, visit www.JimKwik.com/Viome.

THINKING EXPONENTIALLY

So, how does an individual think exponentially? Maybe your goal isn't to solve all the world's problems, invent a new technology, or start a billion-dollar company, but you can see how applying exponential thinking might make a real difference to your school, your business, or your personal growth. How can thinking less linearly and more exponentially make dramatic changes in your life?

The first step is having a good understanding of what the exponential mindset looks like. In a piece for the *Harvard Business Review,* Mark Bonchek, founder and chief epiphany officer of Shift Thinking, describes the linear mindset as a line appearing on a graph that rises gradually over time. He then juxtaposes this with a second line that curves upward, slowly at first, and then shooting over the other line before heading far off the graph. This is his visual depiction of the exponential mindset.

Phase of a Business

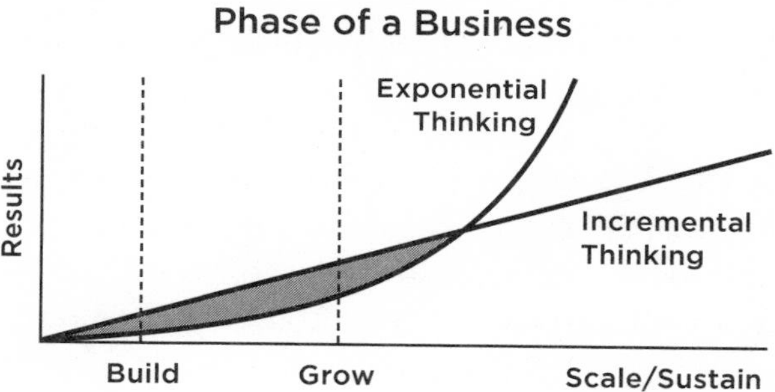

"The incremental mindset focuses on making something *better*, while the exponential mindset is focused on making something *different*," he notes. "Incremental is satisfied with 10 percent. Exponential is out for 10X."[14]

"The incremental mindset draws a straight line from the present to the future," Bonchek continues. "A 'good' incremental business plan enables you to see exactly how you will get from here to there. But exponential models are not straight. They are like a bend in the road that prevents you from seeing around the corner, except in this case the curve goes up."

Bonchek is speaking specifically about applying exponential thinking to business, but the same perception can be brought to bear on thinking in other parts of life. Imagine, for example, that you were trying to figure out how to have everyone in your family at the dinner table at least three times a week. A linear mindset would involve looking at everyone's work schedules, school schedules, activities schedules, and social schedules to try to find a way to clear out some space. But an exponential mindset would take the approach of turning your family's harried schedules into something different.

Maybe "dinner" isn't the goal at all, but rather finding key moments during the week when everyone can be in the same place and focus exclusively on each other. Maybe the issue isn't your schedules at all but how each of you has chosen to commit their time. Progress might not seem much like progress (three months later, you're barely better off than when you started), but then the changes you've been developing start to take shape, and suddenly you have lots more time together.

If you want to fire up your exponential thinking ability—and take a huge step toward unlimiting your genius—consider these four steps the next time you contemplate a problem or task in need of a solution:

Step 1: Get to the Underlying Problem

As Naveen Jain illustrated when addressing the world's water problem, the core issue might not be the surface issue at all. As Jain noted, the underlying problem behind the shortage of fresh water isn't the availability of the water, but rather that so much fresh water is being used for agricultural purposes. Solving the underlying problem allows for a much more workable solution to the surface problem.

Let's go back to our dinner scenario. The surface problem is that the family rarely eats dinner together because everyone's schedules are too busy. The underlying problem might be that your schedules are so busy because your spouse feels compelled to work long hours at work, your daughter feels compelled to be an elite athlete, your son feels compelled to get perfect academic scores so he can attend a college with a 3 percent acceptance rate, and you feel compelled to sit on three nonprofit boards. But maybe even that is not the true underlying problem.

Maybe what's really at issue is that you each feel the pressures you feel not because you personally aspire to these goals but rather because you live in a community that looks down on people who don't have goals of this sort.

Step 2: Posit a New Approach

One of the keys to exponential thinking is filling your thoughts with what-if statements. Evie Mackie of the Innovation Hub at the John Lewis Partnership says that "'What If' statements come into play to bring unruly scenarios into the picture. For example, 'What if the human race needed to adapt and live in a world which was 90 percent underwater' or 'What if we could no longer touch things with our hands to interact.' This helps conceptualize a WHOLE different array of things we may never have thought of otherwise and allows us to imagine what we would need to survive in a future world, which could be a very different place."[15]

In our example, if you've realized the underlying problem is that the prevailing notions in your community have forced you into filling your daily lives with activities that take far too much of your time, you might ask yourselves, "What if we didn't care what everyone else thought?" Or maybe you'd ask, "What if there were only 18 hours in the day instead of 24?" Or you might even ask, "What if we lived somewhere else?"

Step 3: Read about It

As you already know, I am an extremely strong advocate for reading as much as you possibly can. Reading liberates your brain more than virtually any other activity. Reading is especially important when it comes to exponential thinking. You can't make huge cognitive leaps if you don't have a well-rounded view of a subject.

So, now that you've gone through the what-if exercise, read up on alternatives. Maybe your spouse reads a number of books about the connection between corporate success and happiness. Maybe your daughter connects with bloggers and influencers on both the odds of becoming an elite athlete and the lives of elite athletes. Maybe your son reads a number of studies that look at graduation from ultra-competitive universities and occupational and emotional success afterward. Maybe you read books about the causes you're championing via your nonprofits and reconsider how important these causes are to you.

Step 4: Extrapolate

You've now identified the underlying problem, posed questions that allow you to imagine a world without the problem, and done your research. Now, it's time to try out a scenario. Let's play one out here: You're convinced that you've filled your lives with activities because you need these to maintain your status in your community. You've asked the question, "What if we lived somewhere else?" and found that everyone in your family is intrigued by this notion. You've done your reading and discovered that you could be happier and more satisfied if your job/sports/school/philanthropic goals were revised and reconceived.

So, what would happen if you moved a hundred miles away, across the country, or even to a different country? You know that doing something this dramatic might not immediately seem like progress. You've seen the straight line and the curved line, and you realize that it might even seem you've taken a huge step backward because of all the adjustments you'd need to make. But say the four of you play out the scenarios and decide that making a move is the right thing to do. Two years later, the family is thriving—and you have dinner together nearly every night.

BEFORE WE MOVE ON

This is the last of the method chapters, and I'm sure you're itching to put everything you've learned in this book to use. Before we end, I'm going to give you a vision of how this might work for you and a 10-day plan to jump-start applying what you've learned to your life. But before we get to that, let's try a few things:

- Review Howard Gardner's eight forms of intelligence starting on page 258. Which forms on this list align most closely with your own intelligence?
- Now that you know what your learning style is, what can you do to incorporate the other styles into your thinking?
- Try on all six thinking hats during a test case. Give yourself a relatively simple task, and approach it using Edward de Bono's method.

“We shall not cease
from exploration
And the end of all
our exploring
Will be to arrive
where we started
And know the place
for the first time.”

—T. S. ELIOT

AFTERWORD

RETURN OF THE POSSIBLE

If you're anything like the overwhelming majority of people in the world, when you started reading this book you were being governed—either consciously, unconsciously, or both—by a suite of limitations you'd either imposed on yourself or others had imposed on you.

Maybe you wanted to learn a new ability, but you were sure that you didn't have the capacity to do it. Maybe you wanted to throw your hat in the ring for a big work promotion, but your inner voice kept telling you that you really didn't have the competence for it. Maybe you were convinced that you were always going to leave the house without your phone, or you were never going to remember all the names of the people at your next social gathering, or you were forever going to be the boring guy reading his speech from a piece of paper. If this has ever described you in any way, now that you've come to the end of this book, I hope you're ready to wave good-bye to that person.

Instead, let's meet the new limitless you.

The limitless you has a limitless mindset. You no longer believe that there are all sorts of things you can't be, or do. There might be all sorts of things you *haven't done yet,* and there might be all sorts of things that you've had trouble doing in the past, but the limitless you knows your past doesn't equal your future. The limitless you understands that your brain is a much more powerful tool than you might have previously imagined and that, by setting your mind to learning whatever you want to learn, you can conquer just about any skill.

The limitless you also has limitless motivation. In the past, maybe you could conceive of a more ambitious life, but you couldn't actually get yourself to take action. Now, though, you know how to align your habits with your ambitions; you're capable of making a commitment to lifelong learning and lifelong improvement and it's as natural to you as getting dressed in the morning.

You also know how to fuel your brain with food and sleep and exercise so that you start your day in the best place, and you're always ready to take on new and demanding challenges. And you know how to tap into the flow so that, once you start a task, you can dive into it completely. And, perhaps most significantly, the limitless you has unlocked the methods of learning how to learn. By discovering this, you have become exponentially more powerful than you were before. Beyond a few physical limitations, if you can learn it, you can do it. And the tools you now have at your disposal allow you to learn anything faster. When you couple that with the skills you've gained in unlimiting your focus, your memory, your thinking, and your reading, you're in possession of the ultimate superhero toolkit.

A superhero is not just someone who has discovered and developed their superpowers. Every superhero must eventually return to their world and serve. They must bring with them the lessons and wisdom they won through their journey. They must not only integrate their powers into their lives, but they must learn to use their powers to help others. At the end of *The Matrix,* Neo has won the battle and broken free of limits. In his last phone call to the Matrix, Neo says: "I'm going to hang up this phone, and then I'm going to show these people what you don't want them to see. I'm going to show them a world without you. A world without rules or controls, borders or boundaries. A world where anything is possible." He's returning to the ordinary world, but with a mission to help inspire others, to free their minds.

My hope for you is that you not only take what you've learned in this book and make your life better with it, but that you make the lives of those around you better, too. The formula is: Learn. Earn. Return. No hero's journey is exclusively for the benefit of the hero. With your newfound knowledge, help those around you to learn better and faster and unlimit themselves.

In the film *Lucy,* an American student played by Scarlett Johansson develops superhuman powers after the full potential of her brain is unleashed. Professor Norman, played by Morgan Freeman, is a neurologist who helps Lucy cope with the startling changes taking place in her mind and body. When asked by Lucy what to do with her new gifts, Professor Norman replied in Morgan Freeman's unique voice:

> You know . . . If you think about the very nature of life—I mean, in the very beginning, the development of the first cell divided into two cells—the sole purpose of life has been to pass on what was learned. There was no higher purpose. So if you're asking me what to do with all this knowledge you're accumulating, I say . . Pass it on.

So, now the question becomes this: What are you going to do with what you've learned? Solve a challenging problem at work so you and your colleagues have an impact on your industry, and maybe your world? Start a book club? Make a dent in that huge stack of periodicals on your coffee table, and then teach your children what you've just learned? Connect with people in more dynamic ways? Throw a brain-food dinner party? Sign up for the class that is going to open new doors for you? Or maybe sign up to teach a class yourself? Which would you choose?

That's what a superhero would do. That's what the limitless you *can* do.

Throughout this book, you've had the opportunity to take some of your new skills out for a spin. In the pages that follow, I've laid out a program to get you started. Now is the time to start to use all of what you've learned in concert. Start with one thing, but start somewhere. Anywhere. And when you do, I think you're going to be stunned by what you uncover about yourself. The limitless you is the person you truly are and the person who, over time, will become things you can't even conceive of now.

Know yourself. Trust yourself. Love yourself. Be yourself.

And remember, the life you live are the lessons you teach. Be limitless.

With love and learning,
Jim

10-DAY KWIK START PLAN

Congratulations on making it to the end of this book. You are one of the few who completes the task at hand. I applaud you.

We've covered a lot in this book. My advice is to implement everything you learned. If you're not sure where to begin, then this 10-day plan is here to help you jump-start your limitless journey.

You can follow this plan I made for you, or you can hand-pick three top tips you'd like to integrate from each main section: Mindset, Motivation, and Methods. In this way you can focus on the areas where you feel you're currently lacking and need more support. You can also download this 10-Day Kwik Start program in video format from www.LimitlessBook.com/resources.

Thank you for allowing me to be your brain coach through this book. I look forward to hearing about your progress.

DAY 1: LEARN FASTER

Put this acronym (FASTER) into action on day one:

- **Forget**: The key to laser focus is to remove or forget that which distracts you. There are three things you want to forget (at least temporarily).

    1. What you already know
    2. What's not urgent
    3. Your limitations

- **Act**: Traditional education has trained many people to think that learning is a passive experience. But learning is *not* a spectator sport. The human brain does not learn as much by consumption as it does by creation. Knowing that, I want you to ask yourself how you can become more active in your learning. Take notes. Do the exercises in this book.

- **State**: Your state of being is a current snapshot of your emotions. It is highly influenced by your thoughts (psychology) and the physical condition of your body (physiology). Change your posture or the depth of your breathing. Consciously choose states of joy, fascination, and curiosity.
- **Teach**: If you want to cut your learning curve dramatically, learn with the intention of teaching the information to someone else.
- **Enter**: If it's not on your calendar, there's a good chance it's not getting done. Take out your calendar and enter blocks of time to invest in yourself, even if that's only 10 or 15 minutes a day.
- **Review**: You are better able to retain information by reviewing multiple spread-out sessions. Get in the habit of reflecting on your day and do a daily review of what you've learned.

For more on this, reread the section starting on page 50.

DAY 2: KILL YOUR ANTS

Identify the voices in your head that are focusing on what you can't do—those Automatic Negative Thoughts (ANTs). Start talking back to them.

Remember, too, to discount those pesky LIEs: Limiting Ideas Entertained. And consistently check in with your BS, Belief Systems. When you find yourself thinking, *I always screw up this sort of thing,* counter with, *Just because I haven't always been good at this in the past doesn't mean that I can't be great at it now. How can I learn this?*

Don't shrink what's possible to fit your mind, expand your mind to fit what's possible. For more on this, reread the section starting on page 137.

DAY 3: QUESTION YOUR QUESTIONS

Reflect on the power of dominant questions. You likely have one question you're subconsciously asking yourself throughout the day. Identify this question and think about how you can change it to change your behavior. Knowledge itself is not power, it only has that potential when you apply it. Start asking the questions that will help you get the empowering answers you need throughout the day. For more on this, reread the section starting on page 56.

DAY 4: IMAGINE WHAT YOU WANT MOST

Take a moment to write down all the disadvantages you will have when you don't apply what you learned in this book. For example, you could write, "I will have to keep studying hard and settle for the same mediocre results." "I will continue to doubt myself." "I won't be able to show up at my best for my loved ones" or "I won't get a good job."

Now, write down the advantages you will have when you apply what you learned, such as: "I'll be able to learn what I need to learn with confidence, get a great job I love, and make a lot of money so I can give back to the world." "I will have more free time to exercise and get healthy, travel, and spend more time with my significant other." Or something simple like, "I will finally have some free time to just get caught up and relax!"

Get specific. See it, feel it, believe in it, and then work daily for it. Visualize your celebratory champagne moment. For more on this, reread the section starting on page 124.

DAY 5: CONSIDER YOUR PURPOSE

Purpose is about how you relate to other people. Purpose is what you're here to share with the world. What is your why?

Think about who's counting on you to be limitless. Is it your family? Your lover? Your friends? Colleagues? Neighbors? Get specific about who you're letting down by setting limits in your life. Now, think about how you can affect the lives of others when you show up 100 percent. You've found your purpose. For more on this, reread the section starting on page 113.

DAY 6: START A NEW HEALTHY HABIT

Take small, simple steps to create one new healthy habit that will lead you to success. Make it a part of your morning routine. You'll never change your life until you *decide* to change something you do daily. Our daily decisions and habits have a huge impact on both our levels of happiness and success. If you're persistent you can achieve it, if you're consistent you can keep it. Little by little, a little can become a lot. Remember, every professional was once a beginner.

Pick one new habit you will start doing today. How can you break it down to small, simple steps that you can do consistently each day? For more on this, reread the section starting on page 149.

DAY 7: GIVE YOUR BRAIN SOME ENERGY

Harness your energy to win each day. Eat one or more of these brain foods daily. Which one is your favorite, and why? Remember, what you eat matters, especially for your gray matter. Is what you're eating energizing you or depleting you? Write down some creative recipes you can make using the brain foods below:

Avocados
Blueberries
Broccoli
Dark chocolate
Eggs
Green leafy vegetables
Salmon
Turmeric
Walnuts
Water

For more on this, reread the section starting on page 130.

DAY 8: OPTIMIZE YOUR STUDY

Studying isn't just for people in school. We're all lifelong learners. Set the optimal state to study and learn. Remove distractions. Use the HEAR (Halt, Empathy, Anticipate, Review) method to watch a TED video you've never seen before and practice your listening skills. For more on this, reread the section starting on page 196.

DAY 9: ALWAYS REMEMBER MOM

Before you begin any task, always check with your MOM (motivation, observation, methods). Also, check in with your why. What is your motive for remembering that person's name? What do you observe? Remember, most of your memory is not a retention issue; it's an attention issue. Practice remembering the names of everyone you meet today by using the association technique. If you forget someone's name, write down if it was your motivation, observation, or the method that led you to forget that name. Then try again with another person.

You can practice this skill even when you're shopping at a grocery store or walking through the street or watching television, or anything. Assign names to strangers you see and test how many you can remember. For more on this, reread the section starting on page 213.

DAY 10: EMBRACE THE POWER OF READING

Set a daily reading goal, even if it's just for 10 minutes a day. There's power to reading and these benefits compound over time. The key is consistency. Pick a book you've been wanting to read, set a timer for 10 minutes, put away the distractions, and practice reading with a visual pacer. Then schedule your reading time for each day; put it in your calendar as an appointment with yourself.

Leaders are readers. Reading is great exercise for your mind. Remember, you can download decades of experience by reading just one book. For more on this, reread the section starting on page 237.

LIMITLESS CHILDREN

HOW TO APPLY THIS BOOK TO **PARENTING**

"If a child can't learn the way we teach, maybe we should teach the way they learn."

—Ignacio Estrada

It's not how smart your children are, it's how are they smart. Traditional education teaches children what to learn, what to focus on, what to think, what to study, and even what to remember. But not how to learn, how to focus, how to think, how to study, and how to remember.

Having grown up with my own learning difficulties, one of my passions is teaching our youth about their mindset, motivation, and methods of learning.

How can you start? I've put some of my favorite strategies in a "kwik" bonus chapter.

You can download the chapter at:

LimitlessBook.com/parenting

LIMITLESS TEAMS

HOW TO APPLY THIS BOOK TO **BUSINESS**

"An organization's ability to learn, and translate that learning into action rapidly, is the ultimate competitive advantage."

—JACK WELCH

Can you apply the Limitless model to your business? Absolutely! For over two decades, we've used these methods to train organizations of all sizes, from entrepreneurial startups to corporate clients, including Google, Virgin, Nike, GE, Fox Studios, and Zappos.

Human capital (the collective education, skills, knowledge, training) is an organization's most valuable and most underutilized asset. For your business to grow, your team's collective brainpower must grow.

How can you harness your team's limitless cognitive potential? I wrote a bonus chapter to help you on your way.

You can download the chapter at:

LimitlessBook.com/Business

YOUR BONUS RESOURCES

We've assembled the ultimate set of resources that complement this book and will magnify your results.

These include:

- Video tutorials of select lessons (as an example: watch me teach you how to quickly memorize the top brain foods, and demonstrate the remembering names technique in front of a live audience)
- Written exercises and assessments to test your skills
- Brainpower food recipes from meals to teas
- Recommended reading
- Special interviews with top experts delving deeper into the topics covered in this book—sleep, exercise, nutrition, meditation, and others
- And so much more!

For your free access, go to:

LimitlessBook.com/Resources

KWIK LEARNING ONLINE

DO YOU WANT TO DIVE DEEPER INTO THE **5 LIMITLESS METHODS?**

How do you train yourself, your family, or your team the methods of focus, study, memory improvement, speed reading, and thinking skills?

We've created for you the ultimate proven and simple-to-add-into-your-life online training for anyone looking to uplevel their capabilities.

All you need is 15 minutes a day to build a new learning habit in each area.

Visit KwikLearning.com/Online-Courses and use the code "LIMITLESS" to get 25% off your registration as a thank you for purchasing this book.

When you do, you will join our community of Kwik Brains from 195 countries. Your success is our success, every program comes with an unconditional 30-day money-back guarantee.

SUGGESTED READING

Our community is passionate about reading. If someone has decades of experience and puts that knowledge into a book, and you can read their book in a few days, you effectively download decades into days.

Leaders are readers. Many of our Kwik Readers commit to finishing #1bookaweek (52 books each year).

As a bonus for purchasing this book, you can join our one-hour speed-reading masterclass as my gift. It will help you tackle your booklist. Get free access at JimKwik.com/Reading

Here is a "kwik" list of some of my favorite mindset, motivation, and methods books. They are listed in no particular order. For the extensive reading list, go to LimitlessBook.com/resources.

The Magic of Thinking Big by David J. Schwartz
Man's Search for Meaning by Viktor Frankl
Understanding Understanding by Richard Saul Wurman
The Tapping Solution for Manifesting Your Greatest Self by Nick Ortner
Start With Why by Simon Sinek
The 7 Habits of Highly Effective People by Stephen R. Covey
Change Your Brain, Change Your Life by Dr. Daniel Amen
The Motivation Manifesto by Brendon Burchard
Tiny Habits by Dr. BJ Fogg
Brain Food by Lisa Mosconi
Me to We by Marc Kielburger & Craig Kielburger
The Promise of a Pencil by Adam Braun
Miracle Mindset by JJ Virgin
The TB12 Method by Tom Brady
Super Human by Dave Asprey
The Infinite Game by Simon Sinek
The Future Is Faster Than You Think by Steven Kotler & Peter Diamandis
The Code of the Extraordinary Mind by Vishen Lakhiani
The School of Greatness by Lewis Howes

Stress Less, Accomplish More by Emily Fletcher
The Power of When by Dr. Michael Breus
Becoming Super Woman by Nicole Lapin
Chineasy Everyday by Shaolan
#AskGaryVee by Gary Vaynerchuk
Becoming Supernatural by Dr. Joe Dispenza
Moonwalking with Einstein by Joshua Foer
The Brain that Changes Itself by Dr. Norman Doidge
Mindset by Carol Dweck
The Align Method by Aaron Alexander
Super Brain by Deepak Chopra and Rudolph Tanzi
Genius Foods by Max Lugavere
Sleep Smarter by Shawn Stevenson
The UltraMind Solution by Dr. Mark Hyman
Spark by Dr. John Ratey
The 4-Hour Chef by Tim Ferriss
Math Doesn't Suck by Danica Mckellar
Boundless by Ben Greenfield
Six Thinking Hats by Edward de Bono
Thrive by Arianna Huffington
The Element by Sir Ken Robinson with Lou Aronica
TED Talks by Chris Anderson
Atomic Habits by James Clear
Imagine It Forward by Beth Comstock & Tahl Raz
Belong by Radha Agrawal
Disrupt-Her by Miki Agrawal
The Ripple Effect by Dr. Greg Wells
Exponential Transformation by Salim Ismail, Francisco Palao & Michelle Lapierre
Think Like a Monk by Jay Shetty
The Alter Ego Effect by Todd Herman
How to Live a Good Life by Jonathan Fields
The Mind Map Book by Barry Buzan & Tony Buzan
The Principles by Ray Dalio
Re-Create Your Life by Morty Lefkoe
Emotional First Aid by Dr. Guy Winch
A Higher Branch by Sam Makhoul
Cancer-Free with Food by Liana Werner-Gray
Food Can Fix It by Dr. Mehmet Oz

ACKNOWLEDGMENTS

This is the hardest part of the book for me to write because it takes a village to bring a book into the world. One may think it's a solo adventure of sorts but in reality, it was a heroic group effort.

In the pages I'm allotted, it would be impossible to thank by name all those who have led and supported me to this moment. The list is long—you can say it's pretty limitless.

I know this because you all have a special place in my heart and I feel your presence when I do my gratitude exercises.

Let's start with YOU the reader. Thank you for not only getting this book but more importantly for reading and using it.

To our podcast guests, listeners, and anyone who has ever watched and shared one of our videos, thank you for tuning in each week and getting all brainy with me.

To our online students all over the world, so much appreciation for your time and trust. Thank you for allowing our team to fulfill our purpose of building better, brighter brains.

To all our speaking and training clients, gratitude for having me share with your audiences and teams.

To my private coaching clients, you know who you are, thank you for your friendship and for teaching me so much in return.

To my longtime business partner Alexis Banc. This book and this business would not exist without you. You wear every hat imaginable, your dedication is only matched by your vision for a better brighter world, I am eternally grateful.

To James Banc, thank you, brother, for being a brain warrior.

Gratitude to my personal assistant Elena, thank you for being my right hand (and sometimes brain). Appreciate all you do.

To our amazing Kwik Team who works hard every day serving our community. Thank you for your caring and commitment, Jonie, Sasha, Brittany, Jade, Iris, Denyce, Nicole, Jessica, Kyle, Dallas, Jen, Zareen, Jena, Lauren, Louie, Romario, Elizabeth, Miriam, Julia,

Matilda, Alex, Dmitri, Jena, Kristie, LJ, Arthur, Marcin, Angelo, Pawel, Radek, Agata, Natalia, Katia, Hugo, Michal, Chris, Marta, Drew, Kris, Rusty, and the rest of our team past, present, and future. (Yes, our team is mostly made up of incredible females.)

I believe everyone can be your teacher on life's journey. From my college friend's father who got me to read one book a week to the person who said I had a broken brain, thank you for the lessons.

To my friends Brendon Burchard, Scott Hoffman, Lewis Howes, and Nick Ortner, who encouraged and kept on me to write this book. Thank you for inspiring the world, and for inspiring me to transform my mess into my message.

I am grateful to Reid Tracy and Patty Gift, who saw the potential for this book. Honored to be part of the Hay House family. Thank you, Anne, Mary, Margarete, Lindsay, Patricia, Cathy, Alexandra, Sally, Marlene, Perry, Celeste, Tricia, Julie, Yvette, Diane, John, Karen, Steve, and everyone else who had a hand in creating the book what it is.

Special thanks to our creative team, who made significant contributions to this book.

Lou Aronica, thanks for helping me craft these pages and making this book the best it can be.

Sara Stibitz, you were invaluable. Grateful for all the research, interviews, wordsmithing and getting us to the finish line.

Clay Hebert, for years of support and for quarterbacking this project from A to Z. You put the clay in clarity.

Courtney Kenney, thank you for managing and mobilizing so many moving parts.

Jose Alonso, thanks for the new kwik design. Nick Onken, photographer extraordinaire.

Rodrigo and Anna Corral for the beautiful book cover art.

Dr. Mark Hyman, thank you for believing in our work and writing the book's foreword. Appreciate you and Mia so much for your support on this book.

Special thanks to Michael Robertson and the entire team at The Beverly Hilton for hosting me and our events.

To our brain merch team, what we see is what we take care of. Thank you for bringing brain awareness to the world, Daniel, Tom, Mitchell, Jakob, Anthony, and our entire team.

Thank you to the legends and luminaries who inspired my imagination early on this journey—Quincy Jones, Neil Gaiman, Gene Roddenberry, George Lucas, Joseph Cambell, Oprah Winfrey, Piers Anthony, JK Rowling, Napoleon Hill, Bruce Lee, Howard Garner, Tony Buzan, Harry Lorraine, Norman Vincent Peale, Brian Tracy, Jim Rohn, Les Brown, Arianna Huffington, Sir Ken Robinson, Mister Fred Rogers, and of course Stan Lee.

To the original accountability group, Michael Fishman, Brian Kurtz, and Ryan Lee.

Thank you Vishen Lakhiani, team, and all our Super Brains at Mindvalley for helping us share meta-learning with the world.

To my superhero friends and the communities they lead. Giovanni Marsico and ArchAngels. Tom & Lisa Bilyeu and your Impactivists. Ken Rutkowski and METal brothers. Elliot Bisnow and Summit. Chris Winefield & Jen Gottlieb and UAL. Chris Anderson and TED. Roman Tsunder and PTTOW & WORLDZ. Michael Fishman and CHS. Jack Canfield and TLC. JJ Virgin and Mindshare. Cole & Sanja Hatter and Thrive. Dan Fleyshman and Joel Marion and their MME 100 Group. Joe Polish and your Genius Network. Anthony Tjan and On Cue. Gareb Shamus and ACE.

To all my friends who have done everything from checking in on me to helping us share our teachings with the world: Aaron Alexander, Adam Braun, Alex Banayan, Alex & Mimi Ikonn, Alex Ortner, Amy Jo Martin, Andres Roemer, Anna Akana, Ari Meisel, Audrey Hagen, Ben Greenfield, Dr. Ben Lynch, Ben Rawitz, Benny Luo, Beth Comstock, Bing Chen, BJ Fogg, Bo & Dawn Eason, Bob Proctor, Branden Hampton, Brandon Routh, Brian Evans, Brian Florio, Brian Grasso, Brooke Burke, Carrie Campbell, Carlos Gardes, Chalene Johnson, Charles Michael Yim, Chervin, Chloe Flower, Chris & Lori Harder, Christina Rasmussen, Christopher Lee, Chris Pan, Claire Zammit, Collin Chung, Craig & Sarah Clemens, Craig Kielburger, Cynthia Kersey, Cynthia Pasquella, Dr. Daniel Amen, Dan Caldwell, Dandapani, Danica McKellar, Dan Schawbel, Dave Hollis, Dave Nurse, David and Lana Asprey, David Bass, David Goggins, David Meltzer, David Michail, David Wolfe, Dawn Hoang, Dean Graziosi, Derek Halpern, Derek Hough, Dhru Purohit, Donna Steinhorn, Ed Mylett, Elizabeth Gilbert, Emily Fletcher, Emily Morse, Erik Logan, Erin Matlock, Frank & Natalia Kern, Gail Kingsbury, Gary Vaynerchuk, Dr. Halland Chen, Henk Rogers, Hutch Parker, Ian Clark,

IN-Q, Jack Delosa, Jack Hidary, Jacqueline Schaffer, James Altucher, James Colquhoun, Jason Stuber, Jayson Gaignard, Jay Shetty, Jeannie Mai, Jeff Krasno, Jeff Spencer, Jelena & Novak Djokovic, Jesse Itzler, Jessica Ortner, Jim Poole, Dr. Joe Mercola, Joel & Laurin Seiden, John Assaraf, John Lee, John Romaniello, Jon Benson, Jonathan Fields, Jon Fine, Jules Hough, Jon Levy, Kandis Marie, Katie Wells, Keith Ferrazzi, Ken Hertz, Kerwin Rae, Kevin & Annmarie Gianni, Kevin Pearce, Kevin Rose, Khaled Alwaleed, Kimberly Moore, Kimberly & James Van Der Beek, Kris Carr, Kute Blackson, Larry Benet, Larry & Oksana Ostrobsky, Laurel Touby, Leigh Durst, Liana Werner-Gray, Lisa Garr, Dr. Lisa Mosconi, Lisa Nichols, Liz Heller, Luke Storey, Manny Goldman, Marc Kielburger, Marie Forleo, Mariel Hemingway, Mari Smith, Mark Anthony Bates, Mark & Bonita Thompson, Mary Shenouda, Matt Mullenweg, Max Lugavere, Mel Abraham, Mel Robbins, Mia Lux, Dr. Michael Breus, Michael Gelb, Michael Lane, Mike Cline, Mike Koenigs, Mike Wang, Mikkoh Chen, Miki Agrawal, Mimi Pham, Mindpump Guys, Mona Sharma, Montel Williams, Naomi Whittel, Natalie & Glen Ledwell, Naveen Jain, Nick Kuzmich, Nicole Patrice, Nikki Sharp, Nina Sugasawa, Nusa Maal, Ocean Robbins, Oz Garcia, Paul Hoffman, Penni Thow, Pete Vargas, Peter Diamandis, Peter Hoppenfeld, Peter Nguyen, Rachel Goldstein, Radha Agrawal, Ramit Sethi, Randy Gage, Randy Garn, Rene & Akira Chan, Richard Miller, Richard & Veronica Tan, Richard Saul Wurman, Rick Barber, Rick Frishman, Robin Farmanfarmaian, Robin Sharma, Rudy Tanzi, Ryan Holiday, Ryan Kaltman, Ryan Levesque, Sabrina Kay, Sam Horn, Sandy Grigsby, Sashin Govender, Sazan & Stevie Hendrix, Scooter Braun, Scott Flansburg, Sean Croxton, Sean & Mindy Stephenson, Dr. Seeta Narsai, Selena Soo, Shaman Durek, Shannon Elizabeth, Shannon Lee, Seth Godin, ShaoLan, Shawn & Anne Stevenson, Dr. Shefali, Simon Kinberg, Simon Mainwaring, Simon Sinek, Sonia Ricotti, Sony Mordechai, Sophie Chiche, Dr. Stephanie Estima, Stephanie McMahon, Steven Kotler, Steve Sims, Steven Tyler, Sunny Bates, Susan Cain, Tana Amen, Tara Mackey, Thomas Bahler, Tim Chang, Tim Larkin, Tim Ryan, Todd Herman, Tom Ferry, Tony Hsieh, Tracy Anderson, Trent Shelton, Tucker Max, Vani Hari, Whitney Pratt, Will Eppes, Wim Hof, Yanik Silver, Yanjaa Wintersoul, Yue-Sai Kan, Yuka Kobayashi, and so many more.

To the children's education nonprofits we love and support (including with part of the proceeds of this book)—WE Charity,

Pencils of Promise, Unstoppable Foundation and others—thank you for the schools you build and the healthcare and clean water you provide for kids in need.

To the brain health nonprofits who are changing the world funding and conducting research on Alzheimer's—Steve Aoki and the Aoki Foundation, Maria Shriver's Women's Alzheimer's Movement, Dr. Rudy Tanzi, the Cleveland Clinic Lou Ruvo Center for Brain Health, Dr. Lisa Mosconi's Women's Brain Initiative and Alzheimer's Prevention Clinic at Weill Cornell Medical College

To all my school teachers (and teachers everywhere), having worked with so many educators and my mother recently retired in public education, I know it's not easy. Thank you for your caring, compassion, and commitment. You are the true superheroes, we appreciate the capes you wear.

To the original geek squad—Dakota, Morris, and Dave. Thank you for comics, video games, and card play. Not only for your friendship but for all the long tutoring sessions. I wouldn't have made it through school without you.

Sensei Rick for years of martial arts training, wisdom, and friendship. And Bryan Watanabe, you blow me away with your integrity and ability to affect those around you so positively.

Thanks, Rocky, for keeping me company all those early mornings writing, best dog ever!

To my beloved, I'm so lucky to be on this journey with you. Thank you for living through my obsession with all things brain and superheroes. Every day with you is an adventure of learning and laughter, I'm in awe of your limitless love and support. You are the greatest blessing of my life.

To our families, love flows strong and deep, leaving us lifetimes of memories to treasure and keep.

To my sister and brother, thank you for all you do and are. You inspire me as people and as parents. Love you biggest.

Thank you to my parents, my original heroes, not only for your encouragement in this book but also for believing in me from the start. Anything that I've ever become that is decent or done that is good is because of you. Anything less than that is on me.

And again, thank YOU, the reader. It is our honor to serve you as we work together to create a brain, a life, and a world without limits.

ABOUT THE AUTHOR

Jim Kwik (his real name) is a widely recognized world expert in memory improvement, brain optimization, and accelerated learning. After a childhood brain injury left him learning-challenged, Kwik created strategies to dramatically enhance his mental performance. He has since dedicated his life to helping others unleash their true genius and brainpower. For more than two decades, he has served as the brain coach to students, seniors, entrepreneurs, and educators. His work has touched a who's who of Hollywood elite, professional athletes, political leaders, and business magnates, with corporate clients that include Google, Virgin, Nike, Zappos, SpaceX, GE, Twentieth Century Fox, Cleveland Clinic, Wordpress, and such institutions as the United Nations, Caltech, Harvard University, and Singularity University.

Through keynote speeches, he reaches in-person audiences totaling more than 200,000 every year; his online videos have garnered hundreds of millions of views. Kwik is regularly featured in media, including *Forbes,* HuffPost, *Fast Company, Inc.,* and CNBC. He is the host of the acclaimed "Kwik Brain" podcast, which is consistently the top educational training show on iTunes. KwikLearning.com's online courses are used by students in 195 countries.

Kwik, an advocate for brain health and global education, is also a philanthropist funding projects ranging from Alzheimer's research to the creation of schools from Guatemala to Kenya, providing health care, clean water, and learning for children in need. His mission: No brain left behind.

Connect with Jim Kwik at:

JimKwik.com (speaking, coaching, podcast)
KwikLearning.com (online programs)
Twitter: @JimKwik
Facebook: @JimKwik
Instagram: @JimKwik
Text 310-299-9362

ENDNOTES

CHAPTER 2

1. "Digital Overload: Your Brain On Gadgets," NPR, last modified August 24, 2010, www.npr.org/templates/story/story.php?storyId=129384107.

2. Ibid.

3. Ibid; Matt Richtel, "Attached to Technology and Paying a Price," *New York Times*, last modified June 7, 2010, www.nytimes.com/2010/06/07/technology/07brain.html.

4. Paul Waddington, "Dying for Information? A Report on the Effects of Information Overload in the UK and Worldwide," Reuters, accessed December 11, 2019, www.ukoln.ac.uk/services/papers/bl/blri078/content/repor~13.htm.

5. "Digital Distraction," American Psychological Association, last modified August 10, 2018, www.apa.org/news/press/releases/2018/08/digital-distraction.

6. Daniel J. Levitin, *The Organized Mind: Thinking Straight in the Age of Information Overload* (New York: Dutton, 2016).

7. Sean Coughlan, "Digital Dependence 'Eroding Human Memory,'" *BBC News*, BBC, last modified October 7, 2015, www.bbc.com/news/education-34454264.

8. Rony Zarom, "Why Technology Is Affecting Critical Thought in the Workplace and How to Fix It," *Entrepreneur,* September 21 2015, www.entrepreneur.com/article/248925.

9. Jim Taylor, "How Technology Is Changing the Way Children Think and Focus," *Psychology Today*, December 4, 2012, www.psychologytoday.com/us/blog/the-power-prime/201212/how-technology-is-changing-the-way-children-think-and-focus.

10. Patricia M. Greenfield, "Technology and Informal Education: What Is Taught, What Is Learned," *Science,* January 2 2009, https://science.sciencemag.org/content/323/5910/69.full.

11. Richard Foreman, "The Pancake People, or, 'The Gods Are Pounding My Head'," *Edge,* March 8 2005, https://www.edge.org/3rd_culture/foreman05/foreman05_index.html.

CHAPTER 3

1. Tara Swart, *The Source: Open Your Mind, Change Your Life* (New York: Vermilion, 2019).

2. Suzana Herculano-Houzel, "The Human Brain in Numbers: a Linearly Scaled-up Primate Brain," *Frontiers in Human Neuroscience*, November 9, 2009, www.ncbi.nlm.nih.gov/pmc/articles/PMC2776484/.

3. Ferris Jabr, "Cache Cab: Taxi Drivers' Brains Grow to Navigate London's Streets," *Scientific American,* December 8, 2011, www.scientificamerican.com/article/london-taxi-memory/.

4. Courtney E. Ackerman, "What Is Neuroplasticity? A Psychologist Explains [+14 Exercises]," PositivePsychology.com, last modified September 10, 2019, positivepsychology.com/neuroplasticity/.

5. Catharine Paddock, Ph.D., "Not Only Does Our Gut Have Brain Cells It Can Also Grow New Ones, Study," Medical News Today, last modified August 5, 2009, https://www.medicalnewstoday.com/articles/159914.php; Jennifer Wolkin, "Meet Your Second Brain: The Gut," *Mindful*, last modified August 14, 2015, https://www.mindful.org/meet-your-second-brain-the-gut/.

6. Emily Underwood, "Your Gut Is Directly Connected to Your Brain, by a Newly Discovered Neuron Circuit," *Science*, last modified September 20, 2018, https://www.sciencemag.org/news/2018/09/your-gut-directly-connected-your-brain-newly-discovered-neuron-circuit.

7. Ken Robinson and Lou Aronica, *Creative Schools: The Grassroots Revolution That's Transforming Education* (New York: Penguin Books, 2016), xxvii-xxvii.

CHAPTER 4

1. Sonnad, Nikhil. "A Mathematical Model of the 'Forgetting Curve' Proves Learning Is Hard." Quartz, February 28, 2018, qz.com/1213768/the-forgetting-curve-explains-why-humans-struggle-to-memorize/.

2. Francesco Cirillo, "The Pomodoro Technique," Cirillo Consulting, francescocirillo.com/pages/pomodoro-technique.

3. Oliver Wendell Holmes, "The Autocrat of the Breakfast-Table," *Atlantic Monthly* 2, no. 8 (June 1858): 502.

CHAPTER 5

1. "Kwik Brain with Jim Kwik: Break Through Your Beliefs with Shelly Lefkoe," Jim Kwik, May 2, 2019, https://kwikbrain.libsyn.com/114-break-through-your-beliefs-with-shelly-lefkoe/.

2. Jan Bruce, et al., *Mequilibrium: 14 Days to Cooler, Calmer, and Happier* (New York: Harmony Books, 2015), 95.

3. Jennice Vilhauer, "4 Ways to Stop Beating Yourself Up, Once and For All," *Psychology Today*, March 18, 2016, www.psychologytoday.com/us/blog/living-forward/201603/4-ways-stop-beating-yourself-once-and-all.

4. "The Power of Positive Thinking," Johns Hopkins Medicine, www.hopkinsmedicine.org/health/wellness-and-prevention/the-power-of-positive-thinking.

5. Mayo Clinic Staff, "Positive Thinking: Stop Negative Self-Talk to Reduce Stress," Mayo Clinic, last modified February 18, 2017, www.mayoclinic.org/healthy-lifestyle/stress-management/in-depth/positive-thinking/art-20043950.

6. James Clear, "How Positive Thinking Builds Your Skills, Boosts Your Health, and Improves Your Work," James Clear, accessed April 22, 2019, jamesclear.com/positive-thinking.

7. Ibid.

8. Ibid.

9. Barbara L. Fredrickson, "The Broaden-and-Build Theory of Positive Emotions," National Center for Biotechnology Information, last modified August 17, 2004, www.ncbi.nlm.nih.gov/pmc/articles/PMC1693418/pdf/15347528.pdf.

CHAPTER 6

1. Carol S. Dweck, *Mindset: the New Psychology of Success* (New York: Random House, 2006).

2. Daphne Martschenko, "The IQ Test Wars: Why Screening for Intelligence Is Still so Controversial," The Conversation, accessed August 16, 2019, https://theconversation.com/the-iq-test-wars-why-screening-for-intelligence-is-still-so-controversial-81428.

3. Ibid.

4. Ibid.

5. David Shenk, "The Truth About IQ," *The Atlantic*, accessed August 4, 2009, https://www.theatlantic.com/national/archive/2009/07/the-truth-about-iq/22260/.

6. Ibid.

7. Brian Roche, "Your IQ May Not Have Changed, But Are You Any Smarter?", *Psychology Today*, July 15, 2014, www.psychologytoday.com/us/blog/iq-boot-camp/201407/your-iq-may-not-have-changed-are-you-any-smarter.

8. David Shenk, *The Genius in All Of Us* (New York: Anchor Books, 2011) 117.

9. Gabrielle Torre, "The Life and Times of the 10% Neuromyth," Knowing Neurons, last modified February 13, 2018, https://knowingneurons.com/2018/02/13/10-neuromyth/.

10. Eric H. Chudler, "Do We Only Use 10% of Our Brains?," Neuroscience for Kids, https://faculty.washington.edu/chudler/tenper.html.

11. Gabrielle Torre, "The Life and Times of the 10% Neuromyth," Knowing Neurons, last modified February 13, 2018, https://knowingneurons.com/2018/02/13/10-neuromyth/.

12. Eric Westervelt, "Sorry, Lucy: The Myth of the Misused Brain Is 100 Percent False," *NPR*, July 27, 2014, https://www.npr.org/2014/07/27/335868132/sorry-lucy-the-myth-of-the-misused-brain-is-100-percent-false.

13. Barry L. Beyerstein, "Whence Cometh the Myth that We Only Use 10% of our Brains?," in *Mind Myths: Exploring Popular Assumptions About the Mind and Brain*, ed. Sergio Della Sala (Wiley, 1999), 3–24.

14. Ibid.

15. Robynne Boyd, "Do People Only Use 10 Percent of Their Brains?" *Scientific American*, last modified February 7, 2008, https://www.scientificamerican.com/article/do-people-only-use-10-percent-of-their-brains/.

16. Thomas G. West, *In the Mind's Eye: Creative Visual Thinkers, Gifted Dyslexics, and the Rise of Visual Technologies* (Amherst, NY: Prometheus Books, 2009).

17. Ibid.

18. "Einstein's 23 Biggest Mistakes: A New Book Explores the Mistakes of the Legendary Genius," *Discover*, last modified September 1, 2008, http://discovermagazine.com/2008/sep/01-einsteins-23-biggest-mistakes.

19. "About Page," Beth Comstock, https://www.bethcomstock.info/.

20. 99U, "Beth Comstock: Make Heroes Out of the Failures," video, 12:40, September 3, 2015, https://www.youtube.com/watch?v=0GpIlOF-UzA.

21. Thomas Hobbes, *The English Works of Thomas Hobbes of Malmesbury*, ed. William Molesworth (Aalen: Scientia, 1966).

22. "Carol W. Greider," Wikipedia, accessed July 27, 2019, https://en.wikipedia.org/wiki/Carol_W._Greider.

23. "Carol Greider, Ph.D., Director of Molecular Biology & Genetics at Johns Hopkins University," *Yale Dyslexia*, http://dyslexia.yale.edu/story/carol-greider-ph-d/.

24. Mayo Clinic Staff, "Dyslexia," Mayo Clinic, last modified July 22, 2017, https://www.mayoclinic.org/diseases-conditions/dyslexia/symptoms-causes/syc-20353552.

25. Claudia Dreifus, "On Winning a Nobel Prize in Science," *The New York Times*, October 12, 2009, Science section, https://www.nytimes.com/2009/10/13/science/13conv.html.

26. Jim Carrey, commencement address, Maharishi International University, Fairfield, Iowa, May 24, 2014, www.mum.edu/graduation-2014, accessed January 5, 2020.

27. Fred C. Kelly, "They Wouldn't Believe the Wrights Had Flown: A Study in Human Incredulity," Wright Brothers Aeroplane Company, http://www.wright-brothers.org/History_Wing/Aviations_Attic/They_Wouldnt_Believe/They_Wouldnt_Believe_the_Wrights_Had_Flown.htm.

28. Ibid.

29. "Bruce Lee," Biography.com, last modified April 16, 2019, www.biography.com/actor/bruce-lee.

30. Mouse AI, "I Am Bruce Lee," directed by Pete McCormack, video, 1:30:13, last modified June 13, 2015, www.youtube.com/watch?v=2qL-WZ_ATTQ.

31. "I Am Bruce Lee," Leeway Media, 2012, www.youtube.com/watch?v=2qL-WZ_ATTQ.

32. Bruce Lee, Bruce Lee Jeet Kune Do: Bruce Lee's Commentaries on the Martial Way, ed. John Little (Tuttle Publishing, 1997).

33. Daniel Coyle, The Talent Code: Greatness Isn't Born. It's Grown (London: Arrow, 2010); "The Talent Code: Grow Your Own Greatness: Here's How," Daniel Coyle, http://danielcoyle.com/the-talent-code/.

CHAPTER 7

1. "Kind (n.)," Index, www.etymonline.com/word/kind.

2. Christopher J. Bryan, et al., "Motivating Voter Turnout by Invoking the Self," PNAS, last modified August 2, 2011, https://www.pnas.org/content/108/31/12653.

3. Adam Gorlick, "Stanford Researchers Find That a Simple Change in Phrasing Can Increase Voter Turnout," Stanford University, last modified July 19, 2011, https://news.stanford.edu/news/2011/july/increasing-voter-turnout-071911.html.

CHAPTER 8

1. Eva Selhub, "Nutritional Psychiatry: Your Brain on Food," Harvard Health (blog), Harvard Health Publishing, last modified April 5, 2018, www.health.harvard.edu/blog/nutritional-psychiatry-your-brain-on-food-201511168626.

2. Jim Kwik, "Kwik Brain with Jim Kwik: Eating for Your Brain with Dr. Lisa Mosconi," Jim Kwik, last modified January 4, 2019, https://jimkwik.com/kwik-brain-088-eating-for-your-brain-with-dr-lisa-mosconi/.

3. Jim Kwik, "Kwik Brain with Jim Kwik: When to Eat for Optimal Brain Function with Max Lugavere," Jim Kwik, last modified July 19, 2018, https://jimkwik.com/kwik-brain-066-when-to-eat-for-optimal-brain-function-with-max-lugavere/.

4. "Table 1: Select Nutrients that Affect Cognitive Function," National Institutes of Health, www.ncbi.nlm.nih.gov/pmc/articles/PMC2805706/table/T1/?report=objectonly, accessed June 1, 2019.

5. Heidi Godman, "Regular Exercise Changes the Brain to Improve Memory, Thinking Skills," Harvard Health (blog), Harvard Health Publishing, April 5, 2018, www.health.harvard.edu/blog/regular-exercise-changes-brain-improve-memory-thinking-skills-201404097110.

6. Daniel G. Amen, Change Your Brain, Change Your Life: the Breakthrough Program for Conquering Anxiety, Depression, Obsessiveness, Lack of Focus, Anger, and
Memory Problems (New York: Harmony Books, 2015), 109–110.

7. The Lancet Neurology, "Air Pollution and Brain Health: an Emerging Issue," The Lancet 17, no. 2 (February 2018): 103, www.thelancet.com/journals/laneur/article/PIIS1474-4422(17)30462-3/fulltext.

8. Tara Parker-Pope, "Teenagers, Friends and Bad Decisions," Well (blog), The New York Times, February 3, 2011, well.blogs.nytimes.com/2011/02/03/teen-agers
-friends-and-bad-decisions/?scp=6&sq=tara%2Bparker%2Bpope&st=cse.
9. "Protect Your Brain from Stress," Harvard Health (blog), Harvard Health Publishing, last modified August 2018, www.health.harvard.edu/mind-and-mood/protect-your-brain-from-stress.
10. "Brain Basics: Understanding Sleep," National Institute of Neurological Disorders and Stroke, U.S. Department of Health and Human Services, last modified August 13, 2019, www.ninds.nih.gov/Disorders/Patient-Caregiver-Education/Understanding-Sleep.
11. Jean Kim, "The Importance of Sleep: The Brain's Laundry Cycle," Psychology Today, June 28, 2017, www.psychologytoday.com/us/blog/culture-shrink/201706/the-importance-sleep-the-brains-laundry-cycle.
12. Jeff Iliff, "Transcript of 'One More Reason to Get a Good Night's Sleep,'" TED, last modified September 2014, www.ted.com/talks/jeff_iliff_one_more_reason_to_get_a_good_night_s_sleep/transcript.
13. Ibid.
14. Sandee LaMotte, "One in Four Americans Develop Insomnia Each Year: 75 Percent of Those with Insomnia Recover," Science Daily, June 5, 2018, https://www.sciencedaily.com/releases/2018/06/180605154114.htm.
15. Kathryn J. Reid, et al., "Aerobic Exercise Improves Self-Reported Sleep and Quality of Life in Older Adults with Insomnia," Sleep Medicine, U.S. National Library of Medicine, last modified October 2010, www.ncbi.nlm.nih.gov/pmc/articles/PMC2992829/.
16. Michael J. Breus, "Better Sleep Found by Exercising on a Regular Basis," Psychology Today, September 6, 2013, www.psychologytoday.com/us/blog/sleep-newzzz/201309/better-sleep-found-exercising-regular-basis-0.
17. Sandee LaMotte, "The Healthiest Way to Improve Your Sleep: Exercise," CNN, last modified May 30, 2017, www.cnn.com/2017/05/29/health/exer-cise-sleep
-tips/index.html.
18. David S. Black, et al., "Mindfulness Meditation in Sleep-Disturbed Adults," JAMA Internal Medicine 5 (April 2015): 494–501, jamanetwork.com/journals/jamainternalmedicine/fullarticle/2110998.
19. Karen Kaplan, "A Lot More Americans are Meditating Now than Just Five Years Ago," Los Angeles Times, November 8, 2018, www.latimes.com/science/sciencenow/la-sci-sn-americans-meditating-more-20181108-story.html.
20. Jim Kwik, "Kwik Brain with Jim Kwik: How to Make Meditation Easy with Ariel Garten," Jim Kwik, last modified November 8, 2018, https://jimkwik.com/kwik-brain-080-your-brain-on-meditation-with-ariel-garten/.
21. Ibid.

CHAPTER 9

1. Sarah Young, "This Bizarre Phenomenon Can Stop You from Procrastinating," The Independent, last modified March 9, 2018, www.independent.co.uk/life-style/procrastinating-how-to-stop-zeigarnik-effect-phenomenon-at-work-now-a8247076.html.

2. Art Markman, "How to Overcome Procrastination Guilt and Turn It Into Motivation," HBR Ascend, January 7, 2019, hbrascend.org/topics/turn-your-procrastination-guilt-into-motivation/.

3. B. J. Fogg, "When you learn the Tiny Habits method, you can change your life forever," Tiny Habits, last modified 2019, www.tinyhabits.com/.

4. Deepak Agarwal, *Discover the Genius in Your Child* (Delhi: AIETS.com Pvt.Ltd., 2012), 27-28.

5. Charles Duhigg, *The Power of Habit: Why We Do What We Do in Life and Business* (New York: Random House, 2012), 20–21.

6. James Clear, "The Habits Academy," The Habits Academy, habitsacademy.com/.

7. Jim Kwik, "Kwik Brain with Jim Kwik: Understanding Habit Triggers with James Clear," Jim Kwik, October 18, 2018, https://jimkwik.com/kwik-brain-075-understanding-habit-triggers-with-james-clear/.

8. Ibid.

9. Phillippa Lally, et al., "How Are Habits Formed: Modelling Habit Formation in the Real World," *European Journal of Social Psychology*, vol. 40, no. 6 (July 2009): 998–1009, doi:10.1002/ejsp.674.

10. Alison Nastasi, "How Long Does It Really Take to Break a Habit?" Hopes&Fears, accessed November 20, 2015, www.hopesandfears.com/hopes/now/question/216479-how-long-does-it-really-take-to-break-a-habit.

11. Ibid.

12. B. J. Fogg, "A Behavior Model for Persuasive Design," Persuasive '09: *Proceedings of the 4th International Conference on Persuasive Technology*, no. 40 (April 26, 2009), doi:10.1145/1541948.1541999.

13. Ibid.

14. Ibid.

15. Ibid.

CHAPTER 10

1. Mihaly Csikszentmihalyi, *Flow: the Psychology of Optimal Experience* (New York: Harper Row, 2009).

2. Mike Oppland, "8 Ways To Create Flow According to Mihaly Csikszentmihalyi," PositivePsychology.com, accessed February 19, 2019, positivepsychologyprogram.com/mihaly-csikszentmihalyi-father-of-flow/.

3. Susie Cranston and Scott Keller, "Increasing the 'Meaning Quotient' of Work," *McKinsey Quarterly*, January 2013, www.mckinsey.com/business-functions/organization/our-insights/increasing-the-meaning-quotient-of-work.
4. Entrepreneurs Institute Team, "A Genius Insight: The Four Stages of Flow," Entrepreneurs Institute, last modified February 12, 2015, entrepreneurs institute.org/updates/a-genius-insight-the-four-stages-of-flow.
5. Hara Estroff Marano, "Pitfalls of Perfectionism," *Psychology Today*, March 1, 2008, www.psychologytoday.com/us/articles/200803/pitfalls-perfectionism.
6. Travis Bradberry, "Why the Best Leaders Have Conviction," World Economic Forum, last modified December 7, 2015, www.weforum.org/agenda/2015/12/why-the-best-leaders-have-conviction/.

CHAPTER 11

1. Jim Kwik, "Kwik Brain with Jim Kwik: How to Concentrate with Dandapani," Jim Kwik, October 8, 2019, https://jimkwik.com/kwik-brain-149-how-to-concentrate-with-dandapani/.
2. Ibid.
3. Ibid.
4. "A Clean Well-Lighted Place," *BeWell,* accessed January 7, 2020, https://bewell.stanford.edu/a-clean-well-lighted-place/.
5. Melanie Greenberg, "9 Ways to Calm Your Anxious Mind," *Psychology Today*, June 28, 2015, www.psychologytoday.com/us/blog/the-mindful-self-express/201506/9-ways-calm-your-anxious-mind.
6. Donald Miller, "The Brutal Cost of Overload and How to Reclaim the Rest You Need," *Building a StoryBrand*, buildingastorybrand.com/episode-40/.
7. Markham Heid, "The Brains of Highly Distracted People Look Smaller," *VICE*, October 12, 2017, tonic.vice.com/en_us/article/wjxmpx/constant-tech-distractions-are-like-feeding-your-brain-junk-food.
8. Kristin Wong, "How Long It Takes to Get Back on Track After a Distraction," *Lifehacker*, July 29, 2015, lifehacker.com/how-long-it-takes-to-get-back-on-track-after-a-distract-1720708353.
9. "4-7-8 Breath Relaxation Exercise," Council of Residency Directors in Emergency Medicine, February 2010, www.cordem.org/globalassets/files/academic-assembly/2017-aa/handouts/day-three/biofeedback-exercises-for-stress-2---fernances-j.pdf.

CHAPTER 12

1. Ralph Heibutzki, "The Effects of Cramming for a Test," *Education*, November 21, 2017, education.seattlepi.com/effects-cramming-test-2719.html.
2. Mark Wheeler, "Cramming for a Test? Don't Do It, Say UCLA Researchers," UCLA Newsroom, August 22, 2012, newsroom.ucla.edu/releases/cramming-for-a-test-don-t-do-it-237733.

3. William R. Klemm, "Strategic Studying: The Value of Forced Recall," *Psychology Today*, October 9, 2016, www.psychologytoday.com/us/blog/memory-medic/201610/strategic-studying-the-value-forced-recall.
4. Ibid.
5. James Gupta, "Spaced Repetition: a Hack to Make Your Brain Store Information," *The Guardian*, January 23, 2016, www.theguardian.com/education/2016/jan/23/spaced-repetition-a-hack-to-make-your-brain-store-information.
6. Jordan Gaines Lewis, "Smells Ring Bells: How Smell Triggers Memories and Emotions," *Psychology Today*, January 12, 2015, www.psychologytoday.com/us/blog/brain-babble/201501/smells-ring-bells-how-smell-triggers-memories-and-emotions.
7. Wu-Jing He, et al., "Emotional Reactions Mediate the Effect of Music Listening on Creative Thinking: Perspective of the Arousal-and-Mood Hypothesis," *Frontiers in Psychology* 8 (September 26, 2017): 1680, www.ncbi.nlm.nih.gov/pmc/articles/PMC5622952/.
8. Claire Kirsch, "If It's Not Baroque Don't Fix It," *The Belltower*, January 25, 2017, http://belltower.mtaloy.edu/2017/01/if-its-not-baroque-dont-fix-it/.
9. Alina-Mihaela Busan, "Learning Styles of Medical Students—Implications in Education," *Current Health Sciences Journal* 40, no. 2 (April–June 2014): 104–110, www.ncbi.nlm.nih.gov/pmc/articles/PMC4340450/.
10. Bob Sullivan and Hugh Thompson, "Now Hear This! Most People Stink at Listening [Excerpt]," *Scientific American*, May 3, 2013, www.scientificamerican.com/article/plateau-effect-digital-gadget-distraction-attention/.
11. Ibid.
12. Cindi May, "A Learning Secret: Don't Take Notes with a Laptop," *Scientific American,* June 3, 2014, www.scientificamerican.com/article/a-learning-secret-don-t-take-notes-with-a-laptop/

CHAPTER 13

1. Eve Marder, "The Importance of Remembering," *eLife* 6 (August 14, 2017), https://www.ncbi.nlm.nih.gov/pmc/articles/PMC5577906/.
2. William R. Klemm, "Five Reasons That Memory Matters," *Psychology Today*, January 13, 2013, www.psychologytoday.com/us/blog/memory-medic/201301/five-reasons-memory-matters.
3. Joshua Foer, "How to Train Your Mind to Remember Anything," CNN, 11 June 2012, www.cnn.com/2012/06/10/opinion/foer-ted-memory/index.html.

CHAPTER 14

1. Lauren Duzbow, "Watch This. No. Read It!" Oprah.com, June 2008, www.oprah.com/health/how-reading-can-improve-your-memory#ixzz2VYPyX3uU.

2. "Keep Reading to Keep Alzheimer's at Bay," Fisher Center for Alzheimer's Research Foundation, last modified November 12, 2014, www.alzinfo.org/articles/reading-alzheimers-bay/.

CHAPTER 15

1. "Six Thinking Hats," the De Bono Group, www.debonogroup.com/six_thinking_hats.php.

2. "The Components of MI," MI Oasis, www.multipleintelligencesoasis.org/the-components-of-mi, accessed April 10, 2019.

3. Ibid.

4. Ibid.

5. The Mind Tools Content Team, "VAK Learning Styles: Understanding How Team Members Learn," Mind Tools, www.mindtools.com/pages/article/vak-learning-styles.htm, accessed April 10, 2019.

6. Matt Callen, "The 40/70 Rule and How It Applies to You," Digital Kickstart, last modified May 3, 2016, https://digitalkickstart.com/the-4070-rule-and-how-it-applies-to-you/.

7. Ibid.

8. Rimm, Allison, "Taming the Epic To-Do List." Harvard Business Review, June 14, 2018, https://hbr.org/2018/03/taming-the-epic-to-do-list.

9. Peter Bevelin, *Seeking Wisdom: from Darwin to Munger* (PCA Publications LLC, 2018).

10. Ryan Holiday, *Conspiracy: The True Story of Power, Sex, and a Billionaire's Secret Plot to Destroy a Media Empire* (New York: Portfolio, 2018).

11. "Second-Order Thinking: What Smart People Use to Outperform," Farnam Street, accessed January 22, 2019, https://fs.blog/2016/04/second-order-thinking/.

12. "Kwik Brain with Jim Kwik: Exponential Thinking with Naveen Jain," Jim Kwik, May 4, 2018, https://jimkwik.com/kwik-brain-059-exponential-thinking-with-naveen-jain/.

13. Viome.com Home Page, Viome, Inc., accessed February 5, 2020, www.viome.com.

14. Mark Bonchek, "How to Create an Exponential Mindset," Harvard Business Review, October 4, 2017, hbr.org/2016/07/how-to-create-an-exponential-mindset.

15. Evie Mackie, "Exponential Thinking," Medium, Room Y, last modified August 30, 2018, medium.com/room-y/exponential-thinking-8d7cbb8aaf8a.

INDEX

J

K

L

M

T

U

V

W

X

Y

Z

We hope you enjoyed this Hay House book. If you'd like to receive our online catalog featuring additional information on Hay House books and products, or if you'd like to find out more about the Hay Foundation, please contact:

Hay House, Inc., P.O. Box 5100, Carlsbad, CA 92018-5100
(760) 431-7695 or (800) 654-5126
(760) 431-6948 (fax) or (800) 650-5115 (fax)
www.hayhouse.com® • www.hayfoundation.org

Published in Australia by: Hay House Australia Pty. Ltd., 18/36 Ralph St., Alexandria NSW 2015
Phone: 612-9669-4299 • *Fax:* 612-9669-4144
www.hayhouse.com.au

Published in the United Kingdom by: Hay House UK, Ltd., The Sixth Floor, Watson House, 54 Baker Street, London W1U 7BU
Phone: +44 (0)20 3927 7290 • *Fax:* +44 (0)20 3927 7291
www.hayhouse.co.uk

Published in India by: Hay House Publishers India, Muskaan Complex, Plot No. 3, B-2, Vasant Kunj, New Delhi 110 070
Phone: 91-11-4176-1620 • *Fax:* 91-11-4176-1630
www.hayhouse.co.in
